DRESSING GLOBAL BODIES

D1457336

Dressing Global Bodies addresses the complex politics of dress and fashion from a global perspective spanning four centuries, tying the early global to more contemporary times, to reveal clothing practice as a key cultural phenomenon and mechanism of defining one's identity.

This collection of chapters explores how garments reflect the hierarchies of value, collective and personal inclinations, religious norms and conversions. Apparel is now recognized for its seminal role in global, colonial and post-colonial engagements and for its role in personal and collective expression. Patterns of exchange and commerce are discussed by contributing authors to analyse powerful and diverse colonial and postcolonial practices. This volume rejects assumptions surrounding a purportedly all-powerful Western metropolitan fashion system and instead aims to emphasize how diverse populations seized agency through the fashioning of dress.

Dressing Global Bodies contributes to a growing scholarship considering gender and race, place and politics through the close critical analysis of dress and fashion; it is an indispensable volume for students of history and especially those interested in fashion, textiles, material culture and the body across a wide time frame.

Beverly Lemire is Henry Marshall Tory Chair, Department of History and Classics, University of Alberta, Canada. She publishes widely on early modern consumer practice, fashion, material culture, textiles and trade, most recently *Global Trade and the Transformation of Consumer Cultures: The Material World Remade, c.1500–1820* (2018).

Giorgio Riello is Chair of Early Modern Global History at the European University Institute, Italy. Among his books are *Cotton* (2013), *Luxury* (2016) and *Back in Fashion* (2020). Giorgio has published extensively on fashion, textiles and global trade between Europe and Asia in the early modern period.

DRESSING GLOBAL BODIES

The Political Power of Dress in World History

Edited by Beverly Lemire and Giorgio Riello

Routledge
Taylor & Francis Group

LONDON AND NEW YORK

First published 2020
by Routledge
2 Park Square, Milton Park, Abingdon, Oxon OX14 4RN

and by Routledge
52 Vanderbilt Avenue, New York, NY 10017

Routledge is an imprint of the Taylor & Francis Group, an informa business

© 2020 Beverly Lemire and Giorgio Riello

British Library Cataloguing-in-Publication Data
A catalogue record for this book is available from the British Library

Library of Congress Cataloging-in-Publication Data
A catalog record has been requested for this book

ISBN: 978-1-138-49317-9 (hbk)
ISBN: 978-1-138-49318-6 (pbk)
ISBN: 978-1-351-02874-5 (ebk)

Typeset in Bembo
by Swales & Willis, Exeter, Devon, UK

MIX
Paper from
responsible sources
FSC
www.fsc.org   FSC™ C013985

Printed in the United Kingdom
by Henry Ling Limited

CONTENTS

FIGURES

TABLES

CONTRIBUTORS

Hissako Anjo is Lecturer in the Department of Business, Hannan University in Osaka, Japan.

Jody Benjamin is Assistant Professor of History at the University of California, Riverside, United States.

Susanna Burghartz is Professor of Renaissance and Early Modern History at the University of Basel, Switzerland.

Sarah Fee is Senior Curator (Eastern Hemisphere Textiles & Fashion) at the Royal Ontario Museum in Toronto, Canada.

Antonia Finnane is Honorary Professor at the School of Historical and Philosophical Studies, University of Melbourne, Australia.

Karen Tranberg Hansen is Professor Emerita in Department of Anthropology and African Studies, Northwestern University, United States.

Laura Jocic is an independent curator and doctoral researcher at the University of Melbourne, Australia.

Beverly Lemire is Professor and Henry Marshall Tory Chair at the University of Alberta, Canada.

Jane Malthus is Honorary Curator at the Otago Museum, New Zealand.

Tara Mayer is Senior Instructor in the Department of History, University of British Columbia, Canada.

Giorgio Riello is Professor and Chair of Early Modern Global History at the European University Institute, Florence, Italy.

Miki Sugiura is Professor of Global and European Economic History of Hosei University in Tokyo, Japan.

Sophie White is Associate Professor of American Studies at the University of Notre Dame, United States.

Cory Willmott is Professor and Chair in the Department of Anthropology, Southern Illinois University Edwardsville, United States.

INTRODUCTION

Dressing global bodies

Beverly Lemire and Giorgio Riello

Dress is a broad and complex material category that has received much attention over past decades. Its link to the body and reflection of culture, creativity and capacity attract audiences of many kinds to exhibitions, conferences and published works, as well as intriguing students and scholars in many disciplines. Unlike nominally uniform commodities, dress is recognized for its profound variability whether in the form of outer garments or in the shape of small accessories. Attention to global exchange and material culture illuminates the influences that flowed from region to region, people to people, expressed in myriad ways through cultures of dress. Yet, when considered within such a global arena, dress is sometimes contentious, it brings together people as it sets them apart; dress is entangled with power and at times illuminates the persistence and defiance of marginalized peoples and displays the features of industrial and political systems whether in the making of new goods or the circulation of second-hand – all topics explored in this book.

Material culture and global dress

The global, the material and power inform the analyses contained in this collection and weave together a vital intellectual tapestry. There is no better way to approach these issues than through an artefact like this Chinese folding fan, made about 1820–1830 for export to Western markets (Figure 0.1).[1] This amalgam of peacock and painted goose feathers, plus incised bone fan sticks, is part of a long history of fan invention and use in East Asia, a signal marker of status, long incorporated into varied social and cultural forms. A Japanese invention became a Chinese vogue that spread to other regions of Asia, produced in a variety of materials from painted paper and bamboo sticks to more precious media such as ivory suited to a breadth of users. The direct oceanic contacts

FIGURE 0.1   Hand-painted fan, goose feathers tipped with peacock feathers, painted in gouache, pierced bone sticks and guards. Made in China for export, 1820–1830.

Source: Gift of Mrs Henry W. Breyer, Sr. 1967. © Philadelphia Museum of Art, 1967–17–23.

between Europeans and East Asians, from the sixteenth century, encouraged the spread of this elegant accessory, one used with grace and purpose by men and women. Renaissance governments in Italy sought to limit the use of fans made of costly materials to select ranks, as local artisans experimented with making these fashionable notions – parrot feathers, gold, jewels and costly furs or printed paper and cheap fan sticks. At the same time, the trade in Chinese-made fans accelerated to meet demand and continued into the twentieth century, with both European and Chinese artisans working to serve consumers of all ranks.[2] Feather fans amounted to a larger investment than printed or painted paper, even when these included painted goose feathers, as with the example in Figure 0.1. The Renaissance vogue for feather fans, among aspiring Europeans, revived again from the mid-nineteenth century and carried into the twentieth, with feather fans becoming a craze in Western societies.

The sophisticated combination of materials in this fan suggests the ways in which design and the choice of materials were deployed to appeal to various buyers. Equally, the rage for fans in the mid-nineteenth century enabled a wider range of makers to present their take on this fashion accessory, including Native American fashion makers like the Wendat outside Quebec City (Figure 0.2). The whole reflects a type of material dialogue. Fixed-shape feather fans had an ancient lineage among the First Peoples of the Americas and these kinds of stylish feather fans were made and traded from Brazil over the same period, as well

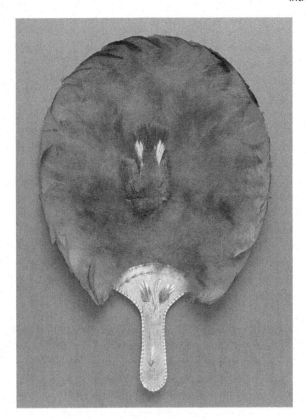

FIGURE 0.2 Canadian (Wendat?) fan, late nineteenth to early twentieth century, 24 × 36 cm. Dyed red marabou feathers mounted on natural turkey feathers, snow bunting at centre. Birchbark handle embroidered with dyed moose hair.

Source: © Museum of Fine Arts, Boston, 1979.446. Gift of Thomas Logan Orser.

as from various communities of Native Americans in territories around the Great Lakes and river systems of central North America. Surveying extant feather fans such as these in major museum collections demonstrate the complexities at work within these global networks.[3] Material evidence powerfully illuminates these global connections, ties that enabled material inspiration in the making of dress; specific modes of dress figured within (colonial) political systems that shaped or attempted to shape the local communities embedded in these networks.[4]

Attention to material culture is pivotal to obtain a full, rich analysis of the many facets of dress considered in this volume. Artefacts contain tacit evidence described as 'extralingual'. Leora Auslander observes the power of things, noting that: 'human beings need things to express and communicate the unsaid and the unsayable ... to situate themselves in space and time ... as well as for sensory pleasure'.[5] At the same time artefacts are also 'active agents in history. In their communicative, performative, emotive, and expressive capacities, they act, [and] have effects in the world'.[6] Extant material evidence and historical representations form the analytical framework for this volume. Material culture study encourages attention to cross-cultural exchange, foregrounding creative actors that might otherwise go unnoticed. The influence of the global takes more tangible form when its materiality is acknowledged and assessed; similarly, the range of actors shaping the local and global are more fully apparent when a material culture approach is mobilized. Materiality opens for us a door into the world of people whose aesthetic, sartorial and material choices were not necessarily conveyed in written documents.

The challenge for us is to look deeply and recognize the myriad sources of knowledge embedded in objects from different places and communities. The Indigenous scholar, Sherry Farrell Racette, considers the many artefacts arising from Native American communities deposited in Western museums and she observes that they are

> encoded with knowledge, although they are sometimes impenetrable and difficult to understand. Most often sleeping on a shelf in a museum storage room, completely decontextualized from their cultures of origin, they are the raw material of women's history. Through the power of colour and design, the objects in museum collections not only speak a powerful aesthetic, they also reveal critical information about the worlds and circumstances in which they were created.[7]

Our collection builds on the findings of scholars such as Emma Tarlo, Sandra Niessen et al. and Jean Allman, among others, which helped recast the meanings of fashion and the politics of dress.[8] They epitomize the generative rethinking taking place in this growing field, part of a flourishing scholarship illuminating gender and race, place and politics, through the close critical analysis of dress. Our contributors offer a wealth of material histories from the rough clothing of Africans enslaved in imperial locales, to the heterogeneous patterns of attire in early nineteenth-century Senegambia and the power of royally mandated uniforms in early nineteenth-century Madagascar. Skin, fur and cloth, plus the shifting spaces of consumption are addressed, along with the patterns of coloniality in North America, New Zealand and Australia. The political practices of dress are likewise considered among late nineteenth-century Indian elites and Native American men and women in the twentieth century, along with the rise of tailored apparel in China and Japan over the same period, with global fashions in post-colonial Zambia also deftly explained. This collection builds the understanding of dress, its power in global, colonial and post-colonial settings and its personal and collective expressions, all of which defined time and place.[9]

A focus on dress provides the opportunity to explore the nuances of historic experiences, including the active engagement of those enveloped in particular dress systems. Interdisciplinarity is critical to this enterprise, building on myriad methodologies and theoretical perspectives. Shared theories and methodologies link this scholarship whether through the assessments of 'object lives' or the 'social skin', blending material culture study, visual and documentary analyses.[10] Recent scholarship of this type has already produced important insights, on which we build, whether of colonial Louisiana, seventeenth-century Europe or nineteenth-century Native American communities.[11] This collection advances scholarship, with an emphasis on global ties and the agency of various world communities in the choices made and expressions of material life.[12]

Present-day scholars recognize the unique capacity of bodily coverings and adornment to explain past practices and politics. Terence Turner defined clothing as 'the social skin',[13] a discursive concept demanding the serious attention to habitual systems along with exceptional material practice, for as Turner states:

> Decorating, covering, uncovering or otherwise altering the human form in accordance with social notions of everyday propriety or sacred dress, beauty or solemnity, status or changes in status, or on occasion of the violation or inversion of such notions, seems to have been a concern of every human society of which we have knowledge.[14]

Karen Tranberg Hansen notes how the concept of the social skin: 'invites us to explore both the individual and collective identities that the dressed body enables'.[15] There is a deeply inherent materiality in this concept, which has been taken up by our contributors, as well as by other scholars. Importantly, material culture study is integrated into historical, art historical and ethnographic studies, topics that also welcome curatorial knowledge. Museum collections are a vital resource in the diverse scholarship that appears in this volume. The challenge to scholars in this field is to untangle the ways in which the clothes that enveloped people in the past reflected their bodily experiences, along with cultural, social and gender priorities, as well as the economies of fashioning and refashioning across place and time.[16]

Within this volume, garments are assessed and intellectually dissected, along with the systems of provisioning or careful self-selection. The economies of identity and self-fashioning reflect hierarchies of value, collective and personal inclinations, political norms and conversions, whether these were enforced or voluntarily enacted. The materialities we address were shaped by global flows of cloth and beads, furs, ready-made and second-hand apparel, in active processes of exchange.[17] Dress was a charged cultural instrument, as evidenced in colonial and decolonization politics, social and political agendas, animated by cross-cultural and commercial flows, industrial and institutional innovations.[18] This fertile foundation inspires the contributions to this collection.

The global: imperial, colonial, post-colonial and the critique

Current global history scholarship rejects long-standing Eurocentric assumptions surrounding a purportedly all-powerful Western metropolitan fashion system and challenges the persistent claim that fashion originated solely in the West. 'Decentring' is part of a decolonization process, responding to cogent critiques in the wider social science fields, as with Dipesh Chakrabarty's call to 'provincialize Europe' and Natalie Zemon Davis' attention to 'decentring history'.[19] Sustained, comparative assessments of clothing systems, to which we contribute, are building a clearer view of historic entanglements, while chronicling the powerful politics of dress, shaping economies and societies. Studies such as these are now recognized for the unique ways in which they illuminate social and political processes, as well as advancing understanding of the dressed body in distinctive spaces.[20] This volume continues the work of redefining national and collective communities as reflected in the practice of dress fashion, seen through the global lens, from the sixteenth through the twentieth century, exploring diverse colonial and post-colonial practices through this uniquely expressive medium.

That said, scholars have recently critiqued the 'global turn', noting that some global histories neglect the national or the local, with one scholar wondering whether global history 'has hit a point of diminishing return'.[21] Debates of this sort indicate the disruptions that accompany a global historical methodology that – while not new – has gained prominence in recent years for its capacity to generate innovative and incisive analyses. Global histories elucidate topics that include national and micro analyses, while attending to connections and intersections across borders, world areas and oceans. It is important to acknowledge that there is a heightened antagonism towards the global in the present day within elite and populist politics in many parts of the word; however, we neglect attention to global histories at our peril, as these studies assess change and continuity, resistance and interruptions, from important vantage points, often with finely parsed assessments. Richard Drayton and David Motadel argue that the value of global history rests on

> a new sensitivity to the historical agents, forces, and factors at scales above and below those of the nation or region ... [For] a self-conscious global history neither neglects 'the small spaces' nor evades the specificity and strangeness of disconnected historical experience.[22]

The global framework of this volume emphasizes sustained imperial systems, as well as subaltern practices and regional norms and resistances as these evolve, producing withal a global history with the politics and practice of apparel at its heart. Connections of many kinds occurred through history, whether through trade, migration, colonization or resistance. Attention to global ties alters our ways of knowing, acknowledging the long history of sometimes-complex relations at every social level, shaped by Indigenous peoples as well as colonial agents of many sorts and subsequent decolonization forces.[23] Think again about the fad for fans that rebounded through world regions from the mid-nineteenth century and consider the significance of those heterogeneous communities engaged in making these elegant trifles. Makers from different cultural origins – Asian and Indigenous American included – expressed culturally based skills and asserted their creative capacities despite sometime colonial attempts to mute such capacities or narrowly direct such expressions (Figures 0.1 and 0.2).

The processes of contact, connection and colonial/post-colonial struggle are illuminated through the deep study of dress, more fully uncovering the discrete politics, cultures and economies of individuals and communities along with their modes of material performance. The power of skin, shirts and snowshoes are juxtaposed against chapters on slave attire, uniforms and tailoring. Dress media – printed cotton, feathers or leather, wool uniforms, suits or blankets – possess a tactility, shape and weight that define their meanings among different communities of wearers and observers. Our contributors attend to material culture, assessed through different disciplinary lenses, providing a clearer analysis of clothing politics across time and place.

It remains the case that some projects on dress reflect (sometimes unwittingly) a Eurocentric intellectual crib. The fixation on Western elite dress remains strong; the preoccupation with courtiers and couturiers remains powerful. Both are subjects worthy of study. But they must be treated with care, for a profound Eurocentrism taints the subject of the 'birth' of fashion. Eurocentric assertions bruited in the 1970s and 1980s equated the birth of fashion with singular Burgundian courts and Parisian salons.[24] This thinking retains its influence. For example, a noted French theorist insisted that fashion 'took hold in the modern West [*c.*1800] and nowhere else'.[25] This viewpoint reverberated into the 2000s.[26] However, this stance is being challenged by comparative and globalist views, including the decolonizing of dress and fashion study.[27] This collection contributes to ongoing revisions, a vital endeavour in this subject area.

Bodies, dressed or adorned, marked expectation or endurance, creativity or tradition and might evoke distaste or revulsion by observers as much as celebration or regard, as political systems were challenged or upheld.[28] Collectively, our contributors dissect political processes and present new histories, revealing cultural persistence, innovations or disjunctures.

We celebrate the fact that over the past generation, the study of dress moved from the lingering shadows of academia to centre stage, driving new analyses of gender, race, economy and culture – revising disciplinary practices. The dressed body is receiving greater academic and public attention than ever before. The active agency of clothing is now recognized as central in the study of colonial and imperial histories, expressions of shifting modernity, cross-cultural exchange, definitions and contestations of race and gender practice. The politics of dress is uniquely suited to the global study provided in this volume, through case studies that emphasize connections or explorations of entanglement. This collection advances the reimagining of social, cultural and gender politics as expressed through this dynamic 'social skin'.

Dressing global bodies: content

The chapters in this volume are arranged in ways that encourages global comparative perspectives with topics moving from the sixteenth through the twentieth century. They address connections, diffusions and accommodations to political power, plus gender and ethnic priorities across time and place. Themes recur, as in the impact of colonization and the subaltern resistance/persistence in the face of sustained political affronts – or successful colonial settlement – expressed through dress. Analyses and narrative themes include ethnography and knowledge, the political dress of slavery, the potential and practice of fashion, settler accommodation, divergent patterns of Westernization and colonization. The materialities of dress are given sustained weight including as expressions of fashion, whether 'power dressing' in colonial India or the adoption of European-influenced uniforms in pre-colonial Madagascar.

The opening two chapters begin the analysis of historically politicized dress in the so-called 'first global age'. In Chapter 1, Susanna Burghartz assesses how at the end of the seventeenth century European travelogues and costume books attempted to define the world's peoples as encountered by European traders and colonizers. These early modern publications employed illustrations and text to explain the societies outside of Europe, a subject of great interest to elite European readers. Distance and difference were emphasized (or downplayed) through dress and bodily adornment, which sometimes pointed to shared traits and other times emphasized hierarchies of difference and race. These 'proto-ethnographic' texts and images demonstrate as well the priorities of the European authors. In Chapter 2, Giorgio Riello uncovers the shared anxieties surrounding fashion and consumption, fears shared by commentators in four parts of the early modern world: Ming China, Edo Japan, Europe and colonial Latin America. Riello teases out the commonalities and distinctive features of this 'fashion world', formed by discrete urban locales. Cosmopolitan city life itself generated shared traits, spaces often knit together by trade. However, Riello argues for distinctive fashion cultures in each of these settings, flourishing separately even while touched by globalism. Rather than seeing them in a hierarchical order, different areas of the world expressed a diverse range of notions of fashion.

The next four chapters examine various facets of dress politics and practice in colonial settings to the turn of the nineteenth century. The perspectives include the priorities of colonizers, as well as enslaved and Indigenous peoples, in addition to those populations touched by colonial forces in West Africa. Chapter 3, by Beverly Lemire, takes two articles of dress – ready-made white linen shirts and Native American-made snowshoes – using these examples of dress technology to interrogate colonial purpose and the technological capacity of Native American communities in northern North America. Snowshoes, in particular, reveal the vital importance of Indigenous technology, knowledge and diplomacy, with Indigenous material culture shared with European allies who were challenged by this new landscape. In Chapter 4,

Sophie White explores the importance of slave clothing in colonial Louisiana, an essential resource required by law to be provided to slaves by their owners – and defining the look and bodily experience of slaves. Deficiencies and dereliction were commonplace in this clothing system, a by-product of irregular shipments from France and often poor-quality goods, though frequently deemed excessive in price by colonial purchasers. Supply networks defined the capacity of imperial systems. Slaves owners innovated as needed, intent on using apparel to subjugate and control; while slaves, themselves, innovated as they could. Slave clothing was a source of perpetual anxiety and legislation throughout European empires, as Miki Sugiura confirms in Chapter 5, in her study of the Dutch Cape and Indian Ocean colonies. The Cape of Good Hope was a crucial victualing stop between Europe and Asia and slave labour was widely employed to serve domestic and agricultural needs in a unique commercial setting. The Cape's position on this sea route integrated this colony into the Dutch commercial networks in the Indian Ocean and Asia. These enabled the colonizers to secure ready-made garments, sourced in Asia, at exceptionally low prices. Imperial politics transformed dress technologies and politics with global implications. In Chapter 6, Jody Benjamin shows the ways in which in the nineteenth-century Senegambia was integrated into West African and global textile networks, including with the transatlantic slave trade. His analysis complicates the picture of the slave trade, by looking at those African communities who profited from this traffic. Wealthy West Africans who profited from the slave systems also distinguished themselves in their dress. However, wealth alone did not fully determine patterns of dressing. Heterogeneous populations and access to official and unofficial trade goods produced a complex history of dress. Benjamin uses the term 'cosmopolitan' to describe consumers in western Africa, linked to diverse markets, within and beyond French imperial networks. Sartorial innovations reflected these shifting and intersecting influences.

The global networks intersecting the Indian Ocean world are a point of interest in a number of chapters and are a specific focus in Chapter 7, where Sarah Fee examines the distinctive sartorial system introduced by the monarch of Madagascar years before the kingdom was colonized. Fee's ethnographic analysis of fashion counters simplistic assumptions about one-way Western influences and emphasizes the strategic way King Radama used, adopted and adapted uniforms to claim authority inside and outside his realm. This king negotiated purposefully with various colonial powers, while enforcing a major sartorial shift within his kingdom. Madagascar emerges as the site of an innovative resistance that employed new sartorial systems for political ends. Tailored wool uniforms, braid and embellishments took on very different meanings in the process.

Colonization and settler colonialism were materialized through systems of dress. This theme is addressed through the introduction of linen shirts in colonial regions and the challenges of providing apparel suitable for slaves, as discussed in earlier chapters. Equally significant were the new dress regimes enacted in colonial regions such as New Zealand and Australia. Chapters 8 and 9 address the challenges and conundrums faced by settlers themselves who worked to modulate their dress in order to reinforce their territorial claims. In Chapter 8, Jane Malthus considers the settlers that formed part of what James Belich terms the 'Angloworld settler revolution'.[29] The imperial networks linking these spaces in turn provided the designs for weighty garments like wedding dresses, many of which are preserved in regional museums. Malthus unpacks the myths and realities of settlement and the geo-politics of textile production, access and use in New Zealand. Tensions of many sorts infused the dress system that emerged. For New Zealand settlers during the nineteenth and early twentieth centuries, a visible allegiance to the imperial centre, demonstrated in dress, was more important than the climate in which they lived. Further, providing clothing fibre for this imperial system remained a compelling purpose in this region. In Chapter 9, Laura Jocic considers the advice would-be settler immigrants received prior to launching themselves across the empire to Australia. What should they wear? What should they bring? And what could they expect in this new sartorial environment? Jocic concludes that the mid-nineteenth-century British guidebooks rarely provided good advice. Fashion was frowned upon in these compendiums, especially for those labouring male and female migrants destined for hard toil. Guidebooks served imperial purposes of hierarchy, including recommendations that bore little relation to the reality on arrival. Indeed, British visitors were shocked at the 'extravagance' of Melbourne ladies, fashionable excesses that overturned the 'natural' order of things, with Britain intended as the apogee of fashion.

Fashion was always political, whether policed by formal legal systems or by informal efforts to shame, ridicule or coerce. Dress styles remained a particularly contentious phenomenon within colonial settings, where the unruly colonized, or the newly wealthy settlers, rejected due modesty and compliance dear to imperial hierarchies. In Chapter 10, Tara Mayer addresses dress politics among the local elites in British India (1750–1830), where the adoption of European-style fashions unleashed extraordinary anxieties among British overseers. The avant-garde European styles adopted by some Indian princes elicited derision in British publications, imperfectly hiding British concerns that these fashions were a claim for political parity between Indians and Britons. The British struggled to demarcate themselves from the colonized. On some occasions, colonizers worked to distinguish dress systems; on other occasions, colonial instruction worked to erase Indigenous sartorial practice. In Chapter 11, Cory Willmott explores the causes and effects of clothing policies in North American missionary assimilationist programs. Many Anishinaabe children were forced into visual assimilation in boarding/residential schools. Some adults, however, chose to adopt or appropriate Western dress. These 'bodily regimes' were freighted with contending meanings and actors, missionary and Anishinaabe. White shirts and leather shoes were weighted with colonial meanings, though the moccasin way persisted in places despite these policies. Cross-cultural exchange was sometimes an amorphous force, a choice on some occasions and site of curiosity. In

Chapter 12, Hissako Anjo and Antonia Finnane explore the expansion of Western-style tailoring in China and Japan in the early twentieth century, an Asian-based focus that illuminates the complexities of knowledge transfer in thorny political circumstances. Anjo and Finnane identify an 'epistemological revolution' in cutting and tailoring that marked this history, where expertise developed amid differing social conditions, and where new hierarchies of skill evolved. Local tailors then served the priorities of cosmopolitan communities of men in China and Japan.

It is fitting that Karen Tranberg Hansen concludes this collection. Hansen pioneered seminal studies of dress, fashion and taste in colonial and post-colonial Africa and she works with a broad reach across disciplines and regional studies. In Chapter 13, she considers the politics of fashion in Zambia, exploring the strategies and innovations that allowed Zambian women and men to shape their sartorial, visual and aesthetic identities. Second-hand became 'new' in new geographies, with adroit adaptations. Western styles were reimagined through entangled relations with Zambian markets. At the same time, local designers 'invented' a traditional style in the *Chitenge*. Both systems of dress served the fashion desires and dress politics of this distinctive region. In sum, the processes of dressing global bodies open powerful histories of innovation and survival that comprise the human past.

Acknowledgements

Chapters in this book were presented at the conference 'Dressing Global Bodies: Clothing Cultures, Politics and Economies in Globalizing Eras, c. 1600s–1900s' held at the University of Alberta, 7–9 July 2016, organised by the editors. We are grateful for the financial and organisational support provided by the Pasold Research Fund (Conference Grant), the Social Sciences and Humanities Research Council of Canada (Connection Grant), and the University of Alberta, allowing us to host 125 presenters over a three-day event. Whilst only a fraction of conference papers are included in this book, we are pleased that many others are being published in various collections and journals internationally. Our thanks also go to Antonia Finnane, Dana Leibsohn, Karen Tranberg Hansen, and the anonymous referees without whom the 'Dressing Global Bodies' conference and this book would have not been possible.

Notes

1 The Philadelphia Museum of Art holds two fans of this type and the Museum of Fine Art, Boston holds two virtually identical examples, with one artefact including the name of the Chinese supplier, Wo & Co. Sui. These extant artifacts suggest the scope of this trade. See www.mfa.org/collections/object/feather-bris%C3%A9-fan-125856; and www.mfa.org/collections/object/feather-bris%C3%A9-fan-125857 (both accessed 21 May 2019).
2 Beverly Lemire, *Global Trade and the Transformation of Consumer Cultures: The Material World Remade, c.1500–1820* (Cambridge, UK: Cambridge University Press, 2018), 148–156; Evelyn Welch, 'Art on the Edge: Hair and Hands in Renaissance Italy' *Renaissance Studies* 23.3 (2009): 260–268.

3 Examples survive of fashionable fans made by the Wendat, a First Nation community resident outside Quebec City. Their works can be found in the McCord Museum, Montreal, the Museum of Fine Arts, Boston and the Canadian Museum of History, among others. For discussion of Native American fashion makers see Lemire, *Global Trade*, 281–287; Anne De Stecher, 'Souvenir Arts, Collectable Crafts, Cultural Heritage: The Huron-Wendat of Wendake, Quebec', in *Craft, Community and Material Culture of Place and Politics, 19th–20th Century*, ed. Janice Helland, Bevery Lemire and Alena Buis (Aldershot, UK: Ashgate, 2014). See also http://collections.musee-mccord.qc.ca/en/collection/artifacts/M12679; www.mfa.org/collections/object/fixed-feather-fan-125289; and www.historymuseum.ca/collections/artifact/36916/?q=feather+fan&page_num=1&item_num=5&media_irn=3069531 (all accessed 21–24 May 2019). Brazilian feather fan, comparable to that made in Wendake can be found in the collection of the Victoria and Albert Museum, London, among other museums. See http://collections.vam.ac.uk/item/O114619/fan-natte-m-e (accessed 24 May 2019).
4 Anne Gerritsen and Giorgio Riello, eds., *The Global Lives of Things: The Material Culture of Connection in the Early Modern World* (London: Routledge, 2016).
5 Leora Auslander, 'Beyond Words', *American Historical Review* 110.4 (2005): 1019.
6 Auslander, 'Beyond Words', 1017; and Leora Auslander, *Cultural Revolutions: Everyday Life and Politics in Britain, North America and France* (Berkeley: University of California Press, 2009). For the value of material culture analysis in historical study see Lemire, *Global Trade*; Karen Harvey, ed., *History and Material Culture: A Student's Guide to Approaching Alternative Sources*, 2nd ed. (Abingdon, UK: Routledge, 2017); Anne Gerritsen and Giorgio Riello, eds., *Writing Material Culture History* (London: Bloomsbury Academic, 2015).
7 Sherry Farrell Racette, 'Looking for Stories and Unbroken Threads: Museum Artifacts as Women's History and Cultural Legacy', in *Restoring the Balance: First Nations Women, Community and Culture*, ed. Gail Guthrie Valaskakis, Madeleine Dion Stout and Eric Guimond (Winnipeg: University of Manitoba Press, 2009), 285.
8 Emma Tarlo, *Clothing Matters: Dress and Identity in India* (Chicago: University of Chicago Press, 1996); Sandra Niessen, Anne Marie Leshkowich and Carla Jones, eds., *Re-Orienting Fashion: The Globalization of Asian Dress* (Oxford: Berg, 2003); Jean Allman, ed., *Fashioning Africa: Power and the Politics of Dress* (Bloomington: Indiana University Press, 2004).
9 See notes 11, 12 and 18 for examples of these works.
10 Arjun Appadurai, *The Social Life of Things: Commodities in Cultural Perspective* (Cambridge, UK: Cambridge University Press, 1986).
11 Michelle Maskeill, 'Consuming Kashmir: Shawls and Empires, 1500–2000', *Journal of World History* 13.1 (2000): 27–65; Antonia Finnane, 'Yangzhou's "Mondernity": Fashion and Consumption in the Early Nineteenth Century', *Positions* 11.2 (2003): 395–425; Robert Ross, *Clothing: A Global History* (Cambridge, UK: Polity, 2008); Beverly Lemire, ed., *The Force of Fashion in Politics and Society: Global Perspectives from Early Modern to Contemporary Times* (Aldershot, UK: Ashgate, 2010); Lemire, *Global Trade*; and Cory Willmott, 'Designing, Producing and Enacting Nationalisms: Contemporary Amerindian Fashion in Canada', in *The Force of Fashion*, ed. Beverly Lemire, 167–190.
12 Sophie White, *Wild Frenchmen and Frenchified Indians: Material Culture and Race in Colonial Louisiana* (Philadelphia: University of Pennsylvania Press, 2012); Zoltán Biedermann, Anne Gerritsen and Giorgio Riello, eds., *Global Gifts: The Material Culture of Diplomacy in Early Modern Eurasia* (Cambridge, UK: Cambridge University Press, 2018); Lemire, *Global Trade*.
13 Terence Turner, 'The Social Skin', *HAU: Journal of Ethnographic Theory* 2.2 (2012): 486–504, reprinted from 1980.
14 Turner, 'The Social Skin', 486.

15 Karen Tranberg Hansen, 'The World of Dress: Anthropological Perspectives on Clothing, Fashion, and Culture', *Annual Review of Anthropology* 33 (2004): 369–392.

16 See note 10.

17 Beverly Lemire, *Dress, Culture and Commerce: The English Clothing Trade Before the Factory, c.1660–1800* (Baskingstoke, UK: Palgrave Macmillan, 1997); Lucy Norris, 'Creative Entrepreneurs: The Re-Cycling of Second-Hand Indian Clothing', in *Old Clothes, New Looks: Second-Hand Fashion*, ed., A. Palmer and H. Clark (Oxford: Berg, 2004), 119–134; Lynne B. Milgram, 'Activating Frontier Livelihoods: Women and the Transnational Secondhand Clothing Trade between Hong Kong and the Philippines', *Urban Anthropology* 37.1 (2008): 5–47; Onur Inal, 'Women's Fashions in Transition: Ottoman Borderlands and the Anglo-Ottoman Exchange of Costumes', *Journal of World History* 22.2 (2011): 243–272; Robert DuPlessis, *The Material Atlantic: Clothing, Commerce, and Colonization in the Atlantic World, 1650–1800* (Cambridge, UK: Cambridge University Press, 2015); Peter McNeil, *Pretty Gentlemen: Macaroni Men and the Eighteenth-Century Fashion World* (New Haven, CT: Yale University Press, 2018).

18 Susanne Küchler and Daniel Miller, *Clothing as Material Culture* (Oxford: Berg, 2005); Timothy Shannon, 'Dressing for Success on the Mohawk Frontier: Hendrick, William Johnson and the Indian Fashion', *William and Mary Quarterly* 53.1 (1996): 13–42; Grace Karskens, 'Red Coat, Blue Jacket, Black Skin: Aboriginal Men and Clothing in Early New South Wales', *Aboriginal History* 35 (2012): 1–36; Chanel Clarke, 'A Māori Perspective on the Wearing of Black', in *Black: History of Black in Fashion, Society and Culture in New Zealand*, ed. D. de Pont (Auckland: Penguin Books, 2012), n.p.; Giorgio Riello and Peter McNeil, eds., *Shoes: A History from Sandals to Sneakers* (Oxford: Berg, 2011); Steeve O. Buckridge, *African Lace-Bark in the Caribbean: The Construction of Race, Class, and Gender* (London: Bloomsbury, 2016).

19 Dipesh Chakrabarty, *Provincializing Europe: Postcolonial Thought and Historical Difference* (Princeton, NJ: Princeton University Press, 2000); Natalie Zemon Davis, 'Decentering History: Local Stories and Cultural Crossings in a Global World', *History and Theory* 50 (May 2011): 188–202; Hansen, 'World of Dress', 372.

20 Dorothy Ko, 'The Body as Attire: The Shifting Meanings of Footbinding in Seventeenth-Century China', *Journal of Women's History* 8.4 (1997): 8–27; Niessen et al., *Re-Orienting Fashion*; Karen Tranberg Hansen, *Salaula: The World of Secondhand Clothing and Zambia* (Chicago: University of Chicago Press, 2000); Sophie White, '"Wearing Three or Four Handkerchiefs Around His Neck and Elsewhere About Him": Slaves' Construction of Masculinity and Ethnicity in French Colonial New Orleans', *Gender & History* 15.3 (2003): 528–549; Antonia Finnane, *Changing Clothes in China: Fashion, History, Nation* (New York: Columbia University Press, 2008); Ulinka Rublack, *Dressing Up: Cultural Identity in Renaissance Europe* (Oxford: Oxford University Press, 2010); Giorgio Riello and Ulinka Rublack, eds., *The Right to Dress: Sumptuary Laws in a Global Perspective, c.1200–1800* (Cambridge, UK: Cambridge University Press, 2019).

21 David Bell, 'This Is What Happens When Historians Overuse the Idea of the Network', *New Republic* 26 October 2013, quoted in Richard Drayton and David Motadel, 'Discussion: The Futures of Global History', *Journal of Global History* 13 (2019): 2; for further debate see Jeremy Adelman, 'What Is Global History Now?', *Aeon*, 2 March 2017, https://aeon.co/essays/is-global-history-still-possible-or-has-it-had-its-moment (accessed 30 August 2018).

22 Drayton and Motadel, 'Discussion: The Futures of Global History', 13.

23 Examples of global, subaltern histories include: Marcel van der Linden, *Workers of the World: Essays Towards a Global Labour History* (Leiden: Brill, 2008); Clare Anderson, *Subaltern Lives: Biographies of Colonialism in the Indian Ocean World* (Cambridge, UK: Cambridge University Press, 2012).

24 Fernand Braudel, *Civilization and Capitalism Fifteenth-Eighteenth Century: The Structure of Everyday Life*, vol. 1, trans. Siàn Reynolds (New York: Harper & Row, 1985), 312–313.

25 Gilles Lipovetsky, *The Empire of Fashion: Dressing Modern Democracy* (Princeton, NJ: Princeton University Press, 1994), 15.

26 For example, Joan DeJean, *The Essence of Style: How the French Invented High Fashion … Sophistication, and Glamour* (New York: Free Press, 2005); Linda Welters and Abby Lillethun, eds., *The Fashion Reader* (Oxford and New York: Berg, 2007); Carlo Marco Belfanti, 'The Civilization of Fashion: At the Origins of a Western Social Institution', *Journal of Social History* 43.2 (2009): 261–283. For a critique see Giorgio Riello, *Back in Fashion: Western Fashion from the Middle Ages to the Present* (London: Yale University Press, 2020).

27 Craig Clunas, 'Modernity Global and Local: Consumption and the Rise of the West', *American Historical Review* 104.5 (1999): 1497–1511; Jack Goody, *The East in the West* (Cambridge, UK: Cambridge University Press, 1996); Jack Goody, *The Theft of History* (Cambridge, UK: Cambridge University Press, 2012); Giorgio Riello and Peter McNeil, eds., *The Fashion History Reader: Global Perspectives* (London: Routledge, 2010); Veronica Dewar, 'Our Clothing, Our Culture, Our Identity', in *Arctic Clothing of North America, Alaska, Canada, Greenland*, ed. J. C. H. King, Birgit Pauksztat and Robert Storrie (Montreal and Kingston: McGill-Queen's University Press, 2010), 23–27; Karen Kramer, Jay Calderin, Madeleine M. Krope and Jessiva R. Metcalfe, *Native Fashion Now: North American Indian Style* (New York: Prestel, 2015).

28 Emma Tarlo and Annelies Moors, eds., *Islamic Fashion and Anti-Fashion: New Perspectives from Europe and North America* (London and New York: Bloomsbury, 2013); Ted Polhemus, *Fashion & Anti-Fashion: Exploring Adornment and Dress from an Anthropological Perspective* (Open Source, 2011).

29 For example, see James Belich, *Replenishing the Earth: The Settler Revolution and the Rise of the Angloworld, 1783–1939* (Oxford: Oxford University Press, 2009).

1

THE FABRIC OF EARLY GLOBALIZATION

Skin, fur and cloth in the de Bry's travel accounts, 1590–1630

Susanna Burghartz

'The island of Virginia in the region of America was discovered in 1587; because of the variety of its dress and customs, I thought I should put it into this book.'[1] This is how Cesare Vecellio explained the addition of Virginia to the 1598 second edition of his extraordinarily successful costume book, which appeared under the title *Habiti antichi et moderni di tutto il mondo*. As the first costume book with an ambition for global coverage, it included the continent of America.[2] Beginning with a detailed description of dress in his native city, Venice, in the first edition of his book published in 1590, Vecellio provided not only a proto-ethnographic overview of Italy and Europe but also of Asia and Africa based on regionally differing clothing styles. In 1598 he added the so-called New World at the end of his encyclopaedic work.[3] The section on Virginia was based on images and information published for the first time just eight years earlier in the first volume of Theodor de Bry's America series. The Calvinist de Bry launched his successful and long-lasting publishing venture in 1590 with a volume dedicated to European voyages to the West, so-called Indiae occidentalis or Americae. His sons expanded it from 1597 onwards with voyages to the East, so-called Indiae orientalis, thus making this richly illustrated travel collection an undertaking of truly global proportions.[4] The two series were published in Frankfurt and appeared in both German and Latin.[5] As a whole they were aimed at scholars and collectors, courts and the wealthy urban elites in Germany and Europe. The engravings in both series became the most extensive and influential pictorial archive of the first globalization.[6]

The connections between the genres of the costume book and the travel collection were no coincidence. Both aimed at cataloguing and categorizing the world. In the course of the sixteenth century, European costume books had developed visual strategies for depicting the grammar of social and regional differences within and between societies through clothing.[7] At the same time, travel accounts, cosmologies and choreographies developed processes for integrating the New World more or less coherently into existing European knowledge systems and revising them in accordance with a stage theory of civilized development.[8]

Taking the example of the de Brys' lavishly illustrated travel collection, this chapter discusses the meaning of clothing and its effects on the formation of identities in what has been called the first age of globalization. The focus will be on imagination as well as knowledge and economics, since around 1600 Europeans like Vecellio were not simply honing a global system of classification based on dress. Europeans were also becoming integrated into an increasingly global system of exchange that included large-scale trade of textiles from Asia to Europe and from Europe to Africa and the Americas. Yet, the economic interest in global exchange and trade could not always be smoothly reconciled with striving to organize the world through clothing according to a system that demonstrated the superiority of European civilization. Europeans employed sometimes surprising narrative and visual strategies involving similarity, otherness and adaptation in order to sketch a reassuring picture of their own superiority. Their aim was to link their own well-established clothing system that organized differences of sex, status and ethnicity with their economic hopes and interests.

In recent years, global history has intensely discussed the role of fashion and fabric for an early age of globalization, c.1400–1800.[9] It has become increasingly clear how important not just actual interactions and opportunities for exchange were, but also their imaginary anticipation, configuration and mastery. Economically, the trade in fabrics and the (raw) materials to produce them grew steadily. Gold and silver, spices and crops were not the only driving forces behind global networking processes. The significance of non-European raw materials, fabrics, skins and furs in the European textile regions and their global interactions also grew apace. They permanently changed early modern consumer cultures and led to the advent of a new 'cosmopolitan material culture'.[10] At the same time, fabrics and clothing also played a key identity-political role for European textile cultures, whose prosperity and long-standing artisanal pride was largely based on the production of and trade in fabrics. By developing a global system of knowledge and classification for clothing with the aid of costume books, cosmologies and travelogues, they could create a more or less coherent context linking their own notions of social order with the positioning of various non-European societies and even those deemed 'savage' on a scale of civilization. Published between 1590 and 1630, the de Bry family's *Eastern* and *Western Voyages* were among the most famous early modern collections of travel accounts and arguably the most beautifully illustrated. They accompanied the entry of England and the Netherlands as colonial competitors. Moreover, they may be read as globally orientated costume books: they processed knowledge from various sources about dress as a globally functioning system of meaning, thereby illustrating developments over the sixteenth century in the global trade in relevant materials – raw materials like dyewoods, wool, silk, furs, skins and feathers but also various fabrics.

The de Brys deployed a range of existing images. Sometimes they simply copied, sometimes they modified their models, and sometimes they used their own imaginations to affirm, and occasionally alter, European stereotypes about non-European societies and their clothing through images. By portraying clothing from all over the world, the de Brys used texture as a major clue for addressing questions of difference and similarity as well as the vast continuum between these poles. Like contemporary costume books,[11] the de Brys used clothing and its opposite, nakedness, to integrate the various peoples and regions visually into a global stage set of historical development. Their illustrated travelogues opened up a wide range of positions between 'civilized' and 'savage' as encoded in dress. But they also reported on the intensive exchange of stuffs and garments between cultures, whether as diplomatic gifts, important commodities or valued means of barter.

Ernst van den Boogaart noted in 2004 that in de Bry, dress 'provides elementary information about the civility of a social group following the rough-and-ready formula "the more dress the more civility, the more nudity the more savagery"'.[12] I take this formula as a point of departure in order to consider the interplay between unambiguous black and white positioning and the artful transgression of this binary logic. In this chapter I ask how skin, fur and fabric were used on a global comparative scale to negotiate similarity, difference and assimilation: how did the engravings use textures, patterns and cuts to dramatize similarities and differences and to cement but also to play with them? What global topography do the two major de Bry travel series create based on clothing and what systems of circulation and exchange do they invoke? And can we understand the clothing discourse of the costume books and collections of travelogues simultaneously as constitutive elements of a theatre of the global and an emerging stage of early globalization in the making?

(Social) skin – pelts – fur

The first volume on Virginia, for which the de Brys relied on drawings by John White, who documented conditions in Roanoke for the Virginia Company, already appears to affirm the formula of the naked savage. The accompanying engraving depicts Indigenous warriors wearing feathers on their heads and animal-skin loincloths (Figure 1.1). The figures' nakedness and the descriptive insistence on their primitive, animalistic loincloths at first seem to underline the uncivilized nature of the inhabitants of Virginia. According to the caption, 'They hange before them the skinne of some beaste verye feinelye dresset in suche sorte, that the tayle hangeth downe behynde'. The text also describes in detail hairstyles, body painting or tattoos.[13] In combination with the images' use of poses and gestures the collection thus refers to a general European image of the primitiveness and wildness of the natives. The particular interest in the nakedness of the 'savages' displayed by de Bry's sons also fits this image.[14] As Michiel van Groesen shows in his comprehensive analysis of the collection, the de Brys' engravers emphasized the natives' Otherness with a few specific changes to the original drawings by White. By attributing feather headdresses to quite diverse ethnic groups in America, Asia and Africa, they additionally underlined the homogeneity of the uncivilized Other.[15]

A weroan or great Lorde of Virginia. III.

THe Princes of Virginia are attyred in suche manner as is expressed in this figure. They weare the haire of their heades long and bynde opp the ende of thesame in a knot vnder thier eares. Yet they cutt the topp of their heades from the forehead to the nape of the necke in manner of a cokscombe, stirkinge a faier longe pecher of some berd att the Begininge of the creste vppun their foreheads, and another short one on bothe seides about their eares. They hange at their eares ether thicke pearles, or somwhat els, as the clawe of some great birde, as cometh in to their fansye. Moreouer They ether pownes, or paynt their forehead, cheeks, chynne, bodye, armes, and leggs, yet in another sorte then the inhabitantz of Florida. They weare a chaine about their necks of pearles or beades of copper, wich they muche esteeme, and ther of wear they also braselets ohn their armes. Vnder their breists about their bellyes appeir certayne spotts, whear they vse to lett them selues bloode, when they are sicke. They hange before the the skinne of some beaste verye feinelye dresset in suche sorte, that the tayle hangeth downe behynde. They carye a quiuer made of small rushes holding their bowe readie bent in on hand, and an arrowe in the other, radie to defend themselues. In this manner they goe to warr, or tho their solemne feasts and banquetts. They take muche pleasure in huntinge of deer wher of theris great store in the contrye, for yt is fruit full, pleasant, and full of Goodly woods. Yt hathe also store of riuers full of diuers sorts of fishe. When they go to battel they paynt their bodyes in the most terible manner that thei can deuise.

FIGURE 1.1 'A Weroan or Great Lorde of Virginia', plate 3 from Theodor de Bry, *America*. Part 1 in English. *A Briefe and True Report of the New Found Land of Virginia, of the Commodities and of the Nature and Manners of the Naturall Inhabitants* … made in English by Thomas Hariot, Frankfurt 1590.

Although this reading, with its emphasis on the construction of Otherness is persuasive, the collection also allows for the reconstruction of further levels of meaning and lines of argumentation less clearly wedded to the logic of binary coding. The first two volumes on Virginia and Florida in particular, which have received by far the most attention, show the Indigenous bodies as idealized, following antique models.[16] The picture heading 'A Weroan or Great Lorde of Virginia', which points to differences of social rank, and the comment on the 'finely dressed' quality of the animal skins, contrast with the first impression of uncivilized savages. Stephanie Pratt has also shown with reference to the 'Renaissance elbow', that this image was a highly artificial, mannerist portrayal, a pose borrowed from the programme of figures of European rulers, warriors and soldiers.[17]

Comparison with Hendrik Goltzius' 1587 'Standard bearer' reveals clear and surprizing similarities of gesture and body language between Indigenous and European warriors – both idealized – in White/de Bry's pictorial invention (Figure 1.2). This

FIGURE 1.2 'The Standard Bearer', by Hendrick Goltzius, 1587.

Source: © Rijksmuseum, Amsterdam, RP-P-OB-4639.

applies to details like feathers, earrings and curls as well as the standard bearer's slashed fabric, which corresponds to the Indigenous chief's body painting. However, the abundant use of fabric in European dress contrasts starkly with the Indigenous man's nakedness and fur loincloth. A first, fine crack appears in the supposedly clear contrast between savage/naked and civilized/clothed. This creates an ambiguity or even contradiction between various attributions, meanings and value judgments, which was typical of proto-ethnographic knowledge production with their varied voices and interests.[18]

The engraving that closes de Bry's series on the inhabitants of Virginia impressively demonstrates the delicate interplay between similarity and difference. 'The Marckes of the Cheif Mene of Virginia' is a presumably freely invented guide to reading Indigenous body modification (Figure 1.3).[19] The engraving elucidates the meaning of the individual tattoos, which function as signs marking their bearers socially and ethnically as members of individual groups or clans, as the subscript explains. Terence Turner uses the concept of 'social skin' to describe the function of body painting for the Amazonian Kayapo: painted or tattooed skin, he claims, 'is the medium most directly and most concretely concerned with the construction of the individual as social actor or cultural "subject"'.[20] Concretely, in this society body painting represents age, gender and social status and thus ultimately the constitution of social classes and their divisions.[21] This corresponds rather precisely to the function attributed to clothing as a marker of difference in Europe since the late Middle Ages. European observers of de Bry's engraving were familiar with coats of arms and clan badges and were accustomed to using clothing to help them organize their world along social and ethnic lines. In the sixteenth century, costume books emerged as a genre in Europe to depict this repertoire, thereby developing an increasingly global semantics that claimed to classify the various societies in and outside Europe according to their place in the history of civilization.

In his reading of this engraving, Michael Gaudio particularly stresses its translation of the tattoo on the Indigenous body and the arrows into the Latin alphabet, interpreting it as de Bry's 'writing lesson ... upon the body of an American Indian'.[22] He also suggests another reading, in which seemingly secure conceptual pairs, such as visual/verbal and savage/civilized, become destabilized.[23] This is because the engraving illustrates 'how a mark inscribed on a body and a letter inscribed on a copper plate might share a common materiality'. Thus 'the letters on the page are *like* the tattoos they index'.[24] This is all the truer if we consider specific material qualities: copperplate and skin, both media for incisions, correspond to materials such as pelts, leather, lace and slashed, painted and pleated fabrics. They all serve as bearers of socially relevant information. Through their shared characteristics as material and medium, they visually produce textures and messages that allow for comparison and produces similarities.

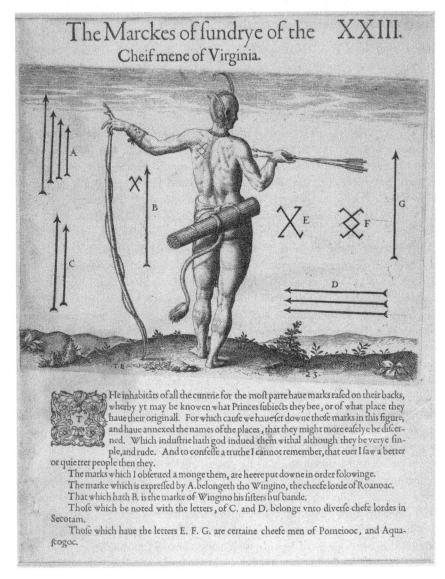

The Marckes of fundrye of the XXIII.
Cheif mene of Virginia.

He inhabitāts of all the cuntrie for the moſt parte haue marks raſed on their backs,
wherby yt may be knowen what Princes ſubieĉts they bee, or of what place they
haue their originall. For which cauſe we haueſet downe thoſe marks in this figure,
and haue annexed the names of the places, that they might more eaſelye be diſcer-
ned. Which induſtrie hath god indued them withal although they be verye ſin-
ple, and rude. And to confeſſe a truthe I cannot remember, that euer I ſaw a better
or quietter people then they.

The marks which I obſerued amonge them, are heere put downe in order folowinge.

The marke which is expreſſed by A. belongeth tho Wingino, the cheefe lorde of Roanoac.

That which hath B. is the marke of Wingino his ſifters huſbande.

Thoſe which be noted with the letters, of C. and D. belonge vnto diverſe chefe lordes in
Secotam.

Thoſe which haue the letters E. F. G. are certaine cheefe men of Pomeiooc, and Aqua-
ſcogoc.

FIGURE 1.3 'The Marckes of Sundrye of the Cheif Mene of Virginia', plate 23 from
Theodor de Bry, *America*. Part 1 in English. *A briefe and True Report of the New Found
Land of Virginia, of the Commodities and of the Nature and Manners of the Naturall Inhabit-
ants* ... made in English by Thomas Hariot, Frankfurt 1590.

Source: © The British Library Board, C.38.i.18, plate 23 page 33.

Textures of convergence: clothing and skin

The second volume of de Bry's *Western Voyages*, dedicated to Florida, takes the meeting between Europe and America still further by converging the surface textures in the portrayal of Indigenous and European leaders. This is all the more surprising since the text and accompanying illustrations depict some disquieting rituals of punishment and sacrifice, emphasizing the cruel idolatry of the Florida natives. In the Virginia volume, the visual analogies between Indigenous and European warriors consist mainly of poses and gestures. In the Florida volume such analogies are evoked quite explicitly through textiles and their surface designs. The representations of the European leaders reveal remarkable similarities between the texture of their clothing and the Indigenous bodies and their tattoos. This becomes particularly obvious in the engraving of Laudonnière[25] and Saturiwa[26] watching a cruel ritual of punishment for inattentive sentries. The clothing worn by the two is at once similar and distinct (Figure 1.4).[27]

There are significant similarities between the headgear of the two leaders, with the feathers on the European's hat resembling the Indigenous man's hairstyle. The hatband and the attachment of the feather headdress are also similar, as the fall of the folds of the European sash and the Indigenous deerskin cape correspond to one another. Particularly interesting is the effect of the tattoos on the king's arms, torso and legs: the Indigenous chief appears almost clothed and thus imply through texture – clothing on the one hand, tattooed skin on the other – the equality between the two leaders (especially in contrast to the naked, smooth skin of the king's subjects, visible in the background). Behind Laudonnière and Saturiwa, European soldiers seem to form a single group with the two leaders. Far less elaborate, the soldiers' clothing nevertheless marks them as civilized. The captions describe the treatment of the king's skin as 'pricks' or 'pricked' and thus as tattooed rather than painted; and yet the designs appear as purely surface ornaments, similar to the king's painted deerskin. The slits in the captain's suit appear primarily as pattern, while the soldier's slashed clothing recalls wounds. The texture of skin and fabric thus plays with approximation and difference.

Admiration for the natives' textile artistry becomes clearer still in a depiction of the king and queen of Florida with their courtiers during an evening stroll in the woods, 'covered with finely prepared/deerskin painted in various colours/such that one can hope to find no finer or more splendid painting'.[28] Clearly just as fascinating as the king's painted cloak, albeit far more alien, was the queen's moss mantle: 'From her shoulders hangs a particular type of moss / which grows on many trees. This moss hangs down like thread / in the manner of a chain / green and sky blue in colour / fine and merry / resembling silken threads'.[29] When it came to the royal clothing, the subscript, with its indications of comparability – the fineness of the painting or the silky and thus precious quality of the moss filaments – sought to comment positively. The subsequent commentary on Floridian tattoo practices, however, which addresses readers directly, reveals the deep ambivalence with which

FIGURE 1.4 'How the Sentries Were Punished for Their Carelessness', detail from plate 32, Theodor de Bry, *America*, vol. 2, Frankfurt 1591.

Source: © Zentralbibliothek Zürich, Re 20: n,2 1 G (www.e-rara.ch/doi/10.3931/e-rara-28677).

Europeans regarded the inhabitants of Florida and their bodily practices: 'Dear reader / you should however know / that all these kings / along with their wives / adorn / the skin of their bodies / with many little dots / creating paintings / [as can be seen from Figure 1.4] / such that they sometimes lie ill for seven or eight days.'[30] And their sharp fingernails and toenails, which they filed with shells, seem to have aroused more disdain than admiration.[31] The engraving thus combines multiple, conflicting messages: acknowledgement and admiration for an alien but fascinating mode of dress and body decoration alternates seamlessly with dismay and indeed perhaps even contempt for unhealthy tattoo practices and body treatments. Once again, closeness and distance are brought into a virtually irresolvable interplay.

Asian textile worlds: similar, superior or different?

Asia presented a different set of interpretative challenges for Europeans. Here, Europeans encountered commercial cloth production and an articulated textile trade. In 1598 Jan Huygen van Linschoten, a Dutch merchant from Haarlem who had served for six years as secretary to the archbishop of Goa, published *Itinerario: Voyage ofte schipvaert van Jan Huyghen van Linschoten naer Oost ofte Portugaels Indien*, which made Portuguese knowledge about India and Asia accessible to Dutch readers and paved the way for Dutch expansion into Asia. By the late sixteenth century, the Portuguese had familiarized themselves not just with the Asian spice markets, but also with Asian textile markets and their workings. European participation in this trade also increased greatly around 1600 with the establishment of the Dutch and English East India companies to rival with the already existing Portuguese Carreira da Índia.[32] The de Bry brothers adopted Linschoten's *Itinerario* with its plentiful information on Asian textile culture in slightly altered form as volumes 2–4 of their collection.[33] Freshly arrived on the Indian Subcontinent, Linschoten was already swooning over the potential of textiles in Cambay (present-day Khambhat):

> Out of the masses of cotton there canvas is made / of all sorts / which have the following names / *cannequins, boffetas, iorins, chautares, cotonias*, which are similar to drill / and are used for sails or other things / and there are also many other kinds, all of them for little money. They make it so finely / that one cannot see a single thread / and it greatly surpasses all Dutch canvas in purity. They also make many carpets / which they call *alcatifas* / but they are not as beautiful / or as fine / as those that come from Persia via Hormuz / They also make other sorts of carpets called *banquans* / rather similar to the striped sheets from Scotland / and they are used to cover boxes and trunks. The coverlets / called *jodorin colchas* / are very finely and beautifully wrought / of silk and also cotton / in all manner of colours and designs.[34]

Cambay in north-west India was a major textile emporium. Linschoten's enthusiasm continued as he journeyed on to Bengal where he admired 'gorgeous cotton canvas / at Negapatan, S. Thomas, and Musulepatan, of all colours and woven with some pictures and leaf-work / very finely and subtly wrought', which were traded by the Portuguese as well as the merchants of Bengal, Pegu, Siam and Malacca.[35] Despite this wealth of information and enthusiasm for the mercantile potential, the illustrations give limited attention to the variety and quality of fabrics. Thus de Bry's first engraving of India shows scantily dressed Brahmans, who demonstrated their highly privileged position with a 'triple cord, like twine'. Outside the house they wore a long skirt, as can be seen from the example of the merchants beside them, who, dressed like Brahmans, traded in velvet, silk and 'similar wares' (Figure 1.5).

FIGURE 1.5 'Of the Brahmans / i.e. the Indian Priests / and of Their Merchants', plate 8 from Johann Theodor and Johann Israel de Bry, *Orientalische Reisen*, vol. 2, Frankfurt 1598.

Source: © Universitätsbibliothek Göttingen, 4° Itin I 3844ᵃ:1 Rara.

In the *Eastern Voyages*, too, the de Brys depicted the costumes of the various people that Europeans encountered on their eastward travels to Africa, India, South East Asia and China. And once again, they used the visual to classify societies according to their perceived degree of civilization.[36] Dominated by an interest in global classification, the visualization of textile diversity, differing textures, patterns and cuts fades into the background.

Linschoten proved himself especially impressed with the wealth of China and its surfeit of silks:

> It is as common in this country for people to wear silk / as for us to wear ordinary coarse linen cloth. They wear silk / and satin down to their shoes / and also brocade, finely worked and embroidered with golden and silver pieces / because silk is in such surplus amongst them / and so common throughout the country.[37]

Linschoten cites a veritable river of silk, which meant more than enough remained in the country despite exports to India, South East Asia and Japan. The corresponding illustration shows the multilayered Chinese clothing culture. The caption underlines the social distinctions within Chinese society, which revealed its sophistication: high-born Chinese donned silk robes of many colours and the middle classes made do with less precious silks, while the common people wore wool–linen blends, light woollens and cotton cloth (Figure 1.6). The image depicts not the sumptuous quality of the silk fabrics but voluminous robes with multiple long folds. As the text by de Brys explains, in this the Chinese sewing patterns resemble those of 'our' (European) forebears.[38] This positions purportedly superior Chinese silk culture behind European developments, since their fashions were said to correspond to an already obsolete phase of European fashion history.

The account published three years later (1602) by Olivier van Noort, the first Dutchman to circumnavigate the globe, as an addendum to volume 9 of the *Western Voyages* operates quite similarly. Having travelled the globe, van Noort had come into contact with artful Asian fabrics, a world dominated primarily by Indian cloth that was exchanged across and beyond Asia. But this world was not merely the equal but superior to European cloth production, which played a central role in the continent's economy and was the pride of the European cities and their textile guilds. After all, second only to spices, Asian cloth was of paramount interest for the Portuguese, Dutch and other European traders throughout the early modern period. The aesthetic and above all the economic significance of these fabrics remain strangely understated in the de Brys' illustrations of India and South East Asia, although various texts in the collection repeatedly report on fabrics and the trade of cloth in Asia. The often superior quality of Indian cloth and of clothing production, its sophistication, high value and fine workmanship were depicted rudimentarily at best.

After crossing the Straits of Magellan and the Pacific Ocean, van Noort ran into a Japanese trading vessel in the Straits of Manila whose crew mightily impressed him, not least because of their clothing: 'the clothing of the captain / who was a nobleman / was of a light silk / very artfully adorned / with all manner of leaves and flowers'.[39] The corresponding engraving, however, does

FIGURE 1.6 'The Form and Dress of Male and Female Persons in China', plate 23 from Johann Theodor and Johann Israel de Bry, *Orientalische Reisen*, vol. 2, Frankfurt 1598.

Source: © Zentralbibliothek Zürich, Rara 52550.

not really reflect the claim that leaf work and flowers were 'very artfully' formed on the light silk, even if the image bears a certain resemblance to known Japanese patterns of the time. Instead of depicting the outstanding quality of Japanese textiles it shows the Japanese in overgowns (Figure 1.7), which interestingly

FIGURE 1.7 'Depiction of the Japanese', plate 12 from Johann Theodor and Johann Israel de Bry, *America*, vol. 9 *additamentum*, Frankfurt 1602.

Source: © Staatliche Bibliothek Regensburg 999/2 Hist.pol. 812/2 (http://mdz-nbn-resolving.de/urn:nbn:de:bvb:12-bsb11056203-5).

enough, the author associated with the 'exotic' costumes of Eastern Europe, namely the long, somewhat old-fashioned garments of the Polish nobility – a comparison that remarkably combined equality with foreignness.[40]

An often reproduced example appears to get far closer to the actual patterns used in South East Asia. It shows the meeting between the Dutch admiral Spielbergen and Vimala Dharma Surya, king of Candy (1590–1604) (Figure 1.8). The Sinhalese monarch is adorned with jewels and as textile historian John Guy observes 'wears a skirt cloth (*tuppotiya*) with a floral border and a sawtooth

X.

Contrafentung vnnd Bildtnuß deß
Königs von Candij vnd deß Admirals.

Jeses ist das wahrhafftige Bildtnuß deß mächti-
gen Königs Fimala Derura Suriada sonst in seiner jugendt zu
Coulombo getaufft/da ihm der Name Don Iean d' Austria
de Coulombo mit getheilet wirdt. Dieser König ist vnter den
seinen eines fürnehmen Geschlechts/von jugendt auff hat er sich
brauchen lassen in Kriegen vnnd der gleichen sachen/ hat sich auch eine zeitlang
zu Goa gehalten : Dieser König helt sich freundtlich gegen dem Admiral/
hatt mit ihm viellerley discurriert beyde in geistlichen vnd weltlichen Sachen
vnd entlich im vnd seinem Herrn alle freundtschafft angelobt/wie in der Histor y
weitleufftig zu ersehen.

FIGURE 1.8 'The King of Kandy and Admiral Spilbergen Meet', plate 10 from Johann
Theodor and Johann Israel de Bry, *Orientalische Reisen*, vol. 7, Frankfurt 1605.

Source: © Universitätsbibliothek Göttingen, 4° Itin I 3844ª:2 Rara.

pattern at each end; the *tumpal* motif came to dominate Indian trade cloths for
the Malay-Indonesian market'.[41] Even if Indo-South East Asian textile production and trade were superior to their European counterparts and accordingly
evoked admiration in the travel accounts,[42] van den Boogaart's use of clothing
as an indicator of civilization for the Europeans also appears to work in this case.
Importantly for European readers, the text explicitly states how far the Ceylonese court had come on the path to Christianization and Europeanization.

The Dutch admiral expresses his countrymen's esteem for Ceylonese culture in the following scene: he had felt extraordinarily honoured to be invited into the queen's private apartments. Like the young princes and princesses, she dressed in the European manner.[43] Spilbergen also reports that the king and the young prince were in the process of learning Dutch, and had explained to him that 'Candy has now become Flanders'.[44] Here he implicitly alludes to a shift of alliance from the Portuguese to the Dutch, but also invokes a European region well known for its export-oriented textile manufacturing.[45] In this way, the text hints once again to European superiority and the great Ceylonese interest in European culture and dress, and ignores the importance of Indian textile production and the South East Asian textile trade for Europeans.

In the accompanying illustrations, the renowned textile markets remain as colourless as the splendid quality of Indian and Asian stuffs repeatedly described in the texts. In the middle and background of the only depiction of the cosmopolitan market of Banten on the island of Java, the viewer sees Javanese fabric sellers, working in separate male and female groups. There are also the stands of Chinese merchants, who according to the detailed description offered a rich assortment of fabrics: 'Silk embroidery thread / of every kind / and all manner of beautiful colours / silks and damasks / velvet / satin / gold thread'.[46] Once more, the text stresses the quality of the fabrics without highlighting the significance of the Asian textile trade for the global economy. At the same time, the etchings render the Asian textiles so that they pale in comparison to European dress, which are depicted as much more refined and valuable (Figure 1.9).

FIGURE 1.9 'The Market at Bantam', plate 32 from Johann Theodor and Johann Israel de Bry, *Orientalische Reisen*, vol. 3, Frankfurt, 1599.

Source: © Universitätsbibliothek Göttingen, 4° Itin I 3844ᵃ:1 Rara.

Adaptation, otherness and the African market

The collection of accounts dedicated to Africa, which the de Bry brothers already announced with the first volume of their *East Indian Voyages* in 1597, emphasizes quite different features. Here they encountered another rich Indigenous textile culture – which the accounts however largely ignore – along with the long-standing textile imports from North Africa, the Near East and India.[47] Pigafetta and Lopez's account of the kingdom of Congo, published in Italian just seven years earlier in 1591, was included in volume 1 of the *Eastern Voyages*. It reports on the Congolese adoption of civilized European dress practices as part of an act of embracing the Christian faith. The resulting textile trade allowed Europeans to make good profits in the trade with Africa/Congo thanks to asymmetrical conditions of exchange.

The Portuguese Duarte Lopez had visited Rome in 1588 as a diplomat for the kingdom of Congo, but the pope had refused to receive him.[48] His account presents the sophisticated textile culture of his kingdom and its neighbouring countries. He begins his description with the production of palm-leaf fabrics, which the Congolese and their neighbours wove into splendid damasks (*incorimbas*) for the king, shot through with leaf work and gold. They also produced velvet (*zachas*), atlas (*maricas*), taffeta (*en-gombos*) and lesser stuffs.[49] When the Congolese lords went to war, they wore hats or berets adorned with ostrich, peacock, cockerel or other plumes. As currency they used Venetian glass beads, which they wore like rosaries around their necks and arms.[50] Lopez devotes a separate chapter to the lasting changes in sartorial customs since the Portuguese arrival. Once again, he begins with the palm-leaf garments worn by the king and court in pre-colonial times, and continues with a description of the 'delicate and precious' furs, 'namely the fur of young tigers / civet cats / sables / martens and similar beasts / whose pelts are put to splendid use', which they laid over their shoulders.[51] The depiction of the animal pelts whose heads the natives attached to their shoulders, recalls the images of Virginia and Florida in the America series. The description of how Congolese women of the middle and upper strata, unlike slaves and servants, wore several layers of cloth one over the other and covered their breasts with 'a little apron' underlines that in the Congo, social status was negatively correlated with nakedness.[52] However, after the arrival of the Portuguese, the court began to dress in the Portuguese manner: the courtiers now wore cloaks and long scarlet coats, hats and berets and slippers or boots. Elegant women also followed Portuguese fashion. While they did not wear cloaks, they donned veils and little black velvet hats adorned with precious stones. Poor women, in contrast, had not adapted their style of clothing to the colonizers, but remained true to traditional forms. In Lopez's eyes the Christianization of the kingdom of Congo in the sixteenth century went hand in hand with the civilizing process, which was in turn revealed in dress.[53]

The texts and above all the images in the *West* and *East Indian Voyages* thus inscribe clothing cultures as disparate as those of the Congolese and the Virginia and Florida natives into a globally applicable European fashion system, which regarded the contrast between naked and clothed as the yardstick for development and civilization. In the case of the Congo, the civilizing process is clearly portrayed as a process of covering up and the result of beneficial European expansion. The alleged nudity of the natives before the arrival of the Europeans corresponds neatly with the systematic dismissal of the significance of the West African textile trade in the pre-European era.[54] At the same time, it is contrasted with several accounts in the de Bry collection that mention the Portuguese textile trade in Africa. Thus, Linschoten reports that on his way to Asia he already encountered Indian cottons imported by the Portuguese to Mozambique. His description of the inhabitants of Mozambique is revealing with respect to the proportions of tattooed/painted skin, fabric and clothing: it places the interest in patterns and textures in a tension-filled relationship with the civilizing process and the trade associated with it (see Figure 1.10). The inhabitants of coastal Mozambique and from Ethiopia to the Cape of Good Hope all went 'entirely naked and uncovered' it is said.[55] However, since contact with the Portuguese, the women in Mozambique had 'covered themselves a little', as the Portuguese brought cotton cloth from India and bartered it for gold and ivory.

The text devotes special attention to Indigenous body modification techniques and the accompanying sense of superiority of the Mozambicans about their own and the Europeans' skin colour:

> Many among them have pricked their entire bodies and faces / with a hot iron / and they are painted all over ... They are inordinately proud of these patterns / believing there are no more beautiful people under the sun/than they: Therefore / when they see ... white clothed people / they can only mock / and laugh at us / as if we were monsters. If they want to paint or imagine the Devil / they paint a white, clothed person: In sum / they ... are wholly convinced / that they have the proper colour for the human form / and that we have a false and bastardised colour.[56]

The author is equally baffled by the practice of some locals who filed their teeth into sharp points. All of these body practices seem to demonstrate the crude and uncivilized nature of the Mozambicans, who also had – Europeans said – a completely erroneous view of skin colour. Unlike the case of Virginia, the textures create no analogy between skin adornment and European fabrics, but simply affirms that any signs of civilization were owed to Portuguese clothing imports. Overall, the inhabitants of Mozambique are represented as especially savage and cruel, as the account and further illustrations demonstrate.

A few years later, the Dutch merchant Pieter de Marees reported his observations of West Africa in Benin and the Ivory and Gold Coast.[57] As a merchant, he was interested in transport routes as well as the customs and mores of his

III.

Beschreibung der Moren in der Insel Mosambique/ so Caffres genennt werden.

Ie Caffres oder Moren bewohnen das gantze Gestad Aethiopien biß an Capo di bona spe: seind pechschwartz/ mit kurtz krausem gesencktē Haar/ mit flachen stumpffen Nasen vnd dicken Lippen/ ober vñ vnder welchen/ wie auch an den Backen etliche gemachte Löcher haben/ dardurch sie ein Beinlein oder etwas anders stecken. Ihren Leib sampt dem Angesicht haben sie gemeinlich mit heissen Eissen gleich wie ein getruckter Damast zerpickt vnnd vermahlet/ gehen sonsten gantz nacket ohne einige scham/ außgenoñen die so in der Insel Mosambigue wohnen/ deren Weiber jre scham/ wegen der Portugaleser Gemeinschafft etwas bedecken / welche jhnen gegen Helffenbein vnd Gold/ baumwollene Tücher/ so sie auß Jmlien bringen / vertauschen/ mit denselbigen bedecken sich die Weiber von der halben Brust biß auff die halben Oberschenckel/ die Männer aber nur mit einem Lümplein gar schlechtlich.

Ihre Religion belangend/ seind in der Insel etliche Mahometisten/ etliche Heyden/ etliche wenige Christen: Die andern aber nach dem Capo di bona spe, mit welchen die Portugaleser noch keine Gemeinschafft gehabt/ leben one einige wissenschafft einiges Gottesdiensts/wie das Vieh/ als solches hievor im 4. vnd 41. Capitel vermeldet worden.

FIGURE 1.10 'Description of the Moors of the Island of Mozambique / Known as Kaffirs', plate 3 from Johann Theodor and Johann Israel de Bry, *Orientalische Reisen*, vol. 2, Frankfurt 1598.

Source: © Universitätsbibliothek Göttingen, 4° Itin I 3844ª:1 Rara.

potential trade partners. He too wrote at length about dress as a form of social distinction and his drawings show different degrees of nakedness according to social status. Thus one engraving depicts four different female types of varying social status from Cabo Corso (Cape Coast Castle) in West Africa (Figure 1.11):

FIGURE 1.11 'Women of Mina and Their Attire', plate 3 from Johann Theodor and Johann Israel de Bry, *Orientalische Reisen*, vol. 6, Frankfurt 1603.

Source: © Universitätsbibliothek Göttingen, 4° Itin I 3844ᵃ:2 Rara.

the carefully dressed Mulatta wife of a Portuguese man with a typical short hair-cut (A); a peasant woman with a bare upper body carrying fruits to market on her head (B); a (still) elegant young maiden in the city, covered with a large linen shawl (C); and a simple wife and mother nursing her child over her shoulder, tattooed and painted with her hair braided, a hairstyle that recalls the little caps worn by unmarried European women (D).

The accompanying text provides explicit references to dress and the accompanying trade practices common on the coast of Ghana: it speaks of stuff, arras, grosgrain and striped linen, but also of Venetian glass corals that the natives attached to their arms and legs with bundles of straw and cords and 'regarded as their fetishes or holy objects'.[58] The concrete reference to the types of fabric in the text points to the vibrant textile trade on the coast of Ghana, in which the Portuguese (and later the Dutch) were involved – a long-established superregional, indeed intercontinental trade.

The text is accompanied by a typical costume picture, which allows the viewer to assess the degree of civilization of the various inhabitants of the Guinea coast. It does so by inserting them into a global grammar of dress. On closer scrutiny, clothing serves once again as a sign of civilized adaptation. Thus the Mulatta wife of a Portuguese from the fortress of Mina is presented as 'finely adorned with garments', while a peasant woman from the country and a 'common woman' with a child, known as 'Hiro', are shown with naked upper bodies and scarified faces and arms. In this way, distance from civilization is linked to social and moral categories, since 'common women' in particular are described in an introductory passage as shameless and unchaste. The text even goes as far as to describe the sexual abuse of native women by the Portuguese colonizers as a civilizing act, as it taught them to feel shame.[59] And here, too, the author is interested in the specific tattoo and body-painting practices of women in Guinea. He describes how they cut their foreheads and coloured the cuts and also painted numerous white spots on their faces, which looked from a distance 'as if their faces were full of beautiful pearls'.[60] For de Marees, the tattoos on their arms and breasts, which they rubbed with different colours in the morning, also awakened positive associations with fabric textures, 'looking from afar like a black-slashed doublet / or women's bodice'.[61] Unlike in the image of the king of Florida, in the engraving these cuts resemble the branding used in Europe to mark marginalized and criminalized outsiders. In contrast to what the text suggests, the engraving allows for no similarity between the texture of the tattoos and those of precious fabrics.

Thus unlike the account on Virginia, the volume on the Gold Coast does not visualize approximation, exchange and association by depicting skin and fabrics in a similar manner. Instead, the portrayal of interactions between Europeans and Africans through market exchanges plays a far more visible role. A further engraving depicts the market of Capocorso (Cape Coast), with a Dutch textile merchant measuring out cloth (Figure 1.12). It portrays the business acumen of the mistrustful locals who are having the cloth they purchased from Europeans remeasured.

FIGURE 1.12 'The Market of Cabo Corso', plate 4 from Johann Theodor and Johann Israel de Bry, *Orientalische Reisen*, vol. 6, Frankfurt, 1603.

In the early seventeenth century, the Cape Coast was a commercial centre for various competing European nations in West Africa, especially in the framework of transatlantic exchange of slaves for cloth. De Marees' account stresses the acumen of Ghanaian traders and describes their business practices and history in detail. Originally, the coastal dwellers had approached the Europeans with gold and 'bought from them what they needed / of canvas and woollen cloth / and the like'.[62] The inhabitants of the interior, in contrast, who 'were quite naked and black', were frightened of the 'white men / who were also clothed'. For that reason they used the coastal dwellers as middlemen, who went to the Portuguese forts and castles to trade 'iron / pewter / copper and brass basins / knives / woollens / canvas / cooking pots / corals / and other goods' on their behalf.[63] When the Dutch arrived, they also entered this lucrative trade. In West Africa around 1600, the text and images suggest, there was a lively trade in textiles that made Europeans and Africans trading partners who interacted from mutual interest, exchanging also gold, slaves, metalwork, glass beads and cowrie shell money.

The prerequisite for this trade was the African interest in European and other non-African textiles. The 'nakedness' of the Indigenous trading partners often emphasized in texts and images left their interest in these textiles largely invisible, while other images revealed it in the context of European 'civilizing efforts'. In this way, texts could ignore the intra- and intercontinental textile trade that had been established long before the Europeans arrived and imagine and portray their relationship to African trading partners as an asymmetrical one of superiority. Thus on the west coast of Africa, the promise of globalized markets (with both its hopes and horrors) had already become a reality.

Conclusion

Richard Hakluyt imagined global trade as a bold wish at the beginning of volume 1 of the de Bry collection, fantasizing about the cultivation of silk grass in Virginia and expressing his hope that the raw material from Virginia would soon be as profitable as silk from Persia.[64] This survey of the *West* and *East Indian Voyages* has underlined how Europeans used fashion and fabrics intensively around 1600 to promote global exchange and global knowledge systems of dress, fabrics and texture. The de Bry travel collections have served here as a costume book of global scope, allowing comparative classifications of societies along an imaginary line of development, which defined clothing, morals and civilization as interdependent factors.

Depending on the economic interests, political context and social status of the people in question, the texts and engravings could, via analogy and texture, initiate a tension-filled interplay between similarity and difference, skin and fabric. This could further cement, but sometimes also loosen, the stereotypical categorizations of societies and groups according to their perceived degree of civilization. Thus, the production of knowledge about textiles in travel accounts served to classify experiences in alien societies within an already familiar fashion system. This system had already proved eminently suitable for Europeans as an ordering concept for their own societies and social distinctions. Texts and images on textiles, dress and fashion did not, however, serve solely to expand their own knowledge system and in this way to imaginatively process increasingly global experiences; they also lent visual form to emerging global markets and the increasingly global practice of commodity exchange. In this way, one of the most important early modern collections of travelogues also functions as a significant repository of information about specific aspects and politics of the global history of dress.

Notes

1 Margaret F. Rosenthal and Ann Rosalind Jones, eds., *Cesare Vecellio's Habiti Antichi et Moderni: The Clothing of the Renaissance World. Europe, Asia, Africa, the Americas* (London and New York: Thames & Hudson, 2008), 562.
2 Rosenthal and Jones, *Cesare Vecellio's Habiti Antichi et Moderni*, 553.
3 Cesare Vecellio, *De gli habiti antichi et moderni di diverse parti del mondo: Libri due* (Venice: Zenaro, 1590); the second edition under the title: *Habiti antichi et moderni di tutto il Mondo* (Venice: Sessa, 1598).
4 On the collection as a whole, see Michiel van Groesen, *The Representations of the Overseas World in the de Bry Collection of Voyages (1590–1634)* (Leiden: Brill, 2008).
5 Volume 1 of the America series appeared in four languages: German, Latin, English and French. All later volumes of the two series appeared only in Latin and German. On the differences between the German and Latin versions see van Groesen, *The Representations of the Overseas World*, esp. ch. 8.
6 Susanna Burghartz, ed., *Staging New Worlds: De Bry's Illustrated Travel Reports, 1590–1630* (Basel: Schwabe, 2004).
7 On costume books, see Daniel Defert, 'Un genre ethnographique profane au XVIe: les livres d'habits', in *Histoires de l'anthropologie, XVIe–XIXe siécles*, ed. Britta Rupp-Eisenreich (Paris: Klincksieck, 1984), 25–41.
8 On knowledge systems, see Sureikha Davies, *Renaissance Ethnography and the Invention of the Human: New Worlds, Maps and Monsters* (Cambridge, UK: Cambridge University Press, 2016); on stage theory, see Anthony Pagden, *The Fall of Natural Man* (Cambridge, UK: Cambridge University Press, 1989).
9 See, for example, Valerie Traub, 'Mapping the Global Body', in *Early Modern Visual Culture: Representation, Race, and Empire in Renaissance England*, ed. Peter Erickson and Clark Hulse (Philadelphia: University of Pennsylvania Press, 2000), 44–97; Robert DuPlessis, *The Material Atlantic: Clothing, Commerce, and Colonization in the Atlantic World, 1650–1800* (Cambridge, UK: Cambridge University Press, 2016); Giorgio Riello, *Cotton: The Fabric That Made the Modern World* (Cambridge, UK: Cambridge University Press, 2013).
10 Beverly Lemire, *Global Trade and the Transformation of Consumer Cultures: The Material World Remade, c.1500–1820* (Cambridge, UK: Cambridge University Press, 2018).
11 See Ulrike Ilg, 'The Cultural Significance of Costume Books in Sixteenth-Century Europe', in *Clothing Culture, 1350–1650*, ed. Catherine Richardson (Aldershot, UK: Ashgate, 2004), 29–47; Margaret F. Rosenthal, 'Cultures of Clothing in Later Medieval and Early Modern Europe', *Journal of Medieval and Early Modern Studies* 39.3 (2009): 460–481; Traub, 'Mapping the Global Body'.
12 Ernst van den Boogaart, 'De Brys' Africa', in *Staging New Worlds*, 97.

13 Theodor de Bry, *A Briefe and True Report of the New Found Land of Virginia* (Frankfurt am Main: De Bry, 1590), plate 3, subscription (British Library: G.6837).
14 van Groesen, *The Representations of the Overseas World*, 195.
15 van Groesen, *The Representations of the Overseas World*, 195–199, esp. 199–205.
16 van Groesen, *The Representations of the Overseas World*, 210ff.
17 Stephanie Pratt, 'Truth and Artifice in the Visualization of Native Peoples: From the Time of John White to the Beginning of the 18th Century', in *European Visions: American Voices*, ed. Kim Sloan (London: British Museum, 2009), 35.
18 Mary Campbell refers to the relevant colonial texts as 'coloniology'. See Michael Gaudio, *Engraving the Savage: The New World and Techniques of Civilization* (Minneapolis and London: University of Minnesota Press, 2008), 1–7.
19 De Bry, *A Briefe and True Report*, plate 23.
20 Terence Turner, 'Social Skin', *HAU: Journal of Ethnographic Theory* 2.2 (2012): 486–504, 501.
21 Turner, 'Social Skin', 503.
22 Gaudio, *Engraving the Savage*, 5.
23 Gaudio, *Engraving the Savage*, 5.
24 Gaudio, *Engraving the Savage*, 6.
25 René Goulaine de Laudonnière (*c.*1529–1574) was a French Huguenot explorer and the founder of the French colony of Fort Caroline.
26 Saturiwa (also spelled Satarioua, Satourioua and Saturiba (*fl.* sixteenth century) was chief of the Saturiwa tribe, a Timucua chiefdom centred at the mouth of the St Johns River in Florida, during the sixteenth century.
27 Maike Christadler, 'Indigenous Skins: Indian Costumes at the Court of Württemberg', in *Visual Representations of Native Americans. Transnational Contexts and Perspectives*, ed. Karsten Fitz (Heidelberg: Universitätsverlag Winter, 2012), 13–27.
28 De Bry, *America* vol. 2 (Frankfurt, 1591), plate 39, subscription.
29 De Bry, *America*, vol. 2, plate 39.
30 De Bry, *America*, vol. 2, plate 39.
31 De Bry, *America*, vol. 2, plate 39.
32 Riello, *Cotton*, 90
33 Ernst van den Boogaart, 'Heathendom and Civility in the Historia Indiae Orientalis: The adaptation by Johan Theodor and Johan Israel de Bry of the Edifying Series of Plates from Linschoten's Itinerario', *Netherlands Yearbook for History of Art* 53.1 (2002): 71–106.
34 Johann Theodor and Johann Israel de Bry, *Orientalische Reisen*, vol. 2 (Frankfurt, 1598), 32.
35 Johann Theodor and Johann Israel de Bry, *Orientalische Reisen*, vol. 2, 44.
36 See also van den Boogaart, 'Heathendom and Civility', 71–106, 79.
37 Johann Theodor and Johann Israel de Bry, *Orientalische Reisen*, vol. 2, 61.
38 Johann Theodor and Johann Israel de Bry, *Orientalische Reisen*, vol. 2, plate 23, subscription.
39 Johann Theodor and Johann Israel de Bry, America vol. 9, add. (Frankfurt am Main, 1602), 74.
40 On polish Early Modern dress see Beata Biedrońska-Słota and Maria Molenda, 'The Emergence of a Polish National Dress and Its Perception', *European History Yearbook* 20 (2019): 113–136.
41 John Guy, '"One thing Leads to Another": Indian Textiles and the Early Globalization of Style', in *Interwoven Globe: The Worldwide Textile Trade, 1500–1800*, ed. Amelia Peck (New York: Metropolitan Museum of Art, 2013), 12–27, 20.
42 Riello, *Cotton*, 20.
43 For a discussion of the cosmopolitan court culture in the kingdom of Candy, see Gananath Obeyesekere, 'Between the Portuguese and the Nayakas: The Many Faces

of the Kandyan Kingdom, 1591–1765', in *Sri Lanka at the Crossroads of History*, ed. Zoltan Biedermann and Alan Strathern (London: UCL Press, 2017), 161–177, 322, esp. 162–164.

44 Johann Theodor and Johann Israel de Bry, *Orientalische Reisen*, vol. 7 (Frankfurt am Main, 1605), 28.

45 Cfr. Herman van der Wee, 'Structural Changes and Specialization in the Industry of the Southern Netherlands, 1100–1600', *Economic History Review* 28.2 (1975): 203–221, 216–217.

46 Johann Theodor and Johann Israel de Bry, *Orientalische Reisen*, vol. 3 (Frankfurt am Main, 1599), 138.

47 On the long tradition of textile imports in precolonial West Africa, see DuPlessis, *Material Atlantic*, 35.

48 Opher Mansour, 'Picturing Global Conversion: Art and Diplomacy at the Court of Paul V (1605–1621)', *Journal of Early Modern History* 17 (2013): 525–559, 540; Teobaldo Filesi, 'Duarte Lopez ambasciatore del re del Congo presso Sist V', *Africa* 23.1 (March 1968): 44–84.

49 Johann Theodor and Johann Israel de Bry, *Orientalische Reisen*, vol. 1 (Frankfurt am Main, 1597), 15. On the various types of fabrics in West Africa, see Colleen E. Krieger, 'Mapping the History of Cotton Textile Production in Precolonial West Africa', *African Economic History* 33 (2005): 87–116; Stanley B. Alpern, 'What Africans Got for Their Slaves: A Master List of European Trade Goods', *History in Africa* 22 (1995): 5–43.

50 Johann Theodor and Johann Israel de Bry, *Orientalische Reisen*, vol. 1, 21.

51 Johann Theodor and Johann Israel de Bry, *Orientalische Reisen*, vol. 1, 61.

52 Johann Theodor and Johann Israel de Bry, *Orientalische Reisen*, vol. 1, 61.

53 With a different emphasis, see van den Boogaart, 'De Bry's Africa', 106–107.

54 DuPlessis, *Material Atlantic*, 35.

55 Johann Theodor and Johann Israel de Bry, *Orientalische Reisen*, vol. 2, 10–11 and plate 3.

56 Johann Theodor and Johann Israel de Bry, *Orientalische Reisen*, vol. 2, 122.

57 On Marees, see van den Boogaart, 'De Bry's Africa', 96–97; DuPlessis, *Material Atlantic*, 34.

58 Johann Theodor and Johann Israel de Bry, *Orientalische Reisen*, vol. 6 (Frankfurt am Main, 1603), 23.

59 Johann Theodor and Johann Israel de Bry, *Orientalische Reisen*, vol. 6, 21–22.

60 Johann Theodor and Johann Israel de Bry, *Orientalische Reisen*, vol. 6, 22.

61 Johann Theodor and Johann Israel de Bry, *Orientalische Reisen*, vol. 6, 22.

62 Johann Theodor and Johannn Israel de Bry, *Orientalische Reisen*, vol. 6, 27.

63 Johann Theodor and Johann Israel de Bry, *Orientalische Reisen*, vol. 6, 27.

64 De Bry, *America*, vol. 1, 7.

2

FASHION IN THE FOUR PARTS OF THE WORLD

Time, space and early modern global change[1]

Giorgio Riello

Fashion and social competition

> In all probability [fashion] started in the families of the gentry, where the maidservants copied it, after which [it was] increasingly borrowed by their relatives until it made its way into the quarters of the neighbourhood. The wealthy and powerful began by considering innovation to be something wonderful and went on to think surpassing their predecessors to be admirable. Those who managed to do so believed it not to be going to excess but prestigious; while those who failed to achieve this did not think it a cause for being at peace with themselves but for shame ... Thus it has become an all but irreversible trend.[2]

Specialists in eighteenth-century British history will easily recognize in this quotation several of the elements that Neil McKendrick, John Brewer and Jack Plumb used in their *The Birth of a Consumer Society* (1982) in explaining the rise of 'modern' British consumerism and fashion in the age of Enlightenment.[3] Fashion was seen as key as to why people in eighteenth-century Britain started to consume a wider range of commodities – well beyond what we might call 'necessities' – and why they privileged new things that were changed increasingly frequently. Their idea of a 'consumer revolution' saw emulation and fashion as key mechanisms in changing consumption patterns and choices. The most memorable example of emulation or 'aping' was that of servants who had the proximity to observe – and very often the means to imitate – the consuming habits of their employers. The maidservant wished to copy the rich outfit of her mistress and sometimes could do so by accepting a discarded petticoat or a bodice that she would proudly parade in the neighbourhood, very much as the opening quotation reports. This allowed a mere servant to acquire prestige: it was not excess per se, but excess aimed at bettering oneself and climbing the social ladder. And as the quotation suggests this was a continuative process (an 'irreversible trend') that excluded those who failed to embrace it.[4]

This quotation is appropriate not just for McKendrick's work, but also for another of the great names of Western fashion theory: Thorstein Veblen. At the end of the nineteenth century it was Veblen who conceptualized fashion as a game of social competition defined by conspicuous consumption and characterized by a shifting process by which those who are emulated move their preferences to something different, something new.[5] His viewpoint was neither Europe, nor the eighteenth century, but the wealthy society of the American nouveau riche of the turn of the century. What both Veblen and McKendrick posited was that social competition characterized fashion in 'modern' societies. And by 'modern' they meant essentially Western.

This chapter thus enters into an analysis of fashion from a rather classic starting point (Western Europe and America) and by using a specific definition of fashion: fashion as a form of emulation. I take one of the key designations of fashion as defined in a European (perhaps Eurocentric) context to establish whether it can be applied to other contexts. The same procedure will be applied to other possible ways of interpreting fashion, always starting with definitions adopted for Europe in order to evaluate in what ways, under what circumstances, and in which forms during the so-called early modern period (c.1500–1800), fashion manifested itself in places as different as China, Japan and Latin America.[6] For reasons of space most of my examples refer mostly to China and Japan, though occasional references are made to other parts of the world.

To this end, it is revealing to note that the opening quotation – a paraphrase of McKendrick and Veblen – is a description of Shanghai by Meng-chu and dated to the mid-seventeenth century. This is not an exceptional quotation, though it is a particularly helpful one. The Shangdon gazetteer in the late Ming period reported that even in small provincial towns and cities, people were 'competing in extravagance'. It added that 'The masses wear the clothing of the gentry, the gentry wear the headgear of the high officials' and all were 'competing with the rich in grandeur and opulence to the extent that they think nothing of emptying their purses'.[7] One could cite several similar sources not just for Ming China and Edo Japan, but also for sixteenth- and seventeenth-century Latin America and the Ottoman Empire and to a lesser extent also for India and the Middle East. The scholarship of Sarah Dauncey, Antonia Finnane, Craig Clunas and Timothy Brook for China; Eiko Ikegami and Timon Screech for Japan; Suraiya Faroqhi, Christopher Neumann and Donald Quataert for the Ottoman Empire; Rebecca Earle and Regina Root for Latin America; and Robert Ross' global analysis – just to cite a few – provide a sufficiently vast body of quotable material, which suggests that both fashion and emulation were present in each of their geographic areas of specialization.[8]

Carlo Marco Belfanti concludes his 2008 article 'Was Fashion a European Invention?' by explaining that it was definitively not in the period here considered, though his assessment still remains equivocal when he adds that fashion 'only fully developed as a social institution in Europe, while in India, China, and Japan it only evolved partially, without being able to obtain full social recognition'.[9] This chapter challenges this statement, first by asking why in the first instance all other places apart from Europe were deemed by default not to have fashion; second, by reflecting as to whether if it is simply a matter of including new world areas into the accepted notion of fashion or if the definition, chronologies and nature of fashion in the early modern period must be questioned and revised if applied globally.

Fashion's Eurocentrism

What appears to be a reclamation of fashion by present-day extra-European historians is in stark contrast with more classic views inherited from a previous generation of historians. The great French historian Fernand Braudel, though attributing great significance to fashion as a motor of historical change, categorically refuted the idea that fashion might have existed in non-European societies before colonialism and imperialism. He conceded that 'political upheavals' might have induced a change of clothing – as for instance with the arrival of the Manchus in China and the beginning of the new Qing dynasty in 1644 – but he was adamant that this could not be considered as fashion.[10] Similarly Gilles Lipovetzky and most sociologists of fashion leave no doubt that fashion has become a global phenomenon – that is to say a homogenous European-inspired and dominated trend – only in recent years.[11]

The appropriation of fashion by Europeans was not invented by historians: most of the primary sources used by European historians deny the existence of fashion outside the borders of Europe. Costume books such as Cesare Vecellio's *Habiti Antichi et Moderni* (1590 and 1598), for instance, provided a vast array of visual material on both European and extra-European dress but also statically pigeonholed the costumes of what we might call 'others'.[12] Antonia Finnane suggests that one of the issues at stake was the inability of Europeans to read meaning into what was distinctively different, and sometimes the opposite of European clothing, like the use of white for mourning.[13] Europeans, in the words of Finnane, were 'inclined to describe Chinese clothes in terms of how they resembled their own', rather than in their own right.[14] And they were keen to criticize other people's attire because they were – in the words of Cesare Vecellio – 'quite contrarie to ours'.[15] In some parts of the world, this led to a campaign on the part of missionaries to clothe Indigenous populations 'decently concealing the nudity of the past' as Braudel puts it.[16] In other places, Europeans saw stability in contrast to ever-changing European fashion. This was the case even in places where it was patently false as in Japan: the Portuguese writer Luís Fróis at the end of the sixteenth century, commented that: 'We invent nearly every year a new type of garment and a new way to dress; in Japan, the shape [of clothing] is always the same and it does hardly change'.[17] European visitors and merchants struggled to make sense of Asian vestimentary systems. Some forms of distinction labelled as barbarous by Europeans, for example the spread of the use of the bow shoe for a bound foot in the closing years of the Ming period, which was symbolic, especially in the wealthy lower Yang-zu delta, of a socially competitive society. Designed to visually set apart the 'humble country folk' from ladies of elevated status, it was not perceived by Europeans to be in any way connected to forms of fashionability.[18]

A tension emerged from the separation between a Western world of fashion and a non-Western world characterized by a rather vague notion of stability under the label of 'costume'. Historians of fashion are correct in observing that the idea of fashion has been used to characterize the industrial and consumer-driven economies of Europe and later North America.[19] However, the case of Europe shows how the notion of fashion has been extended backwards in time to reach the Middle Ages and linked to processes of capitalist development.[20] While this has served to support the lineage of 'modern' industrial societies to the exclusion of all others, there is also a less positive idea of fashion as ephemeral rather than innovative, wasteful rather than economically productive, immoral rather than ethical. In this sense, fashion is seen more as the 'cancer' of modern societies, rather than as a benign force. And this in part explains why the concept and practice of fashion – although embraced in many societies outside the borders of Europe – was sometimes seen by such societies as foreign to their customs. Again scholarship has been faithful to such a preconception with the idea of costume being upheld in the histories of many extra-European countries and empires as a symbol of identity, tradition and the refusal of what was seen as the exogenous force of fashion.

One should not conclude that it was the 'European gaze' alone that established categories of fashion and costumes. Non-European societies were keen observers of European dress. An example is a 1787 Japanese text entitled *Komo zatsuwa* (紅毛雑話; 'A miscellany on the red-hairs'). The title derives from the designation (red hair) of Dutchmen in Japan. *Komo zatsuwa* is divided into five illustrated volumes that discuss a series of topics related to the Dutch, ranging from the microscope to insects, flowers and seeds. The final part of volume 5 includes a discussion of the Dutchmen's attire and the author claims to have sketched the illustrations of a hat, scarf, overcoat, breeches, socks, two types of shoes, belts, etc. from real garments provided by Dutchmen. The book proceeds with a description of the Dutchmen's attire (Figure 2.1): '[T]he upper part is called rok, and the underwear camisole. The overcoat is long and under shorter. There are parts to put things in (pockets) in the lower part. They are made of wool, or plant fibre, upon the wearer's taste'. The images show a fascination for the attire of these red-haired Europeans, though the accompanying text betrays also surprise, noting that such attire 'if ceremonial (official), all of them including the breeches should be made of same cloth ... (there are few lines on

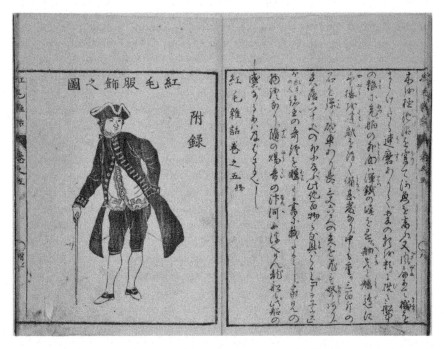

FIGURE 2.1 'Attire of a Dutchman', from *Komo zatsuwa* (紅毛雑話; 'A miscellany on the red-hairs'), 1787.

Source: © Trustees of the British Museum, 1979,0305,0.140.5.

buttons) … The dress system looks as if there are no distinction between the noble and non-nobles'.[21] Japan more than any other country in Asia became a keen observer of European sartorial choices.[22]

Fashion as change

I have so far avoided defining fashion as simple 'change over time'. Braudel cites the observations of a number of early modern European travellers and writers, among them Jean Baptiste Say, who in 1828 wrote that 'the unchanging fashions of the Turks and the other Eastern people do not attract me. It seems that their fashions tend to preserve their stupid despotism'.[23] Two centuries earlier the Englishman Henry Blout (1602–1682), who travelled to Constantinople in 1634, reported that the Ottomans 'to this day vary but little from that long, and loose manner of garment reported to have been ever used in the *East*'.[24] Sartorial stability was considered as characterizing a non-precise group of 'Eastern people' and was deemed to be backward, a form of prevention of the democratic and 'modern' values of fashion.

One could counter these observations and cite the many sources that show instead that dress changed on a regular basis in Asia. The Chinese writer Gu

Qiyuan lived in the first half of the seventeenth century and commented that fashion in Nanjing changed every three to four years instead of every ten years as it had in earlier decades.[25] Others were even more daring and claimed that in the early seventeenth century, in places such as Nanking 'in recent years, strange shapes and outlandish styles are altered with every day, changed with every month'.[26] However the rapid changes of what was purposely defined as 'contemporary style' or 'the look of the moment' in seventeenth-century China,[27] or Japan or Latin America for that matter, should not be matched to a European time frame. Fashion is never static, but should not be forced into a rectilinear chronology. The influence of religious ideas that see time as circular in many Asian cultures presents a notion of time different from that of the West.[28] Similarly, the invocation of antiquity, as was the case in Ming China, was an equally powerful tool of fashion based on what today we would call 'retro'. This was achieved through the use of Han-dynasty (206 BCE–220 CE) caps or Song-dynasty (960–1279 CE) brocades in the fashion of five centuries earlier or the use of antiquities to display taste as pointed out by Craig Clunas.[29]

Timon Screech is even more categorical in warning us against using a Western chronological measure of the impact of fashion. While chartering a complex and multilayered world of fashion in Edo Japan, he is adamant that 'despite the prominence of fashion in Edo urban life, even fairly casual garments altered relatively little in shape over time'.[30] He highlights an historically specific notion of fashion in the early modern world – and one might dare to generalize across most of the globe – that unlike today was about changing shapes, applied rather to cloth, than the cut of clothing.

Fashion as interaction

Clothing, shapes and the cut of a dress change over time, but textiles (their design, colours and patterns) are less about the 'new in time', than the 'new in space': how one gets something new, something different from somewhere else. In the early modern period novelty was not about creativity as such, or the creations of designers; it was about getting one's hands on something that came from somewhere else and was therefore new and different.

Fashion is often described as a self-sustaining force: once unleashed, it becomes a perpetual motor of change, first material (in the form of kaleidoscopic variations in colours and shapes) and second sociocultural (in the changing meaning expressed and created by fashion). It is not by chance that even a century ago Georg Simmel underlined how fashion could not be simply explained by observing the internal dynamics of what later came to be called a 'fashion system'. He explained how in many societies it was the 'foreign' and the 'exotic' – what was not local and part of the system – that provided new and powerful fuel to the bonfire of vanities.[31]

The appeal of the exotic was not just an early modern phenomenon: archaeologist Andrew Sherratt demonstrated that it was already present in prehistoric societies.[32] By the tenth century CE, the geographer al-Muqadassi reported that fashion consciousness was one of the characteristics of the people of Iraq.[33] And fashion was defined not just as any personal attention to what one consumed or wore, but the careful combination of commodities often imported through the extensive long-distance commercial routes dominated by Armenian, Jewish and Indian merchants. They provided linen from Egypt, Chinese silks and cotton cloth from India. The cut of clothes was influenced instead by Persia, especially under the Abbasid rule. China appreciated the appeal of Persian textiles with Greek and Roman design influences as shown by the beautiful double-weave woollen textiles bearing representations of oxen, sheep and naked men adorning a mummy of the Jin Period (206 BCE–420 CE).[34] Ladies of the Chinese court depicted in a tenth-century painting display with grace their elaborate coiffures with hairpins (influenced by foreign metalwork) and silk gowns that are clearly very Chinese products, but with a Persian design not dissimilar to those that we encounter in the dresses of fashionable European ladies a few centuries later.[35]

That fashion acted as a way of connecting sometimes distant places was not new to the sixteenth and seventeenth centuries: for instance, historians of dress and fashion have long underlined the fact that European fashion employed a variety of foreign idioms constructed through the importation of commodities, such as porcelain and lacquer, or the reinterpretation and often 'invention' of otherness as in the case of Chinoiserie and Japonaiserie. Beverly Lemire and I have commented on how Middle and Far Eastern silks first, and later Indian cottons, became integral components in the structuring of new forms and notions of fashionability in Europe between 1200 and 1800.[36] This work, while relativizing and questioning the 'exceptionalism' of European fashion opens the doors to the investigation of similar phenomena across the globe. One might cite for instance the popularization of the *Kosode* – a short-sleeve kimono – in the Heian period Japan (794–1184 CE). It developed as a popularization of elite fashion but was also a reaction – an act against rather than in favour – of foreign customs, in this case the pre-existing reliance on Chinese forms of garments.[37]

The *Kosode* – or Kimono, literally 'thing to wear' (garment) – became the national costume of Japan and as such something that historians of dress see as rather distant from fashion.[38] But later in the seventeenth and eighteenth centuries, the kimono became a fashionable item influenced by designs and aesthetics introduced by Indian cottons, which were also influencing fashion in Europe and elsewhere. The pervasiveness of Indian cottons across Asia was such that – as Kayoko Fujita observes – the available varieties of cotton cloth in Edo Japan were '*bengara(-jima* or *-gôshi)*' (the striped or checked cloth from Bengal), '*santome(-jima)*' (striped cloth from São Thomé) and '*matafû(-jima)*' (striped cloth from Madras).[39]

The Iberian *nanban*, the savages from the West, represented in sixteenth-century Japanese screens might have been indeed uncivilized, but the wearing of outlandish striped clothes, which they had probably acquired in India on their way to Japan, made them the 'coolest guys' of the early modern period (Figure 2.2).[40] Their fashionability was not sensed by the Japanese in terms of change over time but in terms of difference from themselves. This explains why *nanban* fashion became something to be imitated by the locals. Foreign products were so important in Edo fashionability that Japanese legislators thought it wise to ban 'Holland goods' in their 1688 sumptuary law.[41]

The Iberian incursion into Asia did not just proceed eastwards from Europe to the Indian Ocean and the Chinese sea. The Spaniards arrived in the Philippines in the 1560s from across the Pacific Ocean and their colonies in the Americas, where they founded a new trading port at Manila. From the 1570s this was the key node of exchange between China (and more generally East Asia) and the Americas. The Manila to Acapulco route brought to Mexico – and from there to Peru, Panama, China, Ecuador and Nicaragua – all sorts of Asian commodities, silks and cottons among the most important.[42] These elaborate textiles were fashionable among

FIGURE 2.2 'Portuguese Merchants Waiting the Arrival of Japanese Officials Aboard Their Ship', detail from 'Namban' screen attributed to Kano Domi, *c.*1593–1600. Wooden lattice covered with paper, gold leaf, polychrome tempera painting, silk, lacquer, copper gilt, 172.8 × 380.8 × 2 cm.

Source: Museu Nacional de Arte Antiga, Lisbon. Granger Historical Picture Archive/Alamy Stock Photo.

consumers of all social classes as depicted in beautiful *casta* paintings of the seventeenth and eighteenth centuries.[43] While the silks were within the reach of the more affluent, the blue cotton *cambayas* (made in China) or the *mantas* cotton coverings produced in the Philippines, were purchased in large quantities by American consumers in exchange for precious metal.[44] Cottons also came in large quantities from Bengal and Madras in India.[45] This trade influenced design in Latin America. Both in silks and cottons it is possible to observe the mixing of Chinese and Indian motifs, with pre-Hispanic elements or the adoption of ikat-dyed style

FIGURE 2.3 Detail of a folding screen with Indian wedding and flying pole (*Biombo con desposorio indígena y palo volador*), Mexico, *c.*1690. Oil on canvas, 167.64 × 295.28 × 5.08 cm.

Source: Los Angeles County Museum of Art. Purchased with funds provided by the Bernard and Edith Lewin Collection of Mexican Art Deaccession Fund, M.2005.54. © LACMA.

from south-eastern Asian textiles and garments. Second, Asian textiles gave momentum to Latin American fashion.[46] Travellers and visitors to Mexico were impressed
not only by the variety of dress worn by the various ethnic groups, but also by the
riches commonly displayed by the wider strata of society.[47] The Spaniard Artemio
de Valle-Arizpe reported that in eighteenth-century Mexico City 'ordinary worn is
a silk skirt or printed calico decorated with bands of gold and silver, with brightly
coloured ribboned belts with their fringe of gold that tumble down behind and in
front to border the skirt' (Figure 2.3).[48] Quito in Ecuador used both locally produced cottons and the more expensive *ruán* cottons, this time imported not from
Asia, but from the city of Rouen in France.[49]

Cities as islands of fashion

Fashion cannot be defined simply by identifying its mechanisms of generation,
be they imitation and social competition, change over time, or interaction with
other material cultures. Fashion is always characterized by specific spaces and
social dynamics in which it articulates itself.

In terms of sartorial expenditure, the court was surely one of such key spaces of
early modern fashion. The court had a catalytic effect on the urban fashion industry. This is true of the French court of Louis XIV as well as of Edo Japan. Both
had an extensive but ineffective sumptuary system that included the nobility. And
in both countries the sovereign had discovered the importance of keeping friends
close and enemies even closer: thus the idle semi-coerced existence of the French
nobility at Versailles and the imposition of the alternate years of residence for the
Japanese *daimyos* (lords) and their families. In both cases the result was the construction of a court life based on substantial financial investment on the part of
the nobility to please the ruling monarch and conform to etiquette and the rules
of ceremonial occasions. This was not simple luxury but the necessity of a life of
conspicuous consumption centred around the monarch.[50] The relationship
between court and capital city was also important. The demand for luxury and
fashionable goods from the court gave work to thousands of artisans, seamstresses,
weavers and tailors. It created what we could see as a proto-fashion industry: the
gathering together of an unprecedented amount of skills, knowledge, human capital and resources (in terms of materials and credit).[51]

The story constantly repeated to students and the general public sees the present-day position of Paris as the 'capital of fashion' as emerging from the court
culture of the Sun King in the second half of the seventeenth century. Some
historians of fashion have recognized in this a line of evolution and a sort of
'royal pedigree' for the primacy of Paris in the world of fashion.[52] The case of
Japan – and one might expect other important court centres in Asia – show that
this was not the prerogative of Paris alone and that similar concentrations of
fashion production and consumption linked to court life existed in other parts of
pre-modern Eurasia.

Yet for most cities this was a temporary condition that did not lead to the maintenance of a prime position in fashion over more than four centuries as in the case of Paris. One of the explanations put forward for this is that in most cases, court fashion did not have an impact outside the walls of the royal palace. In Paris, and to a certain extent London, urban fashion developed and sometimes reacted against court fashion. Before the 'fossilization' of court fashion in the nineteenth century, the world of the nobility and the sovereign was a point of reference for elite fashion in general and, if we believe imitation theories, for the wider population too. Yet the same was true of Edo Japan, where the *Kindai Sejidan* ('Book of common talk') reports that kimonos decorated with *kanoko* and *surihaku* were first worn by the ladies of the emperor's court, but that, after the mid-seventeenth century, they were worn in the households of *daimyos*. Imitation diffused rapidly and copies were soon worn by wives of the rich bourgeoisie and then the middle ranks.[53] The materials of these kimonos might have been poorer in quality, but it was the visual effect that was important. Even in the case of the more regulated Chinese court where it was the badge of rank to be at the core of a hierarchical system, cases of the inappropriate use of rank symbols, a kind of sartorial symbolic inflation, were already in evidence in the sixteenth century.[54]

The importance of urban life in the history of Western fashion can hardly be overstated: the department store and the *flâneur* in the nineteenth century; the cosmopolitan metropolis of the twentieth century and, to a lesser extent, the formation of a bourgeois sphere in seventeenth- and eighteenth-century cities such as London and Paris are key topics in the history of Western fashion.[55] But was the experience of London or Paris as capitals of fashion before the modern age unique at a global level? Sinologist Antonia Finnane disagrees and observes that 'by the late sixteenth century the lower Yangzi city of Suzhou was performing something of the role played in Europe by Paris'.[56] Like Paris fashion, there was a distinct 'Suzhou style' and like the rivalry between Paris and London, Suzhou style had its alter ego in the Yangzhou style, the other major centre of the Lower Yangzi Delta.[57] The extravagance of Suzhou, Yangzhou and Nanjing are in stark contrast with traditional narratives that assert the Ming and Qing empires as bastions of tradition.[58] These and other cities in Asia were not simply producers of new styles. Seventeenth-century Kyoto was famous both as a place of production (perfecting tie-dye techniques that produced unique forms of shading) and a place of lavish spending, with courtesans and ladies making 'a daily display of beautiful clothes towards earning a living' as represented in Ukiyo-e, the 'pictures of the floating world' (Figure 2.4).[59]

It is however incorrect to say that fashion characterized Japan, China or the Ottoman Empire in the same way in which it is incorrect to say that fashion existed in Italy, France or England. Fashion manifested itself within specific urban spaces: it was especially visible in metropolises and ports where consumer goods were easily available, where shops allured customers and where wealthy merchants and shopkeepers acted as 'brokers of fashion'.[60] This explains why

FIGURE 2.4 'Women and Girls Cooling off on the Waterfront at Evening', woodblock diptych print, Japan, mid–1780s. Inscribed Torii Kiyonaga.

Source: © Trustees of British Museum, Asia Department 1909,0618,0.31.

conservative intellectuals both in China and Japan condemned merchants not just for the increased circulation of luxury and superfluous goods, but also for actively participating in conspicuous consumption with their social superiors.[61] In Chinese cities such as Suzhou and Hangzhou the weavers, the boatmen and the dancing girls were not only part of the world of fashion but also profited from it. The urban environment of these cities – as observed by Clunas – ante-dates by more than a century Mandeville's view that private vice could generate public benefit.[62]

Cultures of fashion

Towns and cities were not just places where fashionable commodities were bought and sold. They were also perfect settings in which fashionable behaviour could be enacted. Today we are well aware that fashion is not just the wearing of something unanimously considered fashionable, but also the act – I would say – of being as good as what you wear. Bourdieu talked about 'fields' not just as social groups with similar ambitions, aims and social standing, but also as social formations based on voluntary participation.[63] If fashion undermined simple birth status as a category of social worth, it strengthened instead the capacity to form new alliances through artefacts, akin to today's youth subcultures sharing similar visual appearances.

Sinologist Tim Brook states that one of the criteria of fashion is that it operates on the principle of constant disappointment and failure.[64] And it was the role of the urban arena to provide the kind of cultural and social interaction that makes possible the production of rules by which some people are in and others are out of fashion. Juan de Viera commented in 1778 that, 'It is marvellous to see [ladies] in [the] church and promenades [of Mexico City] in such a fashion that one cannot tell which is the wife of a count, and which the wife of a tailor'.[65] The city, in this case a populous one in colonial America, provides the very context in which one person's fashion is someone else's vulgarity.

The development of fashion as a way of presenting and representing society was not the prerogative of Europe. Printed texts, even more than printed images, acted as a way to convey not just the concerns over the nature and negative effects of fashion as seen in earlier passages, but also on how to be fashionable. This was done in China through novels, plays and handbooks with detailed descriptions of female clothing, some of which were written by women.[66] In Japan we observe the appearance of 'pattern books' (*hinagata bon*) in the late seventeenth century what were called 'patterns' or 'models' (*On-hiinakata*) the first printed book on *kosode* designs published in 1666–1667. More than 200 of these books were published in the following 150 years, providing a large sample of ready-made patterns that served to guide the consumer choices of customers and the production options of artisans.[67]

Fashion spread also through the display of textiles, clothing and modes of behaviour of a small but important 'fashion elite' that in Europe was defined as the *beau monde* or 'fashion leaders'.[68] To see them as the incarnation of capitalism would be incorrect: they might have been wealthy consumers, rich merchants and wealthy shopkeepers, but they were also courtesans, writers, bureaucrats, as well as servants and professionals in the world of fashion. Rose Bertin, Marie Antoinette's seamstress, or Léonard, the queen's hairdresser are often cited in European fashion history.[69] But similar positions as arbiters of taste and fashion were to be found for instance in Japan where Ogata Kōrin (1658–1716) advised women on matters of fashion. Famously he is credited with having dressed the ladies that he advised in black; this made all other ladies – dressed instead in bright colours – look garish.[70]

Some equated fashion to culture: the late sixteenth-century Ming intellectual Zhang Han, reporting on fashion in Suzhou, said that clothes were 'splendid, as if to be otherwise were to be without culture'.[71] The existence of Breward's notion of a 'culture of fashion' in different cultures – rather than how fashion contributed to culture – should be assessed.[72] Such cultures were urban and commercial in nature and were not limited to the extravagant luxury of courts.

Japanese garments show an influence from the Nō costume (the theatrical costume) but reveal the use of cheaper appliqué techniques when the complex design of the *katami-gawari* and the *dan-wagari* were translated into the *kosode*. This was cheaper and ready-made materials could be used, rather than spending considerable amounts of money especially for the purpose.[73] Similarly both literary and material sources show the use of fake layering. Edo female garments were constructed upon the layering of materials, making the overall attire not just heavy and cumbersome, but also expensive. An alternative was to create garments that showed only the rim of layers that were not actually underneath, a bit like present-day sweaters with a faux T-shirt underneath.

A final issue to be considered in the debates about fashion is technological innovation. European historiography has paid great attention to product innovation as well as process innovation. Maxine Berg, Helen Clifford, John Styles and Evelyn Welch, for instance, see product innovation as key to explaining some of the most important changes in early modern British and Continental European patterns of consumption.[74] Yet, there is substantial evidence to show that in the early modern period, and in particular in the eighteenth century, product innovation in textile production was not limited to Europe. In Japan, for instance, new techniques for stencilling textiles, a process named *Yuzen-zome*, is said to have made, according to one historian, 'a lively contribution to the costumes of the Edo period'.[75] Brands, like the 'Made by the Zhang Family' to be found on Chinese ceramic pillows, were not just a reassurance of quality, but implied a degree of consumer recognition for a product that was not simply another among the many. In a similar way the Yuzen fans, painted by Miyazaki Yuzen in early eighteenth-century Kyoto, were seen as the latest fashion.[76]

The world of fashion and sumptuary laws

So far this chapter has raised two methodological issues. The first is the risk of creating a world of unexplained similarities: the early modern world was not uniform, it was not seamlessly connected and there was no single definition of fashion. Second, histories of fashion tend to be positivistic in nature, chartering the increasing success of fashion and its eventual triumph in structuring modern societies. However, it is noticeable that at a global level the voices of opposition to fashion by its detractors are as strong as those of support by its practitioners. In the Middle Ages and the early modern period sumptuary laws were tools of opposition to fashion. Sumptuary regulations were enacted not just in Europe, but also in many other parts of the world in an attempt to limit conspicuous consumption and to maintain a clear delineation of rank by matching it to precise sartorial categories.[77]

These measures attempted to avoid social climbing and competition through the medium of the most visible of all forms of consumption: clothing. If fashion was fluctuation, the laws could only remedy this situation by stating precise rules and by categorizing people according to their social status. The Ming 'clothing and headwear' law of 1587, for instance, set rules for the styles and materials of clothing in minute detail from the Ming emperor to the courtier, down to the common men and women.[78] This late Ming law illustrates the fact that the legislators' concern was not limited to social climbing, but included the fear of 'social falling'. This law followed previous regulations, the so-called Jiajing's Reforms of 1528 whose rationale claimed that, 'Recently clothing styles have been outlandish, with no distinction between superior and inferior, so that the people's proclivities are without restraints'. Hence, the law stated that:

> We have consulted the regulations on the ancient *xuanduan*, and changed its name to the 'Loyal and Tranquil', alluding to 'Thinking of utmost loyalty when entering, thinking of amending one's faults when retiring'. We have made pictures to instruct on the styles and construction. Officials in the capital above the seventh rank, members of the Hanlin Academy, the Imperial Academy, officials in the Messenger's Office above the eighth rank … are to wear it. Military officials of the rank of commissioner-in-chief or above may wear it. The others are prohibited from exceeding the regulations.[79]

And the problem was not just the fact that commoners wore the 'habits' of the rich, powerful and noble; there was also a general concern about the slippage that luxury was creating among the ruling classes. In Edo Japan, for instance, one could hear the complaint that 'not only the great warlords of today but warriors of every class are concerned with beauty, wearing colourfully woven and embroidered fine silks'.[80]

It has been argued that the existence of similar sumptuary measures in different parts of the world was due to a general change in consumer behaviour characterized by a disrespect of conventional rules or rank and the dismissal of rigid regulations over consumption. Arjun Appadurai observes how 'sumptuary laws constitute an intermediary consumption-regulation device, suited to societies devoted to stable status display in exploding commodity contexts, such as India, China and Europe in the pre-modern period'.[81] By suggesting that an 'exploding commodity context' did not just characterize early modern Europe, Appadurai puts forward the idea of a global framework for consumption in the period 1500 to 1800. Most historians would be critical of such a position, underlining instead the different socio-economic contexts of China, India and Europe.[82] Yet there are important shared features for sumptuary laws across areas as distant as Ming China, the Ottoman Empire, Edo Japan and early modern Europe.[83] Craig Clunas, for instance, observes that Ming sumptuary laws were 'structurally very similar to mechanisms operating in early modern Europe'.[84] Only rarely did the sumptuary laws of a state or empire inform similar legislation in other parts of the world. This is the case in colonial contexts such as Batavia and the Cape (both regulated by the Dutch East India Company's laws) or in North and Latin America where laws drawn from their respective empires were applied.[85]

Shared features should not lead us to think that sumptuary laws belonged to a similar category of legal acts and that such legal acts responded to similar sartorial and consumer issues across the early modern world. There are, as one might expect, substantial differences in sumptuary laws. From a formal point of view, for instance, the European laws were rather moral (influenced by the Church) while the Chinese ones were more attentive to gestures and ceremonies (Figure 2.5). Japanese laws of the Edo period were rather minimal, when compared with the long, precise texts of European laws.[86] In contrast Chinese laws were even more detailed than the European ones.[87] Beyond their formal structure there were at least three major areas of difference: first, the remit of the law (who and what it included); second, the frequency with which they were reissued or repeated over time; and finally the specific period in time when such measures were first enacted in different parts of the world. One can see patterns of similarity and difference that are valid not just for transcontinental comparisons but also for comparisons between cities in geographical proximity as in the case of the Italian city states.

FIGURE 2.5 'A Winter Court Robe Worn by the Emperor', illustrated manuscript. Produced in Beijing, 1736–1795, ink and colour on silk.

Source: © Victorian and Albert Museum, 818–1896.

What exactly fell under the remit of a sumptuary law is a problematic issue as they varied dramatically from place to place and time to time. Negley Harte, for instance, observed that English sumptuary laws always told people what they 'should not' wear and consume, rather than impose what they should (what technically might be called 'clothing laws'). They followed a model similar to that of Japan but not of many other places such as the Ottoman Empire and China.[88] In Latin America, for instance, sumptuary laws actively engaged with birth, rather than status as they targeted different ethnic groups. Rebecca Earle has shown how sumptuary laws, and similarly the visual representations of fashion and race of the casta paintings, became increasingly static and responded to what was seen as a social need as well as the curbing of conspicuous consumption.[89] In the Ottoman Empire sumptuary laws were enacted well into the nineteenth century but assumed a different function from previous laws as they were used by Mahmud II to reform dress by forcing civil servants to wear the fez. In this case the law was exercised not to stop, but to force change as part of a process that we call 'Westernization'.[90]

A second problem is the profound differences in how laws were updated in different parts of the world. While it has been claimed that in Europe sumptuary laws could be read as a catalogue of what was fashionable and desirable, this is not the case in China where they remained unchanged.[91] However, one should not see this as a feature of a society in which fashion did not exist. Craig Clunas argues instead that 'the Chinese empire under the late Ming appears more like the "modern" Netherlands than it does like the great land empire of the Spanish Habsburg'.[92] Fossilization should therefore be interpreted as a defeat of any attempt to control fashion as was the case in the sixteenth- and seventeenth-century Dutch Republic.[93] Japanese sumptuary laws followed instead a more pragmatic line. The 1688 law, for instance, observed how '[e]mbroidery has been prohibited in women's clothing. Its use has become common, however' and established that 'hereafter embroidered robes may be bought and sold if they are not especially sumptuous'. The target of prohibition was moved and the new law prohibited only 'magnificent embroidery'.[94] The Japanese case, similar to the European one, updated the law but instead of reinforcing bans and prohibitions, simply acknowledged the changed circumstances.[95]

A final complication in the interpretation of sumptuary laws is the fact that they were issued at different times. Alan Hunt and Catherine Kovesi observe slight differences in the chronologies of different European states but admit that the phenomenon had a certain degree of unity between 1200 and 1700.[96] In Latin America, however, sumptuary regulations were first enacted in 1628 and became popular in the eighteenth century at a time in which they were on the wane in Iberia.[97] Sumptuary laws became common in Japan in the seventeenth century and in the Ottoman Empire they remained widely in use throughout the eighteenth and nineteenth centuries.

The meaning of these differences, as well as similarities is difficult to appreciate. Does it mean that fashion was present in different parts of the world, but at different times? Are we talking about similar processes and phenomena? And are we giving too much weight to specific concepts and historical interpretations taken from European history?

Conclusion

This chapter has shown that in the early modern period 'instances' of fashion were present in places as different as Japan, the rich cities of China and Latin America, as well as Europe. This is not surprising. Recent scholarship has unearthed sufficient evidence to argue that fashion was not just a 'passing fad' but integral to different world cultures as argued by Carlo Marco Belfanti.[98] Yet we are left with two open issues. First, why do we still think that fashion appeared only in medieval and early modern Europe, and 'nowhere else'? And second, what were the processes, forces and dynamics that explain fashion across the globe?

A reply to the first question has been given by considering Eurocentric views in which fashion was equated with change. Fashion was in this case taken to be integral to a 'modern' process of development that characterized Europe and Europe alone. In this chapter I have repeatedly argued against taking such a narrow explanation of change as the yardstick through which to judge what we might call an 'efflorescence' of fashion in different parts of the world.[99] By adopting instead a multidimensional definition of fashion, this chapter highlights the dynamic forces that shaped fashion in different areas of the world. Rather than seeing fashion as one process, this chapter has adopted different definitions to show how the 'fashion world' in the period c.1500–1800 was formed in different areas, mostly urban, dominated by some shared features (for instance imitation; the role of merchants; the importance of courts), a certain degree of interaction (trade and encounters with other cultures), but also distinctive characteristics (specific socio-economic contexts, and hierarchical structures). The latter point is important because, as Karen Tranberg Hansen reminds us, we should appreciate the subjective and experiential experiences of dress, something still difficult to access in non-European contexts.[100]

The comparative methodology is skewed towards Europe as the continent still provides the most extensive historical evidence and has long provided the research and conceptual toolbox for the analysis of fashion. The adoption of a reciprocal comparative method is not yet possible and entails a great deal of research for all the major extra-European empires and countries.[101] One might conclude that there was no global process called fashion in the early modern world, but that fashion was present in all 'four parts of the world'. Although instances of the conquering force of European fashion were already present in 1500, their consequences were not visible before the end of the early modern period. The worldwide adoption of Western attire as the result of colonial domination or as the acceptance of the 'modernity' of European life became an integral feature of global fashion only from the end of the eighteenth century.[102] And later in the twentieth century Western (this time American) leisurewear secured markets, imposed lifestyles and profited not just from global consumption, but also global production.[103]

Notes

1 This is a revised and updated version of Giorgio Riello, 'Fashion and the Four Parts of the World: Time, Space and Change in the Early Modern Period', in *Linking Cloth/Clothing Globally: The Transformations of Use and Value, Eighteenth to Twentieth Centuries*, ed. Miki Sugiura (Tokyo: Hosei University, 2018), 131–156.

2 Cited in Mark Elvin, 'Blood and Statistics: Reconstructing the Population Dynamics of Late Imperial China from the Biographies of Virtuous Women in Local Gazetteers', in *Chinese Women in the Imperial Past: New Perspectives*, ed. Harriet T. Zurndorfer (Leiden: Brill, 1999), 152.

3 Neil McKendrick, John Brewer and J. H. Plumb, *The Birth of a Consumer Society: The Commercialisation of Eighteenth-Century England* (London: Europa, 1982).

4 This emulative paradigm has been heavily criticized by several historians of consumption and fashion. See in particular John Styles, *The Dress of the People: Everyday Fashion in Eighteenth-Century England* (New Haven, CT and London: Yale University Press, 2007).

5 Thorstein Veblen, *The Theory of the Leisure Class* (Oxford: Oxford University Press, [1899] 2007).

6 Beverly Lemire, *Global Trade and the Transformation of Consumer Cultures: The Material World Remade, c.1500–1820* (Cambridge, UK: Cambridge University Press, 2018).

7 Cited in Sarah Dauncey, 'Illusions of Grandeur: Perceptions of Status and Wealth in Late-Ming Female Clothing and Ornamentation', *East Asian History* 25/26 (2003): 53–54.

8 Craig Clunas, *Superfluous Things: Material Culture and Social Status in Early Modern China* (Honolulu: University of Hawai'i Press, 1991); Donald Quataert, 'Clothing Laws, State, and Society in the Ottoman Empire, 1720–1829', *International Journal of Middle East Studies* 29.3 (1997): 403–425; Timothy Brook, *The Confusions of Pleasure: Commerce and Culture in Ming China* (Berkeley, CA: University of California Press, 1999), esp. 218–238; Eiko Ikegami, *Bonds of Civility: Aesthetic Networks and Political Origins of Japanese Culture* (Cambridge, UK: Cambridge University Press, 2005); Timon Screech, *Sex and the Floating World: Erotic Images in Japan, 1700–1820* (London: Reaktion Books, 1999); Rebecca Earle, '"Two Pairs of Pink Satin Shoes!!" Race, Clothing and Identity in the American (17th–19th Centuries)', *History Workshop Journal* 52 (2001): 175–195; Rebecca Earle, 'Luxury, Clothing and Race in Colonial Spanish America', in *Luxury in the Eighteenth Century: Debates, Desires and Delectable Goods*, ed. Maxine Berg and Elizabeth Eger (Basingstoke, UK: Routledge, 2003), 219–227; Dauncey, 'Illusions of Grandeur', 43–68; Suraiya Faroqhi and Christoph K. Neumann, eds., *Ottoman Costumes: From Textile to Identity* (Istanbul: Iren, 2004); Regina A. Root, ed., *The Latin American Fashion Reader* (Oxford: Berg, 2006); Robert Ross, *Clothing: A Global History* (Cambridge, UK: Polity, 2007); Antonia Finnane, *Changing Clothes in China: Fashion, History, Nation* (New York: Columbia University Press, 2007). See also Ulinka Rublack's excellent attempt at connecting European fashion to a global remit and Adam Geczy's analysis of fashion and orientalism. Ulinka Rublack, *Dressing Up: Cultural Identity in Renaissance Europe* (Oxford: Oxford University Press, 2010); Adam Geczy, *Fashion and Orientalism: Dress, Textiles and Culture from the 17th to the 21st Century* (London: Bloomsbury, 2013).

9 Carlo Marco Belfanti, 'Was Fashion a European Invention?', *Journal of Global History* 3.3 (2008): 443.

10 Fernand Braudel, *Capitalism and Material Life, 1400–1800* (London: Fontana, 1973), 227.

11 Giles Lipovetsky, *The Empire of Fashion: Dressing Modern Democracy* (Princeton, NJ: Princeton University Press, 1994), 15.

12 See Eugenia Paulicelli, 'Mapping the World: The Political Geography of Dress in Cesare Vecellio's Costume Books', *The Italianist* 28 (2003): 24–53; Eugenia Paulicelli, *Writing Fashion in Early Modern Italy: From Sprezzatura to Satire* (Aldershot, UK: Ashgate, 2014); Giorgio Riello, 'The World in a Book: The Creation of the Global in Sixteenth-Century European Costume Books', *Past & Present*, supplement 2019. See also Margaret F. Rosenthal and Ann Rosalind Jones, *The Clothing of the Renaissance World: Europe, Asia, Africa, the Americas* (London: Thames & Hudson, 2008), esp. introduction; and Traci Elizabeth Timmons, 'Habiti Antichi et Moderni di Tutto il Mondo and the "Myth of Venice"', *Athanor* 15 (1997): 28–33; Grazietta Butazzi, 'Tra mode occidentali e "costumi" medio orientali: confronti e riflessioni dai repertori cinquecenteschi alle trasformazioni vestimentarie tra XVII e XVIII secolo', in *Il Vestito dell'Altro: Semiotica, Arti, Costume*, ed. Giovanna Franci and Maria Giuseppina Muzzarelli (Milan: Lupetti, 2005), 251–270.

13 Antonia Finnane, 'Yangshou's "Modernity": Fashion and Consumption in the Early Nineteenth Century', *Positions* 11.2 (2003): 402.

14 Finnane, *Changing Clothes in China*, 20.

15 Cited in Rosenthal and Jones, *Clothing of the Renaissance World*, 36.

16 Braudel, *Capitalism and Material Life*, 228. See also Anthony Reid, *South Asia in the Age of Commerce, 1450–1680: Vol. 1. The Lands Bellow the Winds* (New Haven, CT and London: Yale University Press, 1984), 86–88. See also Chapter 11 by Cory Willmott in this volume.

17 *Européens & Japonais: Traité sur les contradictions & différences de moeurs écrit par le R.P. Luís Fróis au Japon, l'an 1585* (Paris: Chandeigne, 2003), 16. See also *The First European Description of Japan, 1585: A Critical English-Language Edition of Striking Contrasts in the Customs of Europe and Japan by Luis Frois, S.J.*, ed. Richard K. Danford, Robin D. Gill and Daniel T. Reff (London and New York: Routledge, 2014).

18 Dorothy Ko, *Cinderella's Sisters: A Revisionist History of Footbinding* (Berkeley: University of California Press, 2005).

19 Anne Brydon and Sandra Niessen, eds., *Consuming Fashion: Adorning the Transnational Body* (Oxford and New York: Berg, 1998), introduction.

20 Karen Tranberg Hansen, 'The World in Dress: Anthropological Perspectives on Clothing, Fashion, and Culture', *Annual Review of Anthropology* 33 (2004): 372.

21 I thank Miki Sugiura for providing translations of the text. See also Anna Jackson and Amin Jaffer eds., *Encounters: The Meeting of Asia and Europe, 1500–1800* (London: V&A Publications, 2004), 216.

22 Giulia Calvi, 'Cultures of Space: Costume Books, Maps, and Clothing Between Europe and Japan (Sixteenth Through Nineteenth Centuries)', *I Tatti Studies in Italian Renaissance* 20.2 (2017): 331–363.

23 Cited in Braudel, *Capitalism and Material Life*, 229.

24 Cited in Sabine Schülting, 'Strategic Improvisation: Henry Blout in the Ottoman Empire', in *Early Modern Encounters with the Islamic East: Performing Cultures*, ed. Sabine Schülting, Sabine Lucia Müller and Ralf Hertel (Aldershot, UK: Ashgate, 2012), 74.

25 Finnane, *Changing Clothes in China*, 44.

26 Ku Ch'i-yüan, *K'o tso chui yü* (Peking, [1618] 1987), cited in Craig Clunas, 'Regulation of Consumption and the Institution of Correct Morality by the Ming State', in *Norms and the State in China*, ed. Chung-Chieh Huang and Erik Zürcher (Leiden: Brill, 1993), 46.

27 Brook, *The Confusions of Pleasure*, 220.

28 Sanjay Subramaniam, *Explorations in Connected History: From the Tagus to the Ganges* (Oxford: Oxford University Press, 2005), 21.
29 Finnane, *Changing Clothes in China*, 46; Clunas, *Superfluous Things*, 154.
30 Screech, *Sex and the Floating World*, 113.
31 Giorgio Riello, *Back in Fashion: A History of Western Fashion since the Middle Ages* (London and New Haven, CT: Yale University Press, 2020), ch. 2.
32 Andrew Sherratt, 'Reviving the Grand Narrative: Archaeology and Long-Term Change', *Journal of European Archaeology* 3.1 (1995): 1–32.
33 Yedida Kalfon Stillman, *Arab Dress: From the Dawn of Islam to Modern Times*, ed. Norman A. Stillman (Leiden: Brill, 2000), 43.
34 Li Wenying, 'Textiles of the Second to Fifth Centuries Unearthed from Yingpan Cemetery', in *Central Asian Textiles and Their Contexts in the Early Middle Ages*, ed. Regula Schorta (Riggisberg, Switzerland: Abegg-Stiftung, 2006), 246–251.
35 Suzanne E. Cahill, '"Our Women Are Acting like Foreigners' Wives": Western Influences on Tang Dynasty Women's Fashion', in *China Chic: East Meets West*, ed. Valerie Steele and John S. Major (New Haven, CT and London: Yale University Press, 1999), 104–105.
36 Beverly Lemire and Giorgio Riello, 'East and West: Textiles and Fashion in Early Modern Europe', *Journal of Social History* 41.4 (2008): 887–916. This point was later developed in my research on cotton and later silk. See Giorgio Riello, *Cotton: The Fabric That Made the Modern World* (Cambridge, UK: Cambridge University Press, 2013), esp. ch. 6; and Dagmar Schäfer, Giorgio Riello and Luca Molà, eds., *Threads of Global Desire: Silk in the Pre-Modern World* (Woodbridge, UK: Boydell & Brewer, 2018), esp. the introduction and final chapter.
37 Seiroku Noma, *Japanese Costume and Textile Arts* (New York: Weatherill, 1974), 20–21.
38 See in particular Dale Carolyn Gluckman and Sharon Sadako Takeda, *When Art Became Fashion: Kosode in Edo-Period Japan* (Los Angeles, CA: Los Angeles County Museum of Art, 1992).
39 Kayoko Fujita, 'Japan Indianized: The Material Culture of Imported Textiles in Japan, 1550–1850', in *The Spinning World: A Global History of Cotton Textiles, 1200–1850*, ed. Giorgio Riello and Prasannan Parthasarathi (Oxford: Oxford University Press, 2009), 181–203. See also Noma, *Japanese Costume*, 132–133; and Screech, *Sex and the Floating World*, 116.
40 Verity Wilson, 'Western Modes and Asian Clothing: Reflections on Borrowing Other People's Dress', *Costume* 36 (2002): 139. See also Ronald P. Toby, 'The "Indianess" of Iberia and Changing Japanese Iconographies of Other', in *Implicit Understandings: Observing, Reporting, and Reflecting on Encounters Between Europeans and Other Peoples in the Early Modern Era*, ed. Stuart B. Schwartz (Cambridge, UK: Cambridge University Press, 1994), 337.
41 Donald H. Shively, 'Regulation and Status in Early Tokugawa Japan', *Harvard Journal of Asiatic Studies* 25 (1964–1965): 135.
42 Arturo Giráldez, *The Age of Trade: The Manila Galleons and the Dawn of the Global Economy* (Lanham, MA: Rowman & Littlefield, 2015).
43 Ilona Katzev, *Casta Painting: Images of Race in Eighteenth-Century Mexico* (New Haven, CT and London: Yale University Press, 2004).
44 Araceli Tinajero, 'Far Eastern Influences in Latin American Fashions', in *The Latin America Fashion Reader*, ed. Regina A. Root (Oxford and New York: Berg, 2005), 67–68.
45 Bhaswati Bhattacharya, 'Making Money at the Blessed Place of Manila: Armenians in the Madras-Manila Trade in the Eighteenth Century', *Journal of Global History* 3.3 (2008): 13 and 19.
46 Abby Sue Fisher, 'Trade Textiles: Asia and New Spain', in *Asia and Spanish America: Trans-Pacific Artistic and Cultural Exchange, 1500–1850*, ed. Donna Pierce and

Ronald Otsuka (Denver, CO: Denver Art Museum, 2009), 180; and Donna Pierce's contribution in *The Arts in Latin America, 1492–1820*, ed. Joseph. J. Riesel and Susan Stratton-Pruitt (Philadelphia, PA: Philadelphia Museum of Art, 2006), 400. On Chinese silks in Mexico see José L. Gasch-Tomás, 'The Manila Galleon and the Reception of Chinese Silk in New Spain, *c.*1550–1650', in Schäfer et al., *Threads of Global Desire*, 251–264.

47 Rebecca Earle, 'Race, Clothing and Identity: Sumptuary Laws in Colonial Spanish America', in *The Right to Dress: Sumptuary Laws in a Global Perspective, 1200–1800*, ed. Giorgio Riello and Ulinka Rublack (Cambridge, UK: Cambridge University Press, 2019), 325–345.

48 Artemio de Valle-Arizpe, *Historia de la ciudad de México segun los relatos de sus cronistas* (Mexico: Departamento del Distrito Federal, 1998), 173–174.

49 Ross W. Jamieson, 'Bolts of Cloth and Sherds of Pottery: Impressions of Caste in the Material Culture of the Seventeenth Century Audiencia of Quito', *The Americas* 60.3 (2004): 440. See also Riello, *Cotton*, 142.

50 Helen Benton Minnich and Shojiro Momura, *Japanese Costume and the Makers of its Elegant Tradition* (Rutland, VE: Charles E. Tuttle Co., 1963), 198.

51 On European courts, see Philip Mansel, *Dressed to Rule: Royal and Court Costume from Louis XIV to Elizabeth II* (New Haven, CT and London: Yale University Press, 2005); and Isabelle Paresys and Natacha Coquery, eds., *Se vêtir à la cour en Europe, 1400–1815* (Lille: Université Lille 3, 2011). On Japan, see Ikegami, *Bonds of Civility*; Katsuya Hirano, 'Regulating Excess: The Cultural Politics of Consumption in Tokugawa Japan', in Riello and Rublack, *The Right to Dress*, 435–460.

52 Valerie Steele, *Paris Fashion: A Cultural History* (London: Bloomsbury, [1988] 2017).

53 Benton Minnich and Momura, *Japanese Costume*, 199.

54 Dauncey, 'Illusions of Grandeur', 50–51.

55 Christopher Breward and David Gilbert, eds., *Fashion's World Cities* (Oxford: Berg, 2006).

56 Finnane, 'Yangshou's "Modernity"', 400.

57 Finnane, 'Yangshou's "Modernity"', 401.

58 Brook, *Confusions of Pleasure*, 221–222.

59 Helen C. Gunsaulus, *Japanese Textiles* (New York: Japan Society, 1941), 21–22; Shively, 'Regulation and Status', 125.

60 Alan Kennedy, *Japanese Costume: History and Tradition* (Paris: Adam Biro, 1990), 11.

61 Dauncey, 'Illusions of Grandeur', 44; Brook, *Confusions of Pleasure*, 210–237.

62 Clunas, *Superfluous Things*, 146–147.

63 See in particular Pierre Bourdieu, *Distinction: A Social Critique of the Judgment of Taste*, trans. Richard Nice (Cambridge, MA: Harvard University Press, 1984).

64 Brook, *Confusions of Pleasure*, 218.

65 Earle, 'Two Pairs of Pink Satin Shoes!!', 177.

66 Dauncey, 'Illusions of Grandeur', 59; Dorothy Ko, *Teachers of the Inner Chambers: Women and Culture in Seventeenth-Century China* (Stanford, CA: Stanford University Press, 1994), 29–67.

67 Amanda Mayer Stinchecum, *Kosode: 16th–19th Century Textiles from the Nomura Collection* (New York: Japan Society and Kodansha International, 1984), 51.

68 See for the case of London: Hannah Greig, *The Beau Monde: Fashionable Society in Georgian London* (Oxford: Oxford University Press, 2013).

69 Michelle Sapori, *Rose Bertin: ministre des modes de Marie-Antoinette* (Paris: Regard et Institut français de la mode, 2003).

70 Kennedy, *Japanese Costume*, 19. Korin, born into a Kimono merchant's family, was a famous painter and founder of the Rinpa School. He also painted kimonos on several occasions although his patterns only became popular after death. He advised a bureaucrats' lady to wear black with white backing all the time, and let her servant

wear bright colours. This made a good contrast and also made competitors look garish. I thank Miki Sugiura for this information.

71 Craig Clunas, 'The Art of Social Climbing in Sixteenth-Century China', *Burlington Magazine* 133.1059 (1991): 370.

72 Christopher Breward, *The Culture of Fashion: A New History of Fashionable Dress* (Manchester: Manchester University Press, 1995).

73 Noma, *Japanese Costume*, 117.

74 Maxine Berg and Helen Clifford, 'Commerce and the Commodity: Graphic Display and Selling New Consumer Goods in Eighteenth-Century England', in *Art Markets in Europe, 1400–1800*, ed. Michael North and David Ormrod (Aldershot, UK: Ashgate, 1998), 187–200; John Styles, 'Product Innovation in Early Modern London', *Past & Present* 168 (2000): 124–169; Evelyn Welch, ed., *Fashioning the Early Modern: Creativity and Innovation in Europe, 1500–1800* (Oxford: Oxford University Press, 2017),

75 Noma, *Japanese Costume*, 155.

76 Ishimura Hayao and Maruyama Nobuhiko, *Robes of Elegance: Japanese Kimonos of the 16th–20th Centuries* (Raleigh: North Carolina Museum of Art, 1988), 7–8. On painted fans see also Quitman E. Phillips, *The Practices of Painting in Japan, 1475–1500* (Stanford, CA: Stanford University Press, 2000), 44–45.

77 The literature on sumptuary laws in Europe is vast. Alan Hunt, *Governance of the Consuming Passions: A History of Sumptuary Law* (New York: St. Martin's Press, 1996), provides an excellent theoretical and historical overview. For a more recent engagement at a global level see Riello and Rublack, *The Right to Dress*, esp. the introduction, 1–34.

78 Dauncey, 'Illusions of Grandeur', 47.

79 Cited in BuYun Chen, 'Wearing the Hat of Loyalty: Imperial Power and Dress Reform in Ming Dynasty China', in Riello and Rublack, *The Right to Dress*, 424–425.

80 Kennedy, *Japanese Costume*, 17.

81 Arjun Appadurai, 'Introduction: Commodities and the Politics of Value', in *The Social life of Things: Commodities in Cultural Perspective*, ed. Arjun Appadurai (Cambridge, UK: Cambridge University Press, 1986), 25.

82 See for instance Ina Baghdiantz McCabe, *A History of Global Consumption, 1500–1800* (Abingdon, UK and New York: Routledge, 2015).

83 Shively, 'Regulation and Status'; Hunt, *Governance of the Consuming Passions*; Clunas, 'Regulation of Consumption'; Madeleine C. Zilfi, 'Whose Laws? Gendering the Ottoman Sumptuary Laws', in Faroqhi and Neumann, *Ottoman Costumes*, 125–142.

84 Clunas, 'Art of Social Climbing', 370.

85 Riello and Rublack, *The Right to Dress*, esp. the introduction, 1–34, discusses the methodological implications of a comparative framework of analysis. On Batavia and the Cape see Robert Ross, 'Sumptuary Laws in Europe, the Netherlands and the Dutch Colonies', in *Contingent Lives: Social Identity and Material Culture in the VOC World*, ed. Nigel Worden (Cape Town: Rondebosch, 2007), 382–390; Stan Du Plessis, '"Pearls Worth Rds4000 or Less": Reinterpreting Eighteenth-Century Sumptuary Laws at the Cape', *ERSA Working Paper* 336 (2013); and Adam Clulow, '"Splendour and Magnificence": Diplomacy and Sumptuary Codes in Early Modern Batavia', in Riello and Rublack, *The Right to Dress*, 299–323.

86 Cf. the European laws, as for instance in Kim M. Phillips, 'Masculinities and the Medieval English Sumptuary Laws', *Gender and History* 19.1 (2007): 22–42, with Shively, 'Regulation and Status'.

87 Clunas, 'Art of Social Climbing'; Clunas, *Superfluous Things*.

88 Negley B. Harte, 'State Control of Dress and Social Change in Pre-Industrial England', in *Trade, Government and Economy in Pre-Industrial England*, ed. D. C. Coleman and A. H. John (London: Weidenfeld & Nicolson, 1976), 132–165.

89 Earle, 'Race, Clothing and Identity'.

90 This is why Quataert prefers to call them 'clothing laws'. See Quataert, 'Clothing laws' and Chapter 7 by Sarah Fee in this volume.
91 Clunas, 'Regulation of Consumption', 43 and 45.
92 Clunas, 'Regulation of Consumption', 45.
93 Unlike China, attempts at introducing sumptuary laws in the Dutch Republic failed. See Isis Sturtewagen and Bruno Blondé, 'Playing by the Rules? Dressing Without Sumptuary Laws in the Low Countries from the Fourteenth to the Eighteenth Century', in Riello and Rublack, *The Right to Dress*, 74–75.
94 Kennedy, *Japanese Costume*, 18.
95 See Hirano, 'Regulating Excess'.
96 Hunt, *Governance of the Consuming Passions*; Catherine Kovesi Killerby, *Sumptuary Law in Italy, 1200–1500* (Oxford: Oxford University Press, 2002).
97 Earle, '"Two Pairs of Pink Satin Shoes!!"', 178–179; Earle, 'Race, Clothing and Identity', 325–326
98 Belfanti, 'Was Fashion a European Invention?'.
99 On the concept of 'efflorescence' see Jack A. Goldstone, 'Efflorescences and Economic Growth in World History: Rethinking the "Rise of the West" and the Industrial Revolution', *Journal of World History* 13.2 (2002): 323–389.
100 Tranberg Henson, 'World in Dress', 372–373.
101 Kenneth Pomeranz, *The Great Divergence: Europe, China, and the Making of the Modern World Economy* (Princeton, NJ: Princeton University Press, 2000); Roy Bin Wong, *China Transformed: Historical Change and the Limits of European Experience* (Ithaca, NY and London: Cornell University Press, 1997). This is an approach that I am currently developing for the analysis of silk in a joint project with Dagmar Schäfer.
102 Wilbur Zelinsky, 'Globalization Reconsidered: The Historical Geography of Modern Western Male Attire', *Journal of Cultural Geography* 22.1 (2004): 83–134; Ross, *Clothing: A Global History*.
103 Gregory Votolato, *American Design in the Twentieth Century* (Manchester: Manchester University Press, 1998); Regina Lee Blaszczyk, ed., *Producing Fashion: Commerce, Culture, and Consumers* (Philadelphia: University of Pennsylvania Press, 2007); and Regina Lee Blaszczyk and Ben Wubs, eds., *The Fashion Forecasters: A Hidden History of Color and Trend Prediction* (London: Bloomsbury, 2018).

3

SHIRTS AND SNOWSHOES

Imperial agendas and Indigenous agency in globalizing North America, c.1660–1800[1]

Beverly Lemire

Apparel and all its components can illuminate the priorities of makers and needs of the wearers, as well as the political climate in which dress was created and used. In this chapter I reconsider specific garments within a cross-cultural focus, exploring the varied contexts of production and use, sharing and adaptation. Ready-made linen shirts became essential apparel for European sailors and soldiers, involuntary consumers serving imperial agendas globally.[2] This garment became one of the 'ways of "socializing" individuals', including in an imperial context.[3] I will also examine Native American made snowshoes – their use and value – in the colonial military contexts of northern North America, wherein different kinds of socialization might take place. These case studies suggest the complexities of material exchange, revealed in entangled facets of dress.

Technologies of empire: the white linen shirt

In the seventeenth century, English (later British) imperial ventures arose within a developing fiscal military state, with military provisioning sustained through an increasingly effective state finance system. This symbiotic alliance was a catalyst in the dramatic expansion of ready-to-wear garments. Some decades ago, I noted this seminal link, and still more is being uncovered and connections explained, including the roles of other imperial institutions.[4] The impetus to devise effective technologies was strong: the challenges of long supply chains and lengthy military campaigns stretched early modern European states. In the century after 1660, advances did not come from new mechanical systems of production; rather, organizational technologies evolved that shaped the clothing worn by maritime and military men.

The noted historian of technology, Thomas Parke Hughes, defines the social and physical facets of technology as those that combine the talents of a range of occupations aimed at designing and controlling a 'human-built world'. While he notes that the word 'technology' was not used until the early nineteenth century, historians have applied 'the word to activities and things in the past not then known as technology' but that have a powerful commonality with more recent systems. Hughes emphasizes the creative, functional and aesthetic dimensions of technological systems, an analysis that fits the development of the provisioning system I describe. This productive method can be termed a new technological system, linking the Navy Board (responsible for the business of ship production and provisioning) to the cast of contractors and subcontractors, and the tens of thousands of predominantly female labourers employed in crafting the mass of garments. Information and its dissemination were critical to this system, setting new material standards, at the core of the shifting 'human-built world'.[5] After 1660, Chatham, one of the Royal Dockyards, grew into the largest centre of naval production and stores in Britain. Chatham, Woolwich (Figure 3.1) and other royal dockyards, were wondrous sights to contemporaries, as ships were built, launched and supplied. Clothing manufacturing was less public and more diffuse, employing legions of women throughout the southern cities of Britain, the products flowing into naval warehouses.

The Navy Board received endless entreaties from commanders, captains and pursers tasked with keeping men in good physical condition. Appeals produced uncertain results and the battles that erupted around Tangier in the 1670s illustrate the case. Charles II acquired Tangier in 1661 as part of the dowry of his Portuguese

FIGURE 3.1 'At Woolwich with Part of the Town, Geometrical Plan of His Majesty's Dockyard', 1753, engraving by Pierre Charles Canot, c.1710–1777.

Source: © Yale Center for British Art. British Art, Paul Mellon Collection, B1977.14.1292.

wife. It seemed an invaluable strategic location, facing the Atlantic on the tip of North Africa, guarding the Gibraltar Strait. Money was poured into its development and upkeep, though never enough.[6] Building defences required immense expenditure; equally necessary was keeping ships well crewed, including slaves to man the galleys. The British adopted North African style vessels in this locale and the slaves needed clothing. In 1675, garments were requested for 260 oarsmen on the *Margaret* galley; the *Mary Rose* needed 120 slaves 'for the oars' and the captain reported on his arrival in 1676 that the men were 'short of clothes'.[7] The purser of the *Margaret* galley, whose job it was to secure stores, was slow in sending samples of potential slop clothes for the Navy Board's approval. Samples circulated back and forth between Tangier and London, along with written communications. One locally made garment was sent for London's evaluation, along with a mixed assessment of two samples of clothing dispatched from London-based contractors. Faults were found and enumerated. Clothing needs remained.[8] Samples were at the heart of the systematic production of ready-made clothing, the provisioning of the navy and shape the meanings carried by this apparel.

Most naval crews were not slaves and bought their own clothes for voyages, stored in sea chests. The ship's purser sold these goods when at sea. The role of naval administration was to provide sound garments, well sewn, of good-quality fabric, at a reasonable price. These items were infused with rationalism – or at least that was the intent. Cloth was intended to be hard wearing, the garment cut generously for a working body – but not so large as to waste fabric and raise costs. Garments were also made in several sizes – a demand that presumed a close knowledge of standard bodily dimensions, from boy to man. The accepted parameters of this metric came at a time when systematic sizing was in its infancy. The provisioning technology that developed over the seventeenth and eighteenth centuries also rested on the veracity of samples and the standards represented in these objects. The functioning of this system required slop sellers to send samples to the Navy Board. Next, delegates on the Navy Board judged the quality of the sample and whether an order would be given; later, naval staff determined whether the order they received matched the original sample. Samples represented the capacities of the contractor, his talent at sourcing fabric, hiring skilled cutters and finding deft needle workers.

Sample clothing embodied material expectations. However, there was frequent divergence from this ideal, with recurring disappointment. Captain Warren of the ship *Windsor*, disparaged the slops sent to his ship in the spring of 1696, returning them to the slop seller as substandard. The slop seller, in turn, claimed his clothes were good quality, citing the stock he sent to other ships that matched the agreed example. He accused the captain of the *Windsor* of mishandling the clothes he provided, insisting they were 'much abused'.[9] Disputes such as this were common and sample evidence usually decided the case.[10] Its materiality offered the weightiest proof. And, to avoid fraud, samples of garments were also posted in major homeports allowing pursers and captains to gauge how well the full order, once delivered, matched the ideal on which the order was based.[11] The physical proof embedded in the sample, assessed by expert eyes and skilled hands, was fundamental to the functioning of the provisioning system and infused the shirts, coats and trousers with a technological rationality directed to imperial ends.

Bribery might secure contracts for well-placed men like Thomas Beckford, scion of a notable contracting family. But routine dishonesty could not erase the ritual of the sample; it remained central in the formal assessment process within the Royal Navy, used to judge everything from tallow to timber, cloth to rigging.[12] This system provided the foundational architecture of imperial provisioning. A hierarchy of values imbued the resulting clothing, determined by the institutional priorities of the Navy. This system of technology aimed to produce goods that could be replicated for the mass making of garments for naval and other populations of involuntary consumers. Ready-made shirts and trousers intended for maritime wear thus distilled a multiplicity of meanings, beginning with the sequential process of their production. Additionally, the scale of production brought tons of garments to the service of the Navy, creating a mobile clothing ecosystem with global repercussions. I do not calculate the total volumes of the goods made – that is not my focus. Rather, I consider the macro-level impact of a ready-made clothing system that carried garments of particular physical structure, reflecting a defined technological system, into the four corners of the world. Consider the 15 tons of apparel shipped to the Royal Navy's Mediterranean headquarters at Port Mahon, Menorca in 1747.[13] One slop seller alone, Charles James, sold over 435,000 shirts to the Navy between 1760 and 1770; 62 per cent were delivered during a two-year climax of the Seven Years' War (1756–1763). There was pressure to provide at speed; in one instance a Navy Board official noted the need for shirts in Jamaica and Antigua, major British naval bases.[14] A decade later, during renewed warfare, James Wadham, sold even greater quantities of shirts, trousers and jackets to supply a larger maritime force, shipping over 612,000 items to naval storehouses between 1780 and 1782.[15] This diffusion of clothing, channelled through the British navy, supplied ships throughout the world's oceans.[16] And as the manufacturing capacity of this system grew, other trading companies discovered their need for types of ready-made apparel, including shirts.[17]

How did these shirts shape Britain's imperial agenda? First, the shirts themselves enacted cultural priorities. The diffusion of linen shirts brought with them new thinking about apparel and new ways to gauge those who achieved or failed to achieve the principles embedded in the shirt. The physical structure of these assembled rectangles of cloth carried values: the rationality of their making within a purposeful imperialism aligned. Additionally, the cleanness of linens loomed large in early modern European culture, a factor rooted in European mores and extended to colonial settings. Cleanness was a trait that was increasingly lauded in the seventeenth and eighteenth centuries, including by medical men tasked to oversee sailors' health, as well as by ships' officers. They increasingly focused on keeping shirts and clothing clean – or at least there being a sufficiency of clothing that clean garments were available on key occasions.

Attaining such standards was a gradual process, as thinking changed with respect to cleanliness and as plebeian crews adopted regimens of washing. It is well known that for the European elites, white linen became an almost fetishized commodity over this period, a proxy for physical cleanliness and the white body.[18] Shirts also buffered flesh from coarser wool or canvas fabrics, the constrictions of waistcoats, breeches or jackets or the frequent ties and buttons that held outer garments in place. Labouring men, like sailors, were uniquely trained to this understanding of linen and its connection to cleanliness and order, a process gradually followed by other workingmen. Indeed, by the 1770s, Adam Smith noted that 'through the greater part of Europe, a creditable day-labourer would be ashamed to appear in public without a linen shirt; the want of which would be supposed to denote that disgraceful degree of poverty'.[19]

Over the long eighteenth century, generations of seafaring plebeian men were commanded to obey shipboard regimes of cleanliness.[20] The sailor caricatured in Figure 3.2 displays some of the material attributes of his cohort, his half-buttoned shirt, white waistcoat and striped trousers proclaiming his occupation.

FIGURE 3.2 'Caricature of a Sailor', by John Sell Cotman, *c.*1799, watercolour and gouache.
Source: Yale Center for British Art. © British Art, Paul Mellon Collection, B1975.4.180.

By mid-century, naval treatises went so far as promoting the washing of the body, especially in warm climates, and keeping below deck 'sweet, clean and wholesome'.[21] At sea, results were achieved with the routine scouring of sailors' clothes by towing them behind the ship.[22] By the end of the century a medical man reported that: 'sailors value themselves upon appearing neat', adding that, 'in war time, to receive impressed men [it is essential] that they may be properly cloathed [*sic*] [and] scrubbed'.[23] And he urged this system of cleanliness be diligently maintained. Indeed, by at least the later eighteenth century orders for sailors to wash their shirts on long voyages in warm climates were routine, reflecting the sensibilities that had developed regarding sartorial ideals for common mariners.[24] Clean decks, clean sea chests and orderly clothing were the defining traits of this seafaring contingent.[25] Indeed, one junior officer, moved to poetry by his naval service, described the good ship with 'all her gallant seamen neat and clean'. Neatness and cleanliness is a phrase repeated throughout his elegy, where he also notes the defining whiteness of mariners' garments.[26]

Linens provided both tangible and intangible meanings within imperial schemas. Shirts manifested new meanings of 'whiteness', distinguishing adherents of material cleanliness from agnostics, those who ignored these values or held other traditions of bodily purification. Boundaries of race and status were policed through the power of white linen, a demonstrable feature of colonial life in the Americas. For example, early in the 1600s, a Jesuit missionary bemoaned the fact that '[linen] Table napkins were not in vogue among the Indians near Quebec in 1633'.[27] This cavil marked cultural boundaries between French and Native Americans. Kathleen Brown states that:

> The spread of linen shirts to North America and the Caribbean was ... a form of cultural imperialism ... The shirt's penetration into new markets pointed to larger patterns of disruption and adaptation as Indians and Africans integrated and reinterpreted it within cultural traditions that were rapidly adjusting to new geopolitical realities ... performed through material objects as well as through manners.[28]

The ethos of linen shirts travelled widely with British naval, military and colonial bodies. The institutional context of these shirts added other dimensions to the calculus of clean and dirty, orderly or disordered, as gauged by Europeans. Indeed, the linen shirt figured in cross-cultural interactions on a global scale, as mercantile and missionary ventures extended throughout the world and Indigenous peoples adapted and translated these materials.[29] Greenlandic peoples received European whalers with increased frequency in this period, a seafaring contingent that included Basque, Dutch, Danish and British. With repeated contacts came cultural exchanges, including the spreading impact of the European clothing system. The use of linen shirts among Western Greenlandic peoples was routine by the early 1700s, demonstrating material adaptations.[30] More intentional flows of European clothing followed in other northern climes. From the late 1600s, the Hudson's

Bay Company (HBC) dispatched ready-made shirts, coats and hats of various kinds to their trading posts positioned at waterways linking to interior Native American communities. At least 4,000 shirts were exported to HBC trading posts between 1684 and 1694.[31] Gifted and traded, these items were ingredients in the creation of *métissage*, a material and cultural mixing intended by Europeans to sign leading Indigenous partners.[32] Catholic missionaries in North America likewise disbursed clothing to potential Indigenous converts, as part of an acculturation process. Native American men, however, usually chose to wear the shirts loose, down to their thighs, in a manner challenging hegemonic norms of European dress. This mode of dress shaped 'new ways of Indigenous thinking and being'.[33] Indigenous men revised the cultural intentions embedded in European-made shirts within a new context of material exchange.[34]

The systems of making, wearing and using linen shirts, the volume of production and their diffusion through imperial ventures, are epitomized in the vast production technologies of the Royal Navy. Yet, world influences flowed in many directions even within the context of European colonial advances. My next case study examines the provision of footwear – snowshoes – in northern North America and the adaptations embraced by Europeans mediated by alliances with Indigenous peoples. Diplomatic ties shaped this essential apparel.

Essential footwear and diplomatic material production

Europe's colonial projects in North America involved continued contact, interaction and allegiance with Indigenous peoples. Relations were founded on treatises and cemented with what Christian Ayne Crouch terms 'material diplomacy', consolidating alliances crucial for Europeans.[35] From the outset Europeans joined as allies in traditional hostilities among competing Indigenous groups and cemented their commitment with gifts and military resources. Europeans were driven by their passion for furs and their aim to secure the best sources of this commodity; subsequent treaties mingled Indigenous, colonial and European priorities. Diplomacy linked all.[36]

Long before the arrival of Europeans, it was a recurring practice 'for chiefs to visit one another periodically to exchange gifts and renew alliances'.[37] Bruce Trigger observes that in the seventeenth century,

> Chiefs and their supporters competed for prestige with other groups. Because prestige was derived in various ways from the conduct of foreign relations, chiefs within a tribe or confederacy often formed two or more factions that pursued alternative foreign policies, each faction hoping to benefit from its choice.[38]

Diplomacy in this period involved diverse coalitions and ruptures, as Indigenous peoples and Europeans negotiated priorities – a process sometimes understood differently by these parties. The English and French initially struggled to gain a foothold in North America and sought human sources of information in America, kidnapping some to carry to Europe. Sir Ferdinando Gorges, commander of the fort at Plymouth, received five kidnapped Native Americans in 1605. He quizzed them extensively on 'the rivers in the land and men of note who lived on them; how powerful they were, how allied and what enemies they had'.[39]

From the outset, European and Native Americans weighed the value of treaties. Once contracted, they were formalized through the exchange of gifts and the pledging of resources: human and material. The gifting of cloth and clothing took place in many circumstances from first contact through the eighteenth century. Allegiance was signalled by exchanges and adaptations to culture, what has been termed a process of 'de-culturation ... and acculturation ... a synthetic process'.[40] This progression included, in part, the wearing of clothes of different sorts by both parties – the shirt, jacket and handkerchief of the European system or the moccasins, leggings and breechcloth of Native Americans. It also involved the exchange of people, living amid the other's societies, forging ties.[41]

When the French arrived in the St Lawrence River in the 1600s they encountered peoples with ancient trade networks reaching deep into the Great Lakes regions and north to Hudson's Bay. As Ruth Phillips notes: 'These trading networks did not disappear after the injection of European manufactures into the exchange system but were further elaborated.'[42] Interactions took place within geographic contexts that challenged Europeans' knowledge systems and material capacities.[43] Earlier sixteenth-century Arctic and northern voyages by English adventurers revealed life-threatening deficits in knowledge and technology.[44] Survival in northern regions ultimately depended on 'learning what the Natives knew'.[45] French Jesuit accounts likewise reveal a growing respect for Indigenous knowledge for they found

> those barbarians are good soldiers; and the french [sic], who despised ... [them] when they first came here, have changed their minds since they saw them last winter [in 1665] in a hot skirmish; [despite the fact that] the winter, too, was more severe and protracted than it had been for 30 years. The snow lay 4 feet deep.[46]

Accommodation to winter demanded snowshoes, what the French called *raquette*, allowing fierce hunts across the snow-covered woods and fields (Figure 3.3).[47] The French also learned that, unlike life in Europe:

> The Winter season is the most suitable for Hunters, who then enrich themselves, and likewise the country, with the skins of animals ... No less favourable is it for working-people, the snow making all roads smooth, and the frost covering Rivers and Lakes with ice, so that one can go anywhere with safety and draft loads ... . So, too, the walking for pleasure-seekers is at that season very fine, and usually favoured with a beautiful Sun and very clear weather.[48]

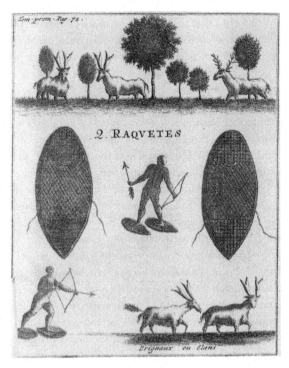

FIGURE 3.3 'Raquette', from *Nouveaux voyages de Mr. le baron de Lahontan, dans l'Amerique Septentrionale, qui contiennent une rélation des différens peuples qui y habitent; la nature de leur gouvernement; leur commerce, leurs coutumes, leur religion, & leur maniére de faire la guerre.* A La Haye: Chez les fréres l'Honoré, 1703–1704, p. 72.

Source: Library of Congress, Prints & Photographs. LC-USZ62-115626 (b & w film copy neg.)

A good winter depended on mastering Indigenous clothing technologies. Footwear was elemental in this equation. Moreover, access to such footwear was determined by the alliances with local people and integration into their existing networks. These factors secured essential knowledge and resources from Native Americans.[49] Here, too, Europeans grafted their interests on to those of their partners, shaping connections generation after generation within the wider dynamic of the colonial fur trade.[50]

If the French, Dutch and English wanted furs, Indigenous leaders, in turn, wanted Europeans' trade goods 'that they could redistribute as a means of enhancing their [own] prestige [among their people]'.[51] Both sought military support. In this manner coalitions were built. The French allied with northern Anishinaabe (Algonquin) peoples, one of many such pacts; and the English allied with the Haudenosaunee (Iroquois) Confederacy. Gift exchanges reinforced such treaties, materializing intentions, part of Indigenous cultural practice and spiritual systems.

'The Jesuit fathers observed that … [gifts] spoke more clearly than lips.'[52] This dip-lomatic context set material relations between Indigenous peoples and Europeans. Moreover, the spread of technologies, like snowshoes, took place within this diplo-matic structure, goods critical to the lives of warriors, including European allies. Snowshoes fascinated the European military and colonial subjects, including among those who initially defined indigeneity with this footwear. Indigenous skills were essential to flourish in this landscape.[53]

Europeans understood nothing of the northern cold and snow, or the land in which they moved. A painful defeat, suffered by the French, is evidence of the importance of knowledge *and* supplies. In 1666, a newly arrived French regi-ment began an ill-fated campaign against the Haudenosaunee to the south. It was a debacle. The Carignan-Salière Regiment had never experienced winter warfare and their leaders took neither advice nor winter equipment, when they set off down the Richelieu River towards the Hudson River Valley and their enemy. Of the 500 men in this campaign 400 died – most from cold and adverse conditions.[54] Local volunteers from French colonial settlements were fully equipped. Knowledge and the appropriate kit were crucial in winter ter-rain, as demonstrated in the image of a French settler in 1720 (Figure 3.4).

Making this footwear combined the skills of Indigenous men who harvested trees and often shaped the wooden frames and women who prepared the sinew, gut and leather and netted the webbing. This was predominantly women's work, aimed at preparing their community for the challenges and opportunities of each season. Indigenous women were in many ways defined by this labour. Snowshoe-making was an essential and strategic part of their duties.[55] Rémy de Courcelle, the driving force behind the disastrous 1666 winter campaign, managed the provi-sioning of the Carignan-Salière Regiment. He rejected a local merchant's offer to secure 50 snowshoes for the mission from local suppliers.[56] As in Europe, com-mercial intermediaries might secure contracts for military supplies from Indigenous allies. Local Europeans were becoming experienced in these commercial affairs, as an adjunct to the fur trade.[57] Snowshoes were a staple.

In 1786, more than a century later, a Scots trader wrote from a new HBC post, noting his need for snowshoes – and the Indigenous women to make them: 'I do not know what to do without these articles [,] see what it is to have no [Indigenous] wives. Try and get Rackets [snowshoes] – there is no stirring without them'.[58] When there was regular contact or proximity to fur trade posts, Indigenous women focused intensively on making moccasins and snowshoes.[59] Thus alliances provided not only the strength and skills of Native American men as warriors, but also the skills and labour of women who made critical war materiel.[60] Snowshoes enabled fur trade life *and* military ventures. Wearing snowshoes in this era, and in this place, did not suggest appropriation of technology by the incomers, but rather an acknow-ledgement of necessity and, for some Europeans, a clear recognition of Indigenous skills. All mention of these goods by colonial correspondents in this period must be understood in the context of the Indigenous makers, within systems of diplomatic accord or informal alliance, in whatever regions that arose. In the St Lawrence

FIGURE 3.4 'Canadiens en raquette allant en guerre sur la neige' ('Canadian going to war on snowshoes'), by J. B. Scotin in Bacqueville De La Potherie and Claude Charles Leroy, *Histoire de l'Amérique septentrionale*, Paris, 1722.
Source: © Alamy Limited, UK.

River territory, the Wendat of Wendake, near Quebec City, and the Montagnas, who treated with the French, structured the material available to military and civilian alike. Alliances were decisive for generations.

Within the next century, greater numbers of Europeans – military, settler and trader – arrived in North America. Ruth Phillips describes the items British military officers typically amassed during their posting to colonial North America. She differentiates sharply between the clothing and other goods acquired as curiosities for European antiquarians, and the apparel and accoutrements used by officers in the conduct of their diplomatic and military affairs.[61] As Phillips notes, 'Tens of thousands of British soldiers spent time in North America between 1750 and 1820'.[62] The male settlers arriving in these regions generally adopted Indigenous attire and skills, as needed. Cultural crossing-dressing was the norm.[63] However, the flow of knowledge and resources from Native American to Europeans has yet to be fully catalogued. It is indisputable, moreover, that Europeans adapted and embraced Indigenous clothing technologies in a variety of circumstances, especially things designed to survive winter cold, storms and deep snow. Diplomacy and material exchange underpinned the myriad networks linking both British and French with their diverse Indigenous allies. Snowshoes symbolized this reliance.

The period of the Little Ice Age around 1700 represented a serious climatic challenge coinciding as well with intrusion by New England settlers into traditional Indigenous lands. Thomas Wickman argues that the frigid years between 1694 and 1706 drove New Englanders to adopt snowshoes in order to survive. The stable snowpack was a boon to the north-eastern Wabanaki, traditionally friendly with the French. Wabanaki oral tradition celebrated good winter snows as a 'season of abundance for skilled members of family hunting bands'. It was equally suitable to attack those deemed enemies, like the New Englanders who encroached on their territory. However, by adopting snowshoes themselves, settlers ultimately challenged the hegemony of that Indigenous community.[64]

New England colonists relearned the importance of snowshoes on several occasions. In 1704, a group of provincial combatants from New Hampshire conducted a winter foray against the Pequawket, another community allied to the French. The value of winter warfare was made plain, with the leader writing that: 'the winter time is the onely [sic] time ever to march against the Indian Enemy ... every man in snow shoes with twenty dayes [sic] provisions'.[65] The lesson was applied repeatedly in colonial conflicts. Clashes between British and French settlers and their Indigenous allies reverberated through the 1700s, often played out on a winter landscape. Snowshoes were critical to combat.[66] Sir William Johnson's life epitomizes material exchange and robust diplomacy with Haudenosaunee peoples. This Anglo-Irish immigrant settled in northern New York province in 1738 and forged close bonds with the Mohawk being adopted into their community. His stature grew among Native American and British administrations because of his mastery of diplomacy. 'Johnson's presents were one of the most powerful conciliatory influences on the Iroquois, the greatest Indian confederacy of the eighteenth century.'[67] Ultimately, in 1746, he convinced the Haudenosaunee Confederacy to act with the British against the French. He materialized his ties with these allies by dressing in the 'Indian fashion' on ceremonial occasions, recognizing the benefits of close collaboration. This perspective was not always realized by his compatriots in their recurring wars with the French.[68] A raid from New England into present-day Nova Scotia, in 1747, was intended to surprise French forces. But, the tables were turned. A force of 700 French and Indigenous allies attacked the 350-strong New England forces during a night when a snowstorm struck that left four feet of snow on the ground. As a correspondent related: 'the want of snow shoes convinced us it was impracticable [to continue the fight] ... the enemy being provided with them, had all the advantage over us as if they had fought on firm ground'.[69] The value of this winter footwear was inestimable.

Supplying the needs of all warriors within an alliance doubtless animated production capacity among Indigenous peoples (as the souvenir trade did in times of peace). In 1754, just prior to the Seven Years' War, a report from New York endorsed close attention to fortifications aligned with 'Indian castles', as he termed fortified Native settlements. He advised small settler garrisons be posted near by and specified the supplies to be stocked, including: 'spare arms [and] snow shoes (with which the French are always provided)'. The author also emphasized the vital importance of shared risks and shoulder-to-shoulder fighting alongside Indigenous allies, employing *their* techniques of war: 'to convince the Indians that we are really in earnest … we must fight along with them … the French seldom fail of this method'.[70] The extended conflict in North America (1756–1763) brought Europeans and colonial militaries in close contact with essential Indigenous warriors. This demanded an adjustment of European diplomatic and martial practice, in keeping with the cultural norms and expectations of their allies. Writing to Colonel Haldiman, William Johnson noted that: 'a friendly behaviour towards all, and a small present well timed, or given on proper occasions to such Indians as have an influence or lead their nation will always have a good effect'.[71]

However, despite the long history of alliances, adjustments were not always readily made. Metropolitan priorities frequently prevailed among some military leaders newly arrived in the Americas, including some French officers who despised guerrilla tactics, fighting in the woods in the Native American style, preferring instead an orderly advance of uniformed men.[72] However, in many instances the advantage went to those adept at Indigenous warfare. War and imminent war brought focused attention on essential goods and those making and using these stores. Indigenous knowledge was invaluable in these contexts, supporting material and military practice in geographically and temporally distinct ways. Those best able to rally these resources fared well.

Settlers, French and British, learned the value of snowshoes, along with the skills of traversing snow-covered forests and ice-bound rivers and some settlers eventually profited by producing these wares.[73] It is also clear that Indigenous communities proximate to trading centres produced significant quantities of goods over sustained periods for settler markets.[74] The Wendat, for example, were noted for their extensive production for proximate populations. As Bruce Trigger observed, the Wendat embedded 'marketing within a framework of political and social relations'.[75] Following the defeat of General Montcalm and the fall of Quebec to the British in September 1759, the French Governor Vaudreuil wondered how he should proceed. Native allies were touched by this defeat.[76] Resistance was proposed in some quarters. And a New York-based correspondent reported that Vaudreuil intended 'to retake Quebec in the winter by storm, for which purpose he gave orders for 20,000 pair of snow shoes to be immediately made'.[77] The scale of the supposed order is noteworthy.

Conclusion

The rumour of the retaking of Quebec proved to be apocryphal – a tale to frighten war-weary Britons and New Englanders. It is notable that snowshoes served as a metaphor for military capacity and Indigenous allies. The enduring relationship between the Wendat and the French governors of Quebec was fully implicated in this assessment. Thus, the production of ready-made clothing and footwear in the long eighteenth century must be assessed with attention to multiple contexts. In Britain, a gendered proto-industrial technology expanded dramatically, dressing ever-larger numbers of mariners and military. This system was premised on ordered, replicable commodities, produced through networks of contractors, subcontractors and a copious female labour force on which they depended. Samples epitomized this system.

Snowshoes suggest other paradigms. In one way, they are embedded in debates about imperial military competence in North America. Historians considered the relative merits of Indigenous and colonial-style woodland warfare versus the proficiencies of European trained troops. Metropolitan perspectives boded large among British officers (and historians of an earlier generation), who discounted provincial and Indigenous combatants. Many French and British professional officers despised guerrilla warfare and the winter dependence on snowshoes. Yet, raiding was a norm for generations, winter raiding in particular, as learned during the indigenization of warfare in North America.[78] Snowshoes defined this combat and were first offered in the context of diplomatic alliances; responses to this footwear defined facets of the colonial process.

Britain claimed extensive territory over much of northern North America, even after 1783 and the resolution of the American Revolution. Thereafter, across this expanse, royalty, nobility, military officers and senior colonial administrators embraced the demonstrable manliness of snowshoe journeys as proof of their right to command these lands. Prince Edward, promoted to major general with a new posting in the Caribbean, headed out from Quebec City to Halifax in this manner in the winter of 1794. He was determined to go in 'as straight a direction as possible, through the woods to Halifax', assisted in this two-week journey by an entourage of 20 Indigenous guides, who also managed the dogs and the sleds packed with gear. Given his Quebec departure site, it is likely that Wendat men steered his path. Following the defeat of the French, the Wendat signed an accord confirming good relations with the incoming British. Senior leaders of this community spoke French and English, as well as their native tongue. It is very likely that, as a member of the royal family, Prince Edward participated in diplomatic ceremonies with Wendat leaders at Wendake. The Wendat were now valued military allies.[79] We can speculate on the prestige within the Wendat community of guiding the royal party, though no mention is made of this in the British press. However, the report did recall a similar expedition from Quebec City in 1789, by Lord Edward Fitzgerald, who was fed and guided by his 'savage' allies.[80] Similarly, in 1813, Lieutenant-Colonel Harvey 'walked in snow shoes, in the depth of last winter, through the wilds lying between the Canadas and New Brunswick', 'so great was the desire of that meritorious officer to arrive at his [new] post'. Harvey was lauded by his commanding officer for his 'zeal, intelligence and gallantry'.[81] Driven by complex imperial agendas, the apparel employed by these men doubtless included white linen shirts as well as snowshoes. The 1840 watercolour of Wendat leader Nicholas Vincent shows him hunting on snowshoes (Figure 3.5). The Wendat's skill as makers and users of this technology is captured in this image.

In colonial northern North America, alliances with Indigenous communities shaped local provisioning for many generations, materialized through gendered Indigenous skills. Native American relationships with Europeans were integrated

FIGURE 3.5 'Portrait of Canadian Indian Nicolas Vincent Wearing Snowshoes', by Philip J. Bainbrigge, 1840, watercolour, 12.7 × 10.2 cm.
Source: © Alamy Limited, UK.

into existing customs and diplomatic systems, continuing throughout this era.[82] The sharing of resources and organization of war materiel took place within this construct. Thus, imperial military institutions, like those of the British and French, worked within two paradigms. A Smithian supply system flourished in Europe (with the products carried to North America), evidence of proto-industrial growth based on low-paid female labour, with stocks of clothing arriving at ports and forts, ideally in sufficient quantities. This model is exemplified in the tons of slop clothes shipped to ports in the Americas, including linen shirts.[83] In North America itself, however, the spread of Indigenous technologies was premised on Native American ritual, custom and skill to which Europeans adapted, until such times as Indigenous allies held no value and colonial manufacturing grew.[84] Indeed, by the later eighteenth century, snowshoeing was 'whitened', increasingly claimed as a marker of imperial masculinity, with men of empire appropriating this technology, though Indigenous cultures remained. This process continued into the century beyond.[85] The power of the white shirt likewise continued its global imperial ascendency. In combination, the snowshoe and the shirt reflect the varied contingent power and material exchange of the early globalizing era.

Notes

1 A version of this work was previously published in: Miki Sugiura, ed., *Linking Cloth/Clothing Globally: Transformations of Use & Value* (Tokyo: ICES Hosei University, 2019).
2 John Styles, 'Involuntary Consumers? The Eighteenth-Century Servant and Her Clothes', *Textile History* 33.1 (2002): 9–21. See also, Beverly Lemire, *Global Trade and the Transformation of Consumer Societies. The Material World Remade, c.1500–1820* (Cambridge, UK: Cambridge University Press, 2018), 124–131.
3 Terence S. Turner, 'The Social Skin', reprinted *HAU: Journal of Ethnographic Theory* 2.2 (2012): 486.
4 John Brewer, The Sinews of Power: War, Money and the English State (London: Unwin Hyman, 1989). Beverly Lemire, *Dress, Culture and Commerce: The English Clothing Trade Before the Factory, c.1660–1800* (Basingstoke, UK: Macmillan, 1997), 1–41; *Global Trade and the Transformation of Consumer Societies*, 122–131. See also Chapter 5 by Miki Sugiura in this volume for the role of the Dutch East India Company (VOC) in sourcing ready-made apparel from Indian Ocean suppliers.
5 Thomas Parke Hughes, *Human-Built World: How to Think About Technology and Culture* (Chicago: University of Chicago Press, 2005), 3–5.
6 Linda Colley, *Captives: Britain, Empire and the World, 1600–1850* (New York: Anchor Books, 2004), 24–25.
7 The National Archives, Kew, London (hereafter TNA): ADM 106/308, f. 236; ADM 106/311, f. 158; ADM 106/318/10.
8 TNA: ADM 106/318/8; ADM 106/308, f. 236.
9 TNA: ADM 106/481/63.
10 Other cases of complaint include TNA: ADM 106/905/73, 31 January 1739, complaint by Captain Long against the slops from Mr Blackmon; TNA: ADM 354/121/177, NMM, 17 March 1743, Vice Admiral Mathews complained of the slops sent to Portsmouth intended for the Mediterranean; TNA: ADM 354/150/216, NMM, 18 June 1755, complaint about slops supplied to the ship *Lancaster*.

11 John Ehrman, *The Navy in the War of William III, 1689–1697* (Cambridge, UK: Cambridge University Press, 1953), 123.

12 TNA: ADM 106/1081/56; ADM 106/1081/60; ADM 106/1203/153; ADM 106/1091/223; ADM 106/927/218; ADM 106/817/186.

13 TNA: ADM 106/1048/312.

14 TNA: ADM 106/1144/137.

15 Lemire, *Dress, Culture and Commerce*, 21–22.

16 For ready-made clothing sent to Atlantic ocean locales including Halifax, Nova Scotia; Boston, Massachusetts; Charleston, South Carolina; Kingston, Jamaica and English Harbour, Antigua, the base for the Royal Navy in the Caribbean, see TNA: ADM 354/160/209, 234; ADM 354/161/128; ADM 106/1088/84; ADM 354/159/219; ADM 106/826/215; ADM 106/875/132; ADM 106/895/44. The National Maritime Museum, Greenwich (hereafter NMM): ADM 354/159/219.

17 For example, the Royal Africa Company, the Hudson's Bay Company and the East India Company Lemire, *Dress, Culture and Commerce*, 34–38.

18 Daniel Roche, *The Culture of Clothing: Dress and Fashion in the Ancien Regime* (Cambridge, UK: Cambridge University Press, 1994), ch. 7.

19 Quoted in Samuel Crumpe, *An Essay on the Best Means of Providing Employment for the People* ... (2nd ed.) (London: G. G. and J. Robinson, 1795), 21.

20 S. A. Cavell, *Midshipmen and Quarterdeck Boys in the British Navy, 1771–1831* (Woodbridge, UK and Rochester, NY: Boydell Press, 2012), 15. Attention to cleanliness also became the focus of military physicians from the mid-1700s.

21 James Lind, *An Essay, on the Most Effectual Means, of Preserving the Health of Seamen, in the Royal Navy* ... (London: A. Millar, 1757), 43, 82.

22 Cumbria Archive Centre, Carlisle: D HUD 13/2/4.

23 Charles Fletcher, *A Maritime State Considered, as to the Health of Seamen* ... (London: M. Vint, 1791), 126.

24 Jean-François de Galaup comte de La Pérouse, *A Voyage Round the World, in the Years 1785, 1786, 1787, and 1788* ... (London: J. Johnson, 1798), 54; Alexander Dirom, *Plans for the Defence of Great Britain and Ireland. By Lieut. Colonel Dirom* ... (Edinburgh, 1797), 136.

25 *The Cruise; A Poetical Sketch, in Eight Cantos, by a Naval Officer* (London: J. Hatchard, 1808).

26 *The Cruise*, 11, 31, 93, 133.

27 Reuben Gold Thwaites, 'The Jesuit Relations', *Queen's Quarterly* 5.4 (April 1898): 266.

28 Kathleen M. Brown, *Foul Bodies: Cleanliness in Early America* (New Haven, CT: Yale University Press, 2009), 98–99.

29 Susanne Küchler and Graeme Were, 'Introduction' in Susanne Küchler and Graeme Were, eds., *The Art of Clothing: A Pacific Experience* (London: Routledge, 2005), ix–xxx.

30 Søren T. Thuesen, 'Dressing Up in Greenland: A Discussion of Change and World Fashion in Early-Colonial West Greenlandic Dress', in J. C. H. King, Birgit Pauksztat and Robert Storrie, eds., *Arctic Clothing* (London: British Museum, 2005), 100–101; Hans Egede, *A Description of Greenland. Shewing the Natural History, Situation, Boundaries, and Face of the Country* ... (London, 1745), 129–130.

31 Lemire, *Dress, Culture and Commerce*, 36.

32 Expenses at Albany Fort from 1 August 1749 to 1 August 1750, 3 May–25 May 1750. Fort Albany Account Book, Hudson's Bay Company, 1749–1750. Available through: Adam Matthew, Marlborough, Global Commodities, www.globalcommodities.amdigital.co.uk Documents/Details/HBCA-B3-d-58 (accessed 11 June 2015). My sincere thanks to Katie Pollock for her work on these records.

33 For example, Reuben Gold Thwaites, *Jesuit Relations and Allied Documents* (Cleveland, OH: Burrows, 1900), vols. 67, 59, 64, 77. Küchler and Were, 'Introduction', xxiii.

34 Sophie White, *Wild Frenchmen and Frenchified Indians: Material Culture and Race in Colonial Louisiana* (Philadelphia: University of Pennsylvania Press, 2013), 204–5.

35 Christian Ayne Crouch, *Nobility Lost: French and Canadian Martial Cultures, Indians, and the End of New France* (Ithaca, NY: Cornell University Press, 2014), 2.

36 For a discussion of the diplomatic processes surrounding the later Seven Years' War in North America see Crouch, *Nobility Lost*, 1–4.

37 Bruce Trigger, *Natives and Newcomers: Canada's 'Heroic Age' Reconsidered* (Montreal and Kingston: McGill-Queen's University Press, 1985), 187–188.

38 Trigger, *Natives and Newcomers*, 171.

39 Quoted in Jace Weaver, 'The Red Atlantic: Trans Oceanic Cultural Exchanges', *American Indian Quarterly* 35.3 (2011): 428–429. See also Charles E. Clark, 'Gorges, Sir Ferdinando (1568–1647)', *Oxford Dictionary of National Biography* (Oxford: Oxford University Press, 2004), www.oxforddnb.com.login.ezproxy.library.ualberta.ca/view/article11098 (accessed 26 June 2015).

40 Ruth B. Phillips, *Trading Identities: The Souvenir in Native North American Art from the Northeast, 1700–1900* (Seattle: University of Washington Press, 1998), 16.

41 Bruce Trigger, *The Children of Aataentsic: A History of the Huron People to 1660*, 2nd ed. (Montreal and Kingston: McGill-Queen's University Press, 1987), vol. 2, ch. 5.

42 Phillips, *Trading Identities*, 22.

43 As noted by the Sieur de Dièrreville in his account *Relation du voyage du Port Royal de l'Acadie suivi de Poésies diverses* (Montreal: Presses de l'Université de Montreal, 1997), 205–206, 225–227, 251.

44 Peter C. Mancall, 'The Raw and the Cold: Five English Sailors in Sixteenth-Century Nunavut', *William and Mary Quarterly* 70.1 (2013): 5–8.

45 Mancall, 'Raw and Cold', 8. For an example of French settlers' attempt in 1663 to fish from canoes see Reuben Gold Thwaites, ed., *The Jesuit Relations and Allied Documents: Travels and Explorations of the Jesuit Missionaries in New France 1610–1791 ... with English Translation and Notes* (Cleveland, OH: Burrows, 1899), vol. 48, 121.

46 Thwaites, *Jesuit Relations*, vol. 50, 169.

47 Dièrreville, *Relation du voyage*, 251.

48 Thwaites, *Jesuit Relations*, vol. 48, 179. For an insightful discussion of Indigenous knowledge of winter and the settler learning process see Thomas Wickman, '"Winters Embittered with Hardships": Severe Cold, Wabanaki Power, and English Adjustments, 1690–1710', *William & Mary Quarterly* 72.1 (2015): 57–98.

49 I thank Anne de Stecher and Jonathan Lainey for beginning my education in Indigenous diplomacy and the role of diplomatic gifts, both scholars of Huron Wendat political history, arts and material culture. Anne de Stecher, 'Souvenir Arts, Collectable Crafts, Cultural Heritage: The Huron-Wendat of Wendake, Quebec', in Janice Helland, Beverly Lemire and Alena Buis, eds., *Craft, Community and Material Culture of Place and Politics, 19th–20th Century* (Farnham, UK: Ashgate, 2014); Jonathan C. Lainey, *La Monnaie des saugaves: les colliers de wampum d'hier à aujourd'hui* (Quebec: Musée de la Civilisation, 2004).

50 For example, The treaty held with the Indians of the Six Nations, at Philadelphia, in July 1742.

51 Trigger, *Natives and Newcomers*, 179.

52 Wilbur R. Jacobs, *Diplomacy and Indian Gifts: Anglo-French Rivalry Along the Ohio and Northwest Frontiers, 1748–1763* (Stanford, CA: Stanford University Press, 1950), 13.

53 The successful transmission of skills, especially in the early years of settlement, often required close contact with Indigenous peoples. Jean Amiot (*c.*1625–1648) exemplifies these traits, living for years in 'Huron country', becoming among the fastest runners in Quebec – on foot or on snowshoes – of Native or European men. Or so it was claimed. Honorius Provost, 'AMIOT (Amyot), JEAN', in *Dictionary of Canadian Biography*, vol. 1 (Toronto: University of Toronto/Université Laval, 2003), www.biographi.ca/en/bio/amiot_jean_1E.html (accessed 23 June 2015).

54 Jack Verney assesses the various accounts of the campaign and determines that aside from the seasoned locals who volunteered, the regiment was not equipped with

snowshoes. Jack Verney, *The Good Regiment: The Carignan-Salière Regiment in Canada, 1665–1668* (Montreal and Kingston: McGill-Queen's University Press, 1991), 44–52.

55 Thwaites, 'Jesuit Relations', 261, 265; Sylvia van Kirk, *Many Tender Ties: Women in the Fur Trade Society, 1670–1870* (Norman: University of Oklahoma Press, 1980), 54–55.

56 Verney, *The Good Regiment*, 47; W. J. Eccles, 'RÉMY DE COURCELLE (Courcelles), DANIEL DE', in *Dictionary of Canadian Biography*, vol. 1 (Toronto: University of Toronto/Université Laval, 2003), www.biographi.ca/enwww.biographi.ca/en/bio (accessed 23 June 2015).

57 Phillips, *Trading Identities*, 22–23.

58 Van Kirk, *Many Tender Ties*, 55.

59 Van Kirk, *Many Tender Ties*, 80–82.

60 Trigger, *The Children of Aataentsic*, 34–40; van Kirk, *Many Tender Ties*; Thwaites, 'Jesuit Relations', 265.

61 Ruth Phillips, 'Reading and Writing Between the Lines', *Winterthur Portfolio* 45.2/3 (2011): 107–124.

62 Phillips, 'Reading', 107.

63 Trigger, *Natives and Newcomers*, 195; Timothy J. Shannon, 'Dressing for Success on the Mohawk Frontier: Hendrick, William Johnson, and the Indian Fashion', *William & Mary Quarterly* 53.1 (1996): 13–42. For the meanings of cross-dressing in the French Illinois territory see White, *Wild Frenchmen and Frenchified Indians*, chs 5 and 6; Catherine Cangany, 'Fashioning Moccasins: Detroit, the Manufacturing Frontier, and the Empire of Consumption, 1701–1835', *William & Mary Quarterly* 69.2 (2012): 265–304.

64 Wickman, 'Winters Embittered with Hardships'.

65 Steven C. Eames, *Rustic Warriors: Warfare and the Provincial Soldier on the New England Frontier, 1689–1748* (New York: New York University Press, 2011), 83.

66 Reports on the campaign of Captain John Lovel and his volunteers, who killed a party of Native warriors in New Hampshire, all of the Indigenous men carrying 'two pairs of snow shoes', *British Journal*, 15 May 1725.

67 Jacobs, *Diplomacy and Indian Gifts*, 88.

68 Timothy J. Shannon, *Iroquois Diplomacy on the Early American Frontier* (New York: Viking, 2008), 62; Daniel K. Richter, 'Johnson, Sir William, First Baronet (1715?–1774)', *Oxford Dictionary of National Biography* (Oxford: Oxford University Press, 2004), www.oxforddnb.com.login.ezproxy.library.ualberta.ca/viewarticle/14925 (accessed 7 July 2015).

69 *London Evening Post*, London, 25–27 June 1747.

70 *Whitehall Evening Post or London Intelligencer*, London, 19–22 October 1754.

71 British Library: Add MS 21670, f. 8.

72 Crouch, *Nobility Lost*, 79.

73 Cangany, 'Fashioning Moccasins'.

74 Catherine Cangany emphasizes the settler production of moccasins in the Detroit region. For examples of Indigenous production, within communities, for trade purposes see Ruth Phillips, *Trading Identities: The Souvenir in Native North American Art from the Northeast, 1700–1900* (Seattle, WA: University of Washington Press, 1998); Anne de Stecher, 'Huron-Wendat Visual Culture: Source of Economic Autonomy and Continuity of Traditional Culture', in *Canada Exposed/Le Canada à découverte*, ed. Pierre Anctil, André Loiselle and Christopher Rolfe (Brussels: Peter Lang, 2009), 131–150; de Stecher, 'Souvenir Art, Collectable Craft, Cultural Heritage'.

75 Trigger, *Children of Aataentsic*, quoted in de Stecher, 'Souvenir Art, Collectable Craft, Cultural Heritage', 43.

76 Crouch, *Nobility Lost*, epilogue; Alain Beaulieu, 'Les Hurons et la Conquête', *Recherches Amérindiennes au Québec* 30.3 (2000): 56–60.

77 *London Evening Post*, London, 24–26 January 1760.

78 Eames, *Rustic Warriors*, 1–16.

79 Wendake was the site of numerous diplomatic ceremonies, given its proximity to Quebec City and the longevity of Wendat relationships with various European powers. Trigger, *The Children of Aataentsic*, 364; de Stecher, 'Souvenir Arts, Collectable Crafts, Cultural Heritage'; Beaulieu, 'Les Hurons et la Conquête', 60.

80 *Sun*, London, 8 May 1794. A full regiment undertook a similar feat in 1812, when it marched 'in snow-shoes from New Brunswick to Quebec, a distance of 260 miles', *Morning Post*, London, 15 February 1817.

81 *Caledonian Mercury*, Edinburgh, 29 July 1813.

82 White, *Middle Ground*, 140–141.

83 TNA: ADM 354/160/209, 234; ADM 354/161/128; ADM 106/1088/84; ADM 354/159/219; ADM 106/826/215; ADM 106/875/132; ADM 106/895/44. NMM: Caird Library ADM 354/159/21. This subject is discussed at length in Beverly Lemire, 'A Question of Trousers: Seafarers, Masculinity and Empire in the Shaping of British Male Dress, *c.*1600–1800', *Cultural and Social History* 31.1 (2016): 1–23.

84 Cangany, 'Fashioning Moccasins'; *Frontier Seaport: Detroit's Transformation into an Atlantic Entrepot* (Chicago: University of Chicago Press, 2014).

85 Reports on the John Franklin and William Parry expeditions are two examples of this process. For Franklin see *Caledonian Mercury*, Edinburgh, 15 May 1823 and for Parry, *Morning Chronicle*, London, 24 March 1827. There is extensive coverage in newspapers around these dates, with repeated mention of the importance of snow-shoes. The role of sport in this process is discussed for the Montreal context in Gillian Poulter, *Becoming Native in a Foreign Land: Sport, Visual Culture & Identity in Montreal 1840–1885* (Vancouver: UBC Press, 2009).

4

DRESSING ENSLAVED AFRICANS IN COLONIAL LOUISIANA

Sophie White

In April 1764, a 60-year-old enslaved African known as Jeanot was arrested. Found begging in the streets of New Orleans, he was prosecuted for having run away from his master. Interrogated about his motives for running away, Jeanot defended his actions on the basis that his master 'had not made any indigo the previous summer, and the maize that the slave was in charge of did not grow'.[1] As a result, Jeanot stated, 'his master was angry and ill-treated him and during the winter he didn't give him the slightest thing, neither coat nor shirt to protect himself from the harsh inclement season'.[2] Jeanot acknowledged being a runaway for about five months. Asked who had fed him, and where he had lived during that time, Jeanot answered that at Bayou St Jean near the barracks he had met the slave Jacob belonging to Mr Dubois, who told him 'stay with me I will feed you and dress you'. He stayed with him for about three months, and afterwards he returned to the town to beg for his bread. Asked if he had stolen anything while a runaway, he answered in the negative and reiterated that if he had acted as he had it was only because 'his master gave him no provisions nor any clothes to protect himself from the cold'.[3]

Three times during his interrogation, Jeanot invoked the matter of clothing, specifically, his lack of it. The court showed no mercy to the elderly Jeanot. Clause 20 of the 1724 code that regulated slavery in Louisiana required that the court prosecute masters who failed to properly feed, clothe and provide for their slaves. Clause 21 was more specific to elderly and infirm slaves: if their masters abandoned them, they were to be adjudged to the nearest hospital, and their masters charged for their food and maintenance. Yet, instead of investigating Jeanot's claims, the judges convicted him and, since he had been a runaway for more than 30 days, he received the mandatory sentence of having his ears cut, being branded with the fleur-de-lys, and then returned to his master.[4] This was colonial justice at work, pronouncing a sentence aimed not only at punishing

Jeanot, but at serving notice to any slaves who wanted to provide a means of support to runaways. Jacob was not prosecuted, but he knew he was taking a risk, yet he nonetheless provided succour to Jeanot, knowing fully that community support was crucial to the survival of the elderly man and other runaways like him. The master suffered no repercussions, beyond the humiliation of his slave being brought to court and, perhaps, greater public scrutiny of his expenditure on a slave whom he clearly considered to be an economic liability.

Commodified bodies   [Slave Clothing: erase individuality erase ethnicity]

[commodity] In a society based on the premise that resources were intended for exploitation and merchandise meant for consumption, slaves, ostensibly, represented yet another commodity. Dress was one of the most visible mechanism through which their commodification and the negation of their individuality and ethnicity was accomplished. Branded in some cases, they were stripped of their own modes of dress and handed European garb. In spite of these challenges, slaves in French colonial Louisiana, as elsewhere, succeeded in using sartorial culture to their own ends.[5] The enslaved deployed a variety of formal and informal means to access clothing. Once in their possession, they could draw on the protean qualities of dress to create a rich and polyvalent means of cultural expression that might equally allow them to forge ties with one another as to thumb their noses at the authority of those who held their lives in their hands. But, if there was a push and a pull in the power dynamic between enslaved and enslavers, access to apparel was the crucial precondition.

The case against Jeanot reminds us of a basic premise: that the enslaved understood well that they had a right to apparel. But the enslaved were not the only ones who brought it up. This chapter is not so much about how the enslaved dressed themselves, as it is about the preconditions for their sartorial acts – namely, how officials and masters saw their role in dressing the bodies of the enslaved.

Focusing on the procedures in place for the supply of apparel to the enslaved does more than illustrate the features of one provisioning system. It allows us to perceive the process that led to some bodies becoming enslaved, and provides a measure by which to evaluate how individuals used dress in their responses to becoming slaves and staying enslaved. In invoking clothing as a necessity, Jeanot alluded to a theme that resonated among enslaved and slavers alike: that of clothing as a 'functional necessity'. For colonists, dress was crucial to the smooth running of slave societies. At its most basic, it ensured the very survival of enslaved individuals. Yet there were further layers that came into play and that illuminate the politics of dress. Colonists may have recognized the functional purpose of apparel, and might have appreciated the problems created when the enslaved were inadequately clothed, even when the courts looked the other way and did not prosecute masters who failed to supply sufficient dress. But they also feared the consequences of insufficient clothing, as seen in the court's interrogation of Jeanot, when he was asked if he had stolen anything while a runaway. For colonists, the right kind of clothing – supplied in the correct way, through prescribed channels – ensured social order. Its absence, or the wearing of apparel outside these parameters, hung over colonists as a perennial risk that could at any point threaten the social and racial order in the colony.

Dressing newly arrived slaves

The slave trade to Louisiana began in 1719, reached a high point in 1730–1731 and virtually halted thereafter.[6] A great consistency is found in the African regions from which slaves were bought. Two-thirds of the slaves sent to Louisiana between 1719 and 1731 came from the area known as Senegambia, in West Africa.[7] In other words, the study of slave's dress has to give attention to differing sartorial backgrounds, of those born in Africa who survived the 'middle passage' and of those born and raised in the cultural space that was Louisiana. For officials, there was no need to consider these factors and they focused instead on the struggle to enforce a new clothing regime that depended on sufficient quantities of textiles and apparel. That struggle was all the more complicated by the fact that the Crown had prohibited the production of textiles in Louisiana, so that all fabric had to be imported.[8]

In Louisiana, the problem of supplying the enslaved was especially acute in the 1720s during the major wave of slave shipments. Writing from New Orleans in April 1728 to the minister of marine in France, the governor of Louisiana mentioned the high mortality rate of slaves both on the slave ships and within a short time of their introduction into the colony. He framed the problem as one in which it was the lack of apparel that was the key factor in the slaves' health problems and eventual demise, asserting that: 'if this vessel had found *capot* coats at the Caye as was supposed to be the case, they would have saved the lives of many'.[9] A *capot* was an overcoat of simple construction, with a hood, made of cheap wool or a blanket. Beyond conveying an early modern mindset about the relationship between clothing and health, the governor's letter also provided information about the clothing supply system that should have been in place to furnish enslaved Africans upon their arrival in Louisiana. In particular, his letter allows us to grasp how critical apparel was to the slave trade, and to the establishment of African slavery in the colony.

The governor's letter reveals that obtaining apparel at La Caye Saint-Louis in Saint-Domingue was seen as preferable to relying on supplies in Louisiana. The practice of using a stopover at one of the more established (and better supplied) ports of the French West Indies to secure slave clothing supplies is confirmed by a reference in another missive sent the following year. In that letter, the governor reported that a further 20 to 30 slaves had died since their arrival on the slave ship *La Galaté* – and this in spite of having coats that had been procured at La Caye. The governor specified that these enslaved individuals had been felled by scurvy, the inference being that clothing was perceived as having protective qualities, but it was not all-powerful.[10]

Slaveholders with large numbers of slaves might plan for apparel to be shipped directly from France to Louisiana, as was the case when the Company of the Indies planned for the shipment of 150 slaves to be delivered to the LeBlanc plantation in 1728:

> As we do not doubt that the Company will attend to sending to Louisiana that which is necessary for the clothing of the slaves, without which they would perish, we request that as the above slaves are delivered to our managers, that there be delivered to them that which they will need for their clothing, promising to pay the Company for the slaves and for the clothes in kind in tobacco or other products.[11]

Here again, clothing was associated with wellness. And, as made explicit in this document, wherever it was acquired, the clothing was only to be issued to the slaves upon arrival in the colony. Prior to their shipment, slaves in *captiveries*, already weakened and usually sick, were kept in poor conditions, with little or no clothing. During the middle passage crossing, as a general rule, their heads were kept shaved, their nails cut, the men naked and the women given only a small cloth to cover their genital area. Slave captains were enjoined to guard the female slaves against sexual 'debauchery' and, especially, to take care of the health of all of the slaves by 'having them provided for properly'.[12] Far from altruism, any measure of care that was to be provided to them during the transatlantic voyage was intended to keep them alive, and saleable.

By the time the ships arrived at their destination, bodies that had suffered during the voyage had to be transformed into commodities fit for sale, and made presentable to prospective buyers. This meant that an enslaved person could not expect any right to the privacy offered by clothing, and that those involved in the slave trade respected no boundaries in claiming the right to handle a slave's body. Wendy Warren describes the process, as

> brought on deck in the bright tropical sun, [slaves] saw their sores masked with a mixture of iron rust and gunpowder … slavers hid the omnipresent diarrhea by inserting oakum hemp treated with tar and used for caulking seams in wooden ships far into an afflicted slave's anus, far enough to avoid detection during the invasive bodily inspections potential buyers inflicted on the human goods.[13]

These were the kinds of practices that aimed to turn humans into property. Access to their bodies did not stop there. Each time they changed hands, enslaved persons could expect to be examined and prodded. As Louisiana planter Antoine-Simon Le Page du Pratz explained, the examination should cover the slave's body down to the genitals: 'from the sole of the feet to the top of the head, between the toes and fingers, in the mouth, in the ears, without excluding those areas that are naturally hidden, though they are at that time uncovered'.[14] Though Le Page du Pratz may have justified this intrusion as necessary for making sound consumer decisions, he did not gloss over the fact that a slave's body was 'at that time uncovered'. Implicit in the presumption that a slaveholder had to clothe his slaves was an equivocal assumption that he or she could at any time unclothe that slave.

When newly arrived slaves were inadequately clothed, it was up to the local storehouses to provide immediate relief, though the enduring shortages of all textile and clothing goods in the colony led to the implementation of creative solutions. In one extreme case in Louisiana, shortages in available clothing in the colony were such that slaves had to be given deerskins to wear, almost certainly traded from Native Americans.[15] The records stay silent on the subject of what garments were fashioned from these skins. It behooved officials to oversee the immediate clothing needs of newly arrived slaves and they were held accountable for these responsibilities. In April 1728, the governor related in detail what measures he and his officials had taken to stave off the death of so many newly arrived slaves. They reported that 20 slaves had died since their arrival at La Balise (the stopping-off point on the Gulf, beyond which ships could not pass, so that slaves and other passengers and all cargo was put on to small vessels to convey them upriver to New Orleans). They had died, he asserted 'in spite of the precautions that were taken'. He had given orders to send 'capots and shirts to La Balize to give [to the slaves] upon arrival, which was done, but it was too late, the cold had already gotten hold of them'.[16] Yet again what these officials underlined was that clothing was a matter of life and death, and therefore, of profit and loss. But we also see that underlying their references to lives lost were concerns about shielding themselves from blame – finding excuses was a time-honoured way for appointed officials to evade censure, accusations of incompetency and other repercussions. After 1731, when transatlantic shipments of enslaved Africans to Louisiana halted, attention veered away from matters of life and death pertaining to the high mortality rate of those who were made to undergo the middle passage. Yet, at the forefront of official policy remained the same preoccupation with ensuring the health of chattel.

Regulating and supplying slaves' clothing

Enslaved individuals were considered movable property, whose ownership could be transferred through wills and donations, and who could be sold, traded or leased and, more rarely, freed through manumission. In French colonies, the matter of their clothing was not to be left to chance, for the French Crown made it a matter for regulation, a topic covered in slave codes. Until 1724, Louisiana was subject to the 1685 slave code (or *code noir*) for the Windward Islands in the Caribbean. Drafted by the governor and intendant in Martinique based on the local jurisprudence that had developed over nearly half a century in the French Caribbean islands, it was only minimally revised in France.[17] In 1724, the French Crown issued a new slave code for Louisiana.[18] Among the changes between the two 1685 and 1724 versions of the *code noir* was the matter of clothing for the enslaved, though both dealt with apparel alongside food rations, underlying the same themes of clothing as functional and protective that the governor's 1728 letters had emphasized. The differences lay in pragmatic concerns about the feasibility of carrying out the goals outlined in the 1685 code.

Namely, the 1685 *code noir* had been specific in mandating a yearly provision of either two linen coats or four ells of cloth to each slave (clause 25), though it was vague enough not to differentiate between male and female dress. While there was much overlap between the 1685 and 1724 slave codes, the provision of apparel was not one of these. Shifting from the specificity of the 1685 code, Clause 18 of the 1724 code stated that:

> We desire that the officers of our Superior Council of Louisiana send their advice as to the quantity of provisions, and the quality of the clothing that masters should supply to their slaves, such provisions to be furnished weekly, and the clothing yearly, so that we can make this a statute, and pending this we permit the said officers to draw up a regulation.[19]

Here again, the subject of clothing was dealt with alongside the other major component of a slave's maintenance – food.

The basic function of clothing as a necessity was reinforced in Clause 20, which granted slaves recourse to the law should their masters fail to provide adequately for their needs (namely 'fed, clothed, maintained'). As with the outcome from the case against Jeanot, no such charges are known to have been brought in French colonial Louisiana, besides which, Clause 24 forbade slaves – like servants – from testifying for or against their master. If a slave was arrested and interrogated, he or she had free rein, and it is in those instances that they might incriminate their masters for not complying with the law. In his 1764 testimony, the 60-year old Jeanot invoked a lack of food and clothing as a motive for running away. Another enslaved African, Bayou, offered a similar defense in 1748:

> Interrogated why he had become a runaway. Answered that it is because his master made him work every day, holiday and Sunday, did not given [*sic*] them to eat nor clothing, did not even give them to time to sleep at night and mistreated them in inappropriate ways.[20]

Both Jeanot and Bayou framed clothing as a necessity, and one that was the responsibility of their master, and both did not hesitate to point out their masters' shortcomings. Yet no defence is known to have succeeded on this basis. As with Jeanot, Bayou's indictment of his master had no impact in his case.

Ultimately, the French Crown never fulfilled the promise given in Article 18 of Louisiana's 1724 *code noir* to legislate the quantity and quality of the food and clothing required for slaves. In practice then, slave owners in Louisiana enjoyed – and exploited – a great flexibility in selecting what items of clothing to furnish, how frequently to do so and how much to spend.

The long-term settler, Le Page du Pratz, addressed this subject in his memoirs. In his chapter on enslaved Africans, he described his manner of governing them:

> When a slave man or women comes to you, it is a good idea to caress them, to give them something good to eat along with a drink of alcohol; it is good to dress them that very day, to give him a blanket and something to sleep on.[21]

It is difficult to know just how representative Le Page Du Pratz's paternalistic view was among the bulk of the slave-owning population. In any case, the repeated complaints about finding adequate resources in the colony of cheap, sturdy clothes suitable for slave use suggest that even the more willing slave owners faced hurdles in providing for their slaves.

It is hard to make sweeping generalizations about the clothing that was actually issued to slaves, in what quantities and at what frequency, since there are no extant plantation ledgers and few other records that attest to the practice rather than the theory. The garments mentioned in those select documents that list the clothing worn by slaves generally included staples such as shirts and *capots* for men and skirts for women.[22] One of the few references to the clothing distributed by owners to their slaves, and the only one to allude directly to the provisions of the *code noir*, dates from 1736. This was a contract passed between a lieutenant in the colonial troops, George Auguste de Vanderech, and a German settler, Christian Grevert, for the latter to manage Vanderech's plantation. Clause 5 of their agreement stated that:

> In order to observe the King's ordinance the said Vanderech requires that it be furnished to each male slave a shirt, a cap and a breechclout, and every two years a capot coat, and to the female slave a shift, a skirt and a bodice each year.[23]

Despite claiming to conform to the regulations of the *code noir*, which called for an annual issue of clothing, some of the garments were to be issued every two years. Perhaps this latitude was a reflection of Vanderech's experience with military dress, whose components were issued in alternate years. It is noteworthy that the garments named in the contract do not differ much from the clothing listed in inventories of poorer settlers. The apparel that Vanderech was to provide the women, for example, matched that of the (white) indigent orphan girls at the Ursuline convent and that consisted of shifts, skirts, handkerchiefs, caps and jackets, all made from the cheapest cloths.[24]

As for males, other than shirts and caps, they were to be supplied with a breechclout and a *capot*. The breechclout was a Native American garment constructed from a hide or piece of wool that covered male genitalia, 'which passes between the legs, hides their nudities, and returns in front and back, with each end passing through a belt tied around the waist, falling back in front and back'.[25] Alexandre de Batz's 'Desseins de Sauvages de Plusieurs Nations' shows both the original incarnation of the breechclout, made from a hide, and its new iteration made from wool cloth (Figure 4.1), The breechclout was adopted by some Frenchmen, especially fur traders, and was here being provided to enslaved Africans. As for the hooded *capot*, it was seen as especially suitable for protection during the mild Louisiana winter. The *capot* derived from sailor's garb but had evolved by the eighteenth century into a distinctive French Canadian form.[26] As seen in Sempronius Stretton's 1805 depiction of a man from Canada in his winter dress (Figure 4.2), it was usually made of a cheap or sturdy woollen fabric, although sometimes cut from a trade blanket (ornamented with distinctive woven bands or stripes). The *capot* followed a basic cut and construction that might not even require the use of buttons, being originally fastened with a sash at the waist. Introduced into Louisiana by the Canadian founders and early inhabitants of the new colony and either imported ready-made into the colony or sewn up locally, the *capot* featured among the articles of clothing traded or

FIGURE 4.1 'Desseins de Sauvages de Plusieurs Nations', by Alexandre de Batz, N^lle Orleans, 1735.

Source: Courtesy of the Peabody Museum of Archaeology and Ethnology, Harvard University, PM41-72-10/20. Gift of the Estate of Belle J. Bushnell, 1941.

FIGURE 4.2 'A Canadian Man and Woman in Their Winter Dress, Quebec Canada', by Sempronius Stretton, 21 November 1805. From Sempronius Stretton, *Sketchbook*, f.19. Watercolour.

Source: Courtesy of the National Archives of Canada.

gifted to Indigenous individuals and communities and was frequently issued to soldiers as a component of their uniforms. It also became a staple of slave dress in the colony, so much so that in the early nineteenth century, a visitor to Louisiana would comment that 'all the inhabitants as well as their slaves ... have capots for wintertime'.[27]

Vanderech was very specific in negotiating the terms of the lease pertaining to dress, but the majority of slave owners were more flexible about which types of garments they provided. In a partnership contract from 1734, it was agreed that each slave was to be supplied with 'a waistcoat, a pair of deerskin *mitasses* [leggings], breeches of *drap a negre* [woolen cloth for slaves], and a shirt of unbleached linen'.[28] Women's clothing was itemized less frequently: in a slave lease from 1747, the lessee promised to give a shirt to each of the four slaves hired. The female slave alone was to be given a skirt.[29] Most documents, however, used the generic phrase '*entretien*' (maintenance) as a blanket term. A three-year lease of slaves from one succession provided only that the lessee 'will feed, maintain and pay any medicine' for the slaves.[30] Other slave leases contained similar generic clauses that required the lessee, rather than the owner, to provide for the maintenance of the slave.[31]

Challenges of provisioning apparel

Once the conditions of a lease or other contract were agreed, or once a slave was bought, where could those responsible for clothing their slaves acquire these items? In some cases, newly arrived slaves were provided with clothing for which the seller was liable. In other cases, the new owners took personal responsibility for this obligation, replacing what clothes were worn by the slaves at the time of their seller with a new issue. Where the establishment of large plantations was concerned, provisions for slave clothing were made in France, even though the slaves themselves had not yet been acquired. In 1719 for example, the clothing for slaves to be delivered in Louisiana for one plantation (which was to include 50 persons and an unspecified number of slaves), was allowed among the shipment of provisions from France sent for the use of the plantation.[32]

The limited information on the clothing supplied by masters to their slaves is, in itself, important and was not solely the result of slave owners' indifference to the question of what their slaves should be expected to wear. Rather, it was precisely because of the irregularity of shipments of European goods to the colony (and therefore fluctuations in the supply of clothing of any kind) that the terms of contracts remained vague. In 1729, and echoing the concerns they had expressed the previous year, officials in the colony wrote to their counterparts in France about the lack of suitable cloth available in the colony:

> You have only sent 2,657 ells of *étoffe à negre* [cloth for slaves], how can you expect us to furnish some to all the inhabitants who have slaves[?], you know approximately how many slaves there are in the colony, [and] there isn't cloth for a third of them, the inhabitants are going to complain about it again this winter if some other vessel doesn't bring us more cloth, since what you have sent will be used to make capot coats for those slaves that will arrive this year, and the inhabitant will be frustrated in his hope to have some cloth, not least because the Beauvais wool that you had already sent is worthless and doesn't even last two or three months, as we have already told you.[33]

Also bearing on the question of the availability of slave clothing are the statements sent from the colony to the minister of marine in France, concerning the quantities of slave clothing that officials anticipated that the colony would require in any given year. In 1735, local officials produced a memorandum detailing all the French merchandise that could profitably be sold in the colony and estimated the needs of the enslaved population at 3,000 ells, in addition to 2,000 woolen caps and 2,000 slave shirts.

Ongoing issues about inadequate supplies within the colony (specifically, for replacing worn-out apparel) made it impossible to be sure what merchandise would be available in the colony at any given time. This helps explain the indeterminate language that *habitants* used in their legal transactions. The frequency of the shortages may also explain the variation in cloths used to clothe slaves, just as shortages in all types of clothing goods may explain the use by white settlers of garments and textiles designed for slaves.[34] *Etoffe à negre* was but one type of textile used for slave dress; in Louisiana, the earliest known reference to this textile was in a document from Illinois from 1723.[35] It was not a generic term since it was sometimes listed side by side with (and therefore distinct from) other cloths used for the enslaved, such as *drap de Beauvais*, thus making a clear distinction between the two.[36] Indeed, while there are a majority of references in different records (lading bills, merchants' records, slave owners' supplies) to *étoffe a negre*, we do find other variants of cloth intended for slave use, such as *drap de Beauvais, limbourg* and *cordillas*.[37]

There is limited information about the origins of textiles and clothing sent to Louisiana for the use of slaves. In the lading bill of merchandise shipped by J. Berard of Bordeaux to the address and consignment of J. Durand, merchant of New Orleans, was a case containing 20 dozen 'slave hats'.[38] A bill for merchandise bought by Sr Labbé from the cargo of the ship *La Reine des Anges* included two entries for slave cloth. The first, dated 28 September 1737, was for 10 ells of 'étoffe à Negre' totaling 23 *livres*, and the second entry, dated 10 October was for an extra ½ ell of the same, at 1.3 *livres*, reflecting a slight reduction on the earlier price. This was marginally more expensive than the lining materials included in the same bill, and almost twice the price of packing cloth, figures that give some idea of the relative worth of slave cloth.[39] Two *voyageurs* (fur traders) owed 3.9 *livres* to the same cargo for 1½ ells of slave cloth.[40] The ship *La Reine des Anges* was from the south-west French port of La Rochelle. The fact that its cargo contained slave cloth suggests that the outfitters recognized its importance as a staple commodity and arranged to have it available for shipment from that port. The merchant-agent for that ship on site in New Orleans was Jean Baptiste Bancio Piemont, a resident of New Orleans, who was familiar with the local market. This presents an instance of the benefits of direct interactions between merchants or agents in New Orleans and outfitters in France, especially at La Rochelle.[41]

The manufacturers who would be interested in making and marketing these low-quality and low-profit-margin goods could well have been the same ones who provided textiles and trade goods for Native Americans and military supplies.[42] Yet, the references to shipments of slave clothing in extant records are infinitesimal in comparison with the references to orders and shipments for Native Americans, for example. Moreover, Native Americans were very particular about the textiles they accepted in trade for their furs. Symptomatic of the lesser status of slaves, this lacuna leaves a large gap in our understanding of the mechanics of manufacturing and marketing cloth and clothing for slaves. But it also touches on one of the essential features of slave clothing: that it was enforced, and therefore did not warrant the same consideration in details of style, colour and comfort afforded to potential allies and trading partners, as Native American nations were perceived. Nor was uniformity an overriding concern, although the semblance of uniformity doubtless occurred when the same cloth or identical articles were issued to the slaves of any one household. Similarly, there were virtually no protests from the colony about the quality of the goods sent for the use of slaves, in contrast to the frequent complaints about the quality of Native American trade items and military dress. On the contrary, we find a number of official documents from the 1730s deriding the quality of trade goods intended for Native Americans as suitable *only* for slaves and no one else. Decades later, Governor Kerlerec complained about the quality of shirts that were not good enough to give to 'the most vile slaves'.[43]

The inference was clear: slaves could have few expectations, stylistically or comfort-wise, about the clothing issued them. That slaves themselves ignored this assumption was expressed in their appropriation of responsibilities that were in theory intended to fall on their masters (namely the duty to provide adequate clothing). They engaged independently in a thriving informal supply system for the making, pawning and reselling of clothing goods and services in the colony and when they did so, they ended up wearing apparel of far greater variety, in terms of patterning, textiles and types of garments.[44] However, slave owners retained the responsibility for handing out clothing supplies on a regular basis and Jeanot's testimony reminds us that the enslaved saw this apparel as their right.

While we would expect a correlation between slave owners' views of slaves' clothing needs and the funds they spent on these, it is impossible, given the available sources, to provide a definitive analysis of the cost aspect. At best, sporadic documents suggest what an owner might have to pay to clothe his slave, even if the actual clothing is not specified or its cost broken down. One such example is the memo of expenses and receipts for two *habitations* from April 1739 to February 1740. Among the entries concerning slaves, we find that one unnamed male slave was leased for 11 months, and that 20 *livres* had been disbursed for his apparel.[45] The specific items included in the 20 *livres* for the slave's clothing are not identified. We do know that three years earlier, in 1737, Paul Rasteau's New Orleans store accounts listed *étoffe a negre* at 50 *sous* (or 2.10 *livres*) per ell and slave hats at 49.3 *sous* (or 2.9.3 *livres*) each.[46]

References to the cost of clothing provisions to slaves were often combined with other expenses making it hard to extrapolate the cost of dressing slaves. In the statement rendered by the legal guardian of two (white) orphaned minor children, for his management of their inheritance, a collective sum of 115 *livres* had been disbursed 'for the apparel provided to the slaves ... the burial of a small slave boy and medicines'. In contrast to the slaves' apparel, a total of 280.15 *livres* had been disbursed for the orphan girls' clothes and 127 *livres* for the orphan boys'.[47] Where masters supplied their slaves with their cast-off apparel rather than new merchandise, the value of the clothes is even harder to quantify. That only limited information exists about the cost to owners of provisioning their slaves suggests that the cost expended on slave clothing, like the character of the clothing itself, was arbitrary. It depended on the funds available at any given time to any given master, on the availability of supplies and on personal whim. And, as we have seen, neither of these was subject to colonial legislation.

Information about the clothing supplied to slaves shows that both ready-made goods and cloth (to be made up locally) were imported into the colony specifically for the purpose. *Etoffe à negre* and other supplies of similarly cheap, low-quality textiles (such as unbleached linen) were imported into the colony in large quantities. But blankets and ready-made clothes were also staple imports. The most prevalent of the ready-made garments were shirts, often, though not always, described as being either for males or females (men's shirts had an open collar, a characteristic not found on women's shifts, whose necklines were however cut lower). Additionally, ships' personnel customarily brought merchandise to sell during their voyage for their own profit. The son of a prominent planter died at sea in 1764 and had among his personal property 'four little bales of slave shirts' that would have been ready-made, and intended for sale.[48] *Capots* were more commonly made in the colony, and there were a number of different ways for slave owners to arrange this. Like the *capots* for Native-Americans, those for slaves could be made on a large scale in the colony when necessary. In the document quoted above, which complained about the insufficient quantity of slave cloth sent to the colony, reference was made by officials in Louisiana to the fact that large quantities of *capots* were to be manufactured in the colony from imported cloth, but it is not clear who would be undertaking this work.[49]

Details of local, small-scale production of slave clothing (including the making of single items) are more prevalent, especially among the notarial records. These are orders from tailors or dressmakers for the making of specific items of clothing. In his will, Pierre Joly, who was described as an indigo maker, included among his debtors Sr. Coquillau, tailor in New Orleans, for 'the making of a capot and a little waistcoat and breeches for a little slave'.[50] In another document bearing on slave clothing, it is the wife of a tailor who is responsible for making shirts (these are not specified as being for the use of slaves), while her husband was responsible for the making of the more tailored articles specified for slaves.[51] It is perhaps consistent with the tailoring trade that Coquillau and Menelet, tailors, should have been commissioned to make structured garments warranting their specialized skills. Menelet's claim was against the estate of his former tenant, Laporte, to recover a total of 1780 *livres*. Most of this claim was for rent owed, and clothing made for, or supplied to, Laporte himself. But there are also two entries, on 15 July and 19 August, for making a jacket and a pair of breeches for Laporte's mulatto slave, at a cost of 50 *livres* on each occasion. As a point of comparison, the four shirts made by Menelet's wife were set at 40 *livres*.[52] It is notable that Menelet's claim was refuted by the Superior Council for lack of proof, with the suggestion that he had exaggerated his demand.[53] Since Menelet was making a claim against a deceased person, without the support of any written agreement or invoice, and without a witness, it is indeed possible that he had inflated the prices. That there had been no formal contract passed between the two underlines the fact that few transactions of this nature were in written format and hints at the limitations of our sources in respect of the making of slave dress.

It is only rarely that we get a glimpse into the vastly underreported practice of having clothes made by female seamstresses. Records of these informal arrangements are generally found as incidental references in other types of documents. In the account rendered of the Kolly estate the executor made an entry relating to slave clothing. On 4 November 1730, a pound of thread was delivered to the wife of Sr Vertut 'to make apparel for the slaves'. While the number of slaves for whom this clothing was to be made is not known, the garments were to be made from three pieces of negro cloth measuring a total of 100 ells, and costing 171.16 *livres*. Estimating that each shirt used approximately 2.5 ells, that would mean at least 40 shirts.[54] Even more elusive was the work undertaken within the household and by the slaves themselves. The purchase in 1748 by Dumont de Montigny, an officer and plantation owner, of a slave 'named Jacques tailor of clothes by profession' suggests that his workload would include the making of apparel for the other slaves. Similarly, the De Noyan plantation records reveal the presence of two laundresses and two seamstresses among the slaves. Extant plantation ledgers from the English Colonies and the French West Indies confirm that the ownership of slave seamstresses and tailors was a common practice, so often essential in managing the apparel needs of these communities.[55]

Given the difficulties in the importation of slave clothing from France, it is not surprising that there were attempts by large slaveholders (who had better channels to the mother country, unlike small-scale, locally based settlers and traders) to contract for their slaves' necessities locally. In 1737, even *Ordonnateur* Salmon, in the name of the king, contracted with the merchant Paul Rasteau to have him supply 297½ ells of negro cloth at 52s/ell for the service of the Crown.[56] Ten years later, we find Governor Vaudreuil justifying his administration's illicit trade with a Dutch ship, on the basis that it was carrying much needed supplies for slaves. He argued that the French ships sent to Louisiana carried none of these supplies, but only the more profitable cloths used in the illicit Spanish trade.[57] In a bolder attempt to secure access to slave-suitable cloth, in 1728, local officials tried to achieve some degree of independence from the vagaries of suppliers in the mother country, argued that settlers in the Illinois Country should be allowed to cultivate hemp for use in clothing for themselves *and their slaves*. This proposal failed to convince officials to rescind their protectionist policies, and did not get off the ground.[58] What each of these instances suggests is that there was a distrust in Louisiana of the ability of French suppliers (including the Ministry of Marine) to provide for the colony's needs. Attempts to have slave clothing manufactured in the colony met with a more positive outcome, understandably since the making of clothing did not fall under the same protectionist policies granted to the French textile industry.

Conclusion

There may well have been difficulties in obtaining adequate quantities of slave-suitable clothing, and there may have been some variants in the attitudes of different masters. But surviving documents show a recurrent preoccupation with keeping slaves adequately clothed. Two distinct factors influenced this. One was the financial stake of owners in the survival of their slaves. The second was a less tangible need to have enslaved Africans conform to their new environment (and their submissive status) by making them adhere to European-style clothing.[59]

Fundamentally, slave clothing was about the politics of subjugation and control; but from the outset, officials and slave owners framed it primarily as a functional need. The fact that they deemed adequate clothing as a matter of life and death only serves to underscore that economic concerns for their chattel were at the root of the preoccupations with supplying apparel to the enslaved. But if the *code noir* legislated against masters who failed to adequately clothe their slaves, in practice none were prosecuted. As in the 1764 case against Jeanot, it was *he* who was interrogated about whether he had stolen apparel, not his master who was investigated for breaking the law.

Emerging from this troubling ideological sleight of hand was a rising anxiety about the ways that the enslaved went well beyond necessity in how they acquired clothing and imbued their dress with meaning. By mid-century, the French, conscious of the loss of social control heralded by slaves' economic interactions and their autonomous sartorial expression, articulated their resistance in a variety of ways. Fortified by the political power of the growing planter elite, local officials enacted new legislation (including the local police code of 1751) that sought to control the movements of slaves, including their access to the market place and the ownership of material possessions. They also prosecuted whites who engaged in commercial transactions with slaves, a hitherto commonplace occurrence condoned by masters.[60] For the enslaved, whites' recognition of their sartorial agency would have terrible consequences, since they were increasingly prosecuted and punished. But ironically, when they acted on their fears, colonists implicitly acknowledged the humanity and individuality of enslaved persons who rejected their commodification by imbuing their own sartorial decisions with meaning: using clothing to participate in the local economy, to forge affective ties and to express their character.

Notes

1 Louisiana State Museum, New Orleans (hereafter LSM): Louisiana Historical Center (hereafter LHC), Records of the Superior Council of Louisiana (hereafter RSCL), 1764041201. On slave testimony in French colonial Louisiana, see Sophie White,

Intimate Voices of the African Diaspora: Narrating Slavery in French Louisiana (Chapel Hill, NC: Omohundro Institute of Early American History and Culture and University of North Carolina Press, forthcoming).

2 RSCL 1764041201.

3 RSCL 1764041201.

4 RSCL 1764041402. Originals of the 1724 *code noir* are located in the LSM: LHC, III 2852.23, March 1724 and AM A, 22: fol. 119, hereafter *code noir*. It has been published in Louis Sala-Molins, *Le code noir, ou le Calvaire de Canaan* (Paris: Quadrige, 1987), on sentencing, see clause 32.

5 On slave dress in French colonial Louisiana, see Sophie White, '"Wearing Three or Four Handkerchiefs Around His Neck, and Elsewhere About Him": Slaves' Constructions of Masculinity and Ethnicity in French Colonial New Orleans', *Gender & History* 15.3 (2003): 528–549; Sophie White, 'Geographies of Slave Consumption: French Colonial Louisiana and a World of Things', *Winterthur Portfolio* 44 (2011): 229–248; Sophie White, 'Slaves' and Poor Whites' Informal Economies in an Atlantic Context', in *Louisiana: Crossroads of the Atlantic World*, ed. Cecile Vidal (Philadelphia: University of Pennsylvania Press, 2014), 89–102. On slave dress in colonial America, see for example Linda Baumgarten, '"Clothes for the People": Slave Clothing in Early Virginia', *Journal of Early Southern Decorative Arts* 14 (1988): 26–70; Steeve O. Buckridge, *The Language of Dress: Resistance and Accommodation in Jamaica, 1760–1890* (Kingston: University of the West Indies Press, 2004); Robert S. DuPlessis, *The Material Atlantic: Clothing, Commerce, and Colonization in the Atlantic World, 1650–1800* (Cambridge, UK: Cambridge University Press, 2016), esp. ch. 4; Chaela Pastore, 'Consumer Choices and Colonial Identity in Saint-Domingue', *French Colonial History* 2 (2002): 77–92; Shane White and Graham White, *Stylin': African American Expressive Culture from Its Beginnings to the Zoo Suit* (Ithaca, NY: Cornell University Press, 2008); Jonathan Prude, 'To Look Upon the "Lower Sort": Runaway Ads and the Appearance of Unfree Laborers in America, 1750–1800', *Journal of American History* 78 (1991): 124–159; David Waldstreicher, 'Reading the Runaways: Self-Fashioning, Print Culture, and Confidence in Slavery in the Eighteenth-Century Mid-Atlantic', *William and Mary Quarterly*, 3rd series, 56 (1999): 241–272.

6 For a chronological listing of the slavers sent to Louisiana, see Gwendolyn Midlo Hall, *Africans in Colonial Louisiana: The Development of Afro-Creole Culture in the Eighteenth Century* (Baton Rouge: Louisiana State University Press, 1992), app. A, 382–397: 'Basic Facts About All Slave-Trade Voyages from Africa to Louisiana During the French Regime'. Though large numbers of slaves were sent to Louisiana before 1731, when shipments of new slaves all but stopped after 1731 and the slave population increased through births, with blacks outnumbering whites by 4,539 to 2,966 in the 1763 census of the population of Lower Louisiana.

7 It was from Senegal that most shipments of slaves to Louisiana were made. Hall discusses the importance of the Senegambia region to the history of Louisiana's slaves in Midlo Hall, *Africans*, 29–34. See also Philip D. Curtin, *The Atlantic Slave Trade: A Census* (Madison: University of Wisconsin Press, 1969), 163–202 for a discussion of the figures available. The bulk of the remaining slaves sent to Louisiana originated in Juda. Midlo Hall, *Africans*, table 2, at p. 60. Occasionally, there are references to Africans arriving from the French West Indies or from the English or Spanish colonies of America, including as runaways.

8 Given the economic importance of France's home textile industry, the Crown prohibited the spinning of yarn and weaving of cloth, with an edict in 1721 even forbidding the cultivation of hemp and flax in the colony since these staples might be used locally rather than exported; see Archives nationales d'outre-mer, Aix-en-Provence, France (hereafter ANOM), Ordonnance id du 9 janvier 1721, fol. 31, vol. 23, ser. A. See also David-Thierry Ruddel, 'Domestic Textile Production in Colonial Québec, 1608–1840', *Material History Bulletin* 31 (1990): 39–49.

9 ANOM, C13A 11, fol. 27, 9 April 1728. The Caye refers to La Caye Saint-Louis in Saint-Domingue, present-day Haiti.

10 ANOM, C13A 11, fol. 305, 30 January 1729. Such a process meant of course that slavers sent from France could carry only that merchandise that they intended to trade in Africa for slaves, rather than being encumbered from the start with cargo meant for the slaves themselves.

11 ANOM, B, vol. 43, pp. 808–809, 31 March 1728: 'Comme nous ne doutons pas que la Compie n'ayt attention a Envoyer a la Louisianne ce qui est necessaire pour l'habillement des Negres, sans quoy ils periroient, nous demandons qu'a mesure que les Negres cy-dessus Seront remis a Nos Regisseurs, il leur soit delivré ce qui convient pour leur habillement promettant de faire payer en Tabac ou autres productions de nos Cultures qui sont reçeües par la Compagnie tant les Negres que l'habillement.'

12 ANOM, B 42bis, pp. 201–202, 4 July 1718. On conditions during the transatlantic passage, see Gaston Martin, *Histoire de l'esclavage dans les colonies françaises* (Paris: Presses universitaires de France, 1948), 73.

13 Wendy Anne Warren, '"The Cause of Her Grief": The Rape of a Slave in Early New England', *Journal of American History* 93.4 (2007): 1031–1049, see esp. 1040.

14 Antoine-Simon Le Page du Pratz, *Histoire de la Louisiane*, vol. 1 (Paris: De Bure l'aîné, 1758), 335.

15 ANOM, C13A 5, fol. 221, [1731?].

16 ANOM, C13A 11, fol. 27, 9 April 1728.

17 Thomas N. Ingersoll, 'Slave Codes and Judicial Practice in New Orleans, 1718–1807', *Law and History Review* 13 (1995): 23–62; Vernon Valentine Palmer, 'The Origins and Authors of the Code Noir', *Louisiana Law Review* 56 (1996): 363–407; and Vernon Valentine Palmer, *Through the Codes Darkly: Slave Law and Civil Law in Louisiana* (Clark, NJ: Lawbook Exchange, 2012); Mathé Allain, 'Slave Policies in French Louisiana', *Louisiana History* 21 (1980): 136–137; Carl A. Brasseaux, 'The Administration of Slave Regulations in French Louisiana, 1724–1766', *Louisiana History* 21.2 (1980): 139–158.

18 LSM: LHC, III 2852.23, March 1724: *code noir*. The 1724 *code noir* was virtually identical, word for word, to the 1723 *code noir* pertaining to African slavery in France's East African island colonies of the Indian Ocean. The issuing of the 1723 and 1724 slave codes heralded a moment when 'the French empire became the first European overseas empire where slave law emanated from a metropolitan edict', even as they reflected the application of the law and the ebb and flow between colony and state, or the push and pull between local elites and court officials. See Guillaume Aubert, '"To Establish One Law and Definite Rules": Race, Religion, and the Transatlantic Origins of the Louisiana Code Noir', in Videl, *Louisiana*, 32–68, esp. p. 33; also Sophie White, 'Les Esclaves et le droit en Louisiane sous le régime français, carrefour entre la Nouvelle-France, les Antilles, et l'océan indien', in *Thémis Outre-Mer: Adapter le droit et rendre la justice aux colonies (16e–19e siècles)*, ed. Eric Wenzel and Eric de Mari (Dijon: Editions universitaires de Dijon, 2015), 57–67. The 1685 and 1724 slave codes have been published in Sala-Molins, *Le code noir*.

19 *Code noir*, 'Voulons que les officiers de notre conseil supérieur de la Louisiane, envoyent leurs avis sur quantité des vivres et la qualité de l'habillement qu'il convient que les maîtres fournissent à leurs esclaves; lesquels vivres doivent leur être fournis par chacune semaine, et l'habillement par chacune année, pour y être statué par nous: et cependant permettons aux dits officiers de régler par provision lesdits vivres et ledit habillement: défendons aux maîtres desdits esclaves de donner aucune sorte d'eau-de-vie pour tenir lieu de ladite subsistance et habillement.'

20 RSCL 1748061102.

21 Antoine Simon Le Page du Pratz, *Histoire de la Louisiane: Contenant la découverte de ce vaste pays; sa description géographique; un voyage dans les terres; l'histoire naturelle; les*

moeurs, coûtumes & religion des naturels, avec leurs origines; deux voyages dans le nord du nouveau Mexique, dont un jusqu'à la mer du sud; ornée de deux cartes & de 40 planches en taille douce, 3 vols. (Paris: De Bure, l'aîné, 1758), vol. 1, 340; Du Pratz does not identify what clothes he deemed suitable. Since he also advises his reader to strip any slave that he is considering purchasing, for a close search of potential disease or defects, we may infer that the slave would be wearing some form of clothing when they arrived.

22 See for example the terms of the lease of a plantation with four male and two female negroes and two slaves to make tar and other labour. The slaves were to be given 'each year to each male a capot and a skirt to each female' (RSCL 1746030602).

23 RSCL 1736022402. In a letter the following year from *Ordonnateur* Salmon to the minister, Vandereck was singled out for his sadism. ANOM C13A 22 fol. 212, 16 December 1737.

24 Ursuline Archives, New Orleans: General Accounts, October 1797–October 1817, p. 13: 'Memoire du linge et hardes des orphelines ce 6 avril 1752'.

25 Newberry Library, Chicago, Ayer MS 257: Jean-François-Benjamin Dumont de Montigny, 'Mémoire de Lxx Dxx officier ingénieur, contenant les evenements qui se sont passés à la Louisiane depuis 1715 jusqu'à present'. On the wearing of the breechclout by colonists, see White, *Wild Frenchmen*, 188–189, 208–218.

26 Francis Back, 'Le capot canadien: Ses origines et son evolution aux XVIIe et XVIIIe siècles', *Canadian Folklore* 10 (1988): 99–127; Jacqueline Beaudoin-Ross, 'A la Canadienne: Some Aspects of 19th Century Habitant Dress', *Dress* 6 (1980): 71–82; René Chartrand, 'The Winter Costume of Soldiers in Canada', *Canadian Folklore* 10 (1988): 155–180.

27 C.C. Robin, *Voyages dans l'interieur de la Louisiane, de la Floride occidentatle et dans les Iles de la Martinique et de Saint Dominique pendant les années 1802, 1803, 1804, 1805 et 1806* (Paris: F. Buisson, 1807), vol. 2, 103. On the use of the *capot* by enslaved Africans in Louisiana, see also M. Perrin du Lac, *Voyage dans les deux Louisianes et les nations sauvages du Mississippi en 1801, 1802 et 1803* (Lyon: Bruysset & Buynand, 1805), 410–411; On the use of the *capot* by enslaved Africans in Louisiana, see Governor Perier and Ordonnateur La Chaise to the Minister of the Marine, 9 April 1728, fol. 27, vol. 11, ser. C13A, ANOM; 30 January 1729, fol. 305, vol. 11, ser. C13A, ANOM; 31 March 1728, pp. 808–809, vol. 43, ser. B, ANOM.

28 RSCL 1734022301.

29 RSCL 1747030901.

30 NONA FM&K-37 (80558–61) 1766/02/21: Succession of late J. B. Eugene Barré.

31 Thus, the lease of a negress and her son by Larche Grandpré to Sr. Francis Haville or Hawill required Haville, the lessee, to pay 200 *livres* per year, and be responsible for her food and maintenance (RSCL 1737072601). In a more unusual case from Kaskaskia, the maintenance to be provided by the lessee to the slave was limited to his footwear needs (KM 37:10:23:1).

32 ANOM G1 465: doc. 169, 26 October 1719.

33 ANOM C13A 11, fol. 351, 26 August 1729.

34 The inventory of the effects of the late Pierre Girard, surgeon major at Fort de Chartres, in the Illinois country, included a listing for 'une paire de culotte d'etoffe à negre' (KM 27:10:17:1). He was not recorded as owning any slaves. Debien comments on the use by '*les petits blancs*' in the West Indies, of the cheap cloths shipped for slaves. *Antilles*, 238.

35 KM 23:7:1:1; see also ANC C13a 11, fol. 134, 3 November 1728, New Orleans and RSCL (after) 1732012601. See also Robert S. DuPlessis, 'Cloth and the Emergence of the Atlantic Economy', in *The Atlantic Economy During the Seventeenth and Eighteenth Centuries: Organization, Operation, Practice, and Personnel*, ed. Peter A. Coclanis (Columbia: University of South Carolina Press, 2005), 72.

36 RSCL 1737080304.
37 *Etoffe à negre* may of course have evolved into a specific and recognizable type of cloth, although the point at which this would have occurred is hard to surmise. In the 1737 inventory of the store of the merchant Paul Rasteau, there is a separate listing for *étoffe à negre* among the 'Draps Divers' (RSCL 1737100201). In the inventory of the estate of the late Jaffre *dit* La Liberté, in 1740, we find another type of coarse cloth, *cordillas*, as well as *limbourg*, used for slave clothing (RSCL 1740032101). This is the only listing of *cordillas* found in the colonial records, perhaps chosen for qualities that made it suitable for work in a tar factory.
38 RSCL 1763082501.
39 RSCL 1738033102. A Jean Labbé was recorded as 'habitant a lanse aux outardes a six ou sept lieurs audessus de cette ville' (RSCL 1738030702).
40 RSCl 1737081405. Since this account was to be due on the return of the Illinois convoy the following year, we can assume that the merchandise purchased, including the negro cloth, was for that market.
41 On Piemont, see John G. Clark, *New Orleans, 1718–1812: An Economic History* (Baton Rouge: Louisiana State University Press, 1970), 92–94.
42 The best account of the manufacturing and supply process for Louisiana, in the broader political, economic and material culture context of the transatlantic trade is Alexandre Dubé, 'Les Biens publics: Culture Politique de la Louisiane française, 1730–1770' (PhD diss., McGill University, 2009).
43 ANOM C13A 17, fol. 187, 1 August 1733 and ANOM C13A 43, fol. 78, no. 308.
44 See White, 'Slaves' and Poor Whites' Informal Economies' and 'Geographies of Slave Consumption'.
45 RSCL 1740022903.
46 RSCL 1737100201. An ell is 18 inches, or approximately 45 cm.
47 RSCL 1739061701.
48 RSCL 1764011201. He was the only son of the Chevalier de Pradel, see Baillardel and Prioult, *Pradel*, 317–318.
49 ANOM C13A 11, fol. 351, 26 August 1729.
50 RSCL 1746020201.
51 See RSCL 1763102501.
52 See the abstract printed in the *Louisiana Historical Quarterly*, 26.1 (24 October 1763): 242–243. The original document has not been located.
53 RSCL 1763110503.
54 RSCL (after 1732012601). The estimate is based on Adrienne Hood's calculations that 3.5 yards were needed to make a shirt; see Adrienne D. Hood, 'The Material World of Cloth: Production and Use in Eighteenth-Century Rural Pennsylvania', *William and Mary Quarterly* 53.1 (1996): table 1, p. 48. A yard measured approximately 2.8 ells, however we can expect that a slave's shirt used a minimal amount of cloth, hence my estimate of 2.5 ells/shirt at most.
55 RSCL 1748020802; RSCL 1763102201. See Linda Baumgarten, 'Plains, Plaid and Cotton: Woollens for Slave Clothing', *Ars Textrina* 15 (1991): 205; and Debien, *Antilles*, 238.
56 RSCL 1737111203.
57 VP, vol. I p. 94v, 24 November 1746 and VP LO 121, 20 March 1748 (see also ANOM C13A 41, fol. 384, 4 May 1759).
58 ANOM C13A 8, Fo 447, 1728.
59 On the significance of the immediate adoption of European apparel by newly arrived slaves in the English Colonies, with its connotations of conferring European notions of decency, see Shane White and Graham White, 'Slave Clothing and African-American Culture in the Eighteenth and Nineteenth Centuries', *Past & Present* 148 (1995): 151–153. The authors also address the impact on slaves themselves of enforced sartorial changes.
60 ANOM C13A, vol. 35, fol. 39, 28 February–1 March 1751.

GARMENTS IN CIRCULATION

The economies of slave clothing in the eighteenth-century Dutch Cape Colony

Miki Sugiura[1]

Contrary to the general belief that garments circulated globally only after the advent of mass production and consumption in the nineteenth century, this chapter explores the contour of such global circulation in the eighteenth century. Global encounters and the European imperial expansion since the sixteenth century created a need for individuals and institutions to provide a mass of clothing of stable quality and as inexpensively as possible. This is the case for the clothing of soldiers, sailors, travelling servants and, as this chapter shows, for slaves. Individuals engaged in these occupations can be deemed 'involuntary consumers' whose needs influenced the circulation of both new and second-hand clothing globally.[2] Beverly Lemire has explored these networks of circulation in a series of innovative and extensive works since the 1980s.[3] Importantly, her later works explored the global outreach this circulation implied; in particular, her research into the provisions of ready-made clothing for sailors and royal marines in the British Empire sheds light on the global scale encompassed by these systems of production and use.

Slave clothing, however, has not been discussed extensively in this context. This is mainly explained by the different and variegated ways of provisioning slave clothing. Clothing for slaves was, for the most part, provided by private individual slave owners and not centrally by large institutions. In this respect, slave clothing could vary significantly according to the wealth and rank of slave owners and thus could not easily be called a unified form of clothing. Nevertheless, two absolutely indispensable elements, namely, the need for their owners to display their bonded and discriminated position by their attire and for their garments to be cheap, contributed to slave clothing being established as a distinguished and standardized category.

Scholars have tended to explain the cheapness of slave clothing, linking it to the creation of cheaper kinds of fabrics, rather than the clothing itself. This holds particularly true for studies of eighteenth-century North America. Scholars analysing the descriptions of runaway slaves in newspapers show the use of specific cheaper linens, most prominently *osnaburgs* or *dowles* used for their shirts.[4] Carole Shammas suggests the average price of *osnaburgs* grew steadily cheaper in the late eighteenth century, becoming almost a third of the price of fabrics generalized as linen and calico.[5] Behind this price decline was the harsh global competition between England, Silesia and Ireland, explored further in recent studies.[6]

The rise of cheaper fabrics designated for slave clothing is well researched for North America, but it would not be justified to simply extend this view to the eighteenth-century Indian Ocean world. As Giorgio Riello suggests, the circulation of low-quality textiles was expanding as barter for West African slave trade.[7] However, whether early modern textile production areas of India, along with Europe, embarked on supplying new, cheaper textiles for slave clothing is yet to be investigated. To determine the precise value of slave clothing we also need to discuss another aspect that was increasing simultaneously: the circulation of clothing. The circulation of fabrics and of clothing has been addressed either in a well-connected fashion or wholly separately for the Indian Ocean world.[8] This chapter examines the dynamic interaction between the cloth and clothing directed at slave populations.

This chapter argues that the circulation of clothing, both at global and local levels, contributed significantly to the creation of the cheaper clothing category of slave clothing, taking the eighteenth-century Dutch Cape Colony as a case study. The Cape Colony started as a resupply port, with provisioning functions for incoming and outgoing ships of the Dutch and other East India Companies (Figure 5.1). Its unique geographical position in the global network, being linked to Asia and Europe, directly shaped slave-clothing provision. Moreover, the Dutch Cape Colony had another distinctive feature unique to colonial settings: it banned retailers in the colony. The Dutch East India Company (VOC) prohibited the establishment of retail shops in the colonies, a ban that lasted until British rule began in 1808. Thus, individual Cape Town slave owners and households had to face this problem in providing textiles and clothing. No professional supplier appears to have specialized in slave cloth or clothing.

Thus, the Cape Colony developed unique textile and clothing circulation mechanisms: highly regulated by the VOC on the one hand, and individually driven on the other. Situated as a unique midpoint between East and West, the Cape Colony relied almost completely on imported textiles brought in by ships that docked regularly, but were absent during the winter months.[9] Despite the ban on retailers, local movement of goods flourished. The supply and distribution of cloth or clothing was executed through non-shop channels and private exchanges. Auctions were held regularly in public spaces, under a specialist VOC officer's supervision, with participation of a broad range of society.[10] So intense and well-developed was private, face-to-face bartering and exchange in the streets and private houses that it amazed contemporary observers, especially visitors to this colony. Slave cloth and clothing circulated in this distinctive

FIGURE 5.1 'Le Cap de Bonne Esperance', coloured engraving by Jacques Gabriel Huquier, Paris, c.1735–1805.

Source: Rijksmuseum Amsterdam, RP-P-1921-789.

manner.[11] By looking at the unique circulation mechanisms of the Cape Colony, this chapter illuminates the roles of institutions and individuals in shaping markets and the provisioning of ready-made clothing at both the local and global levels.

The chapter is composed as follows. The next section demonstrates how the VOC, centred in Batavia, made Indian- and other Asian-manufactured ready-made clothing into trade commodities. The subsequent section presents the details of slave clothing in the Cape Colony and confirms that the cost of slave clothing in the eighteenth-century Cape Colony was surprisingly low. Then, the final section will show how these clothing types were circulated and evaluated in the colony and how these cumulative exchanges contributed to the making of slave clothing in that distinctive locale.

Circulation of ready-made clothing through the Dutch East India Company

Evidence suggests the VOC circulated masses of Indian and South East Asian-made clothing as standardized trade products during the seventeenth and eighteenth centuries. These goods were essentially different in nature from other imported Asian luxury clothing, such as Japanese *kosode* (kimono/overgowns), which were initially attributed as gifts. One of the first prominent standardized clothing genres in circulation was _zijlkleden (sailing clothes)_. By the mid-seventeenth century, _zijlkleden_ were frequently mentioned as staple exchange goods for the slave trade in the Dutch sailing diaries and travel records to the eastern coast of Africa.[12] Their Indian origin is confirmed, as it was often noted in these records that these goods were made in Bengal.[13] Sailing clothes were stockpiled both in VOC warehouses in Batavia and the Cape Colony. Moreover, these items also reached the Netherlands to be auctioned en masse. In 1765, for example, the Amsterdam chamber of the VOC sold 242 pieces of various _zijkleeden_ in total. In October and November of 1783, 940 pieces of _doe-sootjes of zijkleeden_ (_doesootjes_ or sailing clothes) were sold in total at various VOC locales.[14]

At this point, _vrouwen kleedje_, (women's clothing), was becoming an even more popular trade commodity than _zijlkleeden_. The same 1765 list of the Amsterdam chamber of the VOC reported auctioning 1,500 pieces of printed (_gedrukte_) and 1,000 pieces of plain women's clothing in the Netherlands, next to the sailing clothes (_zijkleeden_).[15] Another document of 1753 notes three ships returning from Batavia via Cape Colony that brought 4,200 women's gowns.[16] The sale of imported Asian garments seemed to be routine in the middle of the century, as they were mentioned also in the official price list of Amsterdam VOC's auction in 1763.[17] Their prices were 11.75 guilders per piece for printed women's clothing and 9.25 guilders per piece for plain, both inexpensive garments.[18] They were made of cotton and were four to five times cheaper than silk _Japanse rocken_ (Japanese _kosode_ overgowns), which were sold at 50–100 guilders per piece. Ready-made _vrouwen kleedje_ was an entirely different genre of product from the Japanese silk overgown, also called 'banyan' in English. Moreover, they were less expensive than half of the cotton textiles mentioned in the list (Table 5.1). From these relative prices, _vrouwen kleedjes_ appear to be simply sewn garments made of low-priced printed cotton textile, although their precise style or cut is not entirely clear. However, we can conclude from other descriptions of clothing around that time, '_kleedjes_', which literally means simple clothing, were possibly a long wrap skirt that covered the lower body.[19]

Thus, these records confirm that the VOC traded Asian-made simple clothing as established and standardized products. Importantly, it appears that these categories of ready-made clothing were cheap from the earliest years. The price list published for VOC auction held in 28 April 1689 in Amsterdam listed _Boutonse monster-kleetjes_ (patterned simple clothing from the island of Buton), priced at 5.5 guilders per piece, or about half the price of _vrouwen kleedjes_ in the 1763 auction.[20] This price was not only less than one-seventh of the cheapest sold _kosode_ at the occasion, but also 2–5 guilders lower priced than 'coarse sailcloth made in Bengal'. We cannot know all the elements that determined the price of these garments, from the cost of the cloth to the cost of colonial labour. Still, we can see that VOC adopted printed cotton clothing they encountered in their interregional trade in South East Asia and then made them into a product to be retailed in the Netherlands as early as in the seventeenth century. _Vrouwen_

TABLE 5.1 Clothing specified for orphans and slaves in Batavian orphanages in the regulation issued on 23 May 1750

Article 42: As for clothing, the following should be annually provided

(1) For daughters of European blood	Six tailored (*gemaakte*) shirts (*hemd*) made of common bleached coastal Guineas
	Two chintz skirts (*rokken*), made of common coastal textiles
	Two *cabaaijen* (possibly a jacket made from cotton fabric, usually gingham or chintz)
	Two *waskleedjes* (bathing clothing) or sarong
	Two colourful headscarves/handkerchiefs (*neusdoeken*)
	Two pairs of cotton socks
	Two pairs of shoes
	Two pairs of slippers (*sloopen*)
	One chintz *japon* (dress), provided every two years and a new *keursliyff* every three years
(2) For daughters clothed in a mixed style	Three fine shirts (*baytjes*) made of Guineas or Moeris
	Four coarse of the same
	Three *coetans* or waistcoat (*borstrokken*) made of common Guineas of Moeris
	Four clothing/skirt (*kleedje*) made of fine Bengal *fotas*
	One fine *custkleedje* (coastal clothing/skirts)
	Two colourful headscarves/handkerchiefs
	Two pairs of cotton socks
	Two pairs of shoes or mules
	Two pairs of slippers
(3) For boys	Six shirts (*hemd*) of common bleached coastal Guineas
	One *camisool* (type of short waistcoat), two waistcoats, three trousers (*broeken*) made of Gingang *pinas* or *drangam*
	Two colourful headscarves/handkerchiefs
	Three pairs of cotton socks
	Three pairs of shoes
	Two pairs of slippers
	One hat

Article 43: The following should be provided for the serfs (lijfseigenen) and slaves

(4) For female slaves	Four rough simple-style shirts (*baytjes*) made of common coastal Guineas
	Two jackets (*coetans*)
	One colourful headscarf/handkerchief
	Three clothing/skirts (*kleedje*) made of coarse Bengal *fotas*
(5) For male slaves	Four pairs of trousers made of Surat *niquanias*
	Two simple-style shirts (*baytjes*) made of brown bleached coastal *salempouris*
	One waistcoat made of Surat *niquanias*
	One colourful headscarf/handkerchief

Source: 'Reglement voor het weeshuis te Batavia', in J. A. van der Chijs, ed., *Nederlandsch-Indisch Plakaatboek, 1602–1811: Vol. 6 (1750–54)* (Batavia: Landsdrukkerij, 1886), 238.

kleedjes possibly developed along this line, in tune with demand, within the Netherlands and its colonies, with the VOC diversifying its production areas as well as prices in the process in the next century.

Batavia, the VOC's Asian hub, also became the centre of clothing distribution. *Plakaaten* (regulations) issued by the VOC in Batavia confirm that clothing was a regular and staple of ships' cargo and commodity.[21] Ships' captains were asked to unload and register all the clothing they held upon their arrival in Batavia. Regulations concerning how they should be stored at the VOC warehouse or how they should be provided from the VOC *winkel* (workshops) are also recorded.[22] In addition, Batavia itself manufactured various styles of clothing. A regulation issued on 15 August 1660 declaring the installation of a tailor's guild confirms the coexistence of multiple styles of manufacture.[23] The record recounts that tailors from Coromandel had been settling in Batavia for some years, but once they formed considerable capital they went back to the country, suggesting Coromandel artisans were the basis for clothing manufacturing in Batavia. The VOC felt the need to sort out the situation, stipulating which other tailors would manufacture what type of clothing. Subsequently, it was ruled that only the Christians, who were settled in Batavia, could make clothing for Europeans. The rules for making other styles of clothes were looser. Javanese-, Moor- or Chinese-style clothing could be made by anyone from the same ethnic group. Controlling the flows of these diverse types of clothing required an effort that resembled controlling hectic traffic. In the 1660s, the VOC tried not to accept Muslim-made clothing manufactured outside of Batavia, and also tried to ban the outflow of clothing or cotton products not bought by the VOC into Palembang in the South of Sulaweshi.[24] Moreover, since 1648, the VOC repeatedly issued prohibitions against the vending of clothing inside Batavia.[25] These multidirectional bans and restrictions prove the active interregional and local circulations of many kinds of clothing.

It is therefore not surprising that children and slaves of the orphanage in Batavia were supplied with clothing in the forms of standardized garments. The orphanage ordinance issued in 1752 specified the details for each group.[26] Orphans and slaves were divided into six groups: girls with European bloodline, girls wearing mixed-style attire and of mixed ethnicity (*dogters op de Mixtise wys gekleend gaande*), boys, male slaves and female slaves and each group was specified what they were given. Table 5.1 provides the rich details of these regulations. Notably, the descriptions suggest the tailoring capacity in Batavia and the considerable amount of clothing made with requirements for the fabric used. All the clothing specified for European daughters was made of Indian or South East Asian fabrics. And, while the garments of European girls included sarongs and other Asian-originated clothing, none of the names of the clothing or most of the fabrics used for European girls corresponded with those made for girls of mixed ancestry. Though all the fabrics had Asian origin, the VOC seemed to apply a racialized hierarchy among those Indian fabrics, laying out what was appropriate for girls of European ancestry and those that were adequate for girls of other ethnicities, including mixed ethnicity. Female dress was clearly a matter of concern. Girls were not specified by race but categorized as 'daughters who are clothed in mixed styles,' a suggestive designation. One might assume that all orphans, particularly girls, were more or less mixed race and that if the female orphan did not have a background where her European blood was stressed, she was categorized in this group. As Rebecca Earle observes for colonial New Spain: 'Colonial actors relied on individuals' clothing, overall lifestyle, and social networks to perform the difficult work of translating their existence into the language of caste.'[27] So, too, for orphan girls of Dutch Batavia, where mixed clothing suggested ancestry and upbringing. In contrast, orphan boys were given the same shirt, trousers and waistcoat combinations, regardless of their ethnic origin. Here again, their shirts and trousers were made from Indian fabrics, but these fabrics were not differentiated among the groups. This gender gap and complicated disposition of fabrics not only testifies to Batavia's access to great varieties of fabrics, but also the willingness to display ethnic and social distinctions using those fabrics.

In comparison to the orphans' attire, the garments provided for slaves were distinguished by two distinctive characteristics. First, male slaves were not given shoes, socks or hats. Second, clothing was made solely from coarser fabrics. Most of the slave garment names can also be found in the clothing provided for orphans; but slave clothes were made of plain-coloured, coarse version of these fabrics. Similarly, the shirts and skirts for female slaves were made of the coarser version of the same fabric used for mixed-race orphan girls, such as Bengal *fotas* and coastal *guineas*. For male slaves, a differentiated fabric of Surat-made *niquanias* and plain brown, bleached *salempouris* were specified. *Niquanias* were originally the blue and white striped cotton fabric from the Coromandel region. Possibly Surat produced versions of this cloth. Equally, *salempouris* is linked to the place name near Calcutta, and originally meant colourful chintz-style cotton cloth. But here it is converted into a brown-coloured fabric.[28] Thus, we can conclude that by 1750, Batavian people expected that they could acquire the cheapest and most basic range of ready-made clothing for slaves, utilizing the cloth they obtain through the inter-regional trade in South and South East Asia.

Contemporary depictions of slaves working for VOC employees in Batavia, Ceylon and Bali correspond with the garments specified in the above list, though some variations are included (Figures 5.2–5.6). For male slaves, we see on one hand, in Johan Brandes' portrayal, a short and casually styled short trouser and shirt, with most of his upper body bare (Figure 5.2). On the other hand, an anonymous picture from 1700–1725, presumably in Batavia, of several types of slaves, demonstrates a strong contrast between the attire of seemingly Asian slaves, who wore blue waistcoats with buttons, and that of possibly African slaves whose only covering was a cloth of red patterned fabrics falling from around their waists, with white handkerchiefs around their heads and neck (Figure 5.3). Further, portrayals of female slaves also show varieties in their *kleedjes* (clothing/skirts) and *baaitjes* (shirts) (Figures 5.4 and 5.5). *Kleedje* is assumed to be sarong-like tube of textiles sewn on one side of the fabric, sometimes combined with *baaitjes*, whose

FIGURE 5.2 'Slave with an Indonesian Parasol (*pajoeng*), Child and Dog', pencil and wash drawing, from an album by Jan Brandes, *c*.1779–1785, 19.5 × 15.5 cm.

Source: Rijksmuseum, Amsterdam NG-1985-7-2-53.

length could be long or short. As Figure 5.6 shows, tube-type fabric could be used for covering both upper and lower part of the body. Figure 5.6 is an illustration of a Balinese slave in Batavia around 1700, in the Cornelis de Bruin's travel writing published in 1718. The elements of her apparel are clearly displayed.

The evidence provided in this section demonstrates the routine manufacture, use and circulation of ready-made garments made in Batavia and India, commodities with a global reach. Moreover, these were not the only clothing circulated by the VOC. The ships leaving the ports of the Netherlands not only carried large volumes of shirts and trousers provided for ship crews at the outset, but also other piles of garments were stocked dedicated for distributing later. Moreover, there is a possibility that VOC mass ordered clothing, socks and shoes in the Chinese ports of Canton and in the Cape Colony. For example,

FIGURE 5.3 'Dutch Merchant with Slaves in East Indies Hills', oil on canvas by an unknown artist, *c.*1700–1725, possibly made in Batavia, 48 × 57.2 cm.

Source: Rijksmuseum, Amsterdam SK-A-4988.

the ship crews of *Vrouwe Geertruida* that departed the Netherlands in early 1758 for a voyage to Canton via Cape Town and Batavia received additional provisions of clothing and shoes on at least at two occasions during their voyage that lasted two years and ten months. The first time was in March 1760, only one month after they left Canton. A total of 112 crew members were provided with either one or two shirts and linen trousers. These shirts could have been made and provided from Batavia. However, this scenario is unlikely, given that the ship barely arrived in Batavia from Canton by then. It is more likely that their clothing was prepared during their stay in Canton from autumn 1759 to February 1760. Multiple private inventories confirm that crews of the same ship also purchased and owned multiple Chinese-made similar or upgraded versions of linen trousers in Canton. The second occasion of crew provisioning happened two days after the ship left the Cape Colony after staying there for more than a month. More than 80 crew members of the ship were provided, two days after the departure, with one pair of leather shoes and one or two pairs of woollen knitted socks. This case is not enough to map out the network of clothing supply at each trajectory, but it strongly suggests that the VOC was able to mass

FIGURE 5.4 Detail of 'Living Room with the Son Jantje and Spinning Female Slave Flora', pencil and wash drawing, from an album by Jan Brandes, *c*.1779– 1785, 19.5 × 15.5 cm.

Source: Rijksmuseum, Amsterdam NG-1985-7-2-4.

order standardized clothing and shoes between one and two months of stay at the ports of the Netherlands, Canton, and Cape Colony. Although Batavia served as an important distribution centre to a certain extent, it was certainly not the only place to provide garments that sustained maritime networks. The other episodes of VOC journeys, be it Canton or Cape Town, appeared equally capable of providing ready-made clothing in a short period of time. Thus, we see the VOC directing interactive clothing circulation, globally.

Slave clothing in the Cape Colony

Slave clothing in the Cape Colony was closely interwoven with these clothing networks developed by the VOC. The picture of Greenmarket Square in 1762 or 1764 by Johaness Rach, a Danish VOC draughtsman, displays various types of slave apparel (Figure 5.7). The slaves' origins varied from islands in South East Asia, Bengal and Coromandel on the Indian subcontinent, to locations along the eastern coast of Africa and Madagascar.[29] Indeed, enslaved labourers were so extensively and pervasively employed in this colony that it became a slave-based society. The total slave population in the Cape is estimated to have grown from 337 in 1692 and 891 in 1701 to roughly 6,000 in the mid-

FIGURE 5.5 Detail of 'Clothing of Women and Slaves on Ceylon', with emphasis on hairdress or *konde*, pencil and wash drawing, from an album by Jan Brandes, *c.*1779–1785, 19.5 × 15.5 cm.

Source: Rijksmuseum, Amsterdam NG-1985-7-1-68.

eighteenth century and then grew rapidly to 14,747 by 1793, outnumbering 'free burghers'.[30] On average, from 1696 to 1805, 66 per cent of the settler population owned slaves, a percentage that grew from the beginning of the eighteenth century.[31] This rapid rise in the slave population meant there was a high demand for slave clothing.

Slaves in Cape Town could be roughly divided into three categories: company, urban and farm slaves. Company slaves were those owned by the VOC, living collectively in either the castle (fortress, garrison) or slave lodge in Cape Town. Urban slaves were those owned personally by free burghers or by company officials' households located in the settlement of Cape Town. Farm slaves were those working in burgher gardens or in Table Valley situated at the outskirts of Cape Town, where wheat fields and wineries developed.[32]. Company slaves working at the slave lodge were supplied summer and winter sets of clothing annually from the VOC. Although for some items fabrics were supplied, it was standard to be supplied with ready-made apparel, either tailored in Cape

FIGURE 5.6 'Balinese slave in Batavia in 1700', by Cornelis de Bruin.

Source: Cornelis de Bruin, *Voyages de Corneille le Brun* (Amsterdam: Chez les freres Wetstein, 1718).

Town or manufactured ready-made elsewhere and shipped to the colony. Generally, men were provided fabric for shirts, trousers and doublets; women, for skirts and/or smocks.[33] This clothing was mixed both in the sense that they mixed European and Asian fabrics, but also the clothing styles were mixed, with male slaves tending to be attired in more European-style garments and female slaves more Asian. The list of supplies for 1720–1721 exists for company slave clothing at the lodge. Otto Mentzel, a German traveller who stayed in the Cape Colony in the 1730s, left notes in his later memoir published in 1785. According to these records, each male company slave was annually provided with a doublet and one or two pairs of trousers, tailored by garrison tailors.[34] The doublets were made of both Dutch and Indian fabrics. The outer fabric was a coarse white woollen cloth with black streaks (*pijlaken*; pilot cloth), lined with a cotton cloth called 'sailcloth' (*zijldoeken*), made in India and different locations of Southeast Asia; this garment was embellished with 12 brass buttons.[35] Other than the doublet and trousers, the slaves received either a length of cheaper cotton, or sometimes cut-out loose clothing pieces and cotton thread intended for the making of shirts.

FIGURE 5.7 Greenmarket Square in the early 1760s with the Old Town House in the background, *c.*1761–1764, by Johannes Rach (1721–1783, Danish, VOC draught man).

Source: Atlas of Mutual Heritage, Atlas of Stolk, 2374, Catalogus Tropenmuseum, Wonen in de wijde wereld.

The hierarchy of clothing provision among different ranks of VOC employees reflected what a slave wore in Batavia. Influences differed from one colonial region to another. Indeed, the utilization of Dutch textiles and the mixing of European styles was more pronounced in the Cape Colony than in Batavia, as the company tried to provide Dutch woollen textiles as much as possible for the trousers and doublets, to adjust to the Colony's harsh winters.[36] However, soon they faced a shortage of supply for woollen textiles and found substitutes in blue or other coloured (often brown) coarse worsted material. This substitute still did not solve the shortage and ultimately they substituted them for jackets and trousers made of locally sourced leather and invented an overcoat made of oilcloth (*waakrok*). This new clothing became the Cape's original style of slave apparel. As leather jackets could not be lined, the company added an extra provision of shirts. With these changes, simplified shirts made of coarse cotton circulated more widely.

In contrast, the records indicated that the garments for female company slaves had a stronger Asian character. Mentzel noted that these garments were 'imported smocks from Batavia' that were 'made up of six yards of coarse cotton cloth', thus, ready-made.[37] It is not entirely clear what Mentzel meant by smocks, but as noted in the previous section, by then '*vrouwenkleedje* (women's simplified clothing/skirt)', or '*baaijtes* (Batavian-style shirts)' became a popular product worn at various Dutch locales. It is highly likely that smocks were connected to these. The clothing style of company female slaves was not specified further, with Mentzel simply noting '[the slaves] should wear it according to customs.' The fact that the slave lodge also operated as a brothel and female slaves were often forced into prostitution would have added another dimension

to what they wore. Figure 5.8 is the possible representation of the VOC lodgement in the Cape. Female slaves are shown wearing two different types of attire,
which were distinctively Asian and clearly differentiated from what the Dutch
wives of the employees wore.[38]

The clothing for urban and farm slaves can be traced from probate inventories, auction records and individual account books. These sources confirm that
urban and farm slaves were given garment combinations similar to the clothing
of other slaves: in one record, male slaves were given one unlined pilot cloth
jacket annually, along with a pair of sailcloth breeches; in another record, male
slaves received a 'cloth (*pije*) jacket and some coarse *vaderlandsche* (homeland)
shirts' each year, and they were promised two new sets of clothing per year.
The same record noted female slaves being given skirts (*rokken*), two jackets
(*baytjes* or *cabaaijen*), or half shirts, therefore quite similar to the style of clothing
that Batavian female slaves wore, although we should be careful to determine
that the garments were the same.[39]

Additionally, the clothing of urban and farm slaves could have a range of variations depending on the rank and taste of slave owners. Sumptuary laws provide
hints on the variety allowed for slave clothing, owned by different ranks. Existing regulations were summed up and synthesized in the sumptuary law in 1755,

FIGURE 5.8 'Interior of the Lodgment of Ceylon or Cape with the Employees of the
VOC and their Wives and Servants', by Esaias Boursse (VOC draughtsman),
1662–1671, 14.8 × 19.6 cm.

Source: Rijksmuseum, Amsterdam NG-1996-6-116.

closely following the Batavian code in 1752 and 1755.[40] Table 5.2 summarizes how slaves were supposed to dress according to the status of their owners. Only the highest-ranked officers of VOC, or their wives, were allowed to dress their slaves in livery.[41] Lower-ranked officers were allowed to dress up to a third of their servants in livery. However, to distinguish slaves, it was the custom to forbid shoes and hats among the enslaved, a global practice as a marker of their status, shared in Batavia and the Americas.[42] In the Cape Colony, coachmen were the only exception to this rule.

It is worth mentioning again that slave clothing could be in mixed styles; both Asian and European styles were mentioned in all of the rank groups.[43] Among the slaves of higher-ranked officials, for example, there was a growing trend to costume their slaves in the Malay style, a contrast to the wearing of European-style livery. What 'Malay style' meant was not entirely clear, but given the slave clothing's strong linkage to Batavian styles, they likely reflected the craze adopted in Batavia or Indian colonial settlements of clothing slaves in extravagant style.[44] The usage of gold and silver threads and buttons or silk was repeatedly banned for slaves, but the quest for dressing slaves in connection to the styles in Batavia never ceased. Although multiple sumptuary laws were introduced to restrict slave clothing into simpler forms, ironically, as we have seen, these did not help make slave clothing cheaper. Sumptuary laws for slave clothing were not meant merely to keep clothing simple but had complicated functions to allow clothing to be stratified according to the rank of the owners, updating and strengthening their links with Batavian colonial strata, as well as to underline visually that slaves were different from others. Thus, it was no wonder that sumptuary details for slave clothing became more specific and detailed over time.

These sumptuary laws did not specify the fabrics used for slave clothing as did administrators for the Batavian orphanage. The overall principle was that the fabrics worn by slaves should be 'coarse, cheap and strong'. No specific place names were noted as major suppliers of these cloths, a commodity that could be supplied from many regions.[45] One record indicated that cloth was 'blue or red linen, striped or checked upon desire'. The blue or red 'linen' mentioned here could be *vaderlandsche* (homeland) linen, half-bleached or dyed, but it could also

TABLE 5.2 Sumptuary law for slaves in the Cape

High-rank VOC officials	Livery allowed (without shoes but possibly hats)Or 'Malay style'
Low-rank VOC officials	Livery allowed for up to a third of their slaves
Merchants and below	Blue or red linen, striped or checked as owners' desire No hats or coats except for coachmen No shoes in general Woollen possible, but totally plain, without any colour in the collars or cuffs

be gingham and others that were striped and in blue and/or red that were supplied from a wide range of places in South and South East Asia. It is symbolic
that in the 1730s, VOC Company Official J. N. Dessin ordered 'blue coarse
cloth for slave clothing' from the Netherlands and 'fine and common slave
cloth' from the East. Sumptuary laws approved 'woollen, but totally plain, without any colour in collars or cuffs' for winter clothing.[46]

Obviously, the less the slave owner had a connection with the VOC and the
more remote their residence the more difficult it was to manage slave clothing.
It was at farmhouses where shortages of slave clothing were most often noted.
However, slave clothing in farmhouses in the Table Valley area at least did not
necessarily differ from what was provided for urban slaves. One record indicated
that adult male slaves were provided annually 'two pairs of trousers and a coat
or a camisool (short workman's jacket)', whereas female slaves were given a skirt
and some fabrics for shirts.[47] In another probate inventory of a 1761 Table
Valley household, we see some examples where these items were intended for
domestic slaves. The household had 14 slaves and 4 related slave children. Two
male slaves received six blue and six white slave shirts, respectively, to be divided among the slaves. One female slave called Liesje was provided with two
pieces of printed chintz and one piece of striped gingham, chintz and white
linen. In this case, the goods that the slaves were given fit the previous records
and regulations discussed above. Many farms stored piles of ready-made or semi-
ready-made clothing, for future use, mentioned as 'slave clothing', 'slave trousers' or 'slave frocks' in the records. In addition, they ordered slave clothing,
such as leather trousers, to be made in quantity by Cape Town shoemakers or
bought second-hand clothing when they came to Cape Town.[48]

It is striking that several farm account records indicate that the cost of slave-
clothing expenditure was not necessarily higher than that for company slaves. The
average cost for feeding and clothing slaves in the company was 15–16 *Rijks-
daalders* (Rd), per person, in the mid-eighteenth century. But according to several
account books at that period, farmhouses were managing to keep a slave's annual
clothing expenditure around 5–7 Rd. Moreover, despite the reliance on irregular
import supply and lack of retail shops and professional clothing traders, the annual
slave-clothing expenditure in the middle of eighteenth century Cape Colony was
remarkably inexpensive compared with the later nineteenth century, when bans
for shops were lifted in the colony and general textile price fell. According to the
annual expenditure documents of the slave owners running farms outside of Cape
Town, the annual cost per slave of providing clothing increased significantly at
the turn of the eighteenth century, from 5 Rd in 1744 to 7 Rd in 1787 and 9.4
Rd in another record in 1789. Prices rose as high as 15 Rd by the end of the
eighteenth century and reached 21 Rd in 1827.[49]

Although these records are random and not available from the same farm,
these figures are revealing in three respects. First, the amount of 5–7 Rd was
one-quarter to a sixth of the contemporary clothing expenditure for the lowest
ranks of soldiers of the VOC, which was reported to be 30 Rd.[50] Second,

TABLE 5.3 Price for wheat, white wine and clothing for slaves, 1716–1800

Year	Wheat (per mud)	White wine (per league)	Slave-clothing expenditure, per annum, per person (year of the document) (Rd)
1716	2.0	21	
1720	2.2	22	
1730	2.4	26	
1740	2.4	28	5 (1744)
1750	1.6	30	
1760	1.5	38	
1770	1.0	22	
1780	2.4	38	
1790	2.6	35	7 (1787), 9.4 (1789)
1800	2.8	30	15 (1801)
1827	–	–	21

Source: Nigel Worden, *Slavery in Dutch South Africa* (Cambridge: Cambridge University Press, 1985), 70; and Nigel Worden, ed. *Contingent Lives: Social Identity and Material Culture in the VOC World* (Cape Town: University of Cape Town Press, 2007), 60; MOOC 10/1–10/8 Vendurollen (Auction Records) 1716–1800.

Note: The official price for wheat until 1741 was 2.6 Rd and company price after 1741 was 2.5 Rd. The official price for white wine until 1741 was 27 Rd.

neither the political turmoil accompanying the transition to British rule nor inflation could explain this rise entirely. As shown in Table 5.3, changes in the average nominal auction prices of wheat and white wine from 1716 to 1800, as detailed in the probate inventory, rose much less steeply.[51] Third, it is remarkable for Cape slave owners to achieve such low clothing price before the 1780s, when cotton textile prices dropped sharply in both British and Dutch commercial circuits.[52] Therefore, it can be assumed that Cape slave owners managed, through some means, to develop a cheap range of clothing during the eighteenth century.

Fabrics for slave clothing and their long-term price trends

The secret to this lower cost was in the supply of clothing, rather than cheaper cloth. To investigate the fabrics used for slave clothing in the Cape Colony and how these slave fabrics and clothing were valued (e.g. how much its value could depreciate), this study surveyed the probate inventories and auction records of Cape Town from 1697 to 1779.[53]

An inventory recorded in 1718 provides good evidence that, by this time, there were options available for slave-clothing fabrics that were cheaper than European blue linen that had been customarily used for slave shirts (Table 5.4). Leather, sailcloth (*zijldoek*) and Indian cloth, such as striped *bafta* from Bengal or inferior gingham, were all cheaper than blue linen. Additionally, during the

TABLE 5.4 Slave clothing-related textiles listed in the inventory of 1718

	Amount (Rd)	Quantities (units)	Price per unit (Rd)
Zeemleer (leather possibly sheepskin)	33	22	1.10
Hollants zeyldoek (sailcloth from Holland)	180	5 rolls	4–4.50
Blauw linnen (blue linen)	81	12	6.15
Bengaals zeyldoek (sailcloth from Bengal)	27	4.5	6
Bengaals gestreept bast (striped bast from Bengal)	26.5	7	3.15
Tutucorynsse chitsen (Indian Chintz)	157.10	21	7.10
Gingham	27	3	9
Inferior gingham	4.10	1	4.10

Source: MOOC 8/3.93

eighteenth century, varieties of cotton cloth produced in India or South East Asia were also used for slave clothing. *Fotas (photas)*, *niquanias* and *selamporis* that were used for Batavian orphanage slaves appear in a few probate inventories, and the majority of these were priced considerably lower than the cheapest European alternatives. Besides these textile varieties, *bouling*, *chintz* and *geras*, which commonly featured cheap and strong clothes, often striped or checked in bright colours such as red or blue, or *chelas* or *celas* (red cotton), *mourin* (muslins), were recorded as popularly used for slave clothing.[54] It is, thus, confirmed that a broad range of Indian textiles were used for slave clothing.

We can summarize from here that although various Indian fabrics were actually used for slave clothing, being cheaper than the Dutch fabrics customarily used for slave clothing, sail cloth or leather were the only materials that could have completely met the demand to make clothing as cheap as was suggested in the annual slave-clothing expenditure. However, these materials presented problems with respect to comfort and could not substitute for all categories of slave clothing. Slaves were actually provided with 'linen', both blue or unbleached linen or Indian stripes and checks, according to the consensus of both contemporary observations and historians' accounts. Gingham and other types of cloth did not become established as fixed slave clothing, at least during the eighteenth century. It was impossible to supply a fabric that was reliably cheaper. Other factors came into play to reduce the costs of slave clothing.

The power of local clothing circulation

The supply of imported ready-made and second-hand clothing in Cape played a vital role in making slave clothing cheap. In the first instance, the clothing circulated by the VOC, described in the first section of this chapter, was very popular in the Cape. We can find ample examples of these imports in Cape probate inventories and auction records throughout the eighteenth century. It is easy to confirm that these were used to clothe slaves and were even designated specifically for slave clothing from the outset, especially for female slave clothing. It is worth emphasizing that one VOC regulation decreed that the clothing of female company slaves should be ready-made apparel supplied from Batavia.

What is even more striking is the low price of these garments in the Cape. Overall, the clothing sold at auctions was not very expensive. Despite the ban on the retail shops, Cape residents stockpiled garments sent from elsewhere and dealt in them as a commercial enterprise, even if informally. One such person was Deborah Koning, who is referred to as one of the richest women in the Cape during eighteenth century.[55] At her large-scale probate auctions in the 1730s, 25 new red coats that were imported and arrived from Batavia after her death were later sold on. For this case, we can confirm the products were new. Each coat was valued at around 3 Rd. This study assumed the new items' prices by looking at persons who had stockpiles of them. In a 1751 inventory, '14 rough [sets of] clothing (*groove kleedjes*) were evaluated at 30 Rd', suggesting 2.1 Rd per set, and '7 separate [sets of] coast clothing (*7 enkelde kustkleedjes*)' at 8 Rd, thus 1.1 Rd per set.[56] The latter could have been second-hand (worn-out) clothing, given its description as 'separate'. It is clear that imported ready-made clothing was predominantly cheap; for luxurious apparel, it was more common to import high-quality fabrics and have them tailored in Cape Town. Ready-made items were more commonly directed to the lower class or as items to be sold elsewhere, including as slave apparel.

Popularly traded clothing by the VOC, such as *zijlkleden* (sailing/sailors clothes) mentioned above, circulated through the Cape. At one auction in 1745, two sets of rough *zijlkleden* were sold at 6 Rd and one rough and one fine set for 4.3 Rd. In 1771, seven pieces of 'Bengal sail clothing' were sold for 21 Rd, thus 3 Rd per garment.[57] Deborah Koning, mentioned above, traded in piles of sail clothing. At her estate sale, 73 pieces of 'fine sail clothing' (*doesoetjes of fijne zylkleeden*) were sold at a price of 3.3–4.1 Rd per piece to 37 different buyers. There was such a convenient accessibility to ready-made clothing from Batavia that mid-eighteenth-century citizens of Cape Town could expect to buy brand-new 'wearable' attire supplied from Bengal at about 3–4 Rd. It is then understandable that slave owners would only expect to spend 5 Rd per annum on slave clothing, as they were integrated into a global supply network (Table 5.5).

Furthermore, from the inventories and auction records, we could easily assume second-hand clothing was even cheaper than these ready-made goods. There is a record of three pieces of *gemeene kleedjes* being valued at 2.12 Rd; thus, the price per piece was below 1 Rd. Skirts made of chintz, called *Bengalse rok*, were sold at auction for an average of 2 Rd, but many pieces were sold for 0.3 to 0.4 Rd. Moreover, at an auction in 1735, fabrics and clothing possessed by a household, including eight shirts, eight handkerchiefs, four shirts, two gingham camisoles, two blankets, six pairs of socks and more, were valued at a total of 5 Rd, which is the same amount as the expected

TABLE 5.5 Prices of imported ready-made and second-hand clothing in inventories, 1740–1775

Imported ready-made clothing from Batavia	Price per set (Rd)
1740	Red coats	3
1740	Coarse sets of clothing	2.1
1740	Loose sets of coast clothing (possibly used)	1.1
1751	New sail clothing	3
1745	New fine sail clothing	4.3
Imported second-hand clothing	
1753	Set of general clothing	0.7
1740s	Bengal skirt (skirt made of chintz or other printed cloth)	0.3–2
1735	Eight shirts, eight handkerchiefs, four shirt-wears, two gingham camisoles, two blankets, six pairs of socks	5
1775	Six pairs of standard striped slave trousers and four slave *rok*	1.36

annual expenditure for slave clothing.[58] Second-hand slave apparel was given an even lower valuation, as illustrated in a probate inventory from 1775: six pairs of standard striped slave trousers and four slave *rok* were valued at 1.36 Rd.[59] If such sets were circulated frequently, then finding cheap clothing would not have been difficult. Thus, clothing depreciated in value much faster than cloth through heavy wear. Fabrics could be stored and expected to be traded at a relatively stable price; but once made into clothing and worn, its value declined sharply.[60]

The existence of vibrant second-hand circulation channels is crucial in realizing this depreciation of clothing. It might feel strange that the Cape Colony, where shops were banned by VOC, could demonstrate such active commercial circuits. However, as I have discussed elsewhere, it was precisely the lack of formal retailers that led to flourishing private exchange among individuals and households.[61] Without this category of informal circulation, one could also not explain why Cape Town achieved such a high level of 'luxury item' possession that surpassed even that of Amsterdam, as recently analysed by Johan Fourie.[62] The extent and vigour of private exchange astonished a contemporary observer, Otto Mentzel, whose observations are insightful:

> No matter how [the commodities were] acquired, the fact remains that every man in the town, be he a free burgher, officer, *pasganger* (in transit) or free worker, yea even common soldier is at the same time huckster and trader.[63]

Even slaves themselves were not excluded from joining these transactions. Mentzel observed that even if the slaves received such an outfit (in this case coarse close-fitting woollen doublet and trousers) once a year, the majority of them are so depraved and besotted that they sell this rig-out almost as soon as they get it and go about all the year round in the filthiest rags imaginable.[64]

Selling garments for cash or exchange of goods is a long-held practice. As slaves were often deprived of other means of assets, provided clothing became their important assets.[65] Nigel Worden and Karel Schoeman and other Cape historians generally evaluate clothing provisions, no matter for company, urban or farm slaves, as 'not enough' and that the provision of one set of clothing could easily have worn out in a year. However, they also contemplated why in several contemporary paintings, as well as in travellers' observations, slaves depicted were particularly underdressed.

While graphic depictions of ragged slaved could have served didactic purposes as elsewhere, it is highly likely Cape slaves, with opportunities for exchange, did not use the provided clothing themselves as intended, particularly in the case of urban slaves. Although households needed quite a number of slaves just to keep the basic household activities going, households were not always making enough profit in themselves to make ends meet, given the number of slaves they owned. Thus, in-house slaves often went outside to work with their wages going to their owners. Although operating shops was prohibited, it was legal to let in-house slaves hawk or peddle around Cape Town. As a result, quite a few urban slaves worked as peddlers in the streets and going to ships at anchor. In return they would pay 'coelie geld' to their masters, but they could keep some part for themselves. Moreover, other slaves acquired skills as artisans. Therefore, there was considerable opportunity for slaves to trade their items or to find some rags for exchange.

In 1771, an order was issued that prohibited buying, selling and bartering slave clothing.[66] Thus, although no direct documents were left confirming that they exchanged their annual provisions into other items, urban slaves most likely considered their clothing not only as attire but also as goods for exchange. Furthermore, if slaves had regular access to rags, they would utilize that opportunity to trade as well. Farm slaves, meanwhile, would have had fewer opportunities to peddle their products in Cape Town. Although in principle slave owners had the fullest agency in providing cloth and clothing for slaves, we should not omit the capacity slaves had to serve their own clothing priorities.

Conclusion

This chapter explored the contours and impacts of clothing circulated globally by the VOC in the eighteenth century. It aimed to link the global and local circulation, not only to highlight the connectivity between places and people or the transregional diffusion of the items, but also to see their impact: the co-creation of a new cheaper product range, the place-making and the reformatting of social orders in a colonial settlement where we can observe a hitherto less-studied aspects of circulations.

This chapter focused on trends in slave cloth and clothing in eighteenth-century Cape Town, highlighting the development of a cheaper product range. In a unique colonial environment, such as Cape Town, where no fabrics were manufactured and no shops were allowed, individual slave owners, whether living in a Cape Town settlement or on a farm, faced the task of arranging cheaper cloth and clothing for their slaves. One could not rely on a constant supply of coarse and cheap textiles from the European homeland or other production centres. In addition, no local professional supplier seems to have specialized in slave cloth or clothing. The supply and distribution of cloth and clothing were executed through private exchanges centring on houses and auctions, and slave apparel was no exception to this, not withstanding that the VOC was critically important in the organization of manufacturing and distribution. Attention was paid to balancing price, durability and appropriateness among the varieties of arbitrarily acquired cloth and clothing.

Slave owners in the Cape Colony experienced relatively lower expenditure on annual slave clothing in the eighteenth century than in the first half of the nineteenth century. Slave expenditure increased rapidly at the turn of the century, when Dutch rule was replaced by British rule, and prices for cloth and clothing kept increasing. Worden and other historians attributed the cost increases simply to inflation. However, there are other complexities within the global narrative for this, as the price of cotton both in Britain and the Netherlands was rapidly dropping since the 1780s. The increased availability of cotton cloth towards the turn of the century was not focused on ubiquitous and cheap manufactured cloth, and thus did not lead to lower prices for cloth and clothing everywhere. From the local point of view, there was even the possibility that what was formerly cheap became more expensive or harder to find and as a result even the cheapest range became more expensive. This leads us to question what enabled eighteenth-century Cape Town residents to arrange for cheap slave cloth and clothing.

Suggested answers to this question can be found in probate inventories and auction records and point to the following factors. First, the use of locally available leather as basic, coarse materials is clear; their cost remained low. Second, the wide availability of Indian textiles from multiple areas of India, Malaya and the Indonesian islands was deeply intertwined with provisions for slave clothing. It is impossible to single out a limited range of fabrics solely used for slave clothing. Nor did fabrics used for slave clothing, such as ginghams and guineas, become steadily cheaper and remain fixed for the purpose, as *osnaburgs* or *dowles* did for slave-clothing dress in North America. Each of the Asian fabrics was made in a variety of qualities and prices. Professional traders or shops for both textiles in general or slave clothing in particular were officially banned by regulation; thus, the locals discerned the fabric quality and price by piece and then reached an agreed price according to the condition and quality of the textile in the nexus of their private exchanges. Auctions also remained a vital and consistent part of this commercial paradigm. Under this type of circulation, no fixed labels for slave clothing were established.

Nevertheless, as demonstrated in the third point here, a more institutionalized supply chain supported the provision of slave clothing in the Cape Colony: the practice of ordering ready-made clothing regularly from India. The VOC itself was instrumental in harnessing and mobilizing these resources and facilitating the distribution of these clothing commodities. Here too we can confirm the remarkable existence of a global circulation of simple, basic ready-made clothing. This phenomenon is increasingly observed by researchers seeking to identify the institutional supply chains of clothing for sailors and soldiers in the Indian Ocean territories and beyond.[67] This chapter adds critical new evidence, including the pricing of these ready-made goods at the local level. Despite the long distance they travelled and non-professional and regulated ways they were ordered and distributed, prices were kept low, especially in relation to the local fabric prices. Ready-made clothing supplied from Indian production areas was stockpiled in private homes. Varying in quality and price, they were utilized by a range of individuals in society, in terms of rank, as slave and casual clothing.

Finally, owing to the availability of these ready-made items, clothing in general was valued at relatively cheaper prices. This sheds new light on the wide availability of wearable second-hand clothing in local circulation at this distinctive colonial way station, part of the global trade network. As well, it demonstrates how rapidly this clothing depreciated in its recirculation in comparison to the fabrics. Its sheer low value contributed fundamentally in providing cheaper slave clothing. In sum, the active consumer exchanges in this entrepôt were indispensable in providing low-cost slave apparel in the Cape Colony: private exchanges (auctions, face-to-face trade among acquaintances and bartering) and deals for second-hand items are normally thought to make prices arbitrary and irregular and thus higher. However, private exchanges and estate sales in Cape Town seemed to have provided a platform for pricing that realistically reflected consumers' needs. Cheaper items, like luxury items, were created globally and locally. Reflecting many global contexts, a cheaper range of cloth and clothing was made locally.

Notes

1 I am extremely grateful to Beverly Lemire for her close reading and encouragement to explore broader meanings. Of course, I am responsible for any errors. This work was supported by the Japan Society for the Promotion of Science (JSPS) KAKENHI Grant Numbers 15H03233 and 15KK0059.
2 John Styles, 'Involuntary Consumers? Servants and Their Clothes in Eighteenth-Century England', *Textile History* 33.1 (2002): 9–21.
3 See the latest synthesis in Beverly Lemire, *Global Trade and the Transformations of Consumer Cultures: The Material World Remade* (Cambridge, UK: Cambridge University Press, 2018), 114–135.
4 For the overview on research on runaway slaves, see Rebecca Fifield, '"Had on When She Went Away … ": Expanding the Usefulness of Garment Data in American

Runaway Advertisements 1750–1790 Through Database Analysis', *Textile History* 42.1 (2011): 80–102; and Jonathan Prude, 'To Look Upon the 'Lower Sort': Runaway Ads and the Appearance of Unfree Laborers in America, 1750–1800', *Journal of American History* 78.1 (1991): 124–159. See also Masako Hamada, *A Social Study of the Clothing of the Virginian Slaves in Revolutionary America* (Tokyo: Tokyodō Shuppan, 2002).

5 Carole Shammas, *Pre-Industrial Consumer in England and America* (New York: Oxford University Press, 1990), 99, table 4.9.

6 Izumi Takeda, 'Positioning Irish Coarse Linens in an Eighteenth-Century Global Context', in *Linking Cloth Clothing Globally: Transformations in Use and Value c.1600–1900*, ed. Miki Sugiura (Tokyo: ICES, 2019). See also Izumi Takeda, *Spinning the British Industrial Revolution from Flax and Cotton: The Irish Linen Industry and the Atlantic Market* (Kyoto: Minerva Shobō, 2013). For recent analysis of cheaper linen in Silesia, see Anka Steffen and Klaus Weber, 'Spinning and Weaving for the Slave Trade: Proto-Industry in Eighteenth-Century Silesia', in *Slavery Hinterland: Transatlantic Slavery and Continental Europe, 1680–1850*, ed. Felix Brahm and Eve Rosenhaft (Woodbridge, UK: Boydell, 2016), 87–108; Anka Steffen 'Silesians and Slaves: How Linen Textiles Connected East-Central Europe, Africa and the Americas', paper presented at the Dressing Global Bodies Conference, University of Alberta, Edmonton, 7–9 July 2016.

⑦ Giorgio Riello, *Cotton: The Fabric That Made the Modern World* (Cambridge, UK: Cambridge University Press, 2013), 137–139. For circulation of fabrics by the Dutch East India Company, see Ruurdje Laarhovern, 'The Power of Cloth: The Textile Trade of the Dutch East India Company (VOC), 1600–1780' (Unpublished PhD Thesis, Australian National University, 1994).

8 See Miki Sugiura, 'Garments for Slaves and Fabrics for Sail: Textile Circulations by the Dutch India Company in the Indian Ocean World', in Sugiura, *Linking Cloth-Clothing Globally*, 71–91.

9 In the eighteenth-century probate inventories three is only one record of weaving and nine of the spinning wheel. Schoeman noted one attempt in 1771 to make home-spun slave cloth, which failed. Karel Schoeman, *Portrait of a Slave Society: The Cape of Good Hope, 1717–1795* (Pretoria: Protea Book House, 2012).

10 See a contemporary observer's record on auction in Otto Mentzel, *A Geographical and Topographical Description of the Cape of Good Hope*, vol. II (Cape Town: The Van Riebeeck Society, 1921), originally published in German in 1787, ch. 15. See also Tracy Randle, 'Consuming Identities: Patterns of Consumption at Three Eighteenth-Century Cape Auctions', in *Modernity and the Second-Hand Trade*, ed. Jon Stobart and Ilja van Damme (London: Palgrave Macmillan, 2010), 220–241.

11 Miki Sugiura 'Overflooded with Goods Despite Shops? Women's Private Commodity Exchange in Eighteenth-Century Cape Town', in *Sekaishi no naka no Joseitachi* [Women in world history], ed. Mariko Mizui, Yoko Matsui and Miki Sugiura (Tokyo: Bensei Shuppan, 2015), 195–204; and Miki Sugiura 'Between Material Affluence and Share: Women's Private Commodity Exchange in the Eighteenth Century Cape Town', in *Moving Around: People, Things and Practices in Consumer Culture*, ed. Hiroki Shin, Shinobu Majima and Y. Tanaka (Tokyo: Forum for History of Consumer Culture, 2015), 261–270.

12 E. C. Godée Molsbergen, *Reizen in Zuid-Afrika in de Hollandse tijd. Deel III. Tochten langs de Z.O.-kust en naar het Oosten 1670–1752* (The Hague: Martinus Nijhof, 1922).

13 VOC Archive, The Hague. There are records that ships from Bengal carried a considerable amount of *zijlkleden* and some *zijlkleden* were stocked in a mass at the storage of VOC in Batavia.

14 'Staet van Verscheide Takken van den Nederlandschen Koophandel voor den Jare MDCCLXV', in *Nederlandsche Jaerboken, inhoudende een Verhael an de Merkwaerdigste Gescheidenissen, die voorgevallen zyn binnen den omtrek der vereenigde provintien, federt het begin des jaers MDCCXLVII*, vol. 19 (Leiden: Pieter van der Eyk, 1765); 'Staet van

Verscheidene Tak van den Nderlandschen Koophandel over den Jare 1783', in *Nieuwe Nederlandsche Jaerboken, of Vervolg der merkwaerdigste*, vol. 33 (Leiden: Pieter van der Eyk, 1783), 2216.

15 See note 10. In a 1783 list, 400 pieces of *Sjappafarriers of gedrukte Vrouwe kleedjes* (*sjappafarries*, or pattern-printed women's clothing) were mentioned.

16 *Nederlandsche Gedenkboek of Europische Mercurius*, vol. 1 (The Hague, Netherlands: F. H. Scheurleer, 1753), 221.

17 Prijslijsten van de veilingen, Gedrukut, 1698–1791. N.A. 1.0402/6985; 1763.

18 In the original texts: *Chappa Sari of gedr. Vrouwe Kleedjes tot 11 3/4 gl't ps., Dito of ongedrukte dito tot 9 ¼'t ps*, Prijslijsten van de veilingen, Gedrukut, 1698–1791. N.A. 1.0402/6985; 1763.

19 J. De Rovere van Breugel, 'Beschrijving van Bantam', in *Bijdragen tot de Taal-, Land- en Volkenkunde van Nederlandsch-Indië*, vol. 5 (Amsterdam: F. Muller, 1787), 331.

20 Prijslijsten van de veilingen, Gedrukut, 1698–1791. N.A. 1.0402/6985, 1698. The Island of Buton is situated in the south of Slaweshi, more than 1,000 kilometres away from Batavia.

21 The items categorized as '*kleeren* (clothes)' in this context are better translated as textile manufactures, as they often included both fabrics and clothes and other textile products.

22 Plakaat of 1656, in J. A. van der Chijs, ed., *Nederlandsch-Indisch Plakaatboek, 1602–1811. Vol. 2 (1642–77)* (Batavia: Landsdrukkerij, 1886), 213–215. Also Plakaat of 1664 in the same volume, 384–386.

23 Plakaat of 15 August 1660, in van der Chijs, *Nederlandsch-Indisch Plakaatboek. Vol. 2 (1642–77)*, 316–318.

24 Plakaat of 17 March and 25 March 1669, in van der Chijs, *Nederlandsch-Indisch Plakaatboek. Vol. 2 (1642–62)*, 521 and 536.

25 *Verbod om venden*, see prohibition at 1648, 1653 and 1660, also in van der Chijs, *Nederlandsch-Indisch Plakaatboek. Vol. 2 (1642–62)*.

26 'Reglement voor het weeshuis te Batavia', in J. A. van der Chijs, ed., *Nederlandsch-Indisch Plakaatboek, 1602–1811. Vol. 6 (1750–54)* (Batavia: Landsdrukkerij, 1886), 209–211.

27 Rebecca Earle, 'The Pleasures of Taxonomy: Casta Paintings, Classification, and Colonialism' *William and Mary Quarterly* 73.3 (2016): 434.

28 Definition cited from glossary of VOC terms at http://resources.huygens.knaw.nl/vocglossarium/vocoutp (accessed 30 December 2018).

29 Nigel Worden, *Slavery in Dutch South Africa* (Cambridge, UK: Cambridge University Press, 1985).

30 For the estimation of slaves, see Worden, *Slavery*, 10–11; see also Johan Fourie, 'The Wealth of the Cape Colony: Measurements from Probate Inventories.' *Working Paper 268*, Stellenbosch University, 2012.

31 Johan Fourie and Jan Luiten van Zanden, 'GDP in the Dutch Cape Colony: The National Accounts of a Slave-Based Society', *South African Journal of Economics* 81–84 (2013): 467–490.

32 Further outside the port, the areas of Stellenbosch and Drakenstein developed wineries, but probate inventories from these areas are not addressed extensively in this chapter.

33 For a survey of the VOC records on slave clothing see Karel Schoeman, *Early Slavery at the Cape of Good Hope, 1652–1717* (Pretoria: Protea, 2007), 143–149; Karel Shoeman, *Portrait of a Slave Society*, 112–121. See also Nigel Worden, *Cape Town Between East and West: Social Identities in a Dutch Colonial Town* (Hilversum: Jacana, Verloren, 2012), 92.

34 From 1723, provisioning became annual, but slaves continued to be supplied both summer and winter clothing. The trousers and doublet were tailored first by the company's other soldiers and, later in the century, by private tailors in Cape Town. Shoeman, *Portraits*, 213–215.

35 Valentijn, a contemporary manumitted VOC male slave, referred to cloth distributed twice annually of sailcloth (*zijldoeken*) and blue linen. Schoeman, *Early Slavery*, 145.
36 Therefore, male slave clothing in the Cape Colony is more similar to what was provided for lower-rank sailors of VOC.
37 Worden, *Slavery*, 92; Karel Schoeman, *Early Slavery at the Cape Town*, 148.
38 There is possibility that this is the depiction of lodgement of Ceylon.
39 Karel Schoeman, *Early Slavery*, 146 and 148.
40 For the sumptuary law of 1755 and 1765, see Robert DuPlessis, *The Material Atlantic: Clothing, Commerce, and Colonization in the Atlantic* (Cambridge, UK: Cambridge University Press 2016), Robert Ross, *Clothing. A Global History* (Cambridge, UK: Polity Press, 2008); and Worden, *Cape Town*, among others.
41 Livery is the clothing worn by elites' servants. That adopted by the officers of VOC had a rather outdated extravagance, with hybridized ornamental elements.
42 DuPlessis, *The Material Atlantic*. Manumitted slaves bought hats, stockings and shoes to show they were free.
43 Schoeman noted this style as 'Westernized' or 'semi-Westernized'. Karel Shoeman, *Portrait of a Slave Society*, 212. However, from the above analysis, I stress that it was a 'mixed' style.
44 A distinguishing style was forming interacting with the Batavian colonial settlements in the Malay strata. See Peter Lee, Sarong *Kebaya: Peranakan Fashion in an Interconnected World, 1500–1950* (Singapore: Asian Civilizations Museum, 2014). For Batavian extravagance, Boxer provides detailed account. See Charles R. Boxer, *Dutch Seaborne Empire* (London: Penguin, [1965] 1990).
45 Many fabrics are identified by place names or named with place names (e.g. Chinese linen in the probate inventories). The names ranged from Middle and Far East (Armoesijn = Ormuz (Persia), Gilang = Gilan (Persia), West Africa (Guinees = Guinea), Thailand (Salempoeris/Salemporis/Serampore/Zalemporis/Siamoes) and different locations in India: Coast (= Coromandel Coast), Surat, Bengal, Malay, Tutucorin, Chinese and Japanese.
46 Schoeman, *Portrait of a Slave Society*, 213–215.
47 Schoeman, *Portrait of a Slave Society*, 218.
48 Worden *Slavery*, 92; Schoeman, *Portrait of a Slave Society*, 428.
49 Worden, *Slavery*, 70. There are also random records from rich households that spent 15 Rd annually for slave clothing in 1740s as well.
50 Van der Chijs, *Nederlandsch-Indisch Plakaatboek. Vol. 6 (1750–54)*.
51 Furthermore, demand for slave clothing was not growing at this time: the increase in slave population was much more rapid in the latter half of the eighteenth century. Owing to the lack of direct import records in Cape Town, it is not yet possible to investigate directly why slave clothing did not become cheaper but rather more expensive in the nineteenth century.
52 The 1780s marked the watershed when cotton prices dropped sharply in British commercial circuits, with the value of both calico and muslin almost halved between 1780 and 1800. Stephen Broadberry and Bishnupriya Gupta, 'Cotton Textiles and the Great Divergence: Lancashire, India and Shifting Competitive Advantage, 1600–1850'. Paper presented at IISG, www.iisg.nl/hpw/factormarkets.php (accessed 8 September 2018); Stephen Broadberry and Bishnupriya Gupta, 'Lancashire, India and Shifting Competitive Advantage in Cotton Textiles, 1700–1850: The Neglected Role of Factor Prices', *Economic History Review*, 62.2 (2009): 302.
53 TANAP, Inventories of the Orphan Chamber Cape Town Archives Repository, South Africa, http://databases.tanap.net/mooc (hereforth MOOC) (accessed 25 January 2019).
54 See for explanation of fabrics used for slave clothing, www.tanap.net/_glossary_Kaap DeGoedeHoop/index.html (accessed 18 September 2018).
55 Also assessed in Tracy Randle, 'Consuming Identities: Patterns of Consumption'.

56 MOOC 8/7.18, 1751/6/22.

57 MOOC 8/13.65, 1771.

58 MOOC 10/4.14.

59 MOOC 8/15.41.

60 I have argued elsewhere that when one compares the inventories and auctions, less clothing was sold at auction than any other items, as clothing was more often divided up among household members. Miki Sugiura, 'Women and Her Possessions Second-hand, Cape Town Women's Inventories in the Eighteenth Century', in *World History Written with Women in Perspective*, ed. Miki Sugiura, M. Mizui, Y. Matsui, A. Ota and T. Fushimi (Tokyo: Bensei Shuppan, 2016).

61 Miki Sugiura, 'Between Material Affluence and Share'.

62 Johan Fourie, 'The Remarkable Wealth of the Dutch Cape Colony: Measurements from Eighteenth-Century Probate Inventories', *Economic History Review* 66.2 (2013): 419–448.

63 Otto Mentzel, *A Geographical and Topographical Description*, 75.

64 Mentzel, *A Geographical and Topographical Description*, 124.

65 Although, in the Cape Colony, slaves had regular rations of tobacco. Mentzel, *A Geographical and Topographical Description*, 76 and 86.

66 As Worden points out, the original sentence of this law suggests persons of any rank or race could have been the seller or buyer. See note 60 in Worden, *Cape Town*.

67 Besides the works by Lemire mentioned in note 2, there is inspiring research made on the interactions between institutionally provided clothing and local residents. See G. Karskens, 'Red Coat, Blue Jacket, Black Skin: Aboriginal Men and Clothing in Early New South Wales', *Aboriginal History* 35 (2011): 1–36; Marshall Joseph Becker, 'Match Coats and the Military: Mass-Produced Clothing for Native Americans as Parallel Markets in the Seventeenth Century', *Textile History*, 41, suppl. 1 (2012): 153–181.

6

CLOTHING AS A MAP TO SENEGAMBIA'S GLOBAL EXCHANGES AT THE TURN OF THE NINETEENTH CENTURY

Jody Benjamin

'This cloth is for them such precious merchandise that they remain in admiration as they see pieces unfolded; just as we Europeans do with the gold these Marabouts sometimes bring to sell', wrote Pruneau de Pommegorge in his 1789 *Description de la Nigritie*. Late eighteenth-century written, visual and material sources on Senegambia suggest a broad range of interactions between western African consumers and traders within global textile markets. Large quantities of imported cloth were offloaded from ships near Saint Louis, Senegal and ferried ashore in canoes. They also flowed into Goree Island, and carried to ports along the Petite Cote south of contemporary Dakar and transported to many markets inland. The French slave trader Dominique Lamiral (1751–1800) wrote with equal parts outrage and marvel at how one process of local redistribution from the market to local people occurred as he saw it. Lamiral would receive visits from a local Moorish chief who, on an ordinary day, was not readily distinguishable as a figure of authority, being as 'badly dressed and poorly fed' as the poorest of his subjects. But on a trading day, the chief would turn up with an entourage of officials dressed in beautiful robes made of *pagnes* a locally woven strip-cloth. If the chief had no fine *pagnes* of his own, he would borrow some from a *signare*, one of the prominent female merchants in town known as doyennes of fashionable taste in Saint Louis. Negotiating prices, the chief would, 'march about with gravitas, look around with a disdainful air, and have [Lamiral's] words repeated to him by two interpreters even though he has well understood'.[1]

Once this performance resulted in an acceptable exchange of goods, the Moorish chief and his entourage returned home where, as Lamiral saw it, social distinctions appeared to fade away. Those referred to as 'slaves' in front of Lamiral were free enough to eat from the same bowl and smoke from the same pipe as their chief. Also, the Moorish chief would quickly distribute goods just obtained from the French, with 40 to 50 thousand French livres worth of merchandise – textiles, gunpowder, guns, accessories – given out within an hour or so: 'When the chief had given it all away, if his people were still not satisfied, they would take even his shirt, saying to him, "you can still give up the shirt, the whites will not refuse you something to wear"'.[2]

Lamiral, a staunch advocate for the slave trade during a period of revolutionary change in both France and its largest slave colony, Haiti, was no friendly observer of western Africans, despite his familiarity with Senegal. However, his description of trading suggests how the performance of power and status lubricated commercial negotiations in late eighteenth-century Saint Louis. His and other similar accounts also suggest something of the slipperiness of identification in which particular personas and claims could be made and unmade through dress. In Senegambia, cotton, as woven textiles, tailored garments and raw material, was a vital element of a political and a social economy that engaged a variety of social groupings that was heterogeneous in terms of language, ethnicity, religious practice and degree of wealth. Among them were merchant *signares*, riverboat labourers, European soldiers and merchants, Muslim clerics and itinerant traders, cooks, indigo dyers, enslaved persons, formerly enslaved persons and Catholic missionaries. By considering consumption and the clothing practices of this differentiated population, this chapter reveals something of the cultural logics underpinning western Africans' engagement with late eighteenth-century global markets and offers insight into shifting social relationships over time.

As a vital consumer item, cloth makes historically visible a broad range of West African actors that have sometimes been elided in the historiography of the Atlantic slave trade. Already diverse in ethnic, linguistic and religious affiliation, some western African populations of the late eighteenth century had a wide variety of aesthetic choices and ideological models to choose from in shaping their own identities. This chapter argues that the importation of a wide diversity of textiles, apparel and accessories was shaped substantially by local consumer tastes and contingencies, departing from the tendency to emphasize the impact of external forces. Instead I suggest how contingencies and tastes such as those derived from the Saint Louis *signares'* strategy of cultural alignment with both the French and their Muslim African trading partners, or the demand for indigo dyed cloth at Futa Tooro and at Gajaaga, had an impact on long-distance global exchange networks. People's choices were influenced by environmental change, the rise of an Islamic reform movement, migration caused by war and enslavement and the push–pull dynamics of commerce between the coast and interior regions along the Senegal River. At Saint Louis, numerous observers have noted the urbane, cosmopolitan ethos of merchant *signares* whose clothing and home furnishings combined the material elements and symbols of myriad places to construct themselves as powerful and honourable elites. But this cosmopolitanism was not limited to the Atlantic coast and could also be found in market centres and among certain especially mobile actors throughout the region. Attending to questions of consumption and fashion reveal western African consumers as actively participating in and shaping the global commerce in cotton textiles in the eighteenth and nineteenth centuries. This West African history of consumption and dress is entangled with the defining economic features of the eighteenth and nineteenth century globally: slavery, abolition, colonialism and industrialization. Tracing this history recovers the way dynamics within western Africa could and did make an impact on activities in other parts of the world. It also looks beyond the region's peripheralization by the rise of European capitalism, to historicize the politics of fashion within the region through its complex and cosmopolitan engagements with the global transformations of the turn of the nineteenth century.

In this chapter, I explore consumption and dress within the broader context of Senegambia in three sections. I begin by establishing the social and economic context of Saint Louis, the island trading settlement on the Atlantic coast that was the gateway to the Senegal River, and to the gold, slaves and other commodities sought by European trading companies. I then consider the heterogeneous nature of the settlement's population, the role of Eurafrican or *metis* habitants as merchants and taste makers of a Creole-dominated island society, as well as the range of textiles circulating in its ports and in the Senegal River trade to Gajaaga, several hundred kilometres inland. The following section considers evidence for the dress and material culture of a variety of 'everyday' people who inhabited, visited or worked in Saint Louis and the region with particular attention to *laptots*, a Wolof term for sailors, both enslaved and free, whose labour was critical to the movement of trade goods along the river. The final section reconnects the social transformations evident in coastal Saint Louis to the Islamic history of the broader region.

Saint Louis: cosmopolitanism at the gateway to the West African Sahel

Almost 10,000 people lived on the island of Saint Louis at the turn of the nineteenth century,[3] diverse in both religion and ethnicity, including speakers of Wolof, Hasaniya Arabic, Serer, Fulbe, Bamana, French and English. Its population grew throughout this period as a generation of slave-holding Eurafrican elite families gained wealth and political power from their control of the gum trade on the Senegal River. They did so through their affiliation with the French imperial project, their embrace of Catholicism, their adoption of French civil law, French cultural mores and metropolitan fashions to project respectability and status. Eurafrican *habitants* (the term referred originally to those in houses built close to the European fort on the island) were instrumental in helping France to regain control of Saint Louis by ousting the much-disliked British who controlled the town for two decades.

By the late eighteenth century, consumers in western Africa were enmeshed – along with those in western Europe, Asia and the Americas – in a global market for consumable goods such as textiles and clothing, accessories like glass and coral beads, hats, tools, cooking implements and raw materials such as dye woods, iron, precious metals, cowrie shells, leather hides, alcohol and foodstuff. The last quarter of the eighteenth century is widely associated with the political revolutions reshaping British and French empires, and their American colonies, but it was also a turbulent period within western Africa. In 1776, a group of Fulbe Muslim clerics seized power in Futa Tooro – an interior region that was a key supplier of grain to coastal Saint Louis – from local leaders viewed as corrupt and insufficiently protecting Tukulor Muslim peasants from enslavement. Over the next 30 years, a new state led by the cleric Abdul Qader Kan launched a number of defensive and expansionist military campaigns. The implications of this political revolution were profound, as it proposed to reorder long-standing relations between clerics and rulers. It was part of a longer historical trajectory of Islamic reform in West Africa that, over the course of the nineteenth century, shaped the experience of millions of people.

Yet this was also a period when the mostly Christian community of Eurafrican or *metis* habitants on Saint Louis enjoyed political and economic ascendance in the region, many having gained wealth as intermediaries between European merchants and the African markets of the interior. Living in stone houses near the centre of the town, they were often Catholic and dressed in European clothing, and filled their homes with the material goods obtained through overseas trade. They celebrated their wealth in late-night parties called *folgar* that featured drumming, dancing, palm wine and the ostentatious display of expensive clothing and accessories. According to Antoine Edme Pruneau de Pommegorge, 'The usual way to praise those who have excelled in dancing is to fling a cloth or handkerchief over them, which they return to the person who has thrown it, making a deep bow to thank him'.[4]

Many *signares* and *habitants* often spoke Wolof in addition to French (or more rarely English) and continued to pursue their own economic interests independently of French company traders. Though Catholic, *signares* were often associated with a religious pluralism that acknowledged and participated in both Muslim and Wolof practices such as celebrating Tabaski (the Eid festival), wearing protective talismans known as *gris-gris* or some Wolof naming practices for their children.[5] It was this culturally flexible posture that actively integrated divergent and seemingly incongruous elements, which defines them as cosmopolitan figures.[6] They sent their sons (and less commonly daughters) to be educated in France as was the case with Charles Thevenot, who returned after living for eight years in Paris to serve as both 'mayor' and Catholic priest to the *habitant* community.[7] Thevenot had a brother-in-law, LeJuge, who travelled extensively to both Europe and India.[8] Such Eurafrican men were described as wearing European clothing in Saint Louis. By contrast, the distinctive clothing of many *signares* reflected an urbane ethos that looked outward to the seas but was also rooted in local discourses of taste, propriety and authority. Their signature tall head wraps were perhaps a local distillation of an eighteenth-century trend among French metropolitan elite women for large wigs and turbans, but were localized with an artfully arranged imported cloth in a style that became uniquely associated with Senegal.[9] The use of imported cloth and ribbons to create large turbans was intended to convey the status and leisure of the wearer. The headdress, which Lamiral described as resembling 'a tiara with a triple crown', was said to indicate that the wearer was not a commoner obliged to carry items on her head.[10]

Such local discourses ascribing high social status to the wearers of these headwraps contrasted with proscriptions elsewhere in the Atlantic for African and African-descent women to wear these as a sign of servitude. In 1789, the Spanish governor of Louisiana instituted a law governing the wearing of *tignon* headwraps directed at women of African descent, whether enslaved or free, insisting that they always cover their hair with a handkerchief scarf.[11] The policy was intended especially to limit the social mobility of free women of colour by associating the wearers with the degraded status of the enslaved. Colonial authorities and slave owners alike in many plantation and urban slave societies sought to impose social hierarchy through customary law or less formal policies for clothing the enslaved, naming them or otherwise marking ownership of them such as through branding.[12] But, as noted by scholars of dress in early American colonies, enslaved and free people of African descent often responded to these sartorial constraints with distinctive styles that seemed to undermine the logic of chattel slavery itself. In some cases, enslaved people obtained clothing of better quality and appearance than their officially allotted dress, which was worn for special occasions or celebrations – such as depicted in well-known paintings by Agostino Brunias of enslaved people in the late eighteenth-century Caribbean colonies.[13] For Africans on both sides of the Atlantic Ocean, headwraps and other forms of clothing were frequently made of Indian cottons such as *madras*, a loom-patterned check from southern India. Such cottons were heavily imported to African ports throughout the eighteenth century, and those cotton goods not sold there were commonly sent onward to destinations in the Americas where buyers purchased them to clothe enslaved labourers.[14] Differences across the Atlantic in the meanings attributed to clothing and accessories made from these Indian cottons suggests how such meanings were embedded within specific social and economic contexts, and how differential constructions of class, race and gender emerged from these distinct Atlantic contexts at the turn of the nineteenth century.

In western Africa, women who were successful as merchant *signares* lived and worked at the convergence of at least two broadly different political economies: one European, Christian and Atlantic Ocean/maritime in character; and the other African, Muslim and Sahelian/Saharan. As elite players in a larger community of free Africans, *signares* were not subject to customary laws imposed by the French with whom they still interacted as host partners in commerce, rather than as colonial subjects in the late eighteenth century. As property owners, wives and well-connected merchants, they were able to make demands of French authorities that added to their wealth and prestige. They were often Catholics who adopted aspects of European clothing and material culture and lived according to French civil code; but they were also known to modify that code to fit local understandings and dispensed with some European social mores on occasion. These advantages only evaporated when socio-economic changes increasingly favoured the public visibility of habitant men, that is, the brothers, sons and nephews of *signares* over themselves. These changes occurred as a new generation of French companies began to dominate the region's export commerce and colonial interventions also increased.[15] Nonetheless, *signares* maintained distinctive dress.

The outfits of *signares* featured the wearing of multiple cloths that were accentuated with gold jewellery imported from the interior and leather slippers from Morocco. As such they expressed forms of sartorial creolization. But this was only one iteration of larger regional patterns and should not be used to reify Eurafricans as uniquely 'Creole' and thus distinct from other Africans. Muslim and other residents of Saint Louis tended to reject forms of European cultural assimilation and were often distinguishable by dress even as they, like the Eurafricans, made claims on the French state as citizens.[16] For example, in the late eighteenth century, the resident population of Saint Louis included people like Charles Scipio, a riverboat captain and successful African resident who spoke Wolof, Fulbe, Bamana, Fulbe, Arabic, French and English and was celebrated in Saint Louis for his military, diplomatic and commercial skills.[17] Like the Eurafricans, Africans of diverse ethnic and religious affiliations also expressed forms of sartorial creolization – such as the incorporation of imported textiles and accessories like beads, hats or handkerchiefs into local dress. The island trading port settlement of Saint Louis was a cosmopolitan space because of the convergence and interactions of its diverse residents and visitors. But these residents would have exhibited differing forms and levels of cultural fluidity, linguistic, religious or sartorial, according to their affiliations and capacity.

These eighteenth-century manifestations of cultural accommodation, appropriation and adaptation in Saint Louis can be viewed as part of an older pattern of accommodation between different social groups and interests in the region. As Toby Green has argued, this tradition of cultural pluralism based on the accommodation of difference between hosts and strangers was particularly important to the history of Islam and of trade diasporas in western Africa and was linked to the expansion of the Mali empire in the fourteenth century.[18] This background helps to contextualize the cultural pluralism of the *signares* of the late eighteenth century who are described in contemporary accounts as observing both Easter and Tabaski (the Muslim Eid festival), carrying rosaries as well as amulets known as *gris-gris*.[19] The wealth of *signares* came from their control of enslaved labour that provided goods and services for the European fort, assisted European vessels to navigate the dangerous waters and provided the main labour force for vessels trading along the Senegal River for gum resin, grain, gold and enslaved people. Both the British and the French at Saint Louis relied on them to supply labour that lubricated their imperial commercial projects.

A key commodity imported into Saint Louis and traded along the river were indigo-dyed cotton cloths imported from India known as *guinées*. Africans admired such cloths for the intensity of their dark blue or black with a coppery red sheen visible on the surface produced from over saturation, as well as for added starch – a characteristic that has also been mentioned as desirable to consumers in other parts of West Africa.[20] Like plain white cotton cloth, they were commonly worn on the body as wrappers, turbans or tailored into garments and exchanged as currency against a number of other goods in local and trans-Saharan markets. The cloths may have been particularly desirable because the indigo dye used was said to rub off on the wearer's skin and thus provide protection from the sun's rays or because the indigo colour was believed to repel mosquitoes.[21] European textile manufacturers endeavoured to reproduce indigo cloths for the West African market throughout the period, but the French also relied on manufacturing in their colony at Pondicherry in southern India to supply them to Saint Louis in West Africa, which were preferred by many buyers well into the nineteenth century.[22] The long-term preference for the particular qualities of this cloth, which fed a centuries-old trans-Saharan and regional commerce in indigo cottons, suggests how West African market conditions, consumer tastes and fashion in fact shaped networks of suppliers in Europe, Asia and the Americas.[23]

Beyond indigo *guinées* cloths, an inventory kept by Louis Lamiral, of the Compagnie de la Guyane operating in Saint Louis from 1778 to 1781, gives some sense of the wider variety of textiles, apparel and accessories that were available there and at ports along the Senegal River. They included *gingas* (variously patterned woven cottons from India); two types of cotton stockings; slippers; Moroccan leather; two colours of a coarse linen cloth ('toile'); pieces of Nankeen cotton from China, handkerchiefs from India and from Cholet, France; three colours of Rouen-made *Siamoise* cloths (cotton and silk blends inspired by the visit of ambassadors of the King of Siam to Louis the XIV in 1685); several skeins of silk thread; fine cloth for robes; 'Negro hats' ('Chapeau a negre'); 'Negro smocks' ('Cassaque a negre'); linen sheets and several varieties of coral and glass beads.[24]

Other goods regularly mentioned in similar trade accounts include scarlet wool cloth, Silesian linens, *indiennes* (printed French cotton or cotton-linen blend cloths inspired by Indian prints) and *romals* (loom-patterned Indian cotton handkerchiefs). In Nantes, an Atlantic port city whose economy grew from its links to the slave trade in Africa, manufacturing houses emerged in the mid-eighteenth century producing *indiennes* printed imitations of Indian cottons for export to Europe, Africa and the Americas. One of the city's largest manufacturers, Favre Petitpierre et Compagnie, could produce up to 26,000 pieces of printed cloth in the 1780s.[25] This company produced a book of block-print designs for *indiennes* it intended for commerce in Africa, which features 162 distinct patterns including stripes, flowers, paisley, abstract forms animals and scenes of African villages (Figure 6.1).

The collection of block prints is believed to have been created later in the company's lifespan, after 1815 when illegal slave trading continued to flourish from Nantes until the French state officially ended such activity in 1831.[26] While there are apparent differences in pattern design among these prints from those of *indiennes* typically produced for the European market (such as scenes of African village life), it is not clear the degree to which they were created based on specific information about African consumers or attempting to appeal to tastes in particular markets. No other company documents or correspondence from the company that might provide further insight into its operations or design process were preserved in local archives after it disbanded in 1847. It is not clear whether and how many of these block print designs might have been sold in Senegal. An 1824 cargo list from a French slaver, the *Jeune Louis*, lists cloth prints produced by the company valued at over 35,000 francs, or

FIGURE 6.1 'Costumes de Différents Pays: Petre Sacrificateur du Senegal', hand-tinted engraving on paper by Jacques Grasset de Saint-Sauveur, 1797, 26.35 × 20.32 cm. *Source*: © LACMA, Costume Council Fund M.83.190.281.

65 per cent of all merchandise shipped, being sold in the Bight of Biafra region. However, as Senegal was an important trading port for France throughout the company's existence, it is likely that some of the company's goods arrived there aboard vessels from Nantes, along with the other categories of textiles mentioned above. Each of these goods implies a distinct sector of a diverse consumer market that accessed goods produced in Europe, Asia and other parts of Africa through Saint Louis and the Senegal River trade.

Sailors and everyday dress in a West African Atlantic port

The *habitant* commercial houses of Saint Louis worked for the French factory, but they also traded on their own account and allowed some of their skilled dependents to do the same, especially sailors known by the Wolof-language term *laptots*. These sailors were viewed as critical to navigating the Senegal River and also as a critical source of maritime labour at a time of frequent war when it was in short supply.[27] Seasonal commerce along the river was an essential part of business at Saint Louis because it was how local merchants there accessed enslaved captives, gum resin, gold and even the grain that fed the town, which did not produce its own food. An analysis of a partial mid-century occupational census suggested that 40 per cent of the African men residing in Saint Louis were labourers in the river trade, including riverboat captains, language interpreters and general labourers. Women also laboured as cooks for *laptots* on commercial riverboat voyages.

Although many *laptots* were enslaved, owing a portion of their income to their patron, whether that be the European company or a *signare*, there were also some, such as Charles Scipio mentioned earlier, who were 'free' wage labourers able to keep their earnings for themselves and build wealth. In describing wages for *laptot* sailors conducting trade for the Compagnie du Senegal, Pere Labat noted that: 'in addition to their ordinary wages, we give them a certain profit from their own trading'.[28] When riverboats passed through shallow sections of the river, the disciplined *laptot* crew members pulled the vessel forward from the banks using ropes, work that they performed rhythmically accompanied by drummers, the encouragement of a praise singer and their own singing and dancing. *Laptots* were considered essential to a successful trade voyage to the interior, serving not only as physical labour but also sometimes as negotiators and soldiers armed with rifles or swords. In 1765, a governor of the French colony on Gorée Island formed an auxiliary military unit of 82 *laptots* armed with rifles and led by local free mulatto African residents of the colony. In an image produced of four members of this unit, the *laptots* are distinguishable as either 'free' or enslaved by clear differences in their uniform clothing.[29] Both Eurafrican and African *laptots* who were 'free' appear in company-issued infantry uniforms with a collared top coat, a shorter blue waist coat, knee-length breeches, white stockings and a black felt tricorn hat. By contrast, those enslaved are shown with simpler outfits of undyed, canvas-like cloth: a long-sleeve jacket with cloth buttons and no collar, ankle-length loose-fitting trousers and a round-shaped hat of the same cloth with yellow wool trim or tassels. Unlike, those depicted as 'free', the lower status *laptots* were barefoot. These images suggest some important social distinctions among this group of labourers employed directly by the French, some of whom experienced some mobility during their lifetimes. But numbers of these labourers worked for Eurafricans or Africans, had little contact with Europeans and/or dressed themselves in local rather than European styles such as local breeches known as *dhiata* and loose tunic-like tops called *mboube*.[30] In the 1770s, Gabriel Bray, an artist traveling aboard the British ship *Pallas*, produced a number of images of African sailors he saw in the ports visited between Senegal, Sierra Leone and Ouidah in the present-day Republic of Benin, depicting them wearing locally made white cotton shirts, breechclouts and white caps as they paddled standing in their canoes (Figures 6.2 and 6.3). In addition to this dress for labour, the successful return of a months-long commercial voyage to the interior market of Gajaaga was a cause for celebration during which *laptots* were known to appear on-board the boat in fine clothes newly purchased at interior markets. These included garments such as expensive *ckoussabes* (cloaks) and brightly coloured, wide cloth belts, both specialty products of Soninke-speaking Gajaaga that were often embroidered with wool or silk,[31] suggesting the circulation of regional fashions within western Africa.

The mobility of African *laptots* was not limited to western Africa itself. As sailors aboard British or French ships, some travelled around the Atlantic and the Indian Ocean, wearing the same standardized apparel given to European

FIGURE 6.2 'African Canoe Men Paddling Through the Surf', Pallas, January, 1775, watercolour by Gabriel Bray.

Source: © National Maritime Museum, Greenwich, London, Ref. no. PT2022.

FIGURE 6.3 'A Sailor Bringing Up His Hammock', Pallas, January 1775, watercolour by Gabriel Bray.

Source: © National Maritime Museum, Greenwich, London, ref. no. PT1989.

mariners of their class, which was often deckhand, pilot or cook.[32] Five such sailors were captured off the coast of the Bahamas aboard a British ship by an American privateer at the beginning of hostilities during the American Revolution in November 1776. A manifest for the captured British ship *Swallow* lists five Senegambians among its crew members, all free: Jack Bamberry (Jack Bambara), Mamanly (Momeda) Sana, Alsimeer (Algema), Ganserry (Gansare) and Famsey (Tamsa), who were to be paid, £1 6s per month for their labour on a slaving voyage from Senegal to Barbados and Mississippi that was to return to Senegal.[33] The Americans intercepted the vessel after it had delivered 93 enslaved people to Mississippi and was returning across the Atlantic. After capture, the men were taken to Providence, Rhode Island where they were detained until they were eventually turned over to the British authorities in a prisoner swap, where their trace in the archival record ends.

However, in a further testament to the larger presence of such *laptots* in the eighteenth-century Atlantic and Indian Oceans, the *Swallow* was also found to be carrying four letters – all written by the same hand in ungrammatical French – from other Senegambia sailors (perhaps picked up from a separate vessel) sending messages to their families in Saint Louis. 'Give my compliments to Cuiba Sione Ditwaller', Boubou Birame Guibe wrote to Madame Yaye Birame in one of the recovered letters that give insight into the experience of these sailors and that of their communities.

> Tell her that I am doing well thanks be to God. Tell Birama Jacques to put the tapa ['tapade' from Wolof for 'enclosure' or 'compound'] [in order] that I will pay when I come to Senegal … Madoune [Madame?] Walo promised to give me some things. Tell her to put them at the head of my bed.[34]

Guibe's expressed concern from overseas about his return to the 'tapade' or compound in Senegal, and about contributing to and accessing the material objects within it, demonstrate the ways in which *laptots* were thoroughly embedded in Atlantic commercial networks, through which people, goods and raw materials from Europe, Africa, Asia and the Americas flowed. Though the British vessel *Swallow* had its venture interrupted, the expectation was that sailors on such voyages would have had direct access to some of the best goods circulating through these networks and opportunities through their own private trading or 'smuggling' to bring them to their households and home communities.[35] Although much detailed evidence of their lives is lacking from historical archives, the *laptots* were change agents who took opportunities afforded by their gender, skills, physical capacity and linguistic dexterity to obtain a level of mobility and access to income that other groups of enslaved people or free labourers could not. They would have had an interest in marking themselves as socially distinct in large ways and small – as evidenced by spending on large gatherings and special clothing to celebrate successful trading.

Visual images of West Africans published in the pages of European travel narratives from the period, though limited in number and scope, offer additional insight into the dress habits of diverse groups of West Africans. Most of these images were engravings produced in Europe, and while some were not based on first-hand or detailed information, others such as those by Bray, were sketches made on-site or based on eyewitness reports and sought to convey specific information about a particular place. By the late eighteenth century, Jacques Grasset de Saint Sauveur, a Canadian-born former French diplomat, attempted an encyclopaedic survey of African dress from around the continent, producing several dozen images in a volume entitled *Encyclopedie mondiale du costume*, published in 1784. Later editions appeared under slightly different titles, sometimes featuring additional images in 1788, 1796 and 1806.

In Paris, Saint Sauveur worked with a workshop of engravers to produce his images based on travellers' reports. Though well travelled, and having served as a diplomat in Cairo, Sauveur never visited anywhere else in Africa. The production of these images and the circulation of information about West Africans in Europe was of course part of the larger expansion of Enlightenment ideas about science, nature and commerce throughout the eighteenth century. Information about clothing and material habits, both in narrative descriptions and in images, contributed to the rapid expansion of European knowledge production, often Orientalist in its conceptions of Africa and Asia, while also feeding critical details about regional tastes and cultural practices to commercial actors seeking potential business ventures in Africa. European cloth manufacturers sometimes sent product samples in letters instructing traders travelling to West Africa to determine whether they pleased buyers,[36] and they were among the readers imagined by compilers of encyclopaedia intended for commercial and general audiences. Information about African dress and clothing practices would have interested textile manufacturers in England and France, some of whom became key advocates for imperial expansion in parts of Africa.[37]

The 1796 version of the work, *Encyclopedie des Voyages*, includes 66 engravings depicting a wide range of men and women in different parts of Africa from Egypt and the Maghreb through parts of West, West Central and Southern Africa.[38] But the largest group of subjects depicted are in Senegambia, accounting for 25 of the total number of images. Prefaced by Sauveur's overview of social and economic life in Senegal, the images depict women and men from a range of backgrounds that begin to suggest the heterogeneity of populations in Saint Louis, Gorée and nearby regions such as Waalo and Cayor. Sauveur depicts the clothing of common men and women as incorporating a number of standard elements, such as the wrapper (*pagne*) worn by a woman tending a field, or the two-piece garment consisting of one cotton cloth wrapped around a man's waist, the other tied with a knot over one shoulder and hung on the upper body. Another man was shown in ankle-length cotton breeches over a long tunic of coloured stripes, a matching turban, walking stick and an earring. Accessories for men often included a necklace, an armband and bracelets made of leather adorned by amulets, anklets made of beads, leather sandals and a leather pouch that carried tobacco and a pipe. Commoner women are represented as wearing a wrapper of either striped or printed cloth, while being nude above the waist, except on festival days, when they adorned themselves with beaded earrings and jewellery arranged across the upper body 'with a lot of grace' (Figures 6.4a, 6.4b, 6.5 and 6.6).

Sauveur noted a particular taste for fashion in Saint Louis, stating people's desire to distinguish themselves in society resulted in frequent changes in taste and clothing styles: 'The young people that want to [be attractive] have their tunics and breeches painted with bands of colour, flowers and with other lovely designs'.[39]

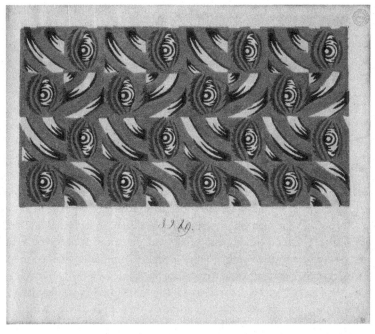

FIGURE 6.4A AND 6.4B Two sample *indiennes* patterns for African trade, Favre Petit-pierre et Compagnie, Nantes, *c.*1815.

Source: © Musée d'Histoire de Nantes ref. no. 941.8.9.

FIGURE 6.5 'Costumes de Différents Pays: Negresse de Qualité de l'Isle St. Louis dans le Sénégal. Accompagnée de son Esclave', hand-tinted engraving on paper by Jacques Grasset de Saint-Sauveur, 1797, 26.3 × 20.3 cm.
Source: © LACMA, Costume Council Fund M.83.190.287.

Sauveur admired the talent of women who painted cloth, which, if his account is to be believed, suggests another artisanal industry adding value to local cloth (and possibly to imported white cloth) to accommodate buyers' changing tastes. Unfortunately, there is no more evidence of what those local cloths he observed were, how they were made or what inspired their designs. However, the desire of buyers for novelty is apparent. In addition to the types of cloth mentioned by Sauveur, the images of his encyclopaedia also depict forms of sartorial creolization as people combined elements of imported and local goods such as men wearing striped or red sashes with fringes or a tricorn hat, as well as how those in traditionally proscribed social roles such as *jeli* praise singers (itinerant performers who were paid with food, iron or cloth) or herbalists created novel assemblages from diverse goods within their reach.

FIGURE 6.6 'Costumes de Différents Pays: Femme du Senegal', hand-tinted engraving on paper by Jacques Grasset de Saint-Sauveur, 1797, 26.3 × 20.3 cm.
Source: © LACMA, Costume Council Fund M.83.190.283.

Some of the sartorial innovations in local dress were mediated and popularized by elites who were sometimes fascinated and charmed by aspects of European dress and military uniforms. The Swedish evangelist and abolitionist Karl Wadström described an encounter in the late 1780s with Buurba Sin, ruler of a Serer-speaking area inland from the Petite Cote south of Saint Louis. As a small token gift, Wadström thought to present Buurba Siin with a few polished metallic sleeve-buttons, manufactured in Birmingham, and used as fasteners and decoration on waist coats, coats, breeches, dresses and shirts. However, Wadström's gift led to an unexpected demonstration of power by the king:

> On my shewing him for what purpose they were intended, he appeared much mortified that his shirt had no button-holes; but observing that that of a mulatto from Gorée was furnished with them ... [the king] insisted

on exchanging shirts with him, in our presence; a demand with which the man was forced to comply. Transported with his new ornaments, the king held up his hands to display them to the people.[40]

Islamic reform in West Africa during the age of Atlantic revolutions

Throughout the nineteenth century, Islam expanded in the interior at the same time as French colonial power and cultural influence expanded from its bases on the Atlantic coast, creating a dynamic between the coast and interior that had profound implications for the history of consumption and fashion. A defining event of the last quarter of the eighteenth century in Senegal was the rise of an Islamic state in the Futa Tooro, which transformed dynamics across the Sahel region supplying food and commercial goods to Saint Louis. The state had emerged from a reformist movement responding to a growing series of conflicts over the capture and sale of enslaved Muslims to Christians at Saint Louis and the lack of resolve of an earlier regime of rulers to prevent it. It represented the culmination of tensions building for years along the 600-mile long Senegal River valley between numerous parties including the Trarza Moors, Wolof rulers in Waalo and Cayor and especially with the French company based on the coastal island of Saint Louis.[41]

In the 1780s, Almamy Abdul Qader Kan, ruler of the Futa Tooro, imposed a ban of all slave trading with Saint Louis – blocking the passage of river and caravan traffic crossing his lands. Further, he escalated his conflict with Saint Louis by banishing slave raiding in his territory and attracting thousands of peasants to resettle there with a promise of lands to farm and protection from capture. French and Eurafrican merchants at Saint Louis were alarmed by these moves and abolitionist observers in Britain, like Thomas Clarkson, cited them as evidence in support of ending the slave trade. However, as a strategic response to the Atlantic and global markets, Kan's embargo of trade with Saint Louis did not fit neatly with the discourses of either French slavers or British abolitionists. Kan's outrage at the enslavement of Muslims did not speak to the enslavement of non-Muslims, who could be legally enslaved. Nor was his conflict with the French a rejection of commerce with Europeans, but an insistence that it should only occur within certain parameters. The emergence of the reformist state of Futa Tooro was part of a longer trajectory of Islamic reform movements that stretched across West Africa, which included the birth of the Sokoto Caliphate in northern Nigeria (1804) and broadly made an impact on ethnic and religious affiliation as well as political relations between Muslim and non-Muslim populations across the Sahel. Although these movements impacted millions of people, they are not usually considered in the context of the 'age of revolutions' transforming Europe and the Americas of the same period. Recent work by Africanist historians has argued for a reconsideration of this general oversight, as neglecting to attend to this African Muslim response to the expanding Atlantic economy dominated by Europe misses a key factor shaping later periods and contemporary global relations.

In responding to a growing European influence on the coast, Kan's aim was not to reject overseas commerce but to control it by harnessing it to a project of Islamic reform, building mosques, establishing Qur'anic schools and promoting agriculture and certain forms of industry. Kan's worldview and social agenda were shaped by his lineage and scholarly background, which connected him to some of the most important scholars and Muslim holy places in western Africa. The physical itineraries of scholars like Kan – which included temporary stays at places in contemporary Senegal, Mauritania, Mali, Guinea and several other countries – give a sense of the vast distances connected by networks of Qur'anic teachers, students and their ideas. The itineraries of these scholars overlapped with those of Muslim merchants who settled in diverse ethnic communities across the region who also participated in long-distance caravans connecting major centres. This pattern helps to explain why European merchants and travellers through the region were often guided by African Muslims who shaped their understanding of the region's social and economic order (Figure 6.7). Both merchants and scholars were purveyors of particular forms of dress – with styles covering more of the body with cloth made of plant fibres rather than of animal skin or by-products – and must be considered for their influence on shaping regional taste and fashions.

Seeking to expand territory in 1796, Almamy Kan sent a white cloth to the Damel of Cayor, Amari Ngoone Ndeela, demanding that he shave his head and wear the turban to symbolize submission to the new state and that he cease his personal consumption of trade liquor, imported French 'eau de vie'.[42] Cayor traded in slaves with the French and *habitants* of Saint Louis in exchange for horses and Spanish piasters that were refashioned into bracelets and other jewellery. Possessing a large cavalry, the Damel and his officials were known to appear in public on horseback and magnificently dressed in garments of local manufacture whose ample sleeves and proportions, along with silver adornments and feathers incorporated into their headwear, signalled their wealth and power.

On receiving the Almamy Kan's demands for submission to his sovereignty, the Damel refused, setting off a bitter military struggle in which the Almamy's fighters were famously routed at the town of Bunguye.[43] Hundreds were reportedly killed, sold into slavery through Saint Louis or scattered in defeat, while the Almamy himself was taken captive. The victorious Damel held the defeated Almamy prisoner for three months before allowing him to return to the Futa Tooro, according to Mungo Park who heard an account of the events several months later from local *jeliw* or praise singers who proclaimed the Damel's actions near the Bafing river in the foothills of the Futa Jallon.[44]

Despite this setback, Almamy Kan recouped his forces and, the following year, his army launched eastward, intervening on one side of a succession dispute in Bundu. This victory was short-lived, however, as respect for the state's authority

FIGURE 6.7 'Diai Boukari (a man), Muslim Marabout from the Futa Tooro', illustration from Gaspard Mollien's *Travels in the Interior of Africa to the Sources of the Senegal and Gambia* (London, 1820).

Source: © Cambridge University Libraries, ref. no. O.24.3.

had begun to fade and internal dissension increased. A strategic alliance between Kan's enemies led to his death during a battle in Bundu in 1806, opening the way once again for increased European commercial presence throughout the Senegal River valley. Nevertheless, his reformist rule left an enduring mark on the social relations in the region. It set the tone for another Islamic reform movement Umar Tal, resisting the expansion of a colonial regime at Saint Louis in the 1850s. The expansion and 'reform' of Islam across the western Sahel and the Senegal River valley shaped the context and the rationale for the region's engagement with global commerce. The turn of the nineteenth century was a pivotal period of transformation in a centuries-long process that also challenged the dynamic of power relations between interior polities, such as at Futa Tooro and Gajaaga and the coast.

Conclusion

In Saint Louis, African-born *habitants* protected their access to foreign sources of wealth and imported commodities by embracing French cultural norms and civil code, which they used to acquire benefits from the French state for themselves and their children. Yet for many, this did not necessarily imply a rejection of alliances with Muslim or other Africans, including sharing in religious celebrations or observances. As merchants, they helped to shape a preference for particular goods such as Indian cottons along lines that were specific to African tastes, such as the preference for indigo cottons.

The cultural ecumene of early nineteenth-century Saint Louis was cosmopolitan in its embrace of overseas and regional influences, but in ways that may have confounded the ideological expectations of their contemporaries both in Paris and in the Futa Tooro. Their festive *folgar* parties were occasions for luxurious displays of wealth through fashion, adornments such as gold jewellery and beads and grooming. At these *folgar* events, which lasted into the early hours of the morning, people drank alcohol, danced to drumming and there was some socializing between people of different backgrounds and social rank. These were spaces where fashion and material culture articulated the negotiation of social status between individuals and groups resident in Saint Louis.

Such a scene suggests, in stark terms, the imbrication of fashion with power in late eighteenth-century Senegal and how this was attached to transregional or 'global' commerce. The appropriation of foreign textiles, clothing and accessories such as Indian indigo cottons, printed French *indiennes* or brass buttons served to express forms of interpersonal or group distinction and sometimes also to project authority. In some places, when permissible by the ruling elite, the appropriation of particular items was accompanied by the popularization of these items among the limited number of people who could access them. This process was also driven by local conditions and consumer tastes, which shaped market trends generally with their preference for cotton cloths with loom patterns or with bright, colourfast dyes that were suitable for West African climate conditions and comparable to local varieties of cotton cloths. The circulation of these goods throughout the region was highly uneven, with different segments of the Senegambian public accessing them only through proximity to certain elite actors or centres of power and wealth. Their adoption as clothing, whether in combination with local textiles and accessories or not, articulates the history of fashion in Senegal at the dawn of an era understood largely as a prelude to a colonial project associated with delivering civilization and modernity. Into the nineteenth century, dress mediated the countervailing forces of an expanding colonial power from the coast, and the expanding influence of Islam from the Sahelian interior – a process informed by a longer tradition of tolerance for cultural pluralism in the region. It is an embodied history of social and economic relations, which reveals pre-modern forms of cosmopolitanism in West Africa linked to the global circulation of people, goods and ideas.

Notes

1 Dominique Harcourt Lamiral, *L'Afrique et Le Peuple Affriquain Considérés Sous Tous Leurs Rapports Avec Notre Commerce & Nos Colonies. De l'abus Des Privilèges Exclusifs, & Notamment de Celui de La Compagnie Du Sénégal. Ce Que c'est Qu'une Société Se Qualifiant d'Amis Des Noirs* (Paris: Dessenne, 1789), 119.

2 Lamiral, *L'Afrique et Le Peuple Affriquain*, 120.

3 James Searing, *West African Slavery and Atlantic Commerce the Senegal River Valley, 1700–1860* (Cambridge, UK: Cambridge University Press, 1993), 165.

4 Antoine Edme Pruneau de Pommegorge, *Description de La Nigritie* (Amsterdam and Paris: Chez Maradan, 1789), 122–123.

5 Hilary Jones, *The Métis of Senegal: Urban Life and Politics in French West Africa* (Bloomington: Indiana University Press, 2013), 37.

6 Laura Fair, 'Remaking Fashion in the Paris of the Indian Ocean: Dress, Performance, and the Cultural Construction of a Cosmopolitan Zanzibari Identity', *Fashioning Africa: Power and the Politics of Dress*, ed. Jean Marie Allman (Bloomington: Indiana University Press, 2004), 13–30; Jeremy Prestholdt, *Domesticating the World: African Consumerism and the Genealogies of Globalization* (Berkeley: University of California Press, 2008).

7 Searing, *West African Slavery*.

8 Saugnier and François Bessire, *Relations de Plusieurs Voyages à La Côte d'Afrique, à Maroc, Au Sénégal, à Gorée, à Galam* (Saint-Etienne: Publications de l'université de Saint-Etienne, 2005).

9 Abdoul Hadir Aïdara, *Saint-Louis Du Sénégal: d'hier à aujourd'hui* (Brinon-sur-Sauldre: Grandvaux, 2004).

10 Lorelle D. Semley, *To Be Free and French: Citizenship in France's Atlantic Empire* (Cambridge, UK and New York: Cambridge University Press, 2017), 94.

11 Beverly Lemire, *Global Trade and the Transformation of Consumer Cultures: The Material World Remade 1500–1820* (Cambridge, UK: Cambridge University Press, 2018).

12 Robert S. DuPlessis, *The Material Atlantic: Clothing, Commerce, and Colonization in the Atlantic World, 1650–1800* (Cambridge, UK: Cambridge University Press, 2016), 156–158.

13 Sophie White, '"Wearing Three or Four Handkerchiefs Around His Collar, and Elsewhere about Him": Slaves' Constructions of Masculinity and Ethnicity in French Colonial New Orleans', *Gender & History* 15.3 (2003): 528–549; Tamara J. Walker, '"He Outfitted His Family in Notable Decency": Slavery, Honour and Dress in Eighteenth-Century Lima, Peru', *Slavery & Abolition* 30.3 (2009): 383–402; Linda Baumgarten, '"Clothes for the People": Slave Clothing in Early Virginia', *Journal of Early Southern Decorative Arts* 15 (November 1988): 26–70.

14 Sandra Lee Evenson, 'A History of Indian Madras Manufacture and Trade: Shifting Patterns of Exchange' (unpublished PhD, University of Minnesota, Minneapolis, 1994).

15 Semley, *To Be Free and French*, 93.

16 Jones, *Métis of Senegal*, 75.

17 Saugnier and Bessire, *Relations de Plusieurs Voyages à La Côte d'Afrique, à Maroc, Au Sénégal, à Gorée, à Galam*.

18 Toby Green, *The Rise of the Trans-Atlantic Slave Trade in Western Africa, 1300–1589*, African Studies Series (Cambridge, UK and New York: Cambridge University Press, 2011), 16.

19 Jones, *Métis of Senegal*, 37–38.

20 Venice Lamb, *West African Weaving* (London: Duckworth, 1975).

21 Ghislaine Krätli Lydon, *The Trans-Saharan Book Trade: Manuscript Culture, Arabic Literacy and Intellectual History in Muslim Africa*, vol. 8, Library of the Written Word (Leiden and Boston, MA: Brill, 2011).

22 Richard Roberts, *Two Worlds of Cotton: Colonialism and the Regional Economy in the French Soudan, 1800–1946* (Stanford, CA: Stanford University Press, 1996).

23 Prestholdt, *Domesticating the World*; Giorgio Riello, *Cotton: The Fabric That Made the Modern World* (Cambridge, UK: Cambridge University Press, 2013).

24 Dominique Lamiral and FR CHAN T1393, 'Papiers de Louis Lamirale. Directeur Compagnie de La Guyane Au Senegal from 1778–1781', n.d., Centre Historique des Archives Nationales, Paris.

25 Thomas David, Bouda Etemad and Janick Marina Schaufelbuehl, *La Suisse et l'esclavage Des Noirs* (Lausanne: Editions Antipodes, 2005), 22.

26 Krystel Gualde, 'Neuchâtel, Nantes et l'Afrique : Une Production Textile Pour La Traite Atlantique', unpublished paper, 2017.

27 James F. Searing, 'The Seven Years' War in West Africa: The End of Company Rule and the Emergence of the Habitants', in *The Seven Years' War: Global Views*, ed. Mark H. Danley and Patrick J. Speelman (Leiden: Brill, 2012), 263–291.

28 Jean Baptiste Labat, *Nouvelle Relation de l'Afrique Occidentale Contenant Une Description Exacte Du Senegal & Des Pais Situes Entre de Cap-Blanc & La Riviere de Serrelionne, Jusqu'a plus de 300. Lieues* (Paris: G. Cavelier, 1974), 243–248.

29 Non-cote, 'Uniformes Des Corps Des Laptots de Goree', 1765, ANOM.

30 P. D. Boilat, *Esquisses Sénégalaises* (Paris: Karthala, 1984), 8.

31 Boilat, *Esquisses Sénégalaises*, 445.

32 Charles Foy, 'The Royal Navy's Employment of Black Mariners and Maritime Workers, 1754–1783', *International Journal of Maritime History* 28.1 (2016): 6–35.

33 'Arnold Family Business Papers; Documents for the *Swallow*', 1776, John Carter Brown Library.

34 'Arnold Family Business Papers; Documents for the Swallow', 22 August 1776.

35 Beverly Lemire, '"Men of the World"': British Mariners, Consumer Practice, and Material Culture in an Era of Global Trade, c.1660–1800', *Journal of British Studies* 54.2 (2015): 288–319.

36 T70/1517, 'Letter from Thomas Norris to William Hollier about Trade in Gambia', 1751, The National Archive, UK.

37 Joseph Inikori, 'Gentlemanly Capitalism and Imperialism in West Africa: Great Britain and Senegambia in the Eighteenth Century', in *Africa, Empire and Globalization: Essays in Honor of A. G. Hopkins*, ed. Toyin Falola, Emily Brownell and A. G. Hopkins (Durham: North Carolina Academic Press, 2011).

38 Jacques Grasset de Saint Sauveur, *Encyclopédie Des Voyages Contenant l'abrégé Historique Des Moeurs, Usages … Religions … Sciences, Arts et Commerce de Tous Les Peuples et La Collection Complette de Leurs Habillemens* (Paris: Deroy, 1796).

39 Grasset de Saint Sauveur, *Encyclopédie Des Voyages*, 44.

40 Carl Bernhard Wadström, *Observations on the Slave Trade: And a Description of Some Part of the Coast of Guinea, During a Voyage, Made in 1787, and 1788, in Company with Doctor A. Sparrman and Captain Arrehenius, by C. B. Wadstrom, Chief Director of the Royal Assay and Refining Office; Member of the Royal Chamber of Commerce, and of the Royal Patriotic Society, for Improving Agriculture, Manufactures, and Commerce in Sweden* (London: printed and sold by James Phillips, George-Yard, Lombard-Street, 1789), 21.

41 Searing, *West African Slavery*.

42 Searing, *West African Slavery*.

43 Searing, *West African Slavery*.

44 Mungo Park, *Travels in the Interior Districts of Africa* (Durham, NC: Duke University Press, 2000), 292–293.

7

THE KING'S NEW CLOTHING

Re-dressing the body politic in Madagascar, c.1815–1861

Sarah Fee[1]

It is an axiom in dress history that nations in Asia were 'the first to develop ways to integrate the Western fashion system into its own fashion system'.[2] Best known are Thailand, Turkey and Japan, where rulers began wearing garments tailored in European silhouettes and imposed the same on their armies. However, 50 years before anywhere in Asia, a pre-colonial African court undertook such dress reforms on an equally grand scale. Radama, the king of central Madagascar, was by 1816 regularly dressing in tailored dress inspired by European prototypes and by 1828 was further requiring it of at least 10,000 men and women in his service. By 1845, his successor Queen Ranavalona I had increased these numbers to perhaps 40,000. The scale of change unsettles claims in particular for the 'exceptionalism' of Meiji Japan, which began its own reforms as late as 1868.

Within Madagascar studies, these fashion shifts are well known, and generally characterized as follows: Radama ascended to the throne of the highland kingdom of Imerina in c.1810, the same year the British took the neighbouring Mauritius island from France during the Napoleonic Wars. As part of a wider abolitionist strategy, British authorities in Mauritius negotiated with Radama to end slave exports in exchange for recognition as sole king of Madagascar, and financial and military aid to expand his rule to the coasts. A treaty signed in 1817, but only actualized from 1820, brought British missionaries, political agents and artisans to the royal seat, Antananarivo, sent Malagasy boys to England for education and supplied Radama and his army with arms and clothing; simultaneously, he developed admiration for Napoleon.[3] As a result of these events and relationships, according to this conventional wisdom, from 1820 Radama broke with 'traditional' wrapper dress to don 'British' or 'European' garments. His court and military soon followed. These and related changes were altogether 'the product of politico-economic developments originating with the European colonial powers' and the start of a long slide of 'cultural erosion'.[4]

Recent studies debunked such colonial historiography to stress Radama's agency in negotiating international alliances, and recognized his many internal cultural and material innovations, in state ceremonies, palace architecture and attempts to industrialize craft production.[5] However, studies have yet to recognize dress as a critical 'technology of change' in Madagascar, to use the expression of Nicholas Thomas. Thomas argues that 'much more than mere markers of identities' clothing has the power to enable novel social forms.[6] This chapter aims to map the actors, timelines, precise garment types, supply chains, grand scale and motivations of Madagascar's early dress reforms under the reigns of Radama and his successor, Queen Ranavalona I (c.1815–1861). It reveals that Radama's sartorial shifts predated British treaties and missionaries, and the Malagasy were the main protagonists in seeking, selecting, procuring, creating and modifying tailored garments. More than some by-product of export trade, new forms of dress were sought as actively as arms and ammunition and mobilized to support entangled local, regional and global agendas. Innovation therefore came not only from Europe, nor was it 'a simple, linear' trajectory or 'dichotomous model' opposing East–West, but instead the recreation of a fashion system in its own right.[7]

Reconnecting Madagascar to the Indian Ocean and beyond

The large island of Madagascar, lying some 400 km off the coast of Mozambique, may appear isolated; but for millennia human networks have connected it to the wider Indian Ocean world. Around 2,000 years ago voyagers arrived on outrigger canoes from today's Indonesia, some 3,000 km to the east. They brought an Austronesian language (Malagasy) and distinctive cultural traits, such as rice cultivation, ancestor veneration and handloom weaving by women. They were joined by Bantu-speaking settlers from eastern Africa. A legacy from both cultures was dress traditions based on rectangular wrappers; Malagasy men and women wore untailored lengths of beaten bark, plaited reed mats or woven cloth – of cotton, silk, bast or raffia leaf – wrapped around hips, chests and shoulders (see Figure 7.1).[8] Further dress influences came through Arab and Swahili traders and clerics who settled on the coasts, followed, from 1500, by Europeans – Portuguese, English, Dutch and French. Generally using the island for provisioning en route to India, Europeans sporadically attempted to establish coastal colonial settlements. More successfully, from 1700 the French colonized two nearby tiny uninhabited offshore islands – Ile de France (Mauritius) and Bourbon (Reunion Island), collectively known as the Mascarenes – importing slave labour to work plantations of sugar cane, coffee and indigo.

Important to this chapter is an appreciation of the sustained exchanges between the Mascarenes and Madagascar's east coast – just a short sailing voyage of a few days or weeks – and the cosmopolitan society that developed at its interface.[9] An influx of European pirates from the late seventeenth century, followed in the eighteenth century by Mascarene traders, shaped political and

FIGURE 7.1 'Habitts att St Lawrence'. This sketch made on the south-west coast of Madagascar in 1642 reveals the body arts practised island-wide at the time: hip wrappers, profuse jewellery and hair braiding for both men and women, with tailored bodices for elite women.

Source: Sir Richard Carnac Temple, *The Travels of Peter Mundy in Europe and Asia, 1608–1667* (London: Printed for the Hakluyt Society, 1919), vol. 3, part 2.

material worlds. Their unions with local women gave rise to a bilingual *métisse* political elite, their offspring occasionally sent to Reunion or Europe for education. As early as 1733, men were observed to be 'dressed and shod' as Englishmen or in 'French style', with women of port towns dressing only in imported blue and 'painted' (*chitte*) Indian cloths.[10] The two-way flow also saw Malagasy elites travelling to, and residing in, the Mascarenes.[11]

Since the 1990s scholars have emphasized the similar entanglements for highland Madagascar, a land-locked area high in the central mountains, 300 km from the coast, home to the Merina Kingdom and today's capital city Antananarivo. Upending the stubborn misconception that this area was isolated prior to British overtures in 1815, their studies show early, regular flows of Arab and European merchants to Imerina, and Merina[12] traders to the coasts.[13] From the 1760s, the booming plantation economies of the Mascarenes put a new premium on enslaved labour and Imerina became the main supplier. The great king Andrianampoinimerina, popularly eulogized as a benevolent unifier, in fact achieved his ends 'through a blend of gentle diplomacy and the force of arms' financed through the slave trade.[14] Altogether, Imerina was by the late eighteenth century globally connected, home to a centrally regulated system of weekly markets and overflowing with local and imported merchandise, especially cloth.

Nevertheless, studies continue to imply that the dress of highland Madagascar remained 'traditional' in the eighteenth century. This can be traced to sparse object and textual evidence – there exists but a single first-hand description of Imerina and Andrianampoinimerina, before 1800 – as well as inaccurate translations of dress terms and the uncritical use of visual sources. The two images routinely adduced as typical of elite Merina male dress prior to 1820 – Andrianampoinimerina dressed in loincloth and shoulder wrapper (Figure 7.2) and Radama's officer Rafaralahy (Figure 7.3) – are both, in fact, anachronistic.[15] The testimony of actual Merina

FIGURE 7.2 An apocryphal painting of the Merina king Andrianampoinimerina, c.1745–1810, father to Radama, painted in 1905 by Ramanakirahina. It depicts him in homespun cloth, but the one first-hand description of Andrianampoinimerina recorded him as dressed in red wrapper and turban, both likely made from imported fabrics.

Source: Musée Andafiavaratra, Ministère de la Culture, Madagascar https://commons. wikimedia.org/wiki/File:Andrianampoinimerina.jpg.

FIGURE 7.3 Rafaralahy Andriatiana, Radama's brother-in-law and governor appointed to the port town of Foule Point, painted in 1821 while on a visit to Mauritius. The outfit he posed in was anachronistic, as by 1821 Rafaralahy had been dressing in tailored military uniforms for three years.

Source: William Ellis, *History of Madagascar*, 2 vols. (London: Fischer & Sons, 1838), vol. 1, frontispiece.

royal garments was, tragically, silenced by the conflagration that largely destroyed Madagascar's palace museum in 1995.

It is clear, however, that by the eighteenth century elite Merina dress was a complex amalgamation of imported fabrics and accessories, drawn from numerous Indian Ocean sources. Imported from India, red umbrellas and red carnelian beads - worn on the forehead, ankles and upper arms - were restricted by sumptuary laws for the use of nobles (*andriana*). Elite headdresses, including that of Rafaralahy in Figure 7.3, may have been based on southern Arabian prototypes.[16] The royal family was marked by, and had sole rights to, an imported scarlet British woollen broadcloth, known locally as *jakimena*.[17]

Assimilated into the category of sacred things, and imbued with mystical force, broadcloth was further gifted by sovereigns to allies and valorous warriors in the form of 'long hats' (*satro-dava*), tall headdresses embellished with imported carnelian or gold braid.[18] Both local histories and the single first-hand European description present Andrianampoinimerina dressed in a mantle of red broadcloth and a red silk turban.[19] Likewise, by the 1770s at least, Merina sovereigns were accepting gifts of frockcoats from Mascarenes traders.[20]

Other Merina elites, meanwhile, dressed mainly in imported silver and Indian silks. With body adornment vital for materializing status, rank and spiritual efficacy (*hasina*), Merina traders typically put 50 per cent of earnings toward arms and ammunition and the other half toward imported dress. They successfully forced Mascarenes merchants to pay them not in despised shoddy trade goods but with silver coins.[21] Wearing the coins directly on the body, or having them melted down and transformed by local smiths into imposing chains, plates and rings, worn around legs, ankles, foreheads and chests, elites might be so weighed down as to require assistants to support them.[22] Silver coins were desired, too, for their exchange value: in the 1780s an estimated 30,000 silver dollars from Imerina annually went to purchasing Indian cloth on the island's west coast.[23]

Tailored garments were also known in Imerina before 1800. As elsewhere in the island, elite Merina women wore small tailored bustiers (*akanjo*), with short or long sleeves.[24] Needles and scissors were produced locally and sewing thread was available in highlands markets by the eighteenth century.[25]

It was into this already hybrid, entangled fashion system that Radama, the son of Merina king Andrianampoinimerina, was born about 1793. Some time around 1810, when Radama was approximately 17, he succeeded his father to the throne. In that same fateful year, Britain took neighbouring Mauritius from France in the Napoleonic Wars. The young king actively sought an alliance from 1811 with this new political force, sending delegations to observe life in Mauritius, and an emissary to parlay with the British agent of Tamatave.[26] In 1815, the British governor of Mauritius, Robert Farquhar, newly tasked with ending the slave trade in the Indian Ocean, reached back to Radama. From 1816 to 1817, numerous Malagasy and British envoys journeyed between the two islands, culminating in a treaty signed in October 1817. Its major provisions had Radama agree to end slave sales in return for money, goods, British military advisors and recognition as the sole king of Madagascar. From 1817 to 1828, with ten major campaigns, Radama invaded and absorbed two-thirds of the islands, including key ports.

Long overlooked by historians in favour of more ostensibly 'serious' material forms such as palace architecture, Radama's refashioning of himself and the body politic with new clothing styles should be recognized as a carefully calculated stratagem and key tool for actualizing his sociopolitical agendas.

The king's new clothing: the hybrid self-fashioning of Radama

Historical works on Madagascar invariably feature the portrait of Radama that he commissioned in late 1825 from French artist André Coppalle (Figure 7.4). In this oil painting, he wears a red British-style military officer's coat with epaulettes, dark trousers and tall parade boots, a striped sash and star-shaped order, with a sword and plumed bicorn hat at his side. Most authors juxtapose this with the apocryphal painting of his father or minister Rafaralahy in 'traditional' garb (see Figure 7.3) to suggest Radama made a radical, definitive sartorial break as a result of the treaty signed with the British in late 1817. However, a critical reading of images, texts and the garments reveals that his self-fashioning with European elements was early, proactive and partial, always hybrid to some degree.

FIGURE 7.4 Radama, dressed in one of his hybrid assemblages, oil painting by Andrée Coppalle, 1825–1826, commissioned by Radama and painted from life.

Source: Musée Andafiavaratra, Ministère de la Culture, Madagascar Used with permission of the Ministère de la Culture.

There is ample evidence that Radama was dressing in imported European-style military coats *before* the 1817 treaty with the British, and throughout his life proactively procured them through a variety of channels. We know little of his dress habits before 1816, beyond that he had pierced ears and ornamental scarification, fashionable Merina body modifications of the previous century.[27] Chardenoux, the first envoy sent to Antananarivo in 1816, regrettably commented little on dress, but his successor, Lesage, had more to say. Radama received him dressed in a crown, sash and uniform, which to Lesage's mortification were more spectacular than the goods he carried as gift, forcing the British envoy to apologize and promise future outfits from England.[28] Not waiting, just months later, in July 1817, on his first visit to Tamatave, Radama paid calls on French slavers (some of whom he'd met as a boy in Antananarivo), complaining of the shoddy English apparel, requesting they bring him French general uniforms and encouraging them to trade in horses and luxury fabrics.[29] He specified the uniforms be 'of the highest rank' and that he purchase them rather than receive them as gifts, so as to avoid obligation and ensure they were to his taste.[30] In October 1817, he instructed his envoys signing the British treaty to visit the same traders and buy 15 horses and all the silver and gold epaulettes they had on hand.[31] Further evidence for the Mascarenes as an important early supplier lies in the fact that most highland Malagasy terms for European-style garments and accessories – frockcoat (*zaby, anaby*), epaulettes (*zepoleta*), waistcoat (*zile*), trousers (*pantaloha*) – derive from French and Creole, and were adopted prior to 1830.[32] Over the years, Radama ordered articles through his representatives in Tamatave, through Farquhar and Hastie and through his many envoys to Mauritius; his treaty delegation returning in the autumn of 1817 brought some 600 tons of merchandise.[33] Further, it was Radama who required that the treaty's 1817 'Equivalent' – compensation for lost revenues from slave sales – include uniforms and horses for himself, directing details of cut, colour and fabric.[34] The 1822 instalment, 'a full dress gold laced military suit with gold epaulettes, etc.', cost an extraordinary $600.[35] In the end, however, the Equivalent brought Radama less than six outfits and only from 1821; some were of dubious value: in 1827 Radama comically modelled for British agent Robert Lyall a recent instalment to show it was 'too big in every way' and 'fits me like a sack'.[36]

By his death in 1828, Radama owned as many as 155 European-style tailored uniforms and coats, in addition to hundreds of related accessories, from stockings to cravats.[37] This concerted accumulation should be viewed as a means rather than an end in itself, central to his interrelated strategies of attaining international recognition as the king of Madagascar and territorial expansion. As recent scholarship has emphasized, the discourse on legitimacy and independence in the global nineteenth century was largely constructed around the concept of 'civilization' and realized by showing competency 'with novel modes of consumption', namely European food, wine, architecture, dance and clothing.[38] Well versed in European and Indian Ocean politics, and the racialized discourse on Africa, Radama carefully choreographed and managed his image for European audiences, at home and abroad. Not coincidentally, he wore blue jackets to receive the French representatives who most resisted his claims.[39] This sartorial strategy surely greatly contributed to popular international praise of Radama as an 'enlightened monarch', so unlike the 'savage', his appearance being 'altogether ... that of the statesman'.[40]

Nevertheless, a fixation on Radama's military uniforms has masked the large and varied nature of his wardrobe and his hybrid assemblages.[41] Unpacking the outfit he chose for his 1826 portrait offers a striking example (Figure 7.4). The red coattee and trousers indeed represent the height of fashionable British officer's dress of the time; but the plumed helmet is likely to be French in origin and the sash based on the French foreign legion.[42] The curved 'Mameluk sword' may be of French or English manufacture, while the breast Order is Radama's own Order of the Hawk, which he created before 1822 and had produced abroad.[43] Written descriptions confirm such admixtures.[44] In August 1817, for instance, for receiving James Hastie, the new British agent, Radama dressed in a 'red Scotch coat and military hat' gifted by the British, combined with blue pantaloons and green boots.[45] Some observers would ridicule as naive or vainglorious these assemblages at variance with European norms. On the one hand, Radama's dress perfectly accorded with nineteenth-century court practices, military officers and monarchs of minor kingdoms in Europe similarly devising personalized uniforms, drawing on French and other international prototypes. On the other hand, this was not – as scholars have shown for similar, later occurrences in the Global South – a matter of failed mimicry, but the selective incorporation of imported elements into a pre-existing discrete fashion system.

For Radama's self-fashioning was also aimed at internal audiences. Even if the silhouette was foreign, his military dress – in a classic instance of authentication – also mobilized local sensibilities. It is not a stretch to suppose that – with scores of uniforms to choose from – he selected British jackets for internal public appearances for their red broadcloth (*jakimena*), which from the eighteenth century was the sacred fabric of the sovereign. The gold braid and epaulettes he fixedly sought represent new incarnations of older 'red' power objects (see above). Indeed, European agents were obliged to participate in the Merina fashion system and industry; Hastie, Robin and others dressed in uniforms 'gaudy with [gold] lace', in order to earn the respect of Radama, even though it brought mockery from their compatriots.[46] At other moments, such as on the military march, or for private dancing parties, the king wore a shoulder wrapper over (or in place of) tailored dress.[47] For large public assemblies, such as tomb visits and official proclamations (*kabary*), with tens of thousands in attendance, he conspicuously removed military uniforms to don the wrapper of royal scarlet broadcloth.[48] At religious ceremonies emphasizing his divine powers, notably the great Annual Royal Bath, his costume changes included black and white headbands and locally woven wrappers of indigenous wild silk.[49]

Radama's tailored garments were further domesticated by home manufacture. As will be discussed below, from 1824 he famously embarked on a program of autarky, exchanging free trade for home industry.[50] Key accessories such as the velvet cap trimmed in gold lace he wore at military reviews, as well as his single surviving military jacket and pair of his boots, appear to have been locally made.

Dress was critical, too, for Radama's innovative political stagecraft that, as Larson shows, he developed early in his reign to assert his new intentions for a British alliance and test public reaction.[51] Larson focuses on the great Royal Bath of 1817, but a large procession several months later, in January, 1818, to the royal tombs outside Antananarivo reveals the central – and multivalent – role of dress at such events. Radama carefully choreographed this 15-mile trek to Ambohimanga, which passed through 60 villages of assembled citizens.[52] He cast British agent Hastie in the subservient role, directing him to dress in garments ('a red coat faced with blue … and a red cloth cap') he supplied from his own wardrobe and strictly instructing Hastie to ride behind him on the horse he likewise provided. Bringing up the rear were four of Radama's officers, also wearing some type of imported apparel, mounted on the horses he had newly purchased in Tamatave.[53] In accordance with local custom, Hastie was made to walk barefoot and bareheaded approaching and leaving the site. Returning to Antananarivo, Radama changed into a new outfit – a velvet suit embroidered with gold – gifted by Farquhar before ascending to the city and waiting crowds. Among the many messages of this complex theatre were the material advantages to be had by the alliance, the king's ability to master the relationship and a promise to share the gains (contrary to local suspicions).

More difficult to interpret are the few European reports of Radama's dressing in 'Arab' costume when delivering public speeches or receiving European dignitaries, particularly in 1821.[54] Radama entertained relations with numerous Islamicized communities residing on the west and south-east coasts – and in his own capital – including Arabo-Swahili traders and the Indigenous Antemoro ethnic group who historically supplied councillors, scribes and tutors to the Merina court. Radama may have merely donned a turban, which his father was known to wear. Given the timing of 1821, his use of 'Arab costume' most likely spoke to his ongoing, costly and bloody attempts to conquer the Islamicized west coast.

Altogether, authentication, domestication and respecting ritual dress codes seem to have eased Merina public acceptance of Radama's innovative garment types and combinations. An associated act, however, brought rebellion. In 1822, Radama cut off his elaborate hair braids, a body modification of great cultural significance practised until that time by all Merina men and women. When he required it soon thereafter for all in his standing army, riots ensued. A sign of mourning, associated with death and disorder, this head shaving caused 2,000 women to march on the capital in protest. Historians continue to debate the causes and meanings of this event – which ended in Radama putting four female leaders to death.[55] Certainly it illustrates the strength of Radama's commitment to new dress: Merina historian Raombana claimed that head shaving was a means not an end, undertaken so the tallow used in hair braiding would not soil shirts and jackets.[56]

Radama's 'abandonment of things Malagasy', observes Larson, has been overdrawn and this certainly applies to his dress.[57] He may have made his anthem 'God save the King', commissioned Mascarenes Creole-style palaces and furnished them with imported European wallpaper, curtains and tableware. But, notes Larson, he was 'successful not because he abandoned highland Malagasy cultural traditions ... but because ... he skillfully employed highland Malagasy cultural symbolism and ritual to set his politics firmly within a highland Malagasy cultural logic'.[58] Although Europeans tended to label his dress as in 'the style of the English',[59] it drew in fact from many sources and in its details, combinations and sourcing spoke to, and shaped, many different constituencies. Far more radical from a dress history perspective was Radama's requiring the new silhouettes of the wider population.

Refashioning the body politic

Many rulers in the Global South were observed to don suit coats and hats of European origin. Radama was precocious and unusual in also requiring tailored clothing for thousands in his service, possibly over 10,000 people by 1828. Here, too, the king directly initiated and realized the reforms, independent of any meaningful external aid. Indeed, the timing of the reforms for his officers and ministers, c.1818–1820, the very moment when the British absented themselves, suggests they were concerned as much with local dynamics as the external gaze, a key tool for restructuring local sociopolitical groupings and thus realizing regional ambitions. Ultimately, as in Thailand decades later, Radama's sartorial reform was culturally innovative but 'politically conservative', a top-down project 'that upheld the sociopolitical status quo of royal absolutism'.[60]

From 1817, Radama devoted special attention to re-outfitting his new professional army.[61] His father had relied on warriors serving under village or clan leaders, called up ad hoc, and a new standing regiment (*voromahery*) drawn from all six provinces and settled in Antananarivo.[62] Their outfits were double loincloths, cross belts, powder horns and amulets, with tall hats, sashes and ornamented silver kits for leaders (Figure 7.5). New dress made manifest Radama's new military organization and ranking system, wherein the common foot soldier was first rank, a leader of ten soldiers claimed fourth rank and up to the tenth rank in charge of 1,000 men, later expanded to 13 honours.[63]

From late 1816, seizing the offer from Lesage, Radama engaged two British sergeants, notably the biracial Jamaican James Brady, to train an elite royal regiment in modern weapons and associated drill formations. Immediately Radama devised for this regiment a new uniform: 'turban, white shirt, tunic, vest, trousers, and a leather belt with a kit covered in silver and beads'.[64] He modelled it – apart from the kit of Malagasy origins – on Lesage's so-called 'sepoy guard', which we know today to have been Indian convict laborers.[65] It was Radama

FIGURE 7.5 Merina men dressed in the ceremonial attire that prevailed before 1815: 'tall hats' decorated with stones and silver, chest sashes with lace and gold trim, shields, ornamental silver and jewelled kits. The 1909 publication labelled the men as officiants at a circumcision ceremony, but more likely they are posing in old costume.

Source: Paul Camboué, 'Les dix premiers ans de l'Enfance chez les Malgaches. Circoncision, nom, éducation', *Anthropos* 4.2 (1909): 377.

who, a few months later, insisted that the Equivalent include outfits for this unit. In private missives to his envoys negotiating the treaty in Tamatave, he instructed them to press for 'beautiful hats, suits of red broadcloth (*jaky mena*), white trousers … a full soldier's dress except for boots' for 400 men.[66] The treaty's final terms modified this to blue trousers, caps, swords and boots instead of shoes. The regiment increased rapidly: from 296 men in 1818 to 3,000 in 1823 and finally over 5,000 by 1828, all dressed in this fashion.[67] Up to several hundred were stationed at the new garrisons built along trade routes and newly conquered coasts, where their dress surely instilled awe.[68] The additional professional regiments formed by Radama in 1821 from 13,000 highland volunteers, were also, by some accounts, provided arms, 'une tunique, un pantalon et un chapeau', although denied shoes.[69] From 1822, they were further required to cut their hair and shave, privileges denied to civilians until the 1860s. Visibly distinguishing irregular, common soldiers was their dress; they were required to remain 'nearly naked, being only girt round the middle with a thin cloth', while the Tsimandoa slave body guard still in 1826 dressed in 'a black and red belt [loincloth], two scarves of the same colour that cross across chest and back, and a fur cap'.[70]

Most conspicuously, dress helped make Radama's new 'officers'. As historians have shown, when Radama took the throne at age 17, he inherited a consultative system of governance and a small circle of advisors from his father's day; these older men from powerful families with deep interests in the export slave trade, were largely inimical to his alliance with the British, which required ending that same trade.[71] When in 1818 the British effectively abandoned the treaty, Radama faced insurrection at home and in the provinces, losing the key port of Tamatave. Refashioning the dress of officers and the professional army at this precise point in time can arguably be read as a declaration of independence from both the internal ancien régime and duplicitous British allies.

In 1816–1817, Europeans observed Radama's 'greats' dressed in wrappers and elaborate silver body ornaments, carried in palanquins.[72] When Hastie returned in late 1820, following the British absence, he found Radama's 34 officers 'mounted and habited as field officers' (Figure 7.6).[73] This radical change marked the dramatic remaking of the political landscape. In the interim, the king had promoted new 'officers' to serve as both military commanders and

11 — Grande revue passée par Radama à Voboasse, en 1823.

FIGURE 7.6 Radama reviewing his troops, 1823, reportedly based on a sketch drawn by Andrée Coppalle.

Source: B. F. Leguével de Lacombe, *Voyage à Madagascar et aux iles Comores, 1823 à 1830* (Paris: Louis Desessart, 1840), vol. 1.

political advisors, men still of high nobility, but chosen mainly through ties of blood or marriage.[74]

The revival of slave exports from Imerina during the suspension of the British treaty, 1818–1820, appears driven as much to obtain horses and uniforms for these men as arms and ammunition. When Hastie returned to Madagascar in fall, 1820, he encountered a caravan heading for Tamatave, led by an officer of Radama, with 2,000 souls to exchange for weapons and other 'merchandize, Horses, etc. and particularly for clothing for Radama's troops'.[75] When Hastie arrived in Antananarivo a few days later, Radama adduced the finery as proof of autonomy, directing ' Mr Hastie to notice the advancement of his subjects, their clothing, conduct and manners and said that all this was created by the intercourse kept up with the Slave Traders'.[76] Officers during this time additionally privately ordered outfits from Mauritius. By sharing the signs and sources of power with officers, Radama further countered a major local suspicion that the treaty was meant to profit him personally.

Officers' wardrobes were also hybrid, personalized and context dependent, with several forms of dress and undress and local rules of combination. For formal occasions, a generic military uniform seemed to suffice, as opposed to one of precise nationality or grade; Rafaralahy was variously observed in the uniform of a naval captain and field marshal.[77] Receiving foreigners at port garrisons, and traveling to Mauritius and Europe, Radama's officers were extensions of him and required to dress and entertain similarly to the court of Antananarivo. Here, again, great value was placed on epaulettes of gold thread, gold braid, tall bicorns and scarlet coats; these accoutrements simultaneously referenced long-standing signs of rank and power while distancing the *ancien régime* in their outmoded silver jewellery and 'long hats', which increasingly fell to the domain of ceremonial wear. For *palavres* (public proclamations organized by the king), shoulder mantles might be worn, while officer undress was characterized by individualized self-fashioning in European cuts.[78]

Officers' wives (polygamy was yet common) and daughters were, from the 1820s at least, designated as 'female soldiers' and observed to wear tailored dresses in fashionable styles, usually in combination with a shoulder mantle (*lamba*).[79] From April 1823, they and their husbands were required to receive instruction in reading and writing at a military college supervised by Robin.[80]

During Radama's reign, the extended royal family came to dress in tailored clothing, at least for ceremonial occasions. Royal wives, the widows of his royal predecessors, all their children, princes and princesses now wore their scarlet broadcloth tailored into jackets, trousers and dresses wearing matching shoes and socks.[81] At other moments, however, royal women might wear 'striped silk tunics' and white cotton cloths, perhaps locally woven, or mantles of red broadcloth.[82] Likewise adjusting to local fashions, Radama's half-brothers, Rahovy and Ratafika, educated in Mauritius for several months in 1817, upon their return abandoned the more restricting elements of the European princely outfits Farquhar had gifted them.[83]

Most unusually, Radama required tailored dress of civilians (*borizano*, from the French 'bourgeois'), the many commoners and minor nobles who laboured in the growing ranks of an extended corvée labour system (*fanampoana*) and who filled the new schools he promoted to feed these ranks. Like the military, the thousands of administrators and artisans he conscripted to supply court, army and garrisons, numbering 40,000 by 1825, were organized into work units of 10, 100 and 1,000, each headed by 'officers' ranked from one to ten, with those above the eighth rank holding official titles or 'honours' (*manamboninahitra*). How dress articulated with this civilian system is less clear. Like common soldiers, court servants from the lowest social orders – singers, cooks, personal attendants – were restricted to wrappers of imported cottons and denied the privilege of tailoring.[84] Decades later, in the 1850s, Ellis observed that high-ranking civilian officers were 'not distinguished by any particular dress, except on public occasion, when those of the highest grade wore some sort of uniform'.[85] However, the expectation for the large group of middling levels appears to have been general European-style dress cuts – shirts for men, dresses for women – worn under shoulder wrappers.

Schools emerged as another major conduit for new dress habits and skills. From the autumn of 1820, Radama welcomed representatives of the London Missionary Society to his capital and supported their teaching boys and girls. It soon became evident he intended schools as a 'branch of public duty', a training ground for crown service, eventually declaring literacy a condition of advancement in both military and civil divisions.[86] According to missionaries, it was the schoolchildren themselves who in 1821 militated to dress in 'clothing similar to that worn by the Europeans', bringing cloth for their wives to sew.[87] The standard uniform became a dark coat, trousers and white shirt for boys and white or print cotton dresses for girls. At first drawn from Antananarivo's elite families, students eventually hailed from across the social orders and Imerina's six provinces. By 1824, 30 schools counted 2,000 students; by 1828 there existed 100 schools with 5,000 students.[88]

In sum, by even a conservative estimate, some 10,000 civilians and military men, their families and retinues, were dressing in some form of tailored garments by Radama's death in 1828.

Many dress studies link the global adoption of Western dress forms to increased garment flows from Europe, while Madagascar historiography tends to accord agency to British agents, missionaries and/or their wives. It is true that Farquhar shared Radama's strategy of using dress to legitimate his standing as ruler of the entire island in the eyes of regional and international players. Farquhar lavished money for the purchase of clothing for a select few in Radama's entourage on their visits to Mauritius to ensure their 'ease' in local society and undoubtedly avoid any confusion with the many enslaved highland Malagasy residing there. In 1821, he famously paid a great sum for Rafaralahy – who, it must be reiterated, had been dressing in tailored garments since at least 1818 –

to be outfitted as 'a proper gentleman' with dozens of shirts, gloves, ties and hats. It is also true that specialty items such as officers' coats, hats and gold lace and trim were most usually procured from the Mascarenes.[89] However, the impact of the British Equivalent has been overestimated. Rarely was the promised annual allotment of 400 soldier outfits paid in full, agents in Mauritius often failing to locate the items from government stores and private vendors in Mauritius and British India.[90] Moreover, the first allotment arrived only in autumn, 1820, by which time the guard had grown to 1,000 men, only to climb to 5,000 or more by 1828.[91] Finally, the Equivalent had made no provisions whatsoever for civilian ranks.

Importantly, the majority of dress worn in the service of Radama was tailored in Imerina itself. Fueled by voracious local demand, needlework was the earliest – of the technology transfers pursued by Radama and, according to Gwyn Campbell, ultimately the most successful.[92] As early as spring, 1817, or even 1816, Radama on his own initiative sent three women to Mauritius for training in needlework; Farquhar sent them home with 'another woman from here' who might assist.[93] Under Radama's urging, they were followed in 1820 by an independent Mauritian Creole tailor who both produced for sale and trained a group of Malagasy boys to fashion the first locally made military coats.[94] From that same year, Mary Hastie, the British agent's spouse, made a fortune privately producing tailored garments, but 'as the Malagasy are very handy, they in a very short time, knew how to cut a gown and to sew as well as her'.[95] Although arriving belatedly, in 1821, the London Missionary Society (LMS) missionary wives, invited by the king for the purpose of teaching needlework, greatly spurred local capacity. Radama required they make sewing part of girls' school curriculum and, from 1824, teach it at the new teacher training college for outlying districts.[96] Girls were observed to make fast 'progress in sewing gowns, pantaloons, shirts, etc. and His Majesty has been pleased to reward some of the best for an encouragement to all the others'.[97] From 1824, a mission shop sold the output of the 40-odd girls of the royal college, being 'small overcoats of twilled calico and bordered woollen cloth, in addition to gowns, trousers, shirts and kerchiefs'.[98] These skills were further appropriated and diffused through local networks. Elite Merina men demanded the best student seamstresses in marriage, while officers were observed to take pride in both the European-style dress of their large retinue and in 'the circumstances of these dresses being entirely prepared and worked by themselves'.[99] By early 1828, 120 girls were removed from the central school to stitch army uniforms and flags directly for the crown.[100]

The queen's clothing: Ranavalona I and 'baroque extravagance'

A brief overview of the long and complex reign of Radama's successor and senior wife, Queen Ranavalona I (b. 1778; r. 1828–1861), confirms the importance of dress politics. She immediately cancelled the British treaty and replaced

Radama's top officers with men from commoner clans. From 1835 she effect-ively ejected the missionaries, persecuted Christian converts and prohibited free trade, granting residence and trade rights to a few select French and American favourites. Provocations included the bombing of Tamatave in 1829 and 1845 by France and Britain, French colonization of the nearby islands of Nosy Be and Mayotte in 1840, with rumours of invasions persisting until the end of her reign. Vilified by some authors as a 'reactionary', 'xenophobe' or even 'psycho-path', she is conversely celebrated by others as a nationalist and remains an enig-matic figure. Most, however, agree that her reign brought a continuation of Radama's policies of autarky, territorial expansion and political independence.[101] Similarly, dress remained central to these pursuits. Overall, her reign was remarkable for the growth in the numbers producing and wearing tailored clothing in general European cuts and the resources invested in self-fashioning.

Establishing what Ranavalona herself wore is not an easy task. Few foreigners were allowed into the capital from 1835 to 1855, and even fewer left written accounts. She refused to be painted or photographed; widely reproduced images of her are either pure inventions or based on a photograph of her successor, Rasoherina.[102] However, first-hand observations, royal wardrobe registers and a few surviving garments show that Ranavalona followed the general sartorial path established by her late husband. Raised at the court of Andrianampoinimer-ina, she had developed a 'taste for luxury items from overseas'.[103] As a royal wife of Radama, she was accustomed to wearing tailored dresses. She, too, invented her own traditions and hybrid assemblages, based on European silhou-ettes, but drawing on Malagasy-informed fabrics, colours, embellishment and combinations. For her coronation on the 27 May 1829, for instance, she alter-nated outfits, variously wearing a 'blue silk peignoir gallooned at the wrists and back' and an older type of ensemble (also of imported materials), composed of bustier (*akanjo*) made of 'purple silk, richly ornamented with gold lace, having round the wrists, and on the back a row of gold buttons' with a waist wrapper (*kitamby*) of white silk, worn with profuse jewellery of coral, carnelian and pre-cious metals. Both outfits were accessorized with white stockings, Moroccan yellow leather shoes, and the royal red broadcloth cloak, gallooned all over with gold lace.[104]

Ranavalona likewise varied her wardrobe according to occasion. For public gatherings and proclamations, she donned as overdress a large wrapper of imported broadcloth and, as the island's other queens, carried a sword, while in religious ceremonies she wore locally woven red indigenous silk.[105] If anything, she increased expenditures on imports.[106] Bypassing the Mascarenes and official French and British agents, she used her hand-selected foreign favourites – French, British and American traders – to order gowns and accessories from the best dressmakers in London, Paris and the United States.[107] Two especially extravagant buying sprees in 1842–1843, in anticipation of her son's circumci-sion ceremony, were covered in the French and Mauritian presses. Via a Tamatave-based merchant, the queen placed orders in Paris for several types of crowns, as well as dresses 'of the finest velvet or scarlet woollen, lined with silk of the same colour', shoes, gloves and stockings of red velvet, silk or broadcloth, all the items heavily embroidered with gold, the metalwork on one dress alone worth £200.[108] She herself designed the crowns and embroidered motifs, which included her initials, crown and rice stalks, an Indigenous play on the international-style oak leaf (Figure 7.7).

Unlike the queen, her court, military and other royals happily posed for photographs from 1853 (Figures 7.8a and 7.8b)[109] They confirm written observations that the extended royal family, including Crown Prince Rakoto (future Radama II), were always 'dressed in the European manner', the adult prince's daily and ceremonial dress being smart cuts in shades of black or blue.[110] More generally, officers and court ladies rejected the restrained ornamentation then fashionable in Europe, craving instead 'the richest and most brilliant materials … loaded with lace at every

FIGURE 7.7 A dress attributed to Queen Ranavalona I made of imported silk satin, with gold thread embroidery depicting rice stalks, crowns and her initials, matching descriptions of items she ordered in 1842 from Paris.

Source: Collections of Andafiavaratra Palace. With permission of the Ministry of Culture, Madagascar.

seam'.[111] Under Ranavalona, the numbers in Crown service increased exponentially, and thus those we can reasonably assume to be participating in the new fashions. The military ballooned alongside large-scale campaigns, with a standing army of 45,000 by 1835 and dozens of Merina garrisons located across much of the island, manned by thousands.[112] Officers above the ninth honour were accorded sometimes hundreds of aides-de-camp – the prime minister reportedly had 2,000 – dependents who worked for their benefit and reflected their glory.[113] The civil administration expanded apace, with administrators, artisans and other labourers conscripted in ever-greater numbers. An industrial complex managed by a French favourite, Jean Laborde, was allocated 20,000 workers to produce arms, soap and dyes. Until 1835, the queen promoted schools, turning instruction over to Malagasy teachers and expanding them into the provinces to 'furnish a supply of better qualified officers for the army, or servants for other departments of government'.[114] By 1840 some 20,000 highlanders were literate.[115] Despite spates of persecution, the number of Christians grew steadily; photographs of the 1850s show their neat tailored dress resembled the undress of state functionaries. Quantifying the numbers of Merina owning and, at least occasionally, dressing in tailored garments, is challenged by lack of sources, but the numbers of the standing army and school graduates would place it conservatively at 40,000, even by 1845.

Four distinctive sartorial trends of her reign deserve mention. First, some standardization appears to have come to the dress of the highest ministers and court officers in the form of a household uniform, consisting of a frock or surtout-coat of dark blue colour, tastefully decorated with black or dark-coloured braid, a cap of the same kind of cloth, with a band of gold lace, or a cocked hat, in general trousers of blue ornamented with broad gold lace.

Higher court servants wore a 'sort of livery of blue jackets bordered with red' (Figure 7.9).[116]

Second, her innovations to political stagecraft and allegiance-profession included not only an augmentation to the scale and expense of existing state ceremonies, but the addition of new ones, notably elaborate masquerade balls. In the early 1850s Ravanalona hosted grandiose afternoon entertainments wherein hundreds of subjects – including European favourites – were made to perform local and foreign dances dressed in elaborate costumes, ranging from the dress of Spanish pages to Turkish princes, complete with enormous turbans and pointed slippers, outfits that she chose from albums she received from abroad.[117] Bewildering to external observers then and now, these balls were an integral feature of what Maurizio Peleggi calls 'the fraternal order of the global monarchy' of the nineteenth century; cosmopolitan rulers of nations stretching from Hawaii to Thailand were connected through gift exchanges and shared conventions such as European-inspired dress, furnishings and entertainments, including dress balls.[118]

Andrianatsitohaina and Raonitsietena

Cheif the Embassy to England in 1837 & member of the Malagasy Government

Noble and member of the Royal Family

FIGURES 7.8A AND 7.8B A pair of photographic portraits of two high-ranking government officials (Andrianatsitohaina and Raonitsietena), which show ceremonial dress and undress, c.1860. Note the white shoulder cloths with silk borders known as *lamba akotso*.

Source: Photograph by William Ellis. Courtesy of the Royal Ontario Museum © Royal Ontario Museum (a) 944 × 72.134 cm, (b) 944 × 72.133 cm.

A third departure during her reign was a more conspicuous use of the shoulder mantle by the sovereign and by officers.[119] Probably nationalist sentiment drove this to a certain degree. Yet, these mantles were always worn *over* tailored garments, and the styles did not hark to the past, but were all recent inventions. Ranavalona was observed to wear a large shawl of white silk with golden sprigs when receiving foreign visitors in the 1850s.[120] Possibly an imported fabric, it may have been locally woven from newly introduced Bombyx sericulture, a monochrome variant of the newly fashionable *akotifahana* brocaded silks, worn by her diplomatic envoys to England in 1838. Another new wrapper style, made of white cotton with blue or green and red bands at the two ends (*lamba akotso*) (see Figure 7.8b), emerged as part of the undress of higher ranked officers.[121] Indeed, there could be no return to former signs of status, and sumptuary laws based on noble birth. The queen's closest allies and supporters, the men now wielding greatest power, who reportedly placed her on the throne, hailed from commoner clans. They moreover controlled the import and transport of foreign cloth.[122] Most influential were brothers Rainijohary and Rainiharo, who successively served as her prime minister and commander of armies, the former ordering from Paris in 1843 a 'uniform of green velvet, with twice more gold embroidery' than that of a French marshall.[123] Surely the new dress styles, with their neutral forms and colours – greens, blues and purples rose in popularity – facilitated the rise of these and thousands of other commoner men; wealth, education and connections, rather than birth, now determined the types and lavishness of dress (Figures 7.10a and 7.10b).[124]

Finally, from Ranavalona's reign comes the first evidence of imported second-hand clothing, especially hats and military outfits.[125] Aside from these specialized garments, the swelling demand for tailored clothing continued to be met locally, by increasing numbers of domestic and professional tailors and seamstresses, some now directly attached to her and the court. The quality of their work was so high, the otherwise contemptuous Austrian traveller Ida Pfeiffer had to admit she had mistaken Crown Prince Rakoto's locally sewn ball dress for the work of Parisian couturiers.[126]

Conclusion

The adoption of ponchos in Polynesian society in the early 1800s, according to Thomas, did not necessarily represent a response to the global, nor was it a mere expression of new identities, but instead was a kind of technology, toward a new way of being in the world. Thousands of miles away, in Hawaii, the Americas and Asia, simultaneous experimentations with new forms of dress were occurring, many playing on European silhouettes: trousers and suit coats for men and dresses for women. If to outside observers (then and now) they seemed evidence of globalizing homogeneity, or naive mimicry, a large body of literature has demonstrated that beneath seemingly similar exteriors lurked very different motivations.

FIGURE 7.9 Private secretaries (palace officers) to Queen Ranavalona I, *c*.1856. Both wear her star-shaped order, 944 × 72.143 cm.

Source: Photograph by William Ellis. Courtesy of the Royal Ontario Museum © Royal Ontario Museum.

The earliest large-scale, state-driven fashion system drawing on European silhouettes developed in pre-colonial Africa, on the island nation of Madagascar. There, from 1816, King Radama remade local fashions to remake the sociopolitical world, by intensifying his own use of tailored dress and requiring it of those in his service, seeking it as actively as arms and ammunition. These dress reforms – long ignored or trivialized – were central to his drive to reconfigure relationships within the island, the region and beyond. Far from imposed by British agents or missionaries, the new dress was appropriated according to local sensibilities and domesticated through proactive provisioning, multiple supply chains and home manufacture.

Scholars have shown that each incoming Merina sovereign devised novel means for subjects to demonstrate allegiance. Assuming the procurement challenges and the heavy costs of the new dress – officers and their wives falling into debt to do so[127] – were embodied acts of obedience and loyalty. Demonstrating

FIGURES 7.10A AND 7.10B A pair of photographic portraits showing ceremonial dress and undress of the aide-de-camp of the prime minister (Rainitompomirary) and his wife (Raizananana), *c.*1860, 944 × 72.145 cm.

Source: Photograph by William Ellis. Courtesy of the Royal Ontario Museum © Royal Ontario Museum.

their own spiritual efficacy through the new finery, 'officers' in turn attracted followers. Clothing, no less than muskets and schools, was a major technology of change in Radama's sociopolitical remaking of his kingdom, further projecting power in the provinces and proving the Merina the equals of their European counterparts, capable of economic and political independence.

Notes

1 I thank colleague Bako Rasoarifetra for her insights and research assistance and Emeline Raharimanana of the Ministry of Culture of Madagascar. Simon Peers and Pier Larson kindly shared archival resources and made comments on earlier drafts of this essay. Gwyn Campbell generously engaged in a discussion on numbers in royal service (our conclusions differ). Nigel Arch, Alexandra Kim and Alexandra Palmer made useful suggestions related to European court and military uniform. All final interpretations remain my own. Research was supported by the ROM Department of World Culture Field Research Grants and an Insight Grant from the Social Science and Humanities Research Council of Canada.

2 Toby Slade, 'Neither East Nor West: Japanese Fashion in Modernity', in *Modern Fashion Traditions: Negotiating Modernity Through Fashion*, ed. M. Angela Jansen and Jennifer Craik (London: Bloomsbury, 2016), 25.

3 On Radama's fascination with Napoleon, see Françoise Raison-Jourde, *Bible et pouvoir à Madagascar au XIXe siècle: invention d'une identité chrétienne et construction de l'Etat, 1780–1880* (Paris: Karthala, 1991), 114; Gwyn Campbell, *David Griffiths and the Missionary 'History of Madagascar'* (Leiden: Brill, 2012), 699.

4 Maurice Bloch, *From Blessing to Violence: History and Ideology in the Circumcision Ritual of the Merina* (Cambridge, UK: Cambridge University Press, 1986), 129; Faly Razafindrangita Andriantsietena, 'Se vêtir à Antananarivo à la fin du XIXe Siècle' (Unpublished MA thesis, University of Antananarivo, 1994). Merina historian Raombana (1809–1855) also attributed dress changes to British intervention. He was not, however, a direct witness, being resident in England during the critical years 1820–1829. Simon Ayache, ed., *Raombana Histoires 1* (Antananarivo: Ambozontany, 1980), 37.

5 L. Munthe, C. Ravoajanahary and S. Ayache, 'Radama Ier et les Anglais: les négociations de 1817 d'après les sources malgaches ("Sorabe" inedits)', *Omaly sy Anio*, 3–4 (1976): 9–104; Gwyn Campbell, *An Economic History of Imperial Madagascar, 1750–1895: The Rise and Fall of an Island Empire* (Cambridge, UK: Cambridge University Press, 2005); Pier M. Larson, *History and Memory in the Age of Enslavement. Becoming Merina in Highlands Madagascar, 1770–1822* (Portsmouth, NH: Heinemann, 2000); Pier M. Larson, 'A Cultural Politics of Bedchamber Construction and Progressive Dining in Antananarivo: Ritual Inversions During the Fandroana of 1817', *Journal of Religion in Africa* 27.3 (1997): 239–269; Didier Nativel, *Maisons Royales, Demeures des Grands à Madagascar* (Paris: Karthala, 2005); Raison-Jourde, *Bible et pouvoir*; Gilbert Ratsivalaka, 'Madagascar dans le Sud-Ouest de l'Océan Indien (circa 1500–1824)' (PhD Thesis, Université de Nice, 1995).

6 Nicholas Thomas, 'The Case of the Misplaced Ponchos: Speculations Concerning the History of Cloth in Polynesia', *Journal of Material Culture* 4.1 (1999): 5–20.

7 M. Angela Jansen and Jennifer Craik, 'Introduction', in Jansen et al., *Modern Fashion Traditions*, 1.

8 John Mack, *Malagasy Textiles* (Princes Risborough, UK: Shire, 1989); Sarah Fee, 'Cloth in Motion: Madagascar's Textiles through History', in *Objects as Envoys: Cloth, Imagery and Diplomacy in Madagascar*, ed. Christime Mullen Kreamer and Sarah Fee (Seattle: University of Washington Press, 2002), 33–94; Christine

The king's new clothing 177

Athenor, 'Lambas et Ikat: une tradition du tissage', in *Arts Anciens de Madagascar*, ed. Bertand Goy (Milan: 5 Continents, 2015), 96–105.

9 See for instance Manassé Esoavelomandroso, 'The "Malagasy Creoles" of Tamatave in the 19th Century', *Diogenes* 111 (1980): 50–64; Pier Larson, 'Fragments of an Indian Ocean Life: Aristide Corroller Between Islands and Empires', *Journal of Social History* 24.2 (2011): 366–389.

10 Ratsivalaka, 'Madagascar', i, 115, 116; M. Legentil, *Voyage dans les Mers de l'Inde* (Paris: Imprimerie Royale, 1779), tome 2, 557.

11 Ratsivalaka, 'Madagascar', 155; Jean Valette, 'La mission de Lesage auprès de Radama Ier', *Bulletin de Madagascar* 275 (1969): 333.

12 While it is an anachronism to use the term 'Merina' in the eighteenth century, I could find no better expression for designating the people today who inhabit Imerina. On the complexity of ethnic terms for this region, see Pier Larons 'Desperately Seeking the Merina (Central Madaascar): Reading Ethnonyms and Their Semantic Fields in African Identity Histories,' *Journal of Southern Africa Studies* 22.4 (1996): 541–560.

13 Ratsivalaka, 'Madagascar'; Gwyn Campbell, 'The Structure of Trade in Madagascar, 1750–1810', *International Journal of African Historical Studies* 26.1 (1993): 111–148; Campbell, *An Economic History*; Larson, *History and Memory*, 148–155.

14 Campbell, *David Griffiths*, 274; Larson, *History and Memory*, 147–155; Raison-Jourde, *Bible et pouvoir*, 97–99.

15 The portrait of Andrianampoinimerina was created only in 1905 (Larson, *History and Memory*, 173). It was based on the sketch of a Sakalava warrior (Simon Peers, personal communication). Rafaralahy was painted from life in Mauritius in 1821, but he dressed in picturesque native garb upon the request of painter Lemaire. Ayach, *Histoires II*, xviii.

16 Simon Peers, 'Robert Townsend Farquhar & Rafaralahy', unpublished manuscript.

17 Scholars typically assume this cloth was the locally woven wild silk *lambamena*, but it clearly refers to British broadcloth. Sarah Fee, 'British Scarlet Broadcloth: The Perfect Red in Eastern Africa, c.1820–1900', in *Colors in Fashion*, ed. Jonathan Faiers and Mary Westerman Bulgarellea (London: Bloomsbury, 2016), 187–198.

18 British Library, Manuscript Division, Add. MSS 18135: La Salle 'Questions sur Madagascar', 1816. R. P Callet, ed., *Tantara ny Andriana eto Madagascar*, 2 vols. (Antananarivo: Académie Malgache, 1908), vol. II, 926.

19 British Library, Manuscript Division, MSS 18137: Hugon, 'Aperçu de mon voyage à Ancova de l'an 1808'; Callet, *Tantara*, vol. II, 926.

20 Nicolas Mayeur, 'Voyage dans le Sud et dans l'Intérieur des Terres et Particulièrement au Pays d'Hancove, Janvier 1777', *Bulletin de l'Académie Malgache* 12.I (1913): 139–176, 156.

21 One Merina trader observed in 1807: 'With our piasters … we will take a musket at one, a stone of cloth at another … because all do not have the same trade goods nor the same quality' (Nicolas Mayeur, quoted in Larson, *History and Memory*, 78).

22 Paul Camboue, 'Les dix premiers ans de l'Enfance chez les Malgaches. Circoncision, nom, éducation', *Anthropos* 4.2 (1902): 377. Larson, *History and Memory*, 136–139.

23 J. P. Dumaine, 'Idée de la côte occidentale de Madagascar', *Annales des Voyages, de la Géographie, et de l'Histoire* 11 (1810): 48.

24 Fee, 'Cloth in Motion'.

25 Campbell, *An Economic History*, 37.

26 Munthe et al., 'Radama Ier et les Anglais', 23–25; Jean Valette, 'La Mission de Chardenoux aurprès de Radam Ier (1816)', *Bulletin de Madagascar* 207 (1963): 691; Jean Valette, *Études sur le régne de Radama I* (Tananarive: Imprimerie Nationale, 1962), 17.

178 Sarah Fee

27 G. S. Chapus and L. Aujas, ed., 'Journal de James Hastie', *Bulletin de l'Académie Malgache* 4 (1918–1919): 150. William Ellis provides no source for his assertion that before 1815 Radama wore wrappers and sat on the floor. *History of Madagascar*, 2 vols. (London: Fischer & Sons, 1838), vol. II, 130. Radama's father used a chair. Hugon 'Apercu de mon voyage'. Local histories, recorded 50 years after his death, assert that Radama dressed for his coronation in 'un bicorne et un pagne garné de soie, noué a son extremité'. Callet, *Tantara*, vol. II.

28 British Library, Manuscript Division, Add. MSS 18135: Valette, 'La mission de Lesage': Lesage's inferior offering was an 'aide-de-camp embroidered coat with epaulet'; 'An account of receipts and expenditures of a special mission to Madagascar'.

29 Chapus and Aujas, 'Journal de James Hastie', 147.

30 Jean Valette, 'Arnoux et le séjour de Radama Ier à Tamatave en Juillet 1817', *Bulletin de Madagascar* 265 (1968): 585; J. Sibree and A. Jully, eds., 'Le Voyage de Tananarive en 1817. Manuscrit de James Hastie', *Bulletin de l'Académie Malgache* 11.4 (1903): 258; Valette, *Études*, 21, 30.

31 Munthe et al., 'Radama Ier et les Anglais', 94–95.

32 David Johns, *Dikisionary Malagasy Mizara Roa, Malagasy sy English* (Antananarivo: Tamy ny Press, 1835). Terms associated with schooling, on the other hand, derive from English and British missionaries.

33 Jean Valette, 'Les débuts de la correspondance entre Radama Ier et Sir R.T. Farquhar', *Bulletin de Madagascar* 274 (1969): 209–212; Anon, *Madagascar Sous Radama 1er* (Antananarivo: Association des Amis du Musée Jean Laborde, 1965), 30.

34 Munthe et al., 'Radama Ier et les Anglais', 82–83. The original 'shirts adorned with gold' and 'beautiful hat' demanded by Radama were formalized in the treaty as 'Un grand habit rouge de drap avec deux epaulettes, chapeaux et bottes pour le Roi'.

35 Mauritius National Archives (hereforth MNA), HB 13: to Hastie, 14 April 1821.

36 *Le journal de Robert Lyall* (Tananarive, Madagascar: Imprimerie Officielle, 1954), 60.

37 Ellis, *History*, vol. I, 254.

38 Maurizio Peleggi, *Lords of Things: The Fashioning of the Siamese Monarchy's Modern Image* (Honolulu: University of Hawai'i Press, 2002); Jeremy Prestholdt, 'Africa and the Global Lives of Things', in *The Oxford Handbook of the History of Consumption*, ed. Frank Trentmann (Oxford: Oxford University Press, 2012), 85–108.

39 André Coppalle, 'Voyage dans l'intérieur de Madagascar et à la capitale du roi Radame pendant les années 1825 et 1826, Suite', *Bulletin de l'Académie Malgache* 8 (1910): 31; 'Imerina en 1825', *Bulletin de Madagascar* 292 (1970): 796.

40 Journal of Lieutenant Boteler quoted in W. F. W. Owen, *Narrative of Voyages to Explore the Shores of Africa, Arabia and Madagascar*, 2 vols. (London: Richard Bentley, 1833) vol. II, 119. Marry Ann Hedge, in her fictionalized *Radama, or the Enlightened African* (London: Harvey & Darton, 1824), however, portrayed him as wearing 'native' dress approximating Central African styles.

41 Observers thus variously recorded he 'dressed simply'. Jean Valette, 'l'Imerina en 1822–1823 d'après les journaux de Bojer et d'Hilsenberg', *Bulletin de Madagascar* 227–228 (1965): 334; or 'loved luxury'.

42 We know he was gifted hats by the French governor of Reunion Island. Alfred Grandidier et al., *Histoire Physique, Naturelle et Politique de Madagascar* (Paris: Imprimerie Paul Brodard, 1942), vol. V, 179.

43 Nigel Arch, personal communication, 22 June 2016; Christian Mantaux, 'Emblèmes malgaches, Sceaux et drapeaux de 1787 à 1897', *Revue de Madagascar* 49–50 (1970): 19.

44 In Foule Point in 1823 Radama was observed to be 'mounted on an Arabian steed, and dressed in the uniform of an English field-officer of engineers, with a cap fitting close to the head, made of crimson velvet, variously ornamented; his boots were of

the same; and over his head a small silk canopy was carried by an attendant'. Captain Moorsom, quoted in Ellis, *History*, vol. II, 311.

45 British National Archives PRO/CO 167/34.
46 Grandidier et al., *Histoire Physique*, 164, 203; Anon, 'A Visit to the Court of Madagascar', *London Magazine*, no. X (January 1829). In 1854, missionary David Griffiths returned to Madagascar as a merchant of gold braid and military stripes. Campbell, *Griffiths*, 905.
47 J. Sibree and A. Jully, eds., 'Le Voyage de Tananarive en 1817. Manuscrits James Hastie', *Bulletin de l'Académie Malgache* 2.2 (1903): 98.
48 Valette, 'L'Imerina en 1822–1823', 325.
49 Sibree and Jully, 'Le Voyage de Tananarive', 175.
50 Campbell, *An Economic History*, 62.
51 Larson, 'Cultural Politics'.
52 I thank Pier Larson for sharing the original source. MNA, HB 10: folder 2, Hastie, 14 November 1817 to 19 May 1818.
53 Chapus and Aujas, 'Journal de James Hastie', 151. Hastie's reference to the fact that Radama's 'captains' changed into 'homemade cloth' suggests they too dressed in uniforms.
54 Grandidier et al., *Histoire Physique*, 179; Ellis, *History*, vol. II, 259, 265.
55 Campbell, *Griffiths*, 292, 639; Raison-Jourde, *Bible et Pouvoir*, 120; Vincent Huyghues-Belrose, *Les Premiers Missionnaires Protestants de Madagascar (1795–1827)* (Paris: Karthala, 2001), 373; Larson, *History and Memory*, 240–253.
56 Ayache, *Raombana. Histoires*, vol. II, 99.
57 Larson, 'Cultural Politics', 261.
58 Larson, 'Cultural Politics', 261.
59 Keturah Jeffreys, *The Widowed Missionary's Journal* (Southampton: Author, 1832), 163.
60 Peleggi, *Lords of Things*, 10.
61 Typically, Berg assumes the new military dress dates only from 1820. Gerald M. Berg, 'Virtù and Fortuna in Radama's Nascent Bureaucracy, 1816–1828', *History in Africa* 23 (1996): 36.
62 Berg, 'Virtù', 33.
63 Ellis, *History*, vol. I, 352.
64 Valette, 'La mission de Lesage', 378. Others observed 300 of Radama's men 'clothed in uniform' by 1817. R. E. Locke Lewis, 'An Account of the Ovahs, a Race of People Residing in the Interior of Madagascar', *Journal of the Royal Geographical Society* 35 (1835): 239.
65 Clare Anderson, *Convicts in the Indian Ocean* (Basingstoke, UK: Palgrave Macmillan, 2000).
66 Munthe et al., 'Radama et les Anglais', 82–83.
67 Sources vary widely on the number of soldiers dressed in tailored uniforms, although all works place it in the thousands as early as 1823. Campbell, *Griffiths*, 663; Grandidier et al., *Histoire*, 180; Coppalle, *Voyage*, 30; Valette, *Etudes*, 18; and Berg, 'Virtu', 37.
68 Campbell, *Griffiths*, 698, 703.
69 Grandidier et al., *Histoire Physique*, 233.
70 Coppalle, 'Voyage', 31; Valette, 'l'Imerina en 1822–1823', 273; Ellis, *History*, vol. II, 311.
71 Berg, 'Virtu'; Larson, 'Culture Politics', 241; Campbell, *Economic History*, 68.
72 Valette, 'La mission de Lesage', 377; Locke Lewis, 'An Account of the Ovahs', 231.
73 They included Ramenataka and Ramorasikina. The National Archives, Kew (hereafter TNA), PRO 167/50: 'Diary of James Hastie', 3 October 1820. Robin's diary from even earlier, in May 1820, puts the number at 36, all mounted on horseback

and dressed 'in the uniform of British captains'. G. S. Chapus, 'Le journal d'une campagne de Radama I', *Bulletin de l'Académie Malgache* 22 (1939): 46.

74 Campbell, *Griffiths*, 637. On this trip Ratefy had his portrait made; more research is required on the published engraving, whether this was done from life and whether he chose the outfit of a shoulder wrapper and tubular hat. Peers, 'Farquhar & Rafaralahy'.

75 TNA, PRO 167/50: 'Diary of James Hastie', 29 September 1820.

76 TNA, PRO 167/50: 'Diary of James Hastie', 3 October 1820.

77 Charles Brand, 'A Visit to the Island of Madagascar', *United Service Journal and Naval Magazine*, 2 (1829): 529; Ellis, *History*, vol. II, 276, 329.

78 *Le journal de Robert Lyall*, 147.

79 Grandidier et al., *Histoire Physique*, 232; Coppalle, 'Voyage dans l'intérieur', 18.

80 Ellis, *History*, vol. II, 309.

81 Previously, in 1816, Lesage observed women wearing red silk, men in belts and silver jewelry. Valette, 'La mission de Lesage', 377.

82 Coppalle, 'Voyage dans l'intérieur', 30, 44.

83 Hastie in Ellis, *History*, vol. II, 169.

84 Ellis, *History*, vol. II, 268.

85 William Ellis, *Three Visits to Madagascar During the Years 1853–1854–1856* (Philadelphia, PA: J. W. Bradley, 1859), 254.

86 Berg, 'Virtu', 34.

87 Ellis, *History*, vol. II, 269, 271.

88 Campbell, *Economic History*, 86–87; Campbell, *Griffiths*, 634; Ellis *History*, vol. II, 351, 353, 415; Berg, 'Virtu', 33.

89 LMS missionary David Jones noted that officers in Radama's army were paying 'excessively dear for these things [clothes] from the Mauritius'. Archives of the London Missionary Society, SOAS, CWM/LMS/Madagascar: Incoming Correspondence David Jones, 24 June 1822.

90 The clothing items of the Equivalent were delivered piecemeal, with many substitutes, and only in 1822 was it apparently paid in full. They were never procured in England as Hastie had urged. Sarah Fee, 'The Equivalent', forthcoming.

91 Grandidier et al., *Histoire Politique*, 231; Berg, *Virtu*, 35.

92 Gwyn Campbell, 'The Decline of the Malagasy Textile Industry', in *Textile Trades, Consumer Cultures and the Textile Worlds of the Indian Ocean: An Ocean of Cloth*, ed. Pedro Machado, Sarah Fee and Gwyn Campbell (London: Palgrave Macmillan, 2018).

93 Jean Valette, 'Documents pour servir à l'histoire des relations entre la Grande-Bretagne et Madagascar sous Radama I', *Revue de Madagascar* 23 (1963): 24.

94 Grandidier et al., *Histoire*, 289; Campbell, *Griffiths*, 612, Valette, *Etudes*, 32.

95 Ayache, *Raombana Histoires*, vol. I, 37.

96 Huyghes-Belrose, *Les Premiers Missionnaires*, 329; Mervyn Brown, *Madagascar Rediscovered* (Hamden, CT: Archon Books, 1979), 158; Ellis, *History*, vol. II, 266.

97 TNA, PRO 167/63: David Jones to Farquhar, 25 March 1822; Ellis, *History*, vol. II, 270.

98 Campbell, *Griffiths*, 613.

99 Campbell, *Griffiths*, 291; Ellis, *History*, vol. II, 329. A plan in 1824 called for Madagascar to export garments to Mauritius. Valette, *Madagascar sous Radama*, vol. I, 32.

100 Campbell, *Griffiths*, 797.

101 Campbell, *Economic History*; P. M. Mutibwa, *The Malagasy and the Europeans* (Atlantic Highlands, NJ: Humanities Press, 1974), 24–27; Gerald M. Berg, 'Writing Ideology: Ranavalona, the Ancestral Bureaucrat', *History in Africa* 22 (1995): 73–92.

102 Simon Peers, *The Working of Miracles: William Ellis Photography in Madagascar 1853–1865* (Antananarivo: British Council, 1995).

103 Campbell, *Griffiths*, 713.
104 Campbell, *Griffiths*, 713. David Jones, cited in Ellis, *History*, vol. II, 428.
105 Bloch, *From Blessing to Violence*, 132.
106 A royal wardrobe register from 1861, kept by a court seamstress (*mpanjaitra*), reveals clothing all of imported fabrics, for the most part velvets and silk-satins (amparasily), but also plain and printed cottons and woolens Archives Royales de Madagascar MM10, Antananarivo 6 asombola 1861, Ary ny isany ny akanjo nan-dRiana tehiriziny mpanjaitra offsDPle.
107 Grandidier et al., *Histoire*, 309. Intermediaries included British missionaries exiled to Capetown, a French trader's wife, and a favoured merchant of the American firm Ropes & Emerton. Campbell, Griffiths, 892; Ayache, *Raombana*, 125.
108 *Morning Post*, 14 April 1843; for even more extravagant 1857 gifts from Lambert see Ida Pfeiffer, *Voyage à Madagascar* (Paris: Hachette, 1862).
109 Peers, *Working of Miracles*.
110 Grandidier, *Histoire*, 299; Ellis, *History*, vol. II, 429; Campbell, *Griffiths*, 754; Ellis, *Three Visits*, 330, 370.
111 *Morning Post*, The historian Raombana was buried with among other clothing articles, purple pants, a pink shirt and a woolen suit embroidered with white.
112 Campbell, *Economic History*, 163.
113 Grandidier et al., *Histoire*, 295.
114 Ellis, *History*, vol. II, 454.
115 Brown, *Madagascar Rediscovered*, 172; Campbell, *Griffiths*, 278.
116 Ellis, *Three Visits*, 282, 347.
117 Pfeiffer, *Voyage*, 239. Similar costumes were sometimes required of the hundreds of subjects who attended the queen on her public outings to the countryside. The 'Arab' costume worn at these balls was fashionable Turkish dress, not austere Omani Arab attire, as some have suggested. Gillian Feeley-Harnik, 'Cloth Production in Madagascar: A Preliminary Inquiry' (Unpublished paper, 1984), 33.
118 Peleggi, *Lords of Things*, 13.
119 Ellis, *Three Visits*, 316, 321, 330, 342; Pfeiffer, *Voyage*, 207.
120 Ellis, *History*, vol. I, 283; Ellis, *Three Visits*, 342, 358; Pfeiffer, *Voyage*.
121 Ellis, *Three Visits*, 330, 377.
122 Andriantsietena, *Se Vêtir*, 58.
123 Raison-Jourde, *Bible et Pouvoir*, 155.
124 Andriantsietena, *Se Vêtir*, 55, 75.
125 Pfeiffer, *Voyage*, 199.
126 Pfeiffer, *Voyage*, 232.
127 *Le Journal de Robert Lyall*, 230; Gustave Julien, *Institutions politques et sociales de Madagascar*, 2 vols. (Paris: Libraire Oriental & Americaine, 1909), vol. II, 120.

8

DRESSING SETTLERS IN NEW ZEALAND

Global interconnections

Jane Malthus

When Catherine Henrietta Elliott Valpy married James Fulton at her parents' home, 'The Forbury', in Dunedin, New Zealand, on 22 September 1852, just four years after organized European settlement of Otago had begun, she wore a cotton organdie dress, with flared sleeves, tiered skirt and a silk under-bodice interlined with calico (Figure 8.1).[1] Her father, William Henry Valpy, had worked for the East India Company and been a judge in Calcutta, returning to England in 1836. He emigrated to Otago in 1849 for health reasons, bringing with him five of his six offspring, a large number of servants and equipment for farming and feeding them all. He also imported a large sum of money, with which he purchased farmland and labour.[2] Catherine's husband, James Fulton (1830–1891), was also born in India where his father was a major in the Bengal Artillery. James, a trained surveyor, travelled to Otago on the same ship as the Valpys.[3]

Although Catherine, born in 1829, was still a small child when the family returned from India, it is worth speculating about her choice of fine cotton fabric for her wedding dress, rather than the increasingly fashionable silk. Did the cream cotton remind her of her Indian upbringing? Did the fibre, fabric or even the made-up dress come from that country, through family connections, or did it come from Sydney, like her older sister's wedding dress the year before?[4] Or were Catherine's ideas about appropriate dress fabric for her wedding more influenced by her English education and European tours before she came to New Zealand, rather than her new environment on the other side of the world? Like most European consumers, Catherine would have been aware of – and probably used – cotton from India or other parts of the world in her everyday life, but the origin of this specific fabric cannot be easily determined.[5]

What *is* known is that Catherine's family and others who came to New Zealand settlements in the nineteenth century came mostly from the British Isles,

FIGURE 8.1 Catherine Valpy's wedding dress.

Source: Otago Museum Collection, Dunedin New Zealand, G86.36. Image credit: Jane Malthus.

while smaller groups arrived from southern and central Europe. They were part of what James Belich has called the Anglo-world settler revolution, creating expanding populations and neo-European economies around the world.[6] Many of those who arrived in New Zealand were not as well off as Catherine's family: most other nineteenth-century wedding dresses in New Zealand museums, while usually silk, resemble good coloured day dresses, which could be worn again.

Why these emigrants came to New Zealand when they could have gone to the United States, Canadian or Australian colonies is still debated, but James Belich argues that they were 'prised out of their British contexts by powerful myths and prophecies'.[7] Proponents of settlement schemes portrayed New Zealand as a Britain of the South, a land benign in its geography and climate and lacking dangerous animals – or people. Māori were claimed as transforming themselves into 'something European-like' with the help of missionaries and others, but also thought to be dying out, and British settlers were praised as much better than those sent to Australia as convicts. People could progress economically and socially and have larger families. At various times between the

1840s and the 1870s provincial governments in New Zealand also offered land grants, assisted passages and ran a nominee system for migration, all of which encouraged settlement.[8]

While the fabric, design and construction of Catherine's wedding dress may have originated elsewhere in the Anglo-world, most Anglo settlers who came to New Zealand shores, including Catherine herself, had to modify their new local environment to provide for their future dress and textile needs, although they assumed that these would follow British or European fashions, rather than be adapted to local conditions. Importers and traders set up shops.[9] Farmers, such as Catherine and her husband, established pastures and grew sheep on their land, and other entrepreneurs appropriated materials for export that Māori had considered theirs, or experimented with plant or protein fibre systems transplanted and acclimatized from elsewhere. Early settlers sent pleas to family back home for supplies of clothing and footwear, but as more people came, goods came with them.

While speculation may be all that is now possible regarding the specific history of the fabric of Catherine's wedding dress, this chapter investigates wider questions of how patterns of settlement, information transfer, shipping and trade affected the supply of textile and apparel goods in nineteenth-century New Zealand. How did materials and technologies arrive and where did they come from? What did settlers think they could do in the textiles and clothing realm to improve their new country's economy and boost their own incomes? How and why did commercial textile businesses such as flax and silk industries develop? How did these patterns and developments affect people's experiences of and ideas about personal appearance and clothes?

Colonial settlement in New Zealand

Nineteenth-century settlers to Aotearoa New Zealand brought their ingrained customs and mores, fashions and etiquette patterns about dress with them, along with as many wardrobe items as they could cram into their trunks. Around 1830 there were fewer than 1,000 Europeans in New Zealand – mainly missionaries, traders, whalers and explorers – among a Māori population estimated at *c*.70,000.[10] The southern South Island was a busy site of interaction between Māori and these very early settlers and transients.[11] Whalers, sealers and commercial ships moved from Port Jackson (Sydney) and Hobart through Foveaux Strait. As historian Michael Stevens has shown, Māori in this area had a networked life as their skills as excellent mariners were in demand, and they quickly adopted European dress, purchasing 'wearing apparel and rum' that had come from American whaling ships as early as the 1830s.[12] They knew about the power and status of clothes. For example, Topi, a young Māori chief, on board the *Acheron* sometime between 1848 and 1851, recorded feeling embarrassed at not being dressed as befitted his status since he was attired in an 'old French marine's grey coat' in the company of the ship's British officers.[13]

From 1850 until the 1880s, Eliza Wohlers (1812–1891), a dressmaker and wife of a missionary, taught Māori women on Ruapuke Island, off the South Island's southern coast, 'European manners' and how to do 'plain sewing and fancy work'.[14] Her husband expressed his concern about European men who married New Zealand (Māori) women but did not provide adequately for them: 'The most they do is to buy them a European woman's dress, whether it fits or is becoming or not'.[15] Presumably these were second-hand or slop garments, maybe from Port Jackson in Australia. Missionaries throughout the country saw it as imperative to clothe Māori as well as teach young Māori women sewing skills, despite Māori customs and expectations being rather different. One mission imported cheap and showy print fabrics for full-length dresses for Māori women.[16] Because they were used to wearing wraps and cloaks that the women made from hand-prepared New Zealand flax, Māori favoured blankets, especially scarlet ones, which they used as wrapping, for tying or for sitting on (Figure 8.2).[17]

Further waves of European settlement occurred between 1830 and 1880, and by 1881 the European population was half a million.[18] The publicity that lured settlers exaggerated the mildness of topography and climate, and the state of progress: people thought they were coming to an established Arcadia, a southern

FIGURE 8.2 Photograph of Māori and Pakeha mourners gather against a backdrop of flax bushes at Ruapuke Island for the tangi and funeral of Teone Tapi Patuki (Topi), 1900. Photographer G. Hicks, Box-146-007.

Source: Hocken Collections – Uare Taoka o Hākena, University of Otago. © Otago Museum Collection, Dunedin New Zealand.

hemisphere paradise with a Mediterranean climate. Instead they found steep hills, bush tracks, high rainfall and harsh winters, especially in the South Island. Lists of clothes and other provisions provided to prospective emigrants suggested that class differences would continue, though other literature promised high wages for all, improved respectability and independence.[19] Some women settlers packed their trunks according to these lists, including dozens of calico night-dresses and nightcaps, several dinner dresses and fancy handkerchiefs that have found their way into museum collections virtually unworn, such was their impracticality for local conditions.

Colonial New Zealand was predominantly an English-speaking working set-tlers' society, attracting those who thought they could improve their economic and social position in a new society.[20] In 1861 two-thirds of the settler popu-lation lived in rural settings, where job opportunities for men were greater, but rapid urbanization throughout the colony meant that, by 1891, 46 per cent of the European population now lived in towns of more than 1,000 inhabitants.[21] Classes had to mix, and while the 'imported' (English, Scottish and Irish) social hierarchy remained and 'distinctions of birth, educa-tion, income, and occupation were acknowledged ... there was little subservi-ence', according to social historian Jeanine Graham.[22] Upward mobility generated an emphasis on propriety, respectability and conformity to the ideals of 'home' (i.e. Britain) that extended to dress as an outward sign of one's abil-ity to adopt the mores associated with the middle class.[23] For example, at a southern hemisphere summer Christmas party in Taranaki in 1858, female members of the Atkinson family attired themselves in black moiré, bronze silk, scarlet llama and black silk dresses, as they might have done in England.[24] Newspaper columnists and retailers both responded to and drove this desire, providing information on fashionable styles, etiquette and appropriate dress and textiles from 'home' wherever possible.

Professional and social etiquette was often referred to in newspapers, with lapses by men criticized or considered 'colonial': too informal or even uncultured.[25] The English satirical publication *Punch*, mocking the earnest lists of outfits for intending settlers, included as part of the indispensable articles for emigrating ladies 'several copies of the *Book of Etiquette*'.[26] However, copies of etiquette manuals (mostly British in origin) in New Zealand museum and library collections – and the number of their mentions in the colonial press – would suggest that considerable attention was paid to published information about social etiquette, behaviour, manners and dress.[27]

Ridicule was a powerful and gendered tool in colonial New Zealand: men ridiculed 'the supreme importance that ladies give to their dress' and grumbled about having to pay the bills: 'But let a woman once neglect her dress, and the masculine eye is ready enough to detect, the masculine voice ready enough to denounce it'. While in terms of their own apparel, men's dislike of 'being rigged out in our best' was 'prompted by some low cravings for animal com-fort ... the ordinary man of unregenerate instincts will not waver long between the choice of existing beautifully and existing in comfort'.[28] Women were less able to exist in comfort, given constraints on their appearance and the dictates of fashion and propriety.

Dressing at a distance from 'home'

Nineteenth-century settlers to New Zealand knew from the experience of travelling by ship to their new country just how far from most sources of goods the country was. As Frances Steel has pointed out in relation to Australia, the sea was both a medium of connection and isolation.[29] Keeping up appearances for women and men was dependent on the supply of materials, information, equipment, tailors and dressmakers, as well as global shipping patterns. As development of industries and commerce occurred in New Zealand, most imports of people and cargo came from Britain as the imperial centre and colonial occupier.

New Zealand newspapers, quickly established as towns grew, published articles (and later illustrations) detailing where materials, clothes and equipment could be purchased, though only occasionally mentioning where they had come from. The gentlemen's dress and accessories available at Alexander Aitken's store in Bridge Street, Nelson, in 1852, for example, included a mix of practical fabrics and garments and the less practical but perhaps more important appearance markers: tweeds, doeskins, cords, moleskins, white and coloured shirts, hosiery, gloves, black and coloured silk handkerchiefs, satin stocks, shirt collars, underclothing, blue cloth caps, felt hats, braces, blue serge shirts and umbrellas.[30] The implication was that men would wear some of these items for the physical work they may have had to do, but still appear as gentlemen for home, civic and family duties.

Women were offered a range of seasonal dress materials and accessories by retailers, such as those advertised by M. Harris of Trafalgar Street, Nelson, in January 1859: bareges (light woollen), linseys, muslins, poplins, alpacas, shot silks and ready-made garments such as mantles and shawls; and from Mr Harris' neighbour, Mrs Green, a dressmaker and milliner, ball and evening dresses in lace, embroidered muslin, tulle, bonnets trimmed and untrimmed and gloves, including Norway Gauntlets.[31] The cottons and blends may have been used for work or housework dresses, but little material or pictorial evidence for these exists in New Zealand.[32]

Ladies' columns in the newspapers reported alterations in dress styles and accessories from British and French sources, and their authors were conscious of women's desire not to look out of date.[33] Similarly, women's letters to and from family members in Britain often went into detail about changes in dress styles.

My own study of 162 nineteenth- and early twentieth-century dresses in New Zealand museum collections revealed that conformity to European/British styles of fashion was more important than adaptation to the New Zealand climatic environment. Changes in fashionable style and colour typical of Europe are represented, including a nostalgic fashion for eighteenth-century designs. Time lags for fashion changes are harder to ascertain, but overall the dresses in these collections are symbolic of the aspirations of many New Zealand settlers in their expression of genteel or middle-class values.[34] Catherine Fulton's wedding dress has survived in such good condition because it was the newly fashionable (in Britain) cream colour, not very practical for her married rural life on the edge of the swampy Taieri Plain near Dunedin, and the tiered skirt style soon went out of fashion. She also had the first of eight children the year after her wedding, so she may not have fitted the dress again. Most of the other dresses in my study show some signs of wear, such as perspiration stains, eyelet hole and buttonhole strains and tears and hem-edge abrasion, but may have been kept for best and gone out of fashion before being worn out. Sarah Falwasser wrote in a letter in 1869 that she had been encouraging her friend Kate Heaphy to order a new dress for the Duke of Edinburgh's visit: 'if I succeed it will be white silk, but the worst of it is there is not much chance of parties afterwards' at which to wear it.[35]

The early supply of tailors and dressmakers and their equipment also came mostly from Britain.[36] Emigration was seen as one solution to the proliferation of needlewomen in Britain, and the imbalance of the sexes in colonial New Zealand was addressed through schemes to bring out single women. A total of 11 'semptresses' arrived in Nelson in 1842 and 32 dressmakers and needle-women landed in Auckland in 1851, some of whom set up dressmaking businesses of their own, while others ended up in domestic service. Settlers looked to these recent arrivals for fashion advice, even if they then made their own clothes. The pull of 'home' was understandable, and family members in Britain were a major source of information about fashions and skills. Most of the nine-teenth- and early twentieth-century how-to books in New Zealand archives come from English tailoring societies.

A Madame Decourtet seems to have been an exception to the predominance of British dressmakers. Although her origins are unknown, she arrived in Dun-edin from Melbourne in 1863, advertising French stays and Parisian nursing stays and samples of the latest Parisian fashions.[37]

Developing textiles and clothing in the colony

For some settlers, becoming rooted to their new land involved cultivating ani-mals or crops as commodities that could earn them income or exploring oppor-tunities to export local flora and fauna. Some followed the example of Mori plant users, while others introduced shrubs and animals from elsewhere to pro-vide business prospects. Entrepreneurs developing textile and clothing businesses, such as those for wool, flax and silk, first looked to Britain and Australia for ideas, plants and the machinery they needed. As Belich has pointed out, this transfer of thought and technology was 'lubricated by language and culture', making communication easier.[38]

Spinning and weaving equipment, and skilled labour for the first woollen mill in the country came from England and Scotland.[39] Established in 1871 at Mosgiel near Dunedin, the new mill processed locally grown wool from sheep introduced multiple times from Captain Cook's visits onwards (Figure 8.3). Sheep farming had developed in New Zealand after its profitable adoption in New South Wales, Australia. As meat and wool production grew, land was developed into grass pasture,[40] so it was perhaps inevitable that factories to process the wool would arise. New Zealand sheep's wool was coarser than that produced in Australia, and was more suited to woollen than worsted cloth, even though equipment had been imported for – and efforts made to produce – both. Blankets, knitting wool and tweed fabrics were more successful, often produced by imitating imported fabric samples and ideas from English mills. Much of New Zealand's wool clip was still exported in a raw state to mills overseas, to be blended with finer fibre or put into carpet production.

Large numbers of sewing machines for domestic and industrial use also came from overseas makers, but not just British ones. Brands including Howe, Singer, Wertheim, Willcox and Gibbs, Frister and Rossmann, Davis, Victory and Jones and Wanzer were imported from England, America, Canada and Germany, with some now part of New Zealand museum collections.[41] But exactly how and when they got to New Zealand is not recorded: import statistics kept by the government only distinguished sewing machines from other machinery for a short period. From 1869 sewing machines were exempt from customs duty, which no doubt helped their sales.[42] As elsewhere, Singer's marketing strategies

FIGURE 8.3 Mosgiel Woollen Mills, showing workers' cottages on the right, *c.*1870s.

Source: © Hocken Collections – Uare Taoka o Hākena, University of Otago.

ensured that its sewing machines were especially popular in New Zealand, being installed at clothing factories such as the New Zealand Clothing Factory in Dunedin, which opened in 1874. Singer machines garnered substantial press coverage and were marketed through weekly payment schemes.[43]

Māori had long used the abundant New Zealand flax (*Phormium tenax*) they called *harakeke* in leaf form to weave *kete* (carrying bags) and other baskets. They were expert at the selection of leaves and had also perfected the technique of hand-scraping with mussel shells to extract fibre (*muka*) of a very high standard with which they wove various wearing apparel, such as cloaks and *piupiu* or skirts.[44] While visiting Europeans and settlers from Captain Cook onwards would not have dreamt of adopting Māori forms of dress, they had seen swathes of flax plants growing near the coasts and recognized its potential for ships' canvas and cordage.[45] Attempts by early settlers to develop flax as a tradable commodity to supply British naval and merchant vessels with ropes utilized imported machinery from Britain. However, problems arose as, for Europeans, flax meant the fibre from linseed (*Linum usitatissimum*), not that from *Phormium tenax*.[46] Processes for extracting the fibre needed to be different. Attempts to scrape or strike the flesh off *Phormium tenax* leaves leaving clean fibre for export usually failed, although many flaxmills were established.[47] Catherine Fulton, living on her farm near Outram, mentions a flaxmill there in her 1875 diary.[48] It was the site of a nasty accident involving one of her nephews, who almost lost his arm in the scutcher.[49] This mill was closed around a year later as flax prices fell, and the scutcher was removed by a Fulton employee.[50]

No doubt the Anglo-world connections of language and culture and the industrial progress of Britain helped facilitate the development of a New Zealand flax industry. Shipments of de-fleshed flax leaves were sent to London or Sydney from the early nineteenth century for ropemaking and some traders employed Māori workers to strip the leaves, paying them with blankets, trinkets or muskets.[51] However, they had little success at developing machinery to replicate the process Māori had invented, which so effectively released the beautiful *muka* (Figure 8.4). Indiscriminate cutting of leaves and lack of experimentation with plants and machinery were identified early on as problems,[52] and later draining of swamps and grazing by cattle affected the quantity of plants available.[53] Two government commissions in 1870 and 1871 investigated how New Zealand flax could become an export crop for ropemaking and possibly for textiles. According to English and Scottish textile and rope manufacturers, the fibres that colonists prepared on their machines were too rough, unclean and 'broke short off like a stick'.[54] *Phormium tenax* was also found to be weaker and rotted faster when exposed to seawater than Manilla hemp, traditionally used for ropes;[55] and the imported machinery, developed for breaking down the woody stems of linseed plants, could not remove all the outside leaf structure or scurf of New Zealand flax, especially from the tip of the leaf.[56]

It was generally recognized that the customary way that Māori chose which leaves to cut (side-leafing) and their methods of preparation produced a far

FIGURE 8.4 Unidentified Māori woman, wearing a *kakahu* (cloak) of *muka* fibre, with decorative taniko borders.

Source: © Hocken Collections – Uare Taoka o Hākena, University of Otago.

superior material and conserved the plant. But preparation and use of flax by Māori had declined as they adopted European dress. The Native Minister, Hon. Donald McLean, even offered prizes, £10 for the best ton, as inducement for Māori to produce dressed flax for export.[57] But when the 1871 commissioners – government scientist James Hector, Colonel Theodore Haultain, retired soldier and member of parliament, and John Kebbell, an industrialist and amateur scientist – ordered a ton or so of fibre prepared in the traditional way from Waikanae Māori, so they could send it to England for experimental weaving, they discovered that it was not economic for Māori to produce it. 'A Native cannot dress more than two or three pounds weight in a day; and at that rate could not earn anything like a sufficient sum' as an incentive.[58]

However, the commissioners asked the government to sponsor an exhibition in Wellington that would show the progress of the industry and encourage both Māori and settlers to get involved and set about collecting samples of

Māori- and settler-made items such as capes, mats, cords, baskets, nets and sails for such a show.[59] The exhibition was held in August 1871 – for the benefit of politicians only, it seems[60] – but colonists persisted with developing fibre, fabric and apparel industries from New Zealand flax, spurred on by the rewards offered by the government. The vigorous Canterbury Flax Association supported entrepreneurs to experiment with extraction, cleaning and creating new products.[61] A fabric woven in Dundee, Scotland, from machine-produced hanks of New Zealand flax, then turned into shirts by an army outfitter in Woolwich, England, created excitement. These shirts were better than other kinds at wicking away moisture, apparently. One shirt, along with breeches and gaiters, was exhibited at the Christchurch rooms of the Flax Association,[62] but nothing further seems to have come of this experiment.[63] Some sample canvas-like fabrics suitable for corn bags and wool sacks were created in England in 1872 to test the idea of establishing production[64] and a display at the London International Exhibition in 1873 for the Canterbury Flax Association included rope, sacking, carpet and a damask tablecloth made by D. Lornie and Sons, Kirkcaldy, from 'native-dressed' flax.[65] Some exhibited items were made from blends of *Phormium tenax* with other fibres and all were intended to raise interest in New Zealand flax as a credible and useful commercial textile.

Nevertheless, strategies such as these did not result in *Phormium tenax* becoming a Pakeha (the New Zealand term for non-Māori) household textile in New Zealand or elsewhere, as production and shipping costs outweighed potential returns. Only wool packs – large sacks for packing fleeces for export – were commercially manufactured from flax fibre into the twentieth century. Even with improved stripping machines and other chemical methods tried, the quality of flax fibre extracted was never as good as that produced by Māori women. It proved impossible to replicate the shell-in-the-hand technique. Māori were not prepared to work at hand-stripping for low wages, and Pakeha could not make the process economic over the long term. Price fluctuations, better quality fibres from elsewhere in the world, and high costs of production and transport reduced the competitiveness of New Zealand flax as a textile commodity.

Finding the most suitable agricultural activities for New Zealand's varied soil and climatic conditions took time and experimentation.[66] Cotton, indigo, rice, wine, pepper, sugar, tea, tobacco and silk were all considered potential export crops for new settler areas with appropriate climatic conditions. These were all crops that British emigrants and traders had been involved with in other parts of the empire.

Early proponents of farming silkworms thought it would provide work for the increasing North Island population, that it might aid the 'civilizing' of Māori, that Māori women and children could be employed cheaply and that silk exports would add to the country's wealth, since it was 'a luxury or semi-luxury product'.[67]

In Britain, developments in cotton fabric production had made cotton more affordable, but silk was still in demand, especially for furnishings and fashionable women's dresses. Debate over which trees to plant (*Ailanthus glandulosa* or white mulberry – *Morus alba*) and which type of silkworm (*Bombyx cynthia* or *Bombyx morus*), seems to have held back progress. Charles Brady, a Sydney resident, promoted the *Ailanthus*-feeding silkworm and was keen to encourage New Zealand settlers to plant trees and then obtain his eggs. As he planned to develop a reeling plant in New South Wales for silk export to Europe, he presumably sought a large number of growers to supply his factory.[68] Cocoons of the *Ailanthus* silkworm from England were shown at the Dunedin International Exhibition of 1865, as were silkworms, eggs and cocoons from 'two ladies from Taranaki'.[69] One of those may have been Helen Ann Wilson, of New Plymouth, who in a letter dated 1863 described how she had prepared a 'beautiful' specimen of silk and sent it with a friend to England to be displayed at the South Kensington Industrial Museum. She encouraged those with gardens in her area to plant mulberry trees.[70]

New Zealand newspapers bolstered the idea of growing trees to support silkworms and farming the worms, in part by publishing articles on the development of silk production in California, Jamaica and Germany.[71] They suggested that such an industry would be profitable, given the diseases affecting worms and trees in other parts of the world, but it seems that few settlers or Māori chose to invest. The *Wanganui Evening Herald* promoted home-based sericulture, enthusing that 'the poorest family in Wanganui can cultivate silk as well as the wealthiest firm. There is practically no limit to its expansion: a market exists in Europe that ever expands with increased supply'.[72] The newspaper gave instructions for raising mulberry trees from seed, cuttings or layers; stated that eggs could be bought from California for 17 shillings an ounce, which would produce 38,000 silkworms; and suggested that, after expenses, growers could make £100 profit per acre. Although the writer pointed out the difficulty of reeling the silk, they thought that the cocoons could be sent to England for unwinding.[73] In a letter to the editor published in the *Daily Southern Cross* in 1856, Mr S. J. Stratford pointed out that China silk (shipped from Shanghai and Canton to France and England) was unlikely to keep up with demand and he suggested that a joint stock company could be formed that would buy up land around Auckland, build houses and encourage Māori to plant mulberry trees and then rear silkworms on the land.[74]

The Victoria International Exhibition held in Melbourne in 1872–1873 included silk in the 'manufactures' section, showcasing the production of several enthusiastic sericulturalists in Victoria. The *Star* newspaper of Christchurch, gleaning its information from the *Australasian*, mentioned displays by Melbournians Mrs A. Timbrell of Silk Farm and Mrs J. Pike of Toorak, both of which showed cocoons and hanks of reeled silk. There was also a 'simple little machine for winding silk on reels', some bleached and dyed silks, and a display aimed at revealing the strength of the fibre.[75] However, a consignment of silk from Victoria sent to England for examination by the Silk Supply Association turned out to be worthless: 'it is to be regretted that the breed of the narrow sharp-pointed yellow cocoons is not stamped out of the Colony'.[76] Only the highest-quality silk was worth producing, and the association recommended getting seed (eggs) from Natal or Mr Brady of Sydney.[77]

In the 1870s, calls for the government to support the development of silk production grew. Mr T. C. Batchelor of Nelson, who had planted and propagated white mulberry, and in 1869 was feeding 6,000 *Bombyx morus* silkworms on leaves from 1,800 trees, published a leaflet about rearing silkworms that he sent to the Hon. W. Gisborne, colonial secretary.[78] Batchelor sought the government's financial help to support his business so that he could expand sericulture in New Zealand. He had researched the industry worldwide, providing information about mulberry trees and silkworms in California, New South Wales, Europe, China and Japan. He proposed that these countries could supply seed and eggs as well as experienced sericulturalists to New Zealand. He suggested that the government also fund acclimatization and agricultural societies to distribute tree seeds, cuttings and eggs.[79]

Questions were raised, however, about the export of cocoons to be reeled or unravelled elsewhere. This had not proved successful in the past, for one British firm at least. In 1886 a Mr F. W. Pennefather presented a paper to the Royal Society of New Zealand on the use of silk cocoons without reeling off the yarn, instead creating silk floss, and in 1887 a report was published noting that silk mills in Yorkshire could deal with cocoons from which silk moths had emerged, and would pay 3–4 shillings per pound for New Zealand-grown cocoons. However, this price was not seen as economic for New Zealand producers.[80]

In 1887 Mr G. A. Schoch, of Auckland reported to the government on his attempts to introduce silk culture. He felt that at a time of economic depression silk cultivation could be a money earner for interested growers. Schoch ascertained that there were 19,000–20,000 white mulberry trees already growing in New Zealand, and imported seeds from Italy to swell tree numbers. Some were planted in Auckland Domain to be distributed to silk raisers as seedlings. He also imported silkworm eggs from Italy and Japan, had a manual of instructions printed and distributed them free of charge. He experimented himself, producing cocoons, some of which he sent to Italy for tests to determine if a regular export pathway could be established.[81] It seems Mr Schoch's efforts were in vain. In 1893 he wrote that while silk production in New Zealand could work and be economic, it would require 'agitation and organization', which he could not undertake himself and that consequently the industry was 'gradually dying out'.[82] Even though Schoch and others made serious efforts, reaching out beyond the Anglo-world in an attempt to gain information, seeds and eggs, it seemed that silk production in New Zealand would be restricted to the level of a backyard hobby.

In developing domestic silk and flax industries, entrepreneurial settlers concentrated on the export potential of the fibres, rather than on making cloth as was being done with wool. Trial-and-error experimentation, assumptions about cheap labour, especially employment of Māori, and high prices all proved to be hurdles not easily overcome. Had silk fibre production been more successful, it could have added materially to New Zealand's income in the later nineteenth century when disease affected production in India and China.[83] But artificial silk development was on the horizon, so it would have been a short-term boom. In both silk and flax production Māori exercised agency in their involvement, aware of the value of their labour and reasons for price fluctuations. They opted not to work for Europeans if the costs were too high for them.[84]

Connecting New Zealand textiles with the world

Determined silk growers utilized the new industrial exhibitions to display their fibre and cocoons and to encourage others to grow mulberry trees. The concept of grand exhibitions showcasing trade, produce and industry was also part of the influence of the Anglo-world. These kinds of exhibitions were an opportunity to expand the 'webs of empire',[85] broaden trade connections and alert the popu-lace to developments both locally and overseas. Following the success of the Great Exhibition held in London in 1851, the planning and opening of which was reported at length in New Zealand newspapers,[86] many British colonies, and countries outside the Anglo-world, launched their own exhibitions, inviting other countries to participate. An invitation from the secretary of the Bombay International Exhibition (held in 1866), printed in the *Otago Daily Times* in 1865, suggested that the proposed exhibition would be 'useful in promoting trade between Bombay and China, the Australian Colonies, the Cape and the United States of America, and [the promoters] are therefore anxious to have New Zealand well represented'.[87]

In New Zealand's South Island, Dunedin citizens decided to host a New Zea-land Exhibition of Produce and Industry in 1865.[88] Dunedin's settlement by Europeans officially dates from 1848, when 344 people arrived on two ships. They reached a harbour site that, as they saw it, was 'beautiful' but undeveloped; it had no roads, streets or boundaries marked for the new town, but received plentiful rainfall that turned the ground to mud.[89] However, when gold was dis-covered inland in 1861, miners from Australia, California and China flocked in, increasing the wealth of Dunedin and fuelling a building boom (Figure 8.5). By 1865 the city was large enough to organize an exhibition that included appointing a certain Mr Morrison, a London agent whose task was to encourage traders, pro-ducers and industries in different countries to send exhibits to Dunedin.

Mr Morrison and his assistant contacted the governors of Mediterranean, West Indian and American colonies; Spanish, French and Netherlands ministers; and representatives of Austria, Italy, the United States, the Argentine, Uruguay, Venezuela, Turkey, Switzerland, Spain, Russia, Prussia, Holland, the Sandwich Isles, Guatemala, Chile, Peru, Brazil, Bolivia and New Granada, along with the secretary of the New York State Agricultural Society.[90] They placed advertise-ments in various trade journals and visited British industrial towns. According to the exhibition reports and prize lists, their efforts at encouraging global

FIGURE 8.5 'View of Part of Dunedin', tinted lithograph by W. & A. K. Johnston, 1862, 175 × 442 mm; on paper 220 × 49 2 mm.

Source: Dr T. M. Hocken's Original Collection, 16,620. © Hocken Collections – Uare Taoka o Hākena, University of Otago.

participation were only partly successful: the vast majority of displays came from within New Zealand and Great Britain. Textiles were dispatched from the Bradford and Manchester regions and others formed part of an exhibit from India. A 'varied and valuable collection of the natural products and manufactures of India' travelled to New Zealand on the *Ramsay*, via London, but was late for the opening.[91] When the consignment did arrive, however, a 'long upright case was filled on each side with Indian textile fabrics ... beautiful ... wonderful gossamer-like muslins, others of more substance finely embroidered, ... [and] cloths of gold and silver'.[92]

Sewing machines (Singer and Wilson brands) imported by local businesses, Queensland cotton, Sydney tweeds, English and New Zealand wool were also shown at the Dunedin exhibition.[93] There was even locally produced raw silk fibre exhibited by Mrs E. Whittaker of Dunedin, as well as that of the Taranaki ladies.[94] According to Mr Morrison, the lack of participation by traders from other parts of the world was to be explained by the distance and expense of sending things to New Zealand, a lack of competitions and prizes, the popularity of trade exhibitions and museums stretching their resources and merchants and agents objecting to manufacturers exhibiting their wares directly.[95]

If Dunedin was only a qualified success, overseas industrial exhibitions were a means by which emerging New Zealand businesses could show off their products and encourage export of their goods. The Mosgiel Woollen Mill, for example, only two years after its establishment, sent 16 varieties of tweed, examples of their underclothing, stockings and other knitting, blankets and travelling rugs, to the Vienna Exhibition of 1873.[96] Mr Thorne's flax exhibit at the London International Exhibition the same year showed his dedication to establishing the industry in New Zealand. Thorne had convinced a number of

European textile companies to incorporate New Zealand flax as weft yarns into materials ranging from women's dress fabric to stair carpet. He had 'peasant women in Gavray, France' spin it into yarn that was then woven to create huckaback towelling; he also showed flax string, cord and fishing line.[97]

Patterns of shipping routes around the globe in the nineteenth century illustrate the distance and the geographically peripheral position of New Zealand in relation to mainstream shipping lanes, but they also indicate the close links of both Australia and New Zealand with Great Britain (Figure 8.6).[98] Shipping was of course predicated on moving people and cargo to their intended destinations, and New Zealand was (and still is) a small market for both. However, according to a letter published in the *New Zealand Herald* in 1881, two large shipping firms in New York had long been interested in the New Zealand and Australian trade. The writer stated that Mailler and Quereau and Cameron and Co. had vessels en route and a further two loading, and would be glad to send vessels more often provided that the amount of freight made it worthwhile.[99] The majority of cargo bound for New Zealand originated, or was reloaded from other sources, in the ports of England and Scotland, especially London and Liverpool, and came to New Zealand via New York and the east coast of America or via the west coast of Africa, Mauritius, and then ports in Australia, especially Melbourne and Sydney.[100]

While scheduled, documented cargo shipping routes were one manifestation of Tony Ballantyne's notion of the 'webs of empire', unscheduled and seasonal sea traffic also brought goods and people to New Zealand, enmeshing the region in a global net. Steam-powered ships aided the imperial expansion of sea routes from the 1840s. As the *Otago Daily Times* explained to its readers in 1865, there had been no direct trade between colonies or territories under British rule until the recent changes in India and the abolition of the East India Company charter. All imperial commerce had passed through Britain, so that tea, sugar, Kashmir shawls and Indian silks

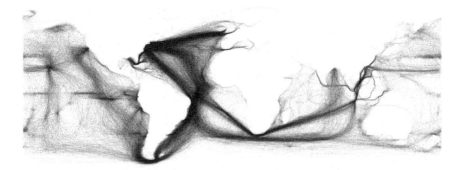

FIGURE 8.6   Nineteenth-century shipping patterns created with US data.

Source: Benjamin M. Schmidt, *Creating Data* [digital monograph] (2018), http://creatingdata.us.

arrived in New Zealand via Britain rather than Macao, Canton, Bombay or Calcutta. The additional costs and taxes entailed in landing and shipping, relanding and reshipping, freight home and freight out again were passed on to consumers. The article argued for greater 'commercial intercourse'. New Zealand was in a good position to trade with any island nation:

> There is no island so barren as not to be capable of producing something in excess of the necessities of its denizens to give in exchange for articles of ornament or dress; and no people are so utterly destitute of industry, as not to endeavour to provide means for purchasing what they need. The position of New Zealand, with regard to many of these groups, is commanding.[101]

However, ships were docking at New Zealand ports from locations other than Britain even before Queen Victoria became Empress of India. For example, some vessels came from Hong Kong either direct to Auckland or via Indonesian ports such as Batavia (Jakarta).[102] A more common route for ships from China was via Sydney, where cargo would have been offloaded, sorted and reloaded on to trans-Tasman boats that plied back and forth between New Zealand and Australian ports. In February 1865, ships docked at the Port of Auckland hailed from London, Sydney, Melbourne, Valparaiso, Cork, the Cape of Good Hope, Newcastle NSW, Adelaide, Hobart, Rarotonga and the South Sea Islands, as well as from other New Zealand ports.[103] In March 1889 it was considered newsworthy to report that 'one of the Union Company's steamers will load at Calcutta for Auckland direct in July next'.[104]

What we do not know, unfortunately, is what textiles (if any) came as cargo from these places, or whether there was even a demand for textiles or dress items from these sources. It is safe to assume, based on knowledge of seafarers' private trade arrangements,[105] that slop garments and fabrics were traded informally with settlers, as were goods including guns and dresses with Māori from the first interactions onwards.[106] A tax of five shillings per cubic foot was applied to most textiles legally entering New Zealand in the Customs Tariff Act of 1866.[107] Avoiding that extra cost may have motivated some, as may the exoticism of the goods. Statistics kept by the New Zealand government on imports during the nineteenth century are patchy, lump together items in ways that are hard to interpret and do not include place of origin. When newspaper advertisements mention provenance, it is almost always Britain. This was no doubt the predominant source of manufactured textiles, but cultural familiarity may have been part of the rationale as well.

Conclusion: dressing globally?

Rather than obtaining goods directly from various parts of the world, dressing globally in nineteenth-century New Zealand settler communities may have been more about wearing fabrics that purported to come from exotic locales. For example, in 1873 Dunedin drapers Herbert, Haynes and Co. were selling 'Danish silk-finished tinted alpacas', 'foreign fibre lustres … for simple morning dress or stylish promenade costume', and 'Krowtree guipure, Turko mohairs, Teheran stripes, Vienna broches … Sicilienne cloths, Thera camlets', as well as 'the Dagmar costume, the Wiesbaden costume' and 'the Viennese costume'.[108] The same year Ballantyne and Co. in Christchurch were offering Indian, Chinese and Japanese silks, French merinos and Italian cloths as part of their summer shipments.[109] Kirkpatrick, Glendining and Co. of Dunedin included prices with their global silk offerings, which indicated quality, and shipping and tariff loadings on imports: Japanese silks from 1s 6d per yard, Chinese silks from 2s per yard, Indian silks from 2s 6d per yard, English silks from 3s per yard, French silks from 4s 6d per yard.[110]

Was there inherent prejudice in this pricing system? Of course, and settlers would have also understood the inferences in the names of fabrics and costumes, even as they realized that they probably came from Britain. Connecting consumers to the world through the names of their textiles was sociocultural marketing, appealing to New Zealand shoppers' desire to appear both fashionable and worldly wise. Prestige may have resided in the descriptive labelling rather than the actual place of manufacture, which was uncertain, since no one was policing the advertising. While the Anglo-world was the major source of imports and ideas throughout the nineteenth century, colonial settlers were having their focus and values regarding textiles and apparel subtly and gradually shifted from the perspective of a British 'homeland' supplier of knowledge and goods to a New Zealand able to produce its own goods. While a cultural cringe about 'colonial' – i.e., New Zealand-produced – wool products was still apparent, local manufacturers of woollen and worsted cloth and men's and boys' apparel, such as the New Zealand Clothing Factory, played their part in this shift, as did newspapers in publicizing the various attempts to establish silk and flax production in New Zealand.[111]

Early European settlers in New Zealand obtained their clothing materials and couturial information via the 'web of empire', with Britain acting as a 'significant and powerful node'.[112] The rise of the 'Anglo-world', as people moved from Britain to North America and Australia, connected New Zealand settlers laterally, too. While connections were made with Australia and across the Pacific to San Francisco, during the early settler period at least, distance, expense and a small population meant that global shipping often bypassed New Zealand ports. The appearances of settler men and women were constrained by their ideas about propriety and desire to improve their situation (as many of them did), and also by the availability of consumer goods. That most of these came from Britain is unsurprising, given the nature of the colony and the local media's tendency to report dress fashions and conditions that reflected British contexts. Some settlers were well connected with people in various parts of the globe, or at least had the ability to find the information and the raw or plant materials they required for textile moneymaking schemes to improve New Zealand's economy from sources other than Britain, if necessary. While some settlers never left New Zealand, a few travelled back and forth across the globe to connect, exchange ideas and goods and arrange tests or experiments to further their domestic textile business aims. But all were still constrained by the patterns of ship traffic in getting their goods and information delivered, while local geography, settlers' and Māori disinterest or other preoccupations and the economic equations challenged the development of textile industries.

As a consequence of these patterns, it is probable that the fabric for Catherine Valpy's wedding dress also came via that British route, possibly to Sydney before reaching Port Chalmers near Dunedin, even if the fibre had been grown in her first homeland of India. Catherine does not mention her own wedding dress in her diary or in her later autobiographical notes, although she does record shopping for clothes sometimes. She was more interested and involved in the adventures and experiences of being a settler, farmer and parent.

Notes

1 Otago Museum Collections G86.36. The wedding was a joint one; Catherine's sister Juliet married William Mackworth at the same ceremony, but her wedding dress has not survived as far as is known.
2 *Southern People: A Dictionary of Otago Southland Biography*, ed. Jane Thomson (Dunedin: Longacre Press, 1998), 526.
3 Thomson, *Southern People*, 173.
4 Catherine Henrietta Elliot Fulton (née Valpy) papers (1849–1919), Dunedin: Hocken Library, University of Otago (hereafter DHLUO) ARC-0379: typescript copy of Fulton's autobiography, MS-0846/002, 12.
5 Melinda Watt, '"Whims and Fancies": Europeans Respond to Textiles from the East', in *Interwoven Globe: The Worldwide Textile Trade, 1500–1800*, ed. Amelia Peck (London: Thames & Hudson, 2013), 82–103.
6 James Belich, *Replenishing the Earth: The Settler Revolution and the Rise of the Anglo-World 1783–1939* (Oxford: Oxford University Press, 2009), 27.
7 James Belich, *Making Peoples: A History of the New Zealanders from Polynesian Settlement to the End of the Nineteenth Century* (Auckland: Allen Lane and the Penguin Press, 1996), 279.
8 Belich, *Making Peoples*, chs 5, 7, 12.
9 E.g., *Colonist*, 7 February 1860, 3.
10 Belich, *Making Peoples*, 178.
11 Another was the area around Russell in Northland.
12 Michael Stevens, 'Muttonbirds and Modernity in Murihiku: Continuity and Change in Kāi Tahu Knowledge' (Unpublished PhD Dissertation, University of Otago, 2010); DHLUO, ARC-0162: MS-582/I/7 (Beattie, James Herries): 'History Collected to Write a Book About Bluff', in 'Papers'.
13 DHLUO, ARC-0467: MS-0968 (Natusch, Sheila): 'George Albert Hansard's Journal of the Voyage of the "Acheron"' (transcribed by Sheila Natusch).
14 Stevens, 'Muttonbirds', 141; Barbara Brookes, *A History of New Zealand Women* (Wellington, NZ: Bridget Williams Books, 2016), 32; Sheila Natusch, 'Eliza Wohlers', in *The Book of New Zealand Women*, ed. Charlotte Macdonald, Merimeri Penfold and Bridget Williams (Wellington, NZ: Bridget Williams Books, 1991), 741–2.

15 Stevens, 'Muttonbirds', 132; DHLUO, MS-0967: North German Missionary Society, Bremen: papers relating to the Reverend J. F. H. Wohlers and the Ruapuke Island Station (1844–1992).
16 Brookes, *A History of New Zealand Women*, ch. 2.
17 Brookes, *A History of New Zealand Women*, 57.
18 Belich, *Making Peoples*, 278.
19 Belich, *Making Peoples*, 309.
20 Jeanine Graham, 'Settler Society', in *The Oxford History of New Zealand*, 2nd ed., ed. Geoffrey W. Rice (Auckland: Oxford University Press, 1992), 112–140.
21 Jeanine Graham, 'Settler Society', 135–136.
22 Jeanine Graham, 'Settler Society', 134–135.
23 Jane Malthus, 'European Women's Dresses in Nineteenth Century New Zealand' (Unpublished PhD Dissertation, University of Otago, 1996).
24 Frances Porter, *Born to New Zealand: A Biography of Jane Maria Atkinson* (Wellington, NZ: Allen & Unwin/Port Nicholson Press, 1989), 109.
25 E.g., *Wellington Independent*, 2 August 1845, 3; *Otago Witness*, 9 October 1852, 3; *Colonist*, 13 November 1857, 2.
26 Reprinted as 'Extracts from *Punch*', in the *New Zealand Spectator and Cook's Strait Guardian*, 26 March 1853, 4.
27 Nancy Swarbrick, 'Manners and Social Behaviour: Nineteenth-Century Manners', *Te Ara – The Encyclopedia of New Zealand*, updated 8 July 2013, www.TeAra.govt. nz/en/manners-and-social-behaviour/page-2 (accessed 1 January 2018). Other examples include: *New Zealand Gazette and Wellington Spectator*, 9 August 1841, 1; *New Zealand Spectator and Cook's Strait Guardian*, 1 November 1854, 3; 'Awful Warning to Bachelors from *Dicken's Household Words*', in *Colonist*, 3 September 1858, 4; *Etiquette for Ladies* in a list of books on sale in Hokitika, *Westport Times*, 30 May 1868, 4; 'Matrimonial Etiquette', in *West Coast Times*, 3 November 1873, 3; *Thames Advertiser*, 18 May 1874, 3; English wedding etiquette is explained in the *Timaru Herald*, 28 May 1877, 3; *New Zealand Herald*, 24 December 1881, 3.
28 *Evening Star*, 6 February 1886, 4.
29 Frances Steel, 'Re-Routing Empire? Steam-Age Circulations and the Making of an Anglo Pacific, c.1850–90', *Australian Historical Studies* 46.3 (2015): 356–373.
30 *Nelson Examiner and New Zealand Chronicle*, 30 October 1852, 141.
31 *Nelson Examiner and New Zealand Chronicle*, 1 January 1859, 1 col. 4; *Nelson Examiner and New Zealand Chronicle*, 1 January 1859, 1 col. 3. A 'race ball' (in association with the Nelson races) was advertised for 4 March 1859 at the Freemasons' hall. In *Nelson Examiner and New Zealand Chronicle*, 26 February 1859, 2.
32 Malthus, 'European Women's Dresses', 293–294.
33 Malthus, 'European Women's Dresses', 72.
34 Malthus, 'European Women's Dresses'. I acknowledge that biases of survival and collection by museums may have affected the results.
35 Alexander Turnbull Library, Wellington, MS 4248: 'Marvin Family Papers', folder 1.
36 Jane Malthus, 'Dressmakers in Nineteenth Century New Zealand', in *Women in History 2*, ed. Barbara Brookes, Charlotte Macdonald and Margaret Tennant (Wellington, NZ: Bridget Williams Books, 1992), 76–97.
37 Her stay in Dunedin seems to have been curtailed by a fire in 1865, which destroyed her premises.
38 Belich, *Replenishing the Earth*, 49.
39 *Evening Star*, 30 October 1871, 2.
40 G. R. Hawke, *The Making of New Zealand* (Cambridge, UK: Cambridge University Press, 1985), 30–35.
41 Megan Melville, 'Nineteenth and Early Twentieth-Century Sewing Machines in New Zealand' (Unpublished Dissertation for PGDip Consumer and Applied Science, University of Otago, 1993), 66.

42 *Lyttleton Times*, 18 March 1869, 4.
43 Andrew Godley, 'Selling the Sewing Machine Around the World: Singer's International Marketing Strategies, 1850–1920', *Enterprise and Society* 7.2 (2006): 266–314. E.g., *Hawera & Normanby Star*, 20 July 1881, 4; *Otago Daily Times*, 7 February 1874, 2: *Otago Witness*, 27 September 1879, 2.
44 Cloaks called *kākahu* were woven with a finger weft-twining technique called *whatu*. See Awhina Tamarapa, ed., *Whatu Kakahu: Māori Cloaks* (Wellington, NZ: Te Papa Press, 2011).
45 A. C. Begg and N. C. Begg, *Port Preservation* (Wellington, NZ: Whitcombe & Tombs, 1973), 127.
46 *Otago Daily Times*, 10 April 1865, 6, discusses growing the European flax and how the fibre is extracted. In New Zealand a smaller species, *Phormium cookianum*, also grew at high elevations and around the coastlines, but was not so useful a fibre. See Gerald Hindmarsh and Peter Quinn, 'Flax: The Enduring Fibre', *New Zealand Geographic* 42 (1999): 20–53.
47 *Otago Witness*, 12 August 1887, 13.
48 ARC-0379 DHLUO, entries for 26 and 29 June 1875.
49 DHLUO typescript copy of Fulton's autobiography MS-0846/002, 38.
50 ARC-0379 DHLUO, entries for 26 and 29 June 1875. A scutcher was used to bash or scrape the outer flesh off the flax leaves.
51 Hindmarsh and Quinn, 'Flax: The Enduring Fibre', 40; Begg and Begg, *Port Preservation*, 130.
52 *New Zealand Spectator and Cook's Strait Guardian*, 25 October 1845, 4.
53 *Otago Witness*, 21 March 1889, 6.
54 Appendices to the *Journals of the House of Representatives* (hereafter AJHR) 1870 D-14a: 'Report from the New Zealand Commissioners Relative to the Manufacture of New Zealand Flax', 2.
55 'New Zealand Commissioners' Report on Flax', *Wellington Independent*, 20 September 1870, 3.
56 Dr Hector presented the issues at a meeting of the Wellington Philosophical Society, *Star*, 15 July 1870, 3.
57 *Nelson Examiner and New Zealand Chronicle*, 9 January 1871, 2.
58 AJHR 1871 G-04: 'Report of the Commissioners Appointed to Enquire into the Preparation of the Phormium Fibre or New Zealand Flax', app. 45, 17. See also *Press*, 29 December 1870, 3 where a letter from Wi Tako Ngatata questions whether the remuneration will be sufficient for the work involved.
59 *Star*, 8 April 1871, 2.
60 *Star*, 14 October 1871, 3.
61 E.g., *Wellington Independent*, 8 February 1871, 3.
62 *Star*, 17 March 1871, 2.
63 *North Otago Times*, 31 March 1871, 6; *Daily Southern Cross*, 7 August 1872, 3.
64 *New Zealand Herald*, 9 February 1872, 2.
65 *New Zealand Herald*, 1 October 1873, 3.
66 Hawke, '*The Making of New Zealand*', 30.
67 *Nelson Examiner*, 11 February 1843, 194. See also a letter from S. J. Stratford of Auckland to the editor, *Daily Southern Cross*, 28 November 1856, 3; Beverly Lemire, *Cotton (Textiles That Changed the World)* (Oxford: Berg, 2011), 77.
68 *Otago Daily Times*, 12 June 1868, 5.
69 AJHR 1870 D-3 No 9; *Lyttleton Times*, 31 January 1865, 5.
70 Nine pages written 22 January 1863 by Helen Ann Wilson in New Plymouth district. Wellington: National Library of New Zealand: 'The Papers of Sir Donald McLean', Series 1, inwards letters.
71 E.g. *Otago Daily Times*, 12 December 1868, supplement; *New Zealand Herald*, 23 March 1871, 2; *Nelson Examiner and New Zealand Chronicle*, 18 April 1846, 25;

Wellington Independent, 13 May 1846, 4; *New Zealand Spectator and Cook's Strait Guardian*, 13 July 1853, 3.

72 *Evening Herald*, 27 March 1871, 2.
73 *Evening Herald*, 27 March 1871, 2.
74 *Daily Southern Cross*, 28 November 1856, 3.
75 *Star*, 18 November 1872, 2.
76 *Colonist*, 21 July 1871, 4.
77 *Colonist*, 21 July 1871, 4.
78 *Nelson Examiner*, 13 January 1869, 2. He also presented a paper at the Royal Society of New Zealand on 3 May 1871, which is recorded in *Transactions and Proceedings of the Royal Society of New Zealand* 1871, 424–426.
79 AJHR 1870 D-3.
80 *Transactions and Proceedings of the Royal Society of New Zealand* (1886), 594; *Otago Daily Times*, 21 February 1887, 3.
81 AJHR 1887, H-11: 'Silk-Culture in New Zealand (Report on)', by Mr G. A. Schoch.
82 *New Zealand Times*, 21 April 1893, 3.
83 *Nelson Evening Mail*, 20 August 1869, 2.
84 Belich, *'Making Peoples'*, 148–152.
85 Tony Ballantyne, *Webs of Empire: Locating New Zealand's Colonial Past* (Wellington, NZ: Bridget Williams Books, 2012).
86 E.g., *New Zealander*, 2 April 1851, 2; 9 July 1851, 2; 23 July 1851, 4; *Daily Southern Cross*, 26 August 1851, 3; *Wellington Independent*, 6 September 1851, 4; *Nelson Examiner and New Zealand Chronicle*, 20 September 1851, 124.
87 *Otago Daily Times*, 14 July 1865, 4.
88 Erik Olssen, *A History of Otago* (Dunedin: McIndoe, 1984), ch. 6; *Otago Daily Times* 17 July 1863, 4.
89 Olssen, *A History of Otago*, ch. 5.
90 *Otago Daily Times*, 28 January 1865, 5.
91 *Otago Daily Times*, 12 January 1865, 5.
92 *Otago Daily Times*, 13 February 1865, 5.
93 *Otago Daily Times*, 13 February 1865, 5; *NZ Spectator and Cook's Strait Guardian*, 14 January 1865, 3.
94 *Otago Daily Times*, 13 February 1865, 5.
95 *Otago Daily Times*, 28 January 1865, 5.
96 *Otago Daily Times*, 26 November 1872, 2; *Daily Southern Cross*, 12 August 1873, 3.
97 *New Zealand Herald*, 1 October 1873, 3.
98 As explained in Steel, 'Re-Routing Empire', 8.
99 E.g. *New Zealand Herald*, 26 October 1881, 6.
100 E.g. *Daily Southern Cross*, 24 July 1855, 3.
101 *Otago Daily Times*, 14 July 1865, 4. The piece was no doubt intended to encourage trade in the Pacific.
102 *Daily Southern Cross*, 2 May 1864, 4. In February 1864 the *Migratas* left Hong Kong bound for Auckland; *Daily Southern Cross*, 5 February 1870, 4. In 1870 the *Waverley*, sailing from Hong Kong to Auckland, had to be repaired at Batavia (Jakarta) en route; *Auckland Star*, 29 August 1890, 4. The *SS Kweiyang* made one trip to New Zealand from Hong Kong in 1890 with a load of teas.
103 *New Zealand Herald*, 14 February 1865, 4.
104 *Auckland Star*, 19 March 1889, 1.
105 E.g. J. Forrest, 'The Invisibility of Crews of Nineteenth Century Australian Shipping in Catalogued collections of Artifacts from Provenanced Sites' (Thesis submitted for BA (Hons) South Australia: Flinders University, 2002), 55.
106 Belich, *Making Peoples*, 153.

107 Return of customs duties collected throughout the colony of New Zealand under the several headings contained in Schedule A. Of 'The Customs Tariff Act, 1866', during the first six months of the operation of that Act. *Appendix to the Journals of the House of Representatives*, 1867 Session I, B-06.

108 *Otago Daily Times*, 15 October 1873, 1.

109 *Press*, 29 November 1873, 3.

110 *Otago Witness*, 16 October 1876, 24.

111 E.g. *Westport Times*, 18 August 1876, 3; *Hawke's Bay Herald*, 9 January 1880, 2.

112 Steel, 'Re-Routing Empire', 10.

9

'ANYTHING FOR MERE SHOW WOULD BE WORSE THAN USELESS'

Emigration, dress and the Australian Colonies, 1820–1860

Laura Jocic

In 1853 the *Emigrant's Guide to Australia* advised prospective emigrants that, 'As regards clothing, the points to consider, for the permanent stock, are utility and durability; anything for mere show would be worse than useless'.[1] The author John Capper was a former clerk and inspector of convict hulks for the Home Office in London.[2] Although he seems to have never been to Australia, Capper portrayed the country as a land of plenty as, 'a land flowing with something better than "milk and honey"', where the climate is

> so favourable to health that medicine is all but unknown, and the death of a young person a most rare occurrence; no taxes, no rent; and with need of so few clothes as to render their cost a matter of little moment.[3]

According to Capper, this was a land where the prospective emigrant would seldom be troubled with the burdens of life in Britain, and fine clothing was either unheard of or not required. In 1853 Australia had become a land of opportunity in more ways than one, since gold had recently been discovered in the inland regions of Bathurst, Ballarat and Bendigo. Although the guide devotes much space to describing the 'latest intelligence from the Gold Fields of Australia', when it comes to the question of who should emigrate, the advice unequivocally recommends that only those who have labouring skills and the determination to apply themselves in their new home should consider emigrating. The aim was that these emigrants were to live in rural areas, carving out a life for themselves and their families on the land.[4] In such an environment it was considered there was no need for fine clothing. Similar notions about dress requirements in Australia were also promulgated about urban areas and for much of the nineteenth century, Australia was generally reckoned by outsiders as a country where there was little need for fashionable dress. Contemporary letters and journals, however, paint a picture of a society where people were attuned to the subtleties of dress and its role in communicating prosperity and respectability. Surviving items of clothing also attest to the existence of a keen fashion sensibility. This chapter investigates the difference between dress expectations and the realities of colonial life, and shows how fashion not only expressed status and prosperity, but also how settlers actively shaped their dress culture within the shifting boundaries of a colonial society-in-the-making.

The value of looking at dress lies in its ability to illuminate the experiences of those who migrated. Integral to this study is the inclusion of surviving items of dress either brought to, or made in, the colonies. As the historian Margaret Maynard points out, 'clothes are not simply a passive reflection of a society and its preferences for display, or even of its class demarcation. They represent the historical constraints and imperatives experienced by individuals and social groups'.[5] Aspects of emigration and dress in the Australian colonial context have been touched upon by Marion Fletcher and Margaret Maynard. Fletcher gives less space to the topic than Maynard and provides an example of the suggested wardrobe for a working-class man or woman published by Henry Capper in his 1838 guide, *South Australia: Containing Hints To Emigrants*.[6] Unlike the men's wardrobe, the women's list contains lengths of fabric, needles, pins, buttons, thread and tape, alluding to the gendered nature of sewing and garment production in the home. In *Fashioned from Penury*, Maynard devotes a chapter to emigration and the response of new arrivals to colonial conditions. She points to a level of misinformation and misconception in Britain about the nature of Australian colonial society.[7] This was especially so for those who settled in urban areas where they found that British standards of dress etiquette were strongly observed. Such findings contradicted the common idea that, being so far from metropolitan centres, Australians had little concern for their appearance.[8]

Emigration and who should come

Capper's advice on who should emigrate supports the British government's approach to populating the Australian colonies. In 1831 the government took official steps to encourage emigration to Australia. With overcrowded cities in Britain and a shortage of labour in Australia, the colonial government ceased granting land to free settlers and instead decided to fund assisted migration through the sale of Crown land.[9] Starting in New South Wales in 1831, formal emigration processes were carried out for the remainder of the century to encourage the passage of suitable people to the Australian colonies. Lobbying for the cessation of penal transportation, the colonies began to shape themselves as free and independent settlements.[10] Prior to 1831, the arrival of free settlers had increased slowly, with the long and costly voyage acting as a deterrent. As of 1830, a total of only 15,700 free migrants had come to Australia since British settlement began in 1788.[11] This was to change: between 1831 and 1850, 170,000 people migrated from Great Britain to the Australian colonies, two-thirds of whom were assisted from land sales in Australia,[12] while from 1831 to 1900 approximately half of all emigrants to Australia received some form of government assistance.[13]

Assisted migration was seen as key to entice free settlers to the far-flung colonies of Australia. Migrants from Britain and Ireland readily paid their passages for the shorter and cheaper voyage across the Atlantic. Costing as little as £3 10s, the passage to the East Coast of America was more affordable than the £15 to £20 required for the lengthy and arduous voyage to Australia.[14] Another deterrent for migrants in selecting Australia as a destination was the distance from home and the likelihood that they would never be able to afford the return passage to see family and friends.[15] For most, the arduous and often dangerous three- to four-month voyage was a one-way trip. All the hopes for the future were vested in the supposed opportunities to be found in the colonies.

In the nineteenth century, however, Australia was seen as the 'working man's paradise' with high wages and opportunities to better oneself, both economically and socially.[16] In December 1838, only three months before his departure for New South Wales, Henry Parkes (who became a prominent politician in Australia) wrote to his sister Sarah, stating,

> The information which we have obtained since we have been here [London] respecting Australia has determined both Clarinda and myself to make up our minds to emigrate to a land which holds out prospects so bright and cheering to unhappy Englishmen.[17]

In the same year George Brunskill, who was planning to emigrate with his wife and children to the newly founded colony of South Australia, wrote to his brother from London with similar high hopes for life in the colony, declaring, 'my mind is made up for Australia … There appears to be no doubt that of our being able to get a comfortable and independent livelihood and a very fair prospect of doing something for our children'.[18] With little means behind them, Parkes and his wife travelled as assisted migrants while the Brunskills paid their way and travelled in intermediate class.

The various assisted migration schemes either offered a free passage for eligible people, or lent the passage money, which was to be repaid by the migrant when he or she was settled in the colony.[19] The contract carriers received a bounty for the safe arrival of each assisted migrant. Commissioners in London ran the scheme via a network of agents located throughout the United Kingdom. In offering assisted passages to prospective emigrants, a strict selection process aimed to ensure only the most suitable were chosen. After years of sending felons to the other side of the world, the British government now wished to ensure that 'a most valuable class of moral and industrious persons might be obtained'.[20]

Particular interest was taken in the 'struggling' and 'sinking' classes who, however hard they worked in Britain, were unable, through overpopulation and lack of employment, to adequately provide for their families.[21] Capper thought such a man,

> who will go out to the southern colonies, having no capital but his labour, with stout arms and a stout heart, with no old-world prejudices hanging about him, determined to work with a will, and to adapt himself to the new country and its ways ... will be sure to find what he seeks and what he cannot get here – certain and constant employment at more than ample wages.[22]

Preferred emigrants were married couples without children and single women of good character trained for domestic or farm service.[23] Assisted or not, it was evident that the emigrant was to roll up their sleeves, leave behind class prejudices and adapt. It was primarily to these people that Capper and other such emigrant's guides addressed their advice. What they should bring with them was part of the ethos of preparing migrants for life in their new home. The advice that only useful and durable clothing was required fitted with the official rhetoric around emigration and what was expected of those who came.

Emigration and dress

As people left for Australia from their homelands, be it England, Scotland, Wales, Ireland or Continental Europe, they prepared themselves for life in the colonies. Some, who had family or friends, had first-hand information about what they should bring with them, particularly in the way of clothing, while others had to rely on the information provided by emigration agents and colonial guides published to inform the increasing tide of emigration. Private journals and newspaper articles provide an insight into the experience of emigration and buried within these accounts are references to clothing requirements for those venturing to Australia. The details of what people brought with them, what they made and how they managed their dress, provides insights into the nature of colonial dress. Existing and sometimes newly made items of clothing were packed by emigrants, while fabrics were stowed away to be made up into garments at a later date. Once in Australia, clothing was altered indicating that clothing could have had a long life, being adapted to changing fashions, mended and reused over many years.

As a basic necessity, which could easily be packed, clothing formed a substantial part of an emigrant's luggage. Charles Masters' journal kept aboard the *Templar* bound for South Australia in 1845 contains itemized lists of the contents of 14 boxes and trunks.[24] Charles and Martha Masters left Britain with their five children. Travelling cabin class, the Masters paid for their passage and brought along eight trunks of clothing, linen and haberdashery. The Masters' clothing consisted of numerous pairs of shoes, shirts, frocks, trousers, stockings, nightgowns, chemises, pinafores, neckerchiefs and stays (corsets). As unassisted migrants, the

Masters were bringing much more with them in the way of clothing than was recommended in the emigrant guides or stipulated by government agencies.

Those selected for an assisted passage to Australia were required to supply a basic wardrobe comprising a selection of practical and durable everyday items of dress.[25] These items were inspected by the agents at the departure depots and if they were wanting, then the emigrant risked rejection for a free passage.[26] Eneas Mackenzie's 1853 edition of his *Emigrant's Guide to Australia* lists this as being

> for men – six shirts, six pairs stockings, two pairs of shoes, and two com-
> plete suits of exterior clothing; for females – six shifts, two flannel petti-
> coats, six pairs stockings, two pairs of shoes, two gowns, as well as sheets
> towels and soap.[27]

Although not discussed in the emigrant guides, those with greater means could purchase a more extensive range of items from one of the many suppliers who advertised emigrant wardrobes. Elias Moses and Son, tailors, clothiers and general outfitters located in Aldgate, London (and with a branch in Melbourne), were in the business of providing complete wardrobes, including a trunk, for emigrants bound for Australia.[28] They offered a choice of price brackets, from the most basic kit, which included bedding and tableware for £3 10s, to the more elaborate.[29] In 1854 Moses and Son advertised a 'Lady's outfit to Australia'.[30] The range of garments, which includes a 'dress improver' (a type of bustle that creates the fashionable shape of the skirt), suggests that the 'Lady's outfit' was aimed at an emigrant who was paying her own passage and wished to maintain a level of fashionable dress. Such items were also easily available for purchase in Australia. In the same year D. Davis of the Old Commercial Store in the New South Wales country town of Goulburn advertised a horsehair dress improver among the 'choice and varied assortment of goods' just brought in from Sydney.[31] The emphasis on 'Australia' in the Moses and Son advertisement suggests that there was something different about dress requirements in the col-onies. However, since the outfitting of emigrants was an important part of Moses and Son's operation,[32] it may have also been a selling point to stimulate sales to the uninformed emigrant who did not know what to expect.

Rather than purchasing emigrant wardrobes, Caroline Chisholm, the philan-thropist and founder of the Family Colonization Society, which was estab-lished in 1849, advised migrants not to waste money on the 'slop shops' when existing clothing could be adapted during the voyage for the changes in cli-mate in Australia.[33] Procuring the basic wardrobe was a considerable outlay for many of those selected for the free government passage. When Henry Parkes and his wife emigrated to Sydney in 1839, Parkes sold some of his beloved books to buy cloth to make into the basic garments they were required to provide.[34] He wrote to his family that his wife Clarinda could make up some of the clothes on the voyage and that she would require 'half a pound of white cotton and shirt buttons', which he wished to have sent to them before they departed.[35] Having no contacts in Australia, Parkes relied on published guides for information about the voyage and the colony of New South Wales.[36] Although almost penniless, Parkes was under the impression that he and his wife would need 15 changes of clothes each for a voyage of about four months, 'as there is no washing allowed on board'.[37] Other deserving emigrants were supported by local charitable societies who funded the mandatory basic kit of clothing that would enable the 'respectable poor' to start a new life in the colonies.[38]

Colonial society

Although prospective emigrants were advised to bring only durable clothing and that anything fashionable would not be required in Australia, contemporary accounts show that from the early years of European colonization settlers were profoundly interested in dress and conscious of its role in defining class. Two months after her arrival in Sydney in January 1826, Fanny Macleay, the daughter of Alexander Macleay, the colonial secretary of New South Wales, wrote to her brother William. She lamented that her time had been occupied with needlework, altering and repairing outfits in order to keep up with local society, because 'people here think of little besides dress'.[39] Over the next ten years Fanny's letters are littered with references to a lively round of parties, balls, dinners and social engagements. Although Fanny describes herself as hating 'all this folly', in 1828 the need to maintain a standard of dress compelled her to write that, 'We are obliged to be at needlework the greatest part of our time for the people here dress so much and clothes wear out so fast that really we are always at work making bonnets or gowns'.[40]

No garments belonging to the Macleay family survive, but Anna Blaxland's wedding dress and accessories do. A contemporary of Fanny's and moving in similar social circles, Anna wore a striking cream silk dress when she married Thomas Walker on 4 January 1823 at St John's Church, Parramatta. Anna was the daughter of the early free settler John Blaxland, who arrived in Sydney in 1806. Taking up pastoral holdings, Blaxland became a prominent colonist and his daughters, having either been born or grown up in Australia from a young age, were known for their genteel upbringing and fashionable taste.[41] It is likely that Anna's wedding dress was made in Australia, as were her bridesmaids' dresses, which no longer survive.[42] The wedding dress is made from a cream silk woven with an alternating matt and satin stripe (Figure 9.1). It comprises a separate bodice and skirt. The bodice has a wide low neckline, short puffed sleeves and fine cord trimmings with acorn tassels. Although the Blaxland girls were known for their stylish dress, Anna's wedding dress, with its high waist and plain straight skirt was, in comparison with the dominant British styles at the time, slightly outdated in 1823. However the fine fabric and detailing on the dress and the accompanying accessories of gloves, shoes, stockings and shawl

FIGURE 9.1 Wedding dress, Australia, 1823.

Source: Vaucluse House Collection, Sydney Living Museums. Photograph © Brenton McGeachie.

indicate that, at this relatively early stage of colonial settlement, access was available to luxurious imported items.

It is conceivable that, with a voyage of four months from Britain to Australia, and a reversal of seasons, information about changing fashions as well as fabrics and accessories could be sent to Australia within the space of six months. Early settlers in Australia with connections back home wrote of receiving boxes of goods from family members that included articles of clothing and books. In addition to items of dress being specially selected from abroad, it is likely that ladies' journals with hand-coloured fashion plates were among the contents that made their way to the colonies. In the early nineteenth-century journals such as *Ackermann's Repository of Arts*, the *Lady's Magazine* and the *World of Fashion* provided a mix of reviews, short stories, domestic tips, needlework designs and information on the latest fashions with accompanying illustrations.[43] Such sources of information on fashions from London and Paris could be interpreted by a competent milliner and dressmaker. As early as 1803 the Sydney-based 'milliner and mantua-maker' M. Hayes advertised her skills in the *Sydney Gazette*. She assured her customers that her work would be 'executed in a Style of fashionable taste and neatness, with the utmost punctuality, and on terms that may recommend her to future favour'.[44]

Some 25 years later, in 1828, Sydney had rapidly grown and the range of goods on offer and modes of dress were a point of comment. The New South Wales settler Christiana Brooks, who had arrived in the colony in 1814, observed that she had

> seen a great improvement in the buildings shops and general appearance, Sydney is becoming a large town, and from the well supplied shops, and the numberless well dressed people you meet in the street you are inclined to fancy yourself in the capital of a flourishing country, and so perfectly is everything English you could almost [feel?] yourself within an [*sic*] hundred mile of London itself.[45]

The colony was progressing and Sydney was emulating English cities. Society followed British protocols of celebrating the king's birthday each year, with a ball at Government House, where 'every person of respectability is asked'. In 1826, Christiana speaks of the commonplace display of beauty and fashion at such a ball, the latter on this particular occasion being unsurpassed.[46] In 1831 Mary Blaxland, who lived in Sydney, wrote to her sister Anna, now living in Van Diemen's Land (Tasmania), describing a ball hosted by Captain Laplace who had docked his ship, *La Favorite*, in Sydney for five weeks during August and September.[47] Attended by what she describes as an '*aristocratic* selection of ladies' (original emphasis), which included Mrs Macleay, all in full dress, wearing book muslin, pelerines silks and satins, Mary emphasizes that her party, who wore tippets and sleeves of book muslin, were complimented on their 'tasteful appropriateness' of dress.[48] At a time when colonial society, in the words of Christiana Brooks, consisted of an 'incongruous mix of bond and free', Mary Blaxland's reference to appropriate dress resonates with notions of respectability.[49] Founded as a penal colony in 1788, by the 1830s the population of New South Wales had become a fluid mix of free settlers, convicts, emancipated convicts and native born. In this environment dress became an important means of reinforcing the position and respectability of the governing class.

In such a society concerns were raised about the general morality of a generation born to convict and emancipated convicts.[50] With this in mind, the governor's wife, Eliza Darling, established the Sydney Female School of Industry in 1826 to educate working-class girls, with an emphasis on needlework and religious instruction. Christiana Brooks reiterated this attitude when she commented rather disparagingly that

yet as the girls will be *tought* [*sic*] to do something useful, they may trans-
mit their knowledge to their offspring and in time become a superior race
to those who lounge over the shop doors in Sydney: A *half* dressed and
over dressed generation – who seem born for no other purpose but to
gossip with their male acquaintenances [*sic*].[51] (Original emphasis)

Was Christiana referring to the class of emancipated convicts or their children,
who, dressing inappropriately, betrayed their base origins and posed a moral
threat to society? While this attempted censoring of dress may not have been
successful, it was nevertheless a point of concern that was regularly raised in the
letters and journals of genteel free settlers. Just as manners were a marker of
acceptability, dress was a tangible means of classifying the types of behaviour
that served to define and also divide society.[52] The fine balance between appropriate and tasteful modes of dress and vulgar over-display was one that caused
considerable unease for the governing class who sought to reinforce social standards that were aligned with those back 'home'.[53] These seemingly idle people
were, under the scheme of assisted migration, to be supplanted by the hard-
working emigrant that Capper speaks of in 1853. This suitable emigrant was not
only to be drawn from the labouring classes, but also extended to anyone who
was prepared to work with their hands. For 'the non-professional farming emigrant – the young gentleman, the lawyer, the clerk, having £1000 to £3000',
there is an opportunity if determined to work provided, 'that he goes out without any stock of kid gloves, or pomatums, or novels'.[54]

More than just useful: dress protocols maintained in rural areas

In 1856 the young squatter George Serocold, who had migrated from England
with funds to purchase a sheep station, bought a property at Cockatoo Creek
on the Dawson River, 200 miles south-west of Rockhampton in Central
Queensland. His letters to his brother Charles describe days filled with hard but
rewarding labour. Serocold fits the above description of a young gentleman who
was prepared to knuckle down and work with his hands. Yet, although living
on a remote station, Serocold did not set aside the niceties of the society in
which he was raised. He endeavoured to maintain a genteel, though practical
level of dress, requesting his brother purchase a mixture of durable working
clothes and better quality items. Serocold ordered his clothes from his London
tailors, shirtmakers and bootmakers who had his measurements on file. The
quality of his clothing, though of a practical nature, would have stood in contrast to the rough ready-made clothing worn by his employees, many of whom
were also migrants. Serocold asked his brother to send him three pairs of best
lace-up shooting boots, 'not over heavy'; three pairs of Wellington boots from
Verity; two dozen good white shirts, 'extra strong both in material and stitch-
ing'; six good strong nightshirts; six plain loose flannel waistcoats; one dozen
shirts of best Scotch twill; three pairs of lighter riding trousers for summer that

'must be strong and able to stand wear' and four plain black neckties. And finally, in contrast to Capper's advice, Serocold asks for '£5 worth of books according to your taste'.[55]

In 1855, when the newly married Jessie Campbell emigrated to New South Wales to live on a rural property near Bathurst, she knew that she would need suitable items of fashionable clothing. Jessie married Australian born pastoralist George Campbell in Glasgow on 10 July 1855 and sailed for Australia two and a half months later. Her choice of wedding dress, which in nineteenth-century tradition was to become her 'best' day wear, indicates that she expected there would be a place in Australia for her fashionable three-tiered crinoline-skirted blue silk dress with wide pagoda sleeves (Figure 9.2). It also appears that a little while later she realized she would also need a ball gown. A separate evening bodice, with a wide, low neckline and short sleeves, which could be interchanged with the day bodice was constructed, either before she departed or after she arrived in Australia, from a well-matched plain blue taffeta of slightly different texture and tone (Figure 9.3). It was not uncommon in the 1850s and

FIGURE 9.2 Wedding dress, Scotland, 1855.

Source: The Cavalcade of History and Fashion, Forestville, NSW, Australia. Timeline Photography © Cavalcade.

FIGURE 9.3 Ball dress, Scotland, 1855.

Source: The Cavalcade of History and Fashion, Forestville, NSW, Australia. Timeline Photography © Cavalcade.

1860s for a 'best' dress to have two bodices, one for daywear and one for evening, thus making economical use of the yards of expensive fabric in the skirt.

In Jessie's dress the fabric and trims of the day bodice match those of the skirt, while those of the evening bodice, though well matched, are different. The three tiers of brocade used in the skirt have been woven *à disposition* with scalloped edges and a deep floral pattern that reflects the fashionable cut of skirts of the day. The Campbells became prominent settlers in the Cowra area and built a large colonial homestead on their property *Jerula*. Wearing her new dress, Jessie was one of many settler women who introduced and maintained the trappings of genteel respectability to rural Australia.[56] Another settler who adhered to common standards of genteel dress was Rachel Henning who, already having spent time on various properties in Australia between 1854 and 1856 with her brother Biddulph, returned to Australia in 1861. In a letter of 1862 Henning describes travelling overland from Rockhampton to her brother's property *Exmoor* where she lived from 1862 to 1865.[57] Situated considerably further north than George Serocold's property, *Exmoor* was located in a part of

Queensland that had only recently been opened up for settlement. Despite its remoteness, Henning packed dresses that conformed to the full-skirted fashions of the day. She wrote that,

> It was raining when we left Rockhampton ... Biddulph had our horses waiting on the other side of the river, and by superhuman effort of packing we crammed our dresses and crinolines into a valise, which he carried before him.[58]

Having spent considerable time in rural Australia on her first sojourn, Henning had first-hand knowledge of dress expectations and protocols in rural settler society. While travelling further afield to North Queensland, Henning introduced these colonial proprieties to a newly settled part of the country. Although Henning wrote of the difficulties of procuring and maintaining items of dress, throughout her three-year sojourn at *Exmoor* she nevertheless was concerned with maintaining acceptable standards of genteel dress and behaviour. In addition, as head of the household, Henning wrote of her brother Biddulph having a 'mortal horror of seeing people shabby'.[59] If women were generally considered a civilizing force in the bush,[60] the examples of Biddulph Henning and George Serocold show that educated pastoralists who lived in remote areas also sought to maintain these standards of dress. Thus, in contrast to the advice that only basic and durable clothing was required, many rural settlers endeavoured to maintain levels of clothing that included adhering to standard fashions of the day. Margaret Maynard has pointed out that the maintenance of appropriate dress and imported fashions in colonial Australia was a sign of 'the triumphant capacity to survive across immense physical and cultural distances'.[61] Settlers and native-born Australians strove to be seen as anything other than 'backward' in appearance and demeanour and dress played a significant role in assuaging this apprehension. Furthermore, in doing so they transplanted and upheld dominant British ideals in newly settled and remote regions. Henning's crinolines may have seemed cumbersome contraptions for life on a remote Queensland station but the steel hoops were, as Lynda Nead points out, symbols of the might of economic and political power of monarchy and empire that supported the layers of expansive fabric.[62]

Dress, society and misleading information

Although it is apparent that settlers such as George Serocold, Jessie Campbell and Rachel Henning had either first-hand knowledge of clothing conditions or were attuned to the current nature of society in Australia, expectations that fine clothing was not required in the colonies was, for many decades, a common source of misleading information. Sarah Bunbury experienced a mismatch between the information she had to hand and the reality of what she found on arrival. In November 1840 Sarah, who was preparing to emigrate to Melbourne with her husband Hanmer, described how Hanmer was making extracts from books and news items about Australia.[63] The information he gleaned still left Sarah relatively uniformed and she was surprised when, soon after they had arrived in Melbourne, they attended a ball in June 1841 to find that people 'dressed as well as at any ball in Europe'. Sarah wore a white satin dress that she had brought with her, stating, 'When I brought it out here I had very little idea of ever having occasion to wear it – but like most people in England, had a very false notion of the state of affairs here'.[64] Although the Port Phillip area had only been colonized six years earlier, the Bunburys found there was a lively social scene that warranted the need for silk dresses and ball gowns.

Some 11 years later the lack of reliable information was still rife when in 1852 Sophy Cooke, who had arrived as an unassisted emigrant in Adelaide in December 1851 to marry her fiancé Edward, was as equally surprised as Sarah Bunbury at the local attention to appropriate and fashionable dress. Sophy commented that she felt decidedly underdressed when attending a concert in Adelaide:

> People at home do not think that we colonists do not dress much. Miss Grocer thought my light silk dress would be useless out here but she was quite mistaken, for people dress genteely and with quite as good taste as at home.[65]

The week after her arrival Sophy was taken to a public concert where she found she, 'did not feel dressed enough when sitting by the side of ladies without bonnets, with lace sleeves and white gloves; it quite put me in mind of England'.[66] Sarah Bunbury and Sophy Cooke were among the many contemporary commentators who expressed surprise at the favourable conditions they met with in Australia.

Recent arrivals often commented on modes of dress as being akin to those in Britain. Although differences were observed, rather than being wildly divergent, these tended to be in the detail and manner of dress. This was particularly the case in urban areas. When Sophy Cooke was greeted by Edward (who had emigrated in 1848 and ran a general goods store in Adelaide) on her arrival she had expected to meet a 'rough-looking creature almost from the bush', but was surprised to find him 'a respectable colonial tradesman' who dressed as he did in England, except for 'a light cap with white calico covering which almost everyone wears for coolness'.[67]

While emigrants often experienced a mismatch between what they were told about Australian society and what they found, they generally packed garments that they already owned and that conformed to their own experience of everyday dress. In 1853 Jane Cannan, who had recently arrived in Melbourne with her husband David during the early years of the gold rush commented that,

The sun has occasionally been hot and glaring but we would not have known that we were not in England so far. I have been wearing the dress & cape that I left home in – with the occasional assistance from the shawl on cold days.[68]

Since a large number of emigrants originated from towns and cities in their homeland their experience of appropriate styles of dress was an urban one and they brought that urban sensibility with them to Australia.[69] Like Jane Cannan, Mary Pearce, who also arrived in Victoria in 1853, brought existing suitable garments and shawls with her. The Pearces had come from London and Mary packed her best silk dress, which she had worn when she married Ephraim Pearce in 1850, and her two paisley shawls into a metal trunk for the voyage to Australia (Figure 9.4). The Pearces, who were assisted migrants, initially settled in a tent in the gold rush town of Ballarat.[70] Ephraim was a carpenter and Mary was the educated daughter of a schoolmaster. The woven and printed paisley shawls made from wool and silk were part of Mary's trousseau. These were cherished items that Mary would have worn with her pale blue silk dress woven with a floral motif. The elegant dress has a long fitted bodice, bell-shaped sleeves and a full skirt flat-pleated at the front and organ-pleated at the back. Rather than go to the considerable expense of

FIGURE 9.4 Wedding dress (England) and shawl (Scotland), *c.*1850.

Source: National Gallery of Victoria, gift of Mrs Betty Blunden, 1979 (D5-1979) and (D123-1979).

purchasing new items, emigrants, whether assisted or unassisted, were inclined to pack what they had and augmented their dress supplies with items they either purchased or sewed themselves.

Clothing, needlework and the voyage

Emigrant guides reinforced the need for general domestic economy. The long voyage provided extended periods of time to fill. Journals kept by first-class and steerage passengers mention how women spent time sewing, knitting and mending. To those emigrating, advice was given with regards to sewing. *The Emigrant's Guide to Australia* recommends that,

> Should a little extra means be at command, let it be expended in laying in small supplies of calicoes, brown holland, camlet, fine canvas, &c.; and it will always be desirable that the wife make as many of her clothes on board ship as possible, as the occupation serves to pass away many otherwise idle, heavy hour.[71]

While sailing from England to New South Wales emigrant Sarah Thomas made a silk plaid skirt (once part of a dress), which is now in the collection of Tongarra Museum, Shellharbour, New South Wales.[72] Sarah and her husband William, who was a carpenter by trade, sailed in 1838 with their four children. They settled on a farm near Albion Park, New South Wales and William also ran a carpentry business.[73] The style of the skirt and the choice of a plaid silk fabric, which was particularly fashionable in the late 1830s and 1840s, suggests that Sarah's dress was made as a 'best' dress, to be worn on Sundays and special occasions in Australia. The pink, purple, green and white plaid taffeta skirt is hand sewn. Sarah took time to create a decorative feature down the centre front of the skirt constructed from bias-cut strips of the plaid silk. The central strip is decorated with eight green fabric-covered buttons that are surrounded with fine pleated fabric of the same colour.

Like Mary Pearce, Sarah also packed two shawls, one a cream-coloured paisley shawl with the distinctive almond-shaped design printed in blues and reds and the other a cashmere shawl with finely woven paisley bands attached along the edges. Being of an older style and finer in quality than the printed shawl, the cashmere shawl may have been a family treasure handed down to Sarah. In making her garment Sarah was constructing a dress that adhered to the fashions of the day. She did not dream up the details of her dress and must have been working from a fashion plate or a similar existing example to the blue and brown silk plaid evening dress in the Museum of Applied Arts and Sciences.[74] The quality of construction and sewing of the latter indicates that the evening dress was professionally made and its provenance points to it either having been made in Australia or brought out with the owner.[75] The striking thing about this dress is its close similarity to Sarah Thomas' skirt and the detail down the front.[76] Both skirts have the same distinctive bias-cut vertical strip applied to the centre front and embellished with handmade decorative button details. Sarah Thomas' industry on the voyage out indicates that she anticipated a place for such a 'best' dress in her new life in Australia.

By the mid-nineteenth century, the major Australian towns such as Sydney, Hobart, Melbourne and Adelaide had developed into prosperous bustling centres that were considered by British visitors to be on a par with English regional towns. Commentators wrote of the well-stocked shops where the latest imports of dress and accessories could be purchased.

As with many other new arrivals to the colonies, Clara Aspinall, who came to Melbourne in 1858 to live with her brother, the lawyer Butler Cole Aspinall, was impressed with the city and its amenities and noted that, 'Melbourne is in reality quite a different place to the Melbourne I had imagined'.[77] She was particularly struck by the extravagant and fashionable display of dress stating,

> All articles of dress are expensive in Melbourne, and yet ladies of Melbourne, generally speaking, are much more extravagant in their toilettes than are ladies at home. I never, even in the gayest English watering-place, saw such elaborate female attire as at Melbourne.[78]

This lavish expenditure on dress has been investigated by Jane Elliot, who asserts that better quality clothing was more easily obtainable to a greater proportion of the colony of Victoria's population than those in England.[79] In 1853 an almost £3 million worth of clothing and clothing materials were imported into Melbourne for a population of less than 100,000.[80] This was the very same year that Capper was advising prospective emigrants that anything other than durable dress would be useless in their new home. Unlike Christiana Brooks' disapproving comments of an over-dressed generation in Sydney in 1826, Aspinall's observances some 30 years later express pleasant surprise at the level of attention paid to fashion by Melbourne 'ladies' compared with their sisters in England. For the emigrant and visitor, Australian society envisaged from afar was essentially an imagined one, which proved to be quite different on arrival.[81] Those born in Australia and some who emigrated made decisions about dress that were at odds with the advice found in the emigrant guides. In doing so they harboured an expectation for their colonial life that was different from the stereotype set by mother England.

Conclusion

As emigrants selected clothing for the long voyage out to Australia, what they often found on arrival was a mismatch between what they were advised to bring, either by word of mouth or in the emigrant manuals, and what they encountered. While emigrant's guides promised opportunities for those prepared to cast aside fine broadcloth for coarse fustian,[82] work hard and adapt, those arriving in Australia found a society that was well attuned to the protocols of dress. From early on, local shops supplied fashionable items and people from all walks of life were able to engage with fashionable dress to suit their means. What are we to make then of the austere claims that anything for mere show would be worse than useless? By emphasizing the need for only simple, hard-wearing clothing, were the published guides attempting to reinforce the role that particular emigrants were to play in the advancement of the Australian colonies? In these guides, clothing is often used as an example of how the emigrant should adapt and throw off past prejudices. The message is that life will be different in Australia and clothing is part of that difference. Far from Britain the new emigrant did indeed contribute to the creation of a related but distinctive society. With an interest in fashionable dress though, Australian colonials ultimately challenged the imperial order of things. Far from having no need of and therefore no interest in fine clothing, those living at a great distance from the traditional centres of fashion were keen to engage with and maintain fashionable levels of dress. In doing so they developed a separate fashion culture that was shaped by local conditions and responses to colonial circumstances.

Notes

1 John Capper, *The Emigrant's Guide to Australia*, 2nd ed. (Liverpool: George Philip & Son, 1853), 94.
2 Museum Victoria Collections, 'John Henry Capper, Home Office Clerk & Author (*c.*1780s–?)', https://collections.museumvictoria.com.au/articles/2137 (accessed 19 May 2019).
3 Capper, *The Emigrant's Guide*, iii and 80.
4 Capper, *The Emigrant's Guide*, 79.
5 Margaret Maynard, 'Australian Dress: Perceptions and Stereotypes', *Journal of Australian Studies* 18.41 (1994): 3–4.
6 Marion Fletcher, *Costume in Australia 1788–1901* (Melbourne: Oxford University Press, 1984), 63–64; Henry Capper, *South Australia: Containing Hints To Emigrants*, 2nd ed. (London: n.p., 1838), the author may have been the same John Henry Capper of the 1850s emigrants' guides.
7 Margaret Maynard, *Fashioned from Penury: Dress as Cultural Practice in Colonial Australia* (Melbourne: Cambridge University Press, 1994), 138.
8 Maynard, *Fashioned from Penury*, 137.
9 Ken Inglis, *Australian Colonists* (Carlton: Melbourne University Press, 1993), 21; James Jupp, ed. *The Australian People: An Encyclopedia of the Nation, Its People and Their Origins* (Cambridge, UK: Cambridge University Press, 2001), 39.
10 Helen Irving, 'Making the Federal Commonwealth, 1890–1901', in *The Cambridge History of Australia Volume 1: Indigenous and Colonial Australia*, ed. Alison Bashford and Stuart Macintyre (Cambridge, UK: Cambridge University Press, 2013), 242–243. The six independent, self-governing British colonies of Australia became states on 1 January 1901 when they were federated under the newly created Commonwealth of Australia. After Federation powers were divided under a constitutional monarchy between a central government that was responsible for national concerns and state governments that looked after regional matters.

11 Andrew Seltzer, 'Labour, Skills and Migration', in *The Cambridge Economic History of Australia*, ed. Simon Ville and Glenn Withers (Port Melbourne: Cambridge University Press, 2015), 181.

12 Inglis, *Australian Colonists*, 21.

13 Seltzer, 'Labour, Skills and Migration', 180.

14 Anthea Jarvis, 'Kitted Out for Australia: Dress and Chattels for British Emigrants, 1840–70', *Costume* 44.1 (2010): 82.

15 Don Charlwood, *The Long Farewell* (Melbourne: Allen Lane, 1981), 12.

16 Seltzer, 'Labour, Skills and Migration', 187.

17 Henry Parkes, *An Emigrant's Home Letters* (Sydney: Angus & Robertson, 1896), 22.

18 State Library of South Australia, Letters from George and Sarah Brunskill, D5203(L): George Brunskill to his brother, 31 March 1838.

19 Deborah Oxley, *Convict Maids: The Forced Migration of Women to Australia* (Cambridge, UK: Cambridge University Press, 1996), 172.

20 'New South Wales Final Report of the Committee of the Legislative Council on Emigration, and Minutes of Evidence 18 May 1835', quoted in Oxley, *Convict Maids*, 176.

21 Capper, *The Emigrant's Guide*, 78.

22 Capper, *The Emigrant's Guide*, 80.

23 Capper, *The Emigrant's Guide*, 83.

24 State Library of South Australia: Charles Masters, D6070(L): 'Journal of Charles Masters', 1845.

25 Robin F. Haines, *Emigration and the Labouring Poor: Australian Recruitment in Britain and Ireland, 1831–1860* (Basingstoke, UK: Macmillan Press, 1997), 24.

26 E. Mackenzie, *The Emigrant's Guide to Australia: With a Memoir of Mrs. Chisholm* (London: Clarke, Beeton & Co., 1853), 179.

27 Mackenzie, *The Emigrant's Guide to Australia*, 179.

28 Jarvis, 'Kitted Out for Australia', 85. On Moses, see Stanley Chapman, 'The "Revolution" in the Manufacture of Ready-Made Clothing 1840–60', *London Journal* 29.1 (2004): 44–61.

29 Jarvis, 'Kitted Out for Australia', 85.

30 Jarvis, 'Kitted Out for Australia', 86.

31 D. Davis, 'Important Notice', *Goulburn Herald and County of Argyle Advertiser*, 7 January 1854, 1.

32 Stanley, 'The "Revolution" in the Manufacture of Ready-Made Clothing', 45.

33 Mackenzie, *The Emigrant's Guide to Australia*, 57.

34 Parkes, *An Emigrant's Home Letters*, 25.

35 Parkes, *An Emigrant's Home Letters*, 38–39.

36 Parkes, *An Emigrant's Home Letters*, 32.

37 Parkes, *An Emigrant's Home Letters*, 25.

38 Haines, *Emigration and the Labouring Poor*, 22.

39 Beverley Earnshaw and Joy Hughes, eds., *Fanny to William: The Letters of Frances Leonora Macleay 1812–1836* (Sydney: Historic Houses Trust of New South Wales, Macleay Museum, 1993), 51.

40 Earnshaw and Huges, *Fanny to William*, 52 and 103.

41 James Broadbent, Suzanne Rickard and Margaret Steven, *India, China, Australia: Trade and Society 1788–1850* (Sydney: Historic Houses Trust of New South Wales, 2003), 161.

42 Maynard, *Fashioned from Penury*, 51.

43 Ann Pullan, '"Conversations on the Arts": Writing a Space for the Female Viewer in the "Repository of Arts" 1809–15', *Oxford Art Journal* 15.2 (1992): 15–26.

44 M. Hayes, 'M. Hayes, Milliner and Mantua-Maker', *Sydney Gazette*, 17 April 1803, 4.

45 National Library of Australia, Brooks Family Papers (hereafter BFP), MS 1559: Christiana Brooks, 'Diary 1825–1830', 10 July 1828.

46 BFP, MS 1559: Brooks, 'Diary', 20 April 1826.

47 Colin Dyer, *The French Explorers and Sydney* (St Lucia: Queensland University Press, 2009), 169.

48 Mitchell Library, State Library of New South Wales, Walker Family Papers, MLMSS 462: Mary Blaxland to Anna Walker, 28 September 1831.

49 BFP, MS 1559: Brooks, 'Diary', 13 October 1825.

50 Elizabeth Windschuttle, 'Discipline, Domestic Training and Social Control: The Female School of Industry, Sydney, 1826–1847', *Labour History* 39 (1980): 4. The colony of New South Wales was the first to abolish the transportation of convicts to Australia in 1840 and Western Australia was the last in 1868. Michael Bogle, *Convicts: Transportation and Australia* (Sydney: Historic Houses Trust of New South Wales, 2008), 95–96.

51 BFP, MS 1559: Brooks, 'Diary', March 1826.

52 Penny Russell, *Savage or Civilised? Manners in Colonial Australia* (Sydney: University of New South Wales Press, 2010), 2–3, discusses the importance of manners as a marker of acceptability within the fluid nature of colonial society. Although Russell does not focus on modes of dress, these were also crucial markers that served to either include or exclude sectors of society.

53 See Maynard, 'Australian Dress: Perceptions and Stereotypes', 10, for a discussion about the importance of appearance in a penal colony where the demarcation between acceptable and inappropriate dress was linked to notions of female sexuality and morality.

54 Capper, *The Emigrant's Guide*, 89.

55 John Oxley Library, State Library of Queensland, George Edward Pearce Serocold papers: George Serocold to Charles Serocold, 26 March 1857.

56 Lisa Ford and David Andrew Roberts, 'Expansion, 1820–1850', in Bashford and Macintyre, *The Cambridge History of Australia*, vol. I, 136.

57 Australian National University: Margaret Caldwell, 'Henning, Rachel Biddulph (1826–1914)', http://adb.anu.edu.au/biography/henning-rachel-biddulph-3753/text5437 (accessed 19 May 2019).

58 Rachel Henning, *The Letters of Rachel Henning* (Sydney: Bulletin Newspaper, 1952), 42.

59 Henning, *The Letters of Rachel Henning*, 41.

60 See Emma Floyd, 'Without Artificial Constraint: Gentility and British Gentlewomen in Rural Australia', in *Imperial Objects: Essays on Victorian Women's Emigration and the Unauthorized Imperial Experience*, ed. Rita S. Kranidis, (New York: Twayne, 1998), 85–107.

61 Maynard, 'Australian Dress: Perceptions and Stereotypes', 9.

62 Lynda Nead, 'The Layering of Pleasure: Women, Fashionable Dress and Visual Culture in the Mid-Nineteenth Century', *Nineteenth Century Contexts* 36.5 (2013): 504.

63 State Library of Victoria, Bunbury Family Correspondence, MS 13530: Sarah Bunbury to her father Robert Clement Sconce, *c.*1840. Sarah noted that Hanmer read the *Australian Record*. This was probably the periodical called the *South Australian Record*, published between 1837 and 1841.

64 State Library of Victoria, MS 13530 Bunbury Family Correspondence: Sarah Bunbury to her father Robert Clement Sconce, 8 June 1841.

65 Irene C. Taylor, *Sophy Under Sail* (Sydney: Hodder & Stoughton, 1969), 133.

66 Taylor, *Sophy Under Sail*, 134.

67 Taylor, *Sophy Under Sail*, 143.

68 National Library of Australia, Letters of Jane and David Cannan, MS 401: Jane Cannan to Jeannette du Bois Raymond, 21 September 1853.

69 For the urban origins of emigrants, see Ford and Roberts, 'Expansion 1820–50', 135. See also 'Report: Distressed Mechanics and Labourers', *The Australian*, 30 November 1843, 3.

70 Rowena Clark, *Hatches, Matches and Dispatches: Christening, Bridal and Mourning Fashions* (Melbourne: National Gallery of Victoria, 1987), 57 and 88.

71 Capper, *The Emigrant's Guide*, 96.
72 Rebecca Evans, 'Tartan Skirt Worn by Sarah Thomas', www.australiandressregister.org/garment/31 (accessed 19 May 2010).
73 Evans, 'Tartan Skirt'.
74 Museum of Applied Arts and Sciences, 'Evening Dress, Silk, Australia, *c*.1845', https://collection.maas.museum/object/195651 (accessed 19 May 2019).
75 The day dress was purchased by the collector Anne Schofield in Tasmania and donated to the Museum of Applied Arts and Sciences in 1983.
76 Rebecca Evans, 'Inside the Collection: Pattern Recognition', https://maas.museum/inside-the-collection/2010/01/13/pattern-recognition (accessed 19 May 2019).
77 Clara Aspinall, *Three Years in Melbourne* (London: L. Booth, 1862), 7.
78 Aspinall, *Three Years in Melbourne*, 125.
79 Jane Elliott, 'The Politics of Antipodean Dress: Consumer Interests in Nineteenth-Century Victoria', *Journal of Australian Studies* 52 (1997): 20.
80 Elliott, 'The Politics of Antipodean Dress', 20.
81 Penny Russell, 'The Brash Colonial: Class and Comportment in Nineteenth-Century Australia', *Transactions of the Royal Historical Society* 12 (2002): 438. Russell points out that this was also the case for those in Australia who created an imagined England by which they judged their own colonial society.
82 Capper, *The Emigrant's Guide*, 90. Broadcloth was a high-quality woollen cloth woven with a smooth face. Fustian was a strong and sturdy cotton cloth with a short nap or pile. The former was used for fine suiting and the latter for durable working-class clothing.

10

DRESSING APART

Indian elites and the politics of fashion in British India, c.1750–1850

Tara Mayer

The regulation of dress was a hallmark of imperialism. The enforcement, adaptation and subversion of sartorial policies was often the most visible arena in which claims to, and contestations of, imperial authority were enacted. Whether in the coerced imposition of Western-style clothing on subject populations, as was the case for African slaves in Spanish Latin America, or in its restriction to only Europeans and Christian converts, as practised for example in South East Asia under Dutch rule, dress was an important currency in what Harish Trivedi has termed 'colonial transactions': the praxis, reception and representation of colonialism.[1]

The most extensively documented case study of this dynamic is British India. British reactions to 'cultural cross-dressing' reveal the anxieties and hypocrisies underlying colonial rule. These became especially clear in the nineteenth century through various efforts to restrict such perceived sartorial transgressions. The concerns about not dressing the part cut both ways. They were projected on to European officials, who were afraid to 'go native', that is become morally and physically corrupted by adopting local mores. But they were also applied to Indian elites, whose espousal of European dress was seen as transgressing racial boundaries and diminishing their utility as colonial intermediaries. The anxieties around the implications of dress for individual and collective identities were played out through a number of common tropes. For instance, the commonplace denouncement of Western-educated, suit-wearing Indians as *babus* – mockingly portrayed as caricature ersatz Englishmen aping European demeanours – was designed to reassert hierarchies of power and status.[2] Any blurring of the visible demarcation lines between imperial master and colonial subject was perceived as a potential challenge to the underlying hierarchy:

By his mimicry of English manners, the *babu* reminded the British of a similarity they always sought to disavow; and, steeped in English liberalism, he posed by implication, if not by outright assertion, a challenge to the legitimacy of the Raj.[3]

Homi Bhabha identifies in such trepidations about colonial imitation the very source of the European desire to create imperial subjects that were 'almost the same, but not quite'.[4] In his view, Europeans only ever intended a partial reform of education, religion and practices in their colonies in order to safeguard and perpetuate this degree of difference, which formed the ultimate tenet of their right to rule. And in the same vein, Indian efforts at mimicry, which is only ever a degree removed from mockery, can be read not just as impersonation but as subversion, as an attempt to call into question the outward markers of difference that were meant to distinguish the master from his subjects (Figure 10.1).

The politics of dress were central to both the policing as well as the contravention of the tenuous boundaries of these outward distinctions. This is evident not only in discourses about *babus* and other Western-educated Indian elites but can also be linked to an earlier period, the late eighteenth to early nineteenth

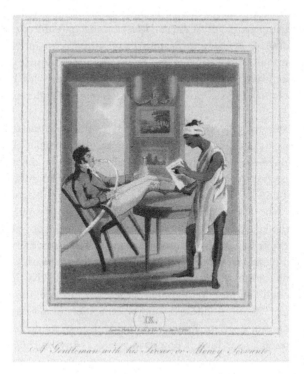

FIGURE 10.1 'A Gentleman and His Sircar'.

Source: Charles Doyley, *The Costume and Customs of Modern India* (London: Edward Orme, 1825), plate 9.

century, a time that is otherwise associated with a more open and experimental regime of cultural interaction. The focus of these earlier concerns about cultural cross-dressing, of Indians mimicking European styles, were the Indian princes. Usually referred to by the Mughal title of Nawab, these regional sovereigns were the bedrock of Britain's system of indirect rule under the East India Company; in many parts of the subcontinent, they continued to serve as key intermediaries of colonial rule even after the establishment of the British Raj in 1858. India's princes occupied a highly ambiguous place within the constellation of colonial rule: in many cases, they served to legitimize and shore up imperial authority, but, especially in times of crisis, they could also serve as an antipode to British claims to sovereignty.

Clothes, class and colonial identity politics

In the eighteenth and early nineteenth centuries, concerns about the ambivalent role of Indian princes within the imperial system were often expressed in terms of modernization versus tradition. The idea of moral and physical 'improvement' of India (and other colonies) was central to the European justification of imperialism. Rationalizing the militaries, bureaucracies, and courts of princes along the European model was therefore seen as a key part of Britain's imperial mission in India. On the other hand, the authority of the Nawabs was based on precedent and traditional titles, which in almost all cases had been established during the Mughal period.[5] While the British eagerly hollowed out the actual power of the princes, they were keen to maintain their symbolic authority in order to lend legitimacy to their own presence and treaties. For the same reason that the British maintained the façade of a Mughal empire – at least until the events of 1857/1858 demonstrated the very real risk that an Indian emperor could serve as the figurehead of an anti-British uprising – they affirmed the traditional role and prestige of the regional Nawabs.

The tension between modernization and tradition engendered by the Nawabs found expression in a vocabulary of visual distinction. The traditional Nawab presented himself in gold-embroidered garbs, elaborate headdresses and all the pomp of a princely retinue; the 'modern prince', by contrast, appeared in a carriage rather than on horseback and wore a suit. Clothing and other forms of material culture became emblematic of the differing and often contradictory attitudes Europeans held about India's princes, which reflect more general concerns, quandaries and misgivings about Indians. Trepidations about what different classes of Indians should, or should not, be wearing are some of the earliest indicants of an imperial ideology that is usually seen as a product of the later nineteenth century.

Not all Indians were seen as potential threats to the fragile social order Britain sought to impose on its largest and most important colony. What the British regarded as the lower rungs of Indian society – poor city dwellers and the overwhelming majority of the rural population – were either criticized for their perceived backwardness or heralded for the picturesque splendour of their 'traditional ways', which were being eagerly surveyed and catalogued by British officials (Figure 10.2). A representative example is a description by William Hodges from 1780 of a ship's arrival at Madras:

> This is the moment in which an European feels the great distinction between Asia and his own country. The rustling of fine linen, and the general hum of unusual conversation, presents to the mind for a moment the idea of an assembly of females. When he ascends upon the deck, he is struck with the long muslin dresses, and black faces adorned with very large gold earrings and white turbans. The first salutation he receives from these strangers is by bending their bodies very low, touching the deck with the back of the hand, and the forehead three times.[6]

The clichéd description of these Indian men in terms of both appearance (their gold-adorned 'black faces' evocatively contrasting with their white turbans) as well as deportment (their bodies prostrated before the arriving Europeans) signals hierarchy and buttresses what Ann Stoler has termed 'the colonial order of

FIGURE 10.2   'A Grassyara' ('A Grasscutter').

Source: François Balthazar Solvyns, *A Collection of Two Hundred and Fifty Coloured Etchings: Descriptive of the Manners, Customs and Dresses of the Hindoos* (Calcutta: [n.p.], 1799), sec. I, no. 29.

things'.[7] Similar attitudes are projected onto Indian men. The most common first impression of Indians found in many European travel accounts is of their nakedness. Descriptions of manual labourers, who constituted the vast majority of the population, focus almost invariably on the show of bare skin – as well as on the complexion of that skin: 'Their dark and glossy skins, their bare heads ... and bodies destitute of clothing, with the exception of a piece of cotton cloth folded about the loins'.[8] For Indians not engaged in manual work, the focus shifts to their supposed meekness; Hodges, for example, describes them as 'delicately framed', 'mild', 'tranquil' and 'sedulously attentive'.[9] This characterization is also extended to their dress, such as in the amused descriptions of their 'white robes and soft limbs [that] look unfit for even the exertion of driving' or of a shawl that makes a Hindu man look 'very lady-like'.[10] In these accounts, the contrast between these Indian men and Europeans is depicted as so stark and so obvious that it poses no concern to British worldviews.

By contrast, the physical and oftentimes functional proximity of Europeans to another class of colonial subjects – Indians in British military, administrative or domestic employ – required a more conscious articulation of difference. This was achieved primarily through the careful regulation of their respective sartorial regimes. These could be geared towards supposed 'improvement' (as seen in military uniforms, which were meant to impose a sense of order and discipline) or towards maintaining and even heightening India's inherent 'otherness' (as evident in the colourful, often deliberately exoticized liveries of domestic servants). In either case, dress served as the clear visible marker of subservience and difference. In spite of the overarching strength of British economic, political and cultural hegemony, however, there existed another class of Indians whose wealth and social status placed them above British sartorial mandate. It was these Indian elites who were perceived as the greatest threat to an imperial order that was made manifest through visual differentiation.

Unlike conscripts, employees and servants, upper-class Indians enjoyed the freedom to make their own sartorial choices; unlike the poor, they also had the means to match and even outdo the fashions of their European counterparts. Their socially elevated vantage point also allowed them to understand the changes taking place in colonial identity politics. By the eighteenth century, the notion of personal identity had become central to the colonial enterprise. The creation of colonial knowledge was predicated on the ability to assign people to distinct and defined categories.[11] These categories had to be fixed because 'by claiming belonging to one or another group recognised by the colonial rulers, one could obtain certain entitlements'.[12] The idea of colonial subjects as free agents able to traverse and exchange markers of personal identity was fundamentally threatening, not only to the European image of India and Indians, but also to the European *self*-image. For if Indians could become European, what did this say about the essential and superior identity of being European? In the late eighteenth century, when Europe's military and economic superiority was apparent but not yet overwhelming, this posed a pressing question.

In answer to this question, the British expended considerable efforts to restrict, reproach and ridicule the dress choices of upper-class Indians. European condescension toward the hybrid appearance of Indian elites reveals the profound anxiety and insecurity that dwelt just under the surface of imperial conceit. The perceived threat of cultural cross-dressers, encapsulated by their ostensible abandonment of tradition in favour of imitation, seems to have served as an impetus for the growing rigidity and regulation of European dress in India.[13] The fact that elite Indians operated outside of British sartorial control – neither liveried, nor uniformed, nor conforming to romantic stereotypes about 'traditional costume' – meant that their experimentation with British clothing and material culture was seen to blur the boundaries between colonizer and colonized. In reaction, many Europeans sought to portray a proper adherence to the latest fashions and an in-depth knowledge of rapidly changing European modes as an exclusively European domain.

Courtly culture and the conservation of difference

From the earliest colonial encounters until the last days of imperial rule, there existed a class of elite Indians whose elevated social status protected them (to varying degrees) from direct sartorial mandate. Yet, while these Indian elites may have escaped formal dress regulations, they were profoundly influenced by the prestige and status that came to be increasingly associated with European manufactured goods. European military victories in the late eighteenth century served to increase the prestige of Western-style discipline as well as European technology in the eyes of native elites. As an example of this, Indian military leaders such as Ranjit Singh (1780–1839) hired European freelancers to discipline their troops along the Western model. Crucially, the increasing respect given to the perceived superiority of European military technology was also transferred to European material goods and manufactures. Not surprisingly, fashionable European attire also became popular with native elites. To British eyes, this adaptation often appeared farcical, for example when a North Indian Nawab visited Calcutta on a shopping spree that included the purchases of an admiral's uniform, two canonicals and a pair of wigs.[14]

The trajectory by which European symbols of wealth and status came to be adopted by Indian elites can be observed particularly well in the case of Awadh (Oudh), a princely state centred in today's Uttar Pradesh. In 1764 the reigning Nawab of Awadh, Shuja-ud-Daula, was defeated by East India Company forces. A subsequent treaty established him as a de facto puppet ruler and obliged him to deliver various forms of tribute to the company. Concurrent to the rise of British power in the region, the Nawab and his courtly elite developed a marked interest in acquiring the latest objects and fashions that were flaunted by European residents such as Antoine Polier and Claude Martin. Shuja-ud-Daula was especially enthralled by the latest technological curiosities sent from Europe.[15] Polier gained his favour by offering him a costly European organ and Martin executed a number of special commissions for the Nawab including, among other things, a puppet theatre, gold-plated pocket watches and reading spectacles.[16]

Shuja-ud-Daula's son, Asaf-ud-Daula, was likewise fascinated by European material culture and greatly expanded on his father's collection, to such a degree that even well-appointed Europeans were astounded by what they saw at his palace. In the first decade of the nineteenth century, a British aristocrat recorded his perceptions of a breakfast he attended at the Nawab's palace in Lucknow:

> The scene was so singular, and so contrary to all my ideas of Asiatic manners, that I could hardly persuade myself that the whole was not a masquerade. An English apartment, a band in English regimentals, playing English tunes; a room lighted by magnificent English girandoles, English tables, chairs, and looking-glasses; an English service of plate; English knives, forks, spoons, wine glasses, decanters and cut glass vases – How could these convey any idea that we were seated in the court of an Asiatic Prince?[17]

When dressed for public, ceremonial occasions, the Nawab of Awadh wore a pointed crown in the European style, paired with an ermine cape; he is said to have been 'highly gratified by any comparison between himself and the Prince of Wales'.[18]

While the elaborate displays of traditional material culture at India's princely courts were regularly chastised by European commentators as emblematic of the decadence and corruption associated with Indian 'despots', the adoption of European forms of dress and decoration was not necessarily welcomed either. Such endeavours were not depicted as sensible efforts at improvement and modernization; instead, Europeanized Indian elites were portrayed as emulating Western material culture with an irrational, effeminate and greedy zeal that, in its excess, was seen as typically Indian.[19] The extensive discourse in English sources about the Nawab Asaf-ud-Daula's consumption was emblematic of this attitude. In their letters from India, British writers depicted him as 'anxious to procure everything that was singular, or that he heard praised; the price was of no consequence; and the imbecility of his mind rendered him a dupe of those who, like General Martin, placed no bounds to their extortions'.[20]

The purportedly indiscriminate consumption of Indian elites suggested that they were neither capable of appreciating the inherent value of an article nor its intended purpose. Such perceptions were often articulated in terms of incongruity. The display of European objects by Indians was commonly described in terms of their 'misuse' that stemmed from the inadequate understanding of the apposite manner, setting, or context in which a particular item of clothing should be worn or a household object employed. Even in the realm of gadgets, of which the Nawab of Awadh was so fond, the acknowledgement that he possessed 'every instrument and every machine, of every art and science' was accompanied by the disdainful qualifier, 'but he knows none'.[21]

Even if individual items were used appropriately, their unusual combination, or perhaps only their unfamiliar context, could evoke a sense of bewilderment. Honoria Lawrence wrote that a collection of European artefacts belonging to a wealthy Indian, which included everything from English furnishings and portraits to telescopes and dressed dolls, was utterly 'incongruous' and represented 'the most curious sample of wasted money' she had ever seen.[22] Similarly, Emma Roberts noted that

> English visitors at Hurdwar [Haridwar, in present-day Uttarakhand] are made to smile at the base uses to which the refinements of European luxury are degraded; nothing appears to be employed for the precise purpose for which it was originally intended.[23]

An excerpt from a letter dating from 1818 that describes the encounter with another Indian prince sums up this attitude:

> It required all the good breeding I was master of to refrain from laughing. A modern equipped Othello stood before us. He had on an immense cocked hat, with a long queue doubled up to his head, hanging in an enormous loop. He was dressed in a red coat laced with silver, very large epaulettes, a silver star embroidered on his right breast, and a French grey pair of loose trousers, not long enough to hide another pair of red silk under them, the latter dangling over his shoes upon the ground, for he had no boots; and to complete his toilet, he had a grenadier officer's regulation sword. He shook hands with both of us, as it appears to be his anxious wish to copy all our manners and customs ... His was a grotesque imitation of European dress.[24]

This 'grotesque imitation' extended to the food that was served (the idea of English cuisine was represented by a plate of hard-boiled eggs accompanied by an uncooked head of cabbage) and the palace's interior decorations (arranged 'without either taste or judgement, and of no particular pattern').[25] The apparent paradox of Europeans who otherwise were staunch advocates for the 'improvement' of Indians, including in particular sartorial reform, reacting with such sarcasm and scorn to the adoption of European material culture by elite Indians speaks to considerable doubts over ambiguous, hybrid forms of individual self-fashioning by their colonial subjects.

'European' style and sartorial tensions

The emulation of European styles extended far beyond princes and rulers. By the mid-1800s, many successful businessmen and Western-educated Indians had taken to wearing European clothes in public.[26] British commentators noted that young Indian elites were 'giving every day fresh proofs of zeal, if not for the very spirit, at least for the outward show of Western civilisation'.[27] This included 'a taste for reading English books, for speaking the English language, for dressing, dining, disporting after the English fashion', all in the service of 'a thorough assimilation of himself to his English neighbour'.[28] This supposed zeal for assimilation extended beyond dress to other facets of material representation:

> Some of the native traders have made or inherited large fortunes, and the public apartments of a few are furnished after the European fashion, with elegant chandeliers, pier glasses, couches, chests of drawers, writing-desks, and two or three hundred chairs ... Some have taken to drinking tea, some keep English coaches and equipages, and one individual was noted for having an English coachman.[29]

Despite official efforts to improve the native condition by promoting Western education, language, and material culture, efforts by individual Indians to adopt European lifestyles were generally met with haughty disdain. (Incidentally, no such judgment was placed on the often malapropos manner in which Europeans appropriated Indian objects and fashions.) While European-led reform was acceptable, independent initiatives of Indian elites to incorporate Western material culture into their self-representation were derided as naïve, pathetic and inherently flawed. In the words of Nirad Chaudhuri, the British 'were violently repelled by English in our mouths, and even more violently by English clothes on our back'.[30] Although undoubtedly rooted in arrogance and condescension, the frequency and urgency of these critiques carry with them a note of acute discomfort – a sense of anxiety on the part of British observers about witnessing the apparent irreverence with which native elites (and other aspiring groups) could imitate and appropriate European modes and manners. The sarcastic reportage of the risible incongruities of Indians emulating English manners is also indicative of a careful guarding of British markers of identity against imitation.

In order to fully understand these reactions, the supposed sartorial transgressions of native elites must be situated against the background of other social and cultural transgressions of that period. While the modern conception of colonial society as racially divided is, on the whole, accurate, it is vital to acknowledge that the upper echelons of colonial Indian society remained, at least to some degree, culturally permeable. The diverse inhabitants of India's bustling commercial towns blurred aesthetic boundaries in ways that complicated clear cultural distinctions. In the late eighteenth and early nineteenth centuries, upper-class Indians, mixed-race Eurasians, Armenians and Parsees often attended the same public functions as Europeans. In 1797, Reverend William Tennant noted that

> some of the respectable Armenians are commonly invited to the public balls and entertainments given in Calcutta, where they invariably behave with all that decorum and correctness which a knowledge of mankind generally produces ... In their fondness for show and elegance, the Armenians approach nearer the English than any merchants here.[31]

In the early years of the nineteenth century, Maria Graham (later Callcott) described a distinguished Parsee family of Calcutta by noting that its members 'speak and write English so well, that if I did not see their dark faces and foreign dress, or read their unusual names at the end of a letter, I should *never guess* that they were not Englishmen'.[32] The ability of non-Europeans to almost erase the markers of difference and superiority by assuming Western manners, fashions and fluency in the English language was met with astonishment, but also concern and opprobrium.

On a political level, there was concern that the adoption of European styles by Indian elites would ultimately undermine their role as useful intermediaries, as the pivots for a system of indirect rule. This concern was especially acute for the Nawabs. To the consternation of British observers, at the court of Lucknow the local ruler was reported to have altogether abandoned traditional protocol in his obsessive efforts to mimic English manners. This development was encapsulated by his attending an Islamic religious ceremony not in his customary royal garb but 'in his ordinary European dress, his black London hat in hand'.[33] The fear was that by such excessive adoption of Western material culture, the Nawabs risked replacing their elite Indian identity with an imperfect European one (Figure 10.3).

To British eyes, the customary aesthetic trappings of power represented continuity with the past and was therefore suited to legitimize the new political status quo of British suzerainty. As part of Queen Victoria's Golden Jubilee celebrations in London

FIGURE 10.3 'Nawab Sheik Imam-u-din' (late governor of Kashmir), watercolour on paper by William Carpenter, India, *c.*1855, 9.75 × 13.62 inches.
Source: © Victoria and Albert Museum, No. IS.152–1882.

in June 1887, a series of Indian princes were paraded before the British public. Their faithful adherence to their traditional costumes was reported as a particularly resonant marker of this direct link between the glories of India's ancient past and the new imperial order:

> The gold brocades, the harmonious boldness of colour in the rich fabrics of the dress, the barbaric wealth of diamonds and gems, testified that, even in the Victorian age, the East was still the East. We must say frankly that the native Princes had probably no great opinion of the show to which they lent so much *éclat*, and let us add, to which they gave so much meaning ... By their dress alone – but most eloquently by their dress – the native Princes showed, that if they were loyal feudatories of the Imperial Crown, they were still faithful to the customs of their ancestors.[34]

In contrast to such celebrations of traditional garb, Indian rulers who styled themselves in the European fashion were depicted as pathetic figures (Figure 10.4):

FIGURE 10.4 Photograph (albumen print from collodion negative), 'Maharaja Duleep Singh' (in Western dress), by Horne & Thornthwaite, London, *c.*1850.
Source: © Victoria and Albert Museum No. PH.192–1982.

The Nawab's carriage passed us, an old landau, drawn by four horses, with a coachman and postillion in red liveries, and some horse-guards in red also with high ugly caps, like those of the old grenadiers, with gilt plates in front and very ill mounted. The great men of India evidently lose in point of effect, by an injudicious and imperfect adoption of European fashions. An Eastern cavalier with his turban and flowing robes, is a striking object; and an Eastern prince on horseback and attended by his usual train of white-staved and high-capped janizaries, a still more noble one; but an Eastern prince in a shabby carriage, guarded by men dressed like an equestrian troop at a fair is nothing more than ridiculous and melancholy. It is, however, but natural that these unfortunate sovereigns should imitate, as far as they can, those costumes which the example of their conquerors has associated with their most recent ideas of power and splendour.[35]

Aside from the familiar denouncement of imperfect Indian mimicry, the loss of stature and status associated with the rejection of traditional dress is here directly linked to the notion of power. But whereas Indian princes, the author suggests, may believe that they join in the power of the imperial suzerain by dressing in the Western style, in actual fact they risk losing whatever standing they still enjoy.

Indian princes adopting European dress were clearly seen as a rupture in the image that, despite British overrule, 'the East was still the East'. The visual reaffirmation of political continuity through the figures of the Nawabs was regarded as critical not only to the continued deference of Indian subjects to established hierarchies but also to the British themselves. For it was not only distinctions of race that were at stake, but also those of class. It was feared that the zeal with which some Indian princes assumed European customs erased the class boundaries on which the sociopolitical order ultimately rested. By adopting Western fashions, it was feared, Indian elites exposed themselves to the influence of European charlatans, who now shared common markers of identity with Indian princes from whom previously they would have been clearly set apart in rank, appearance and manner. Asaf-ud-Daula, for example, was said to have 'carried his European predilection too far in abandoning the forms of an Asiatic court, and in living with Europeans as an equal'.[36]

As a result, even the 'lowest European gentleman seems to consider himself as on an equality with his Highness, and does not always treat him with that respect, which is his due'.[37] This impression was confirmed by the appointment of his English barber to an unprecedented rank at court: he was designated as comptroller of the royal household and master of His Majesty's pleasure boats, royal wardrobe (which, by then, was predominantly in the European fashion), royal menagerie and much else. By small degrees, an English commoner had elevated himself to the status of a royal co-equal, who eventually took to sitting down at the prince's dinner table as a matter of right.[38] This permeability of what were meant to be eternal, hereditary distinctions between the estates of society – royalty, aristocracy, commoners – was alarming in and of itself and all the more so if it implied a possible analogous breakdown of the barriers between colonial master and subject, between European and Oriental.

Conclusion

Indian princely authority, which was essential to the system of indirect rule and legitimization of British power, was perceived to be under threat from cross-cultural admixture and the abandonment of traditional displays. British rule depended on the maintenance of a social order in India that was predicated on the survival of traditional hierarchies. These hierarchies needed to be continuously reaffirmed by displays of pomp and status, in the language of dress, ceremony and custom. The blurring of sartorial boundaries by Indian elites was associated with other forms of cultural and social transgression that had the potential to upset the established norms of order and authority that underpinned effective colonial rule.

British anxieties over the sartorial expression by Indians predate the era of Indian nationalism that began in the middle of the nineteenth century and culminated in 1947 with India's independence. Elite Indians whose wealth and status allowed them to traverse visible cultural boundaries were met with derision but also consternation. The malleability of personal identity that Indian elites demonstrated by adopting 'unsuitable' forms of (European) dress had the potential to challenge and even upset the colonial order. Fashionable display, elegance, education, decorum and correctness were subjective and mutable categories during the late eighteenth to early nineteenth century; which meant that European identity in India was far from impermeable to encroachment. The integrity of European aesthetic and sartorial identity was seen to be undermined not only by a perceived laxity on the part of Britons who adopted Indian dress but especially by a potential blurring of boundaries by colonial subjects. Of those, the native princes were of special concern, not only because their wealth and status allowed them to elevate themselves to British sartorial regulation but also because their identity as hereditary Indian princes was seen as crucial to Britain's claims to political legitimacy.

The phenomenon of elite Indians dressing and behaving like Europeans prompted the British to more rigidly regulate their own modes of dress, in order to maintain the demarcation between native and European. As Emma Tarlo argues, by making their own sartorial codes and customs less accessible to the Indian elite, the British 'were trying to escape "imitation"'.[39] In an effort to avoid the emulative sartorial display of India's native elite, many Europeans sought to portray the in-depth knowledge of, and proper adherence to, the latest fashions as an exclusively European domain. British sartorial norms were constantly being made and remade in reaction to a perceived Indian threat of mimicry Through an ever-quickening cycle of change, fashion itself could make visible mimicry, and thereby render permanent the hierarchy of power engendered in 'dressing apart'.

Notes

1 Harish Trivedi, *Colonial Transactions: English Literature and India* (Manchester: Manchester University Press, 1995).

2 See for example, Mrinalini Sinha, *Colonial Masculinity: The 'Manly Englishman' and the 'Effeminate' Bengali in the Late Nineteenth Century* (Manchester: Manchester University Press, 1995); Emma Tarlo, *Clothing Matters: Dress and Identity in India* (Chicago: University of Chicago Press, 1996); Revathi Krishnaswamy, *Effeminism: The Economy of Colonial Desire* (Ann Arbor: University of Michigan Press, 1998).

3 Thomas R. Metcalf, *Ideologies of the Raj* (Cambridge, UK: Cambridge University Press, 1995), 106.

4 Homi K. Bhabha, 'Of Mimicry and Man: The Ambivalence of Colonial Discourse', *October* 28 (1984): 126; original emphasis. On this theme, see also Natasha Eaton, 'Between Mimesis and Alterity: Art, Gift, and Diplomacy in Colonial India, 1770–1800', *Comparative Studies in Society and History* 46.4 (2004): 816–844.

5 See for example, Peter J. Marshall, *Bengal: The British Bridgehead: Eastern India 1740–1828* (Cambridge, UK: Cambridge University Press, 1987), ch. 3; Christoper A. Bayly, *Indian Society and the Making of the British Empire* (Cambridge, UK: Cambridge University Press, 1988), chs 1–2.

6 William Hodges, *Travels in India, During 1780, 1781, 1782 & 1783* (London: [n.p.], 1793), 2.

7 Ann L. Stoler, *Race and the Education of Desire: Foucault's History of Sexuality and the Colonial Order of Things* (Durham, NC: Duke University Press, 1995), 46.

8 John M. MacMullen, *Camp and Barrack-Room; Or the British Army As It Is* (London: Chapman & Hall, 1846), 66.

9 Hodges, *Travels in India*, 3.

10 John Lawrence and Audrey Woodiwiss, eds., *The Journals of Honoria Lawrence: India Observed, 1837–1854* (Sevenoaks, UK: Hodder & Stoughton, 1980), 45; Godfrey C. Mundy, *Pen and Pencil Sketches: Being the Journal of a Tour in India*, 2 vols. (London: John Murray, 1832), vol. II, 211.

11 Bernard S. Cohn, *Colonialism and Its Forms of Knowledge* (Princeton, NJ: Princeton University Press, 1996).

12 Nira Wickramasinghe, *Dressing the Colonial Body: Politics, Clothing and Identity in Sri Lanka* (Hyderabad: Orient Blackswan, 2003), 70–71.

13 On the notion of cultural cross-dressing, see for example Tara Mayer, 'Cultural Cross-Dressing: Posing and Performance in Orientalist Portraits', *Journal of the Royal Asiatic Society*, series 3, 22.2 (2012): 281–298.

14 P. Thankappan Nair, ed., *British Social Life in Ancient Calcutta (1750–1850)* (Calcutta: Sanskrit Pustak Bhandar, 1983), 30–31.

15 On the dynamics of this exchange between Britain and its empire during this period, see for example Natasha Eaton, 'Nostagia for the Exotic: Creating an Imperial Art in London, 1750–1793', *Eighteenth-Century Studies* 39.2 (2006): 227–250.

16 Claude Martin, 'Letter to Messrs. William & Thomas Raikes & Co.' (8 September 1796), in *A Man of the Enlightenment in Eighteenth Century India: The Letters of Claude Martin, 1766–1800*, ed. Rosie Llewellyn-Jones (New Delhi: Permanent Black, 2003), 304–305.

17 George, Viscount Valentia, *Voyages and Travels to India, Ceylon, the Red Sea, Abyssinia, and Egypt (1802–1806)*, 4 vols. (London: William Miller, 1811), vol. I, 109.

18 Valentia, *Voyages and Travel*, vol. I, 112; Amin Jaffer, 'Dressed for Success: Indian Princes and Western Symbols of Power', in *Portraits in Princely India, 1700–1947*, ed. Rosie Llewellyn-Jones (Mumbai: Marg, 2010), 78–79.

19 On this point, see Maya Jasanoff, *Edge of Empire: Lives, Culture, and Conquest in the East, 1750–1850* (New York: Vintage, 2006), 75–80.

20 Valentia, *Voyages and Travels*, vol. I, 119.

21 Quoted in Mildred Archer, *India in British Portraiture, 1770–1825* (London: Russell Chambers for Sotheby Parke Bernet, 1979), 142–143.

22 Lawrence and Woodiwiss, *Journals of Honoria Lawrence*, 82.

23 Emma Roberts, *Scenes and Characteristics of Hindostan with Sketches of Anglo-Indian Society*, 3 vols., 2nd ed. (London: W. H. Allen, 1835), vol. III, 213.

24 George A. F. Fitzclarence, *Journal of a Route Across India, Through Egypt, to England, in the Latter End of the Year 1817 and the Beginning of 1818* (London: John Murray, 1819), 148–149.

25 Fitzclarence, *Journal of a Route Across India*, 151–152.

26 See for example, Bernard Cohn, 'Cloth, Clothes, and Colonialism: Indian in the Nineteenth Century', in *Consumption: Critical Studies in the Social Sciences*, ed. Daniel Miller, 4 vols. (London: Routledge, 2001), vol. II, 415.

27 Lionel J. Trotter, *The History of the British Empire in India from the Appointment of Lord Hardinge to the Political Extinction of the East India Company, 1844 to 1862* (London: W. H. Allen, 1866), 3.

28 Trotter, *The History of the British Empire*, 4.

29 Walter Hamilton, *The East-India Gazetteer*, 2 vols., 2nd ed. (London: Parbury, Allen & Co., 1828), vol. I, 324.

30 Nirad C. Chaudhuri, *Culture in the Vanity Bag: Being an Essay on Clothing and Adornment in Passing and Abiding India* (Bombay: Jaico Publishing, 1976), 58.

31 William Tennant, *Indian Recreations: Consisting Chiefly of Strictures on the Domestic and Rural Economy of the Mahomedans & Hindoos*, 8 vols., 2nd ed. (London: Longman, Hurst, Rees & Orme, 1804–1808), vol. I, 54.

32 Maria Graham, *Journal of a Residence in India* (Edinburgh: George Ramsay & Co, 1812), 44.

33 William Knighton, *The Private Life of an Eastern King, by a Member of the Household of His Late Majesty, Nussir-u-Deen, King of Oude* (New York: Redfield, 1855), 302.

34 William F. B. Laurie, *Sketches of Some Distinguished Anglo-Indians (Second Series)* (London: W. H. Allen, 1888), 301.

35 Reginald Heber, *Narrative of a Journey Through the Upper Provinces of India, from Calcutta to Bombay, 1824–1825*, 2 vols. (London: J. Murray, 1829), vol. I, 146.

36 Valentia, *Voyages and Travels*, vol. I, 135.

37 Valentia, *Voyages and Travels*, vol. I, 135.

38 Knighton, *Private Life of an Eastern King*, 19.

39 Tarlo, *Clothing Matters*, 39.

11

VISUAL ASSIMILATION AND BODILY REGIMES

Protestant programmes and Anishinaabe everyday dress in North America, 1830s–1950s

Cory Willmott

Introduction

This chapter interrogates colonial bodily regimes instituted through missionary conversion and education aimed at erasing the cultural identity of the Anishinaabek, Native American peoples resident in lands around the Great Lakes.[1] It takes its direction from theories that explain social identities through the embodied and performative aspects of dress, where 'dress' entails not only clothing but also accessories, extensions, body modifications, body confinements, body movement, posture and facial expression – the total dressed appearance of individuals.[2] Dress, understood as total clothed appearance, is a strategic site for both deployment of forced culture-change programmes and individual identity enactments. Ralph Linton identified dress as an agent in creating and maintaining social structures.[3] In his view, societies function as collectives through individuals' repetitive daily performance of collectively shared social roles. In this way, dressed appearances help to construct, maintain and/or modify the identity structures that make up societies. Irving Goffman shifted the focus of role theory to individuals' enactments. He saw this process as a 'daily cycle' of social interactions with greater and lesser degrees of mutual recognition.[4] Some dress studies have followed Goffman's symbolic interactionist examination of dress in individual identity performances.[5] Similarly highlighting individual enactments, Judith Butler emphasized the process through which the repetition of quotidian acts in everyday life can subvert and transform the structure of identity categories that is falsely reified as an impermeable social structure. In this way, Butler's spin on performative identity explains the dynamic relationship between social structure and individual agency by transforming the vision of structure into an embodied process of identity creation and recreation.[6] In this chapter, I reintegrate Linton's interest in structural forces with Goffman's and Butler's focus on individual agency to turn attention to the role of dress in an intentional and sustained culture change regime. Additionally, reframing the discussion of cultural genocide beyond boarding/residential schools, this chapter critically examines the broader context of missionary assimilation programmes through the particular lens of the Protestant beliefs and values that drove them.

Few directed culture-change programmes could be more explicit about role expectations than the assimilation programmes inflicted upon Native Americans beginning in the early nineteenth and tapering off only in the late twentieth century. Following recent scholarship that calls for self-reflexive examination of performing 'whiteness' and 'settler identities',[7] this chapter explores the ways in which missionaries imposed Protestant beliefs and values upon Anishinaabe peoples through bodily regimes that transformed their entire visual appearance to conform with white 'civilized' norms. As such, it supports George E. Tinker's contention that missionaries' 'good intentions' resulted in the implementation of cultural genocide, defined as

> the effective destruction of a people by systematically or systemically (intentionally or unintentionally in order to achieve other goals) destroying, eroding, or undermining the integrity of the culture and system of values that defines a people and gives them life.[8]

General Richard Henry Pratt, founder of the first American government-sponsored Indian boarding school in 1879, expressed this vision in his adage: 'Kill the Indian to save the man'.[9] In Canada, the harm done to First Nations individuals and communities by cultural genocide was recognized and, to some extent addressed, by the Truth and Reconciliation Commission (TRC).[10] Yet, discussion of the role of visual assimilation in cultural genocide is conspicuously absent in the TRC report.[11] South of the border, the toothless apology 'on behalf of the people of the United States to all Native Peoples for the many instances of violence, maltreatment, and neglect inflicted on Native peoples by citizens of the United States' removes responsibility from the federal government programmes and places it on individual citizens.[12] Moreover, Protestant visual assimilation programmes had been implemented decades before R. H. Pratt and extended far beyond the walls of residential schools.

Why have the methods of visual assimilation been absent from analyses of attempted cultural genocide? Assimilationist programmes that enacted and re-enacted class, race and gender relationships were prescribed and enforced in patterns of everyday practices.[13] Unlike historical events that are unique and can be pinpointed in time, everyday practices mould sensibilities and relationships almost imperceptibly. By employing these tactics in educational programmes and beyond, Protestant and other missionaries, plus government policies, aimed to restructure the roles and status of Amerindians in the emerging North American social order. However, attempts to control dress and bodily regimes did not thoroughly achieve the desired goal of assimilation into settler colonial culture and society. Administrators did not foresee the tenacity and flexibility of American Indian cultures.[14]

This chapter will focus on the Anishinaabe nation of the Great Lakes region to explore the values and processes of Protestant visual assimilation programmes. It will also engage Anishinaabe responses that reveal how they often enthusiastically adopted and indigenized dress practices. However, while the Protestant visual assimilation programme could not overcome indigenization as a performative practice, its bodily regimes have left a legacy of 'groundlessness' that permanently transformed Indigenous quotidian cultural practices.

Protestant values: from self-sufficiency to providence

Missionary presence in the Great Lakes brought about cleavages between different religious factions within Anishinaabe society. The three main contenders were Anishinaabe religion, Catholicism and various types of Protestantism. Whereas Anishinaabe religion is pluralistic and therefore tends to be inclusive of new ideas and practices, all forms of Christianity are exclusive because the premise of a singular all-encompassing truth means that only one sect's beliefs can be right. The increasing presence of British and American Protestant missionaries in Anishinaabe country during the nineteenth century magnified the divisive effect on the social fabric that French Jesuit missionaries had begun in the seventeenth century. Missionaries fought as viciously over Anishinaabe souls as had the fur trade companies over their furs in a previous era. A major difference, however, was that whereas the production of furs for barter was a group endeavour, conversion to Christianity took place at the level of the individual. The religious warfare therefore created divisions within families that were often painful and traumatic for the individuals involved.[15] At Mackinac Island during the 1840s, Protestant missionary Reverend John Pitezel 'found an influence which is deadly against the spread of a pure Christianity – it is Catholicism'.[16] At Manitoulin Island in 1853, the Catholic missionary Father Hanipaux complained bitterly of the 'Satanic trap of Protestantism' into which innocent orphans fell. He petitioned his superior for nuns for his mission so that they might 'snatch [the orphans back] from the serpent's teeth'.[17] On Manitoulin Island during the 1860s, Reverend Jabez Sims 'expostulated with [Washakezhik] on the evil he had done' when he took his two children to the Catholic priest at Wikwemikong to be baptised. Washakezhik explained that the priest had been 'after him for two years' to turn away from Protestantism. Nonetheless, he repented and brought his children back to Manitowaning, where the Protestant mission and government agency were located.[18]

In the last quarter of the nineteenth century, American and Canadian governments took control of residential and day-school policy while contracting various Christian denominations to run them. Reverend Alban Jones bemoans the fact that the American federal government awarded Catholic missions only 8 of the 38 claims they submitted as 'first missions', causing 80,000 Catholic Indians to come 'under the control of non-Catholic agents and ministers'.[19] Although students at such schools were sometimes free to attend church services of the denominations of their choice,[20] both governments strongly favoured Protestant practices. At St Joseph's Industrial School on the Menominee reservation in Wisconsin, *c*.1890s–1920s, Catholic administrators were frustrated by the fact that the government disallowed Catholic religious instruction in the school, even though government schools elsewhere routinely included Protestant education and services.[21] Government favouritism affected boarding school clothing policies because Protestants viewed dress as an outward indicator of the moral state and religious affiliation of the wearer.[22] When the Métis at White Earth lobbied for a Catholic missionary in 1868, a group of Episcopalian Anishinaabek wrote to Bishop Whipple that if 'the general government will insist [on] sending us Romanist missionaries ... We want to inform you ... not a single indian [*sic*] will ever have his blanket off'.[23] Based on this same premise, Reverend Peter Jones remarked that he had 'never discovered any real difference between the Roman Catholic Indian and the pagan, other than the wearing of the cross'.[24] The pattern of Protestant assimilation was established early in the nineteenth century. The 1820s visitors to Mackinac Island could see 'a mixture of people clad in a wide array of clothing styles and colour speaking French, Odawa, Chippewa and English'. By the 1830s, however, Evangelical Protestants had established a boarding school where they routinely stripped new students of their clothes, scrubbed them down with soap and water and dressed them in clothes made in eastern American cities. At the same time, they renamed these children with English names and began teaching them English language.[25]

In contrast, although Catholic missionaries promoted sedentary agricultural lifestyles in communities such as Lorette, Quebec, Wikwemikong, Ontario, and L'Arbre Croche, Michigan, dress reform was not a strong component of Catholic conversion. During the first half of the nineteenth century, fur-trade dress styles were characteristic of the Catholic village of Lorette, Quebec, and the Métis communities of Mackinac, Sault Ste Marie and Green Bay. By the last few decades of the nineteenth century, however, Catholic missions were often constrained by government school contracts to 'supply the pupils with ... suitable and sufficient clothing'.[26] Despite differences in the role of dress between Protestant and Catholic theology, Protestant-driven government policies dominated reservation-era assimilation programmes. For this reason, the story of missionary influence on Anishinaabe dress is closely tied to the history of Protestant missions.

Nineteenth-century Protestant values were formed around a belief in different moral virtues for different social classes. Protestants also believed that visual appearances expressed these class-based moral virtues.[27] In England, there was a centuries-old system of occupational dress that visually distinguished and supported class difference. In North America, when Europeans viewed Native peoples through this lens of moral class order, they saw them stereotypically as 'nomadic savages'. Eighteenth- and nineteenth-century paintings reveal a series of interrelated stereotypes that depict racializing characteristics such as 'savagery' (nudity, exotic body modifications, sitting on the ground, grotesque movements) and nomadism (canoes, paddles, sleds, temporary housing). Gendered stereotypes are also apparent, such as male 'indolence' (inactivity, smoking, etc.) and female 'promiscuity' (nudity, revealing postures, etc.). In this light, nineteenth-century Protestant missionaries equated Native peoples with, at best, the lower classes within their own societies and at worst subhumans comparable to monkeys or apes.[28] Assimilation was considered the humanitarian choice compared to its alternative, annihilation. However, assimilation had a very precise limitation where it concerned race and class. Missionizing and educational efforts encompassed a two-pronged programme of behavioural and visual reform aimed at producing lower class members of the labour force. Insofar as these programmes did not succeed in erasing Indigenous identities and cultures, Alice Littlefield refers to this process as 'proletarianization'.[29] Clearly, a driving force was to relieve the government of the economic burden of fulfilling treaty obligations, which often entailed annuities in perpetuity and training in agriculture and other occupations associated with sedentary societies. In contrast to philanthropic sentiments that underlay nineteenth-century British poor laws, this goal was in keeping with the American Protestant ethic of 'self-reliance'.[30]

In the context of American Indian missionizing, Protestants and Catholics alike believed the moral value of self-reliance could only be obtained through agricultural pursuits. Consequently, missionaries did not recognize Indigenous hunting and gathering strategies as self-sufficiency. Instead, they focused on the negative moral impact of 'dependency' on trade goods in the fur trade economy. They viewed the Anishinaabe ability to trade the products of their hunting and trapping to acquire a wide variety of ready-made textiles, as well as a few types of ready-made clothing and accessories, as a degenerative influence that condemned them to their evil paganism and 'indolent' nomadism. Consequently, the first step towards missionaries' goal of 'self-sufficiency' was to encourage their own version of agricultural self-subsistence among their converts in order to 'wean' them from traditional ways of life. In the Great Lakes climate of the Anishinaabek, this generally meant keeping sheep for woollen clothing and cattle to provide cowhide for footwear. Although occasionally settlers had some success growing flax for linen, the climate was simply too cold to grow cotton.[31]

Flocks of sheep were a particularly powerful metaphor for the Protestant fellowship.[32] Accordingly, the early residential schools kept flocks of sheep and taught the girls carding and spinning. During the 1830s, 12 female students were boarded with Reverend William Case at Alnwick, north of Lake Ontario, where they spun, wove and sewed their own clothing from the fleece belonging to the mission.[33] During this same period another Protestant residential school near present-day Grand Rapids, Michigan, had a flock of 100 sheep from which the children harvested wool that the girls spun, wove, sewed and knit into Western-style garments. In 1839, when the British colonial government opened its Anglican missionary 'Establishment' at Manitowaning on Manitoulin Island, Lake Huron, the missionaries likewise brought a flock of sheep. The government hired a woman to teach the Anishinaabe women carding and spinning, which they were 'quick to learn and [they] delighted in being able to knit their own socks and stockings'.[34] Some 25 years later, a woman from the Manitowaning band put this skill to good use by spinning yarn for Reverend Sims in exchange for meat, corn and flour.[35] Catholic priests at Wikwemikong, Manitoulin Island, also kept sheep with the intention of providing the means to liberate Anishinaabek from what they perceived as enslavement to the traders. In addition to knitting, therefore, they sought to train Anishinaabe women to weave woollen cloth. The plan went awry, however, when their weaver forgot his trade while they were waiting for their small flock of sheep to grow large enough to supply wool for the loom.[36]

A daily account book from Mount Elgin Industrial School, in southern Ontario, from 1851 to 1856 provides a unique window into Protestant missionary budgetary priorities during this period.[37] The book records many instances of paying individuals for services related to clothing the students. Although details are not available to calculate precise amounts for each category of service, counting the number of instances of payments for each category is instructive. The preparation of wool and woollen products composed 46 per cent of the payments. The next largest category is shoemaking and mending at 34 per cent and finally sewing comprises 20 per cent of payments. The prominence of wool processing in these accounts suggests that the school not only kept flocks of sheep, but that it was also relatively successful at producing its own woollen cloth. This is supported by comparison with the number of purchases of different types of fabrics during the same period. At 46 per cent, cotton fabric far outnumbered all others, while the next highest type of fabric purchased was woollens at only 14.5 per cent.[38]

By the last quarter of the nineteenth century, the great influx of inexpensive woollens and blended fabrics from Canadian and American mills, as well as the increasing importance of cotton 'wash goods', meant that it was no longer cost efficient to produce one's own woollen cloth. Throughout the Great Lakes region industrially produced fabrics had replaced home-made ones.[39] As early as the late 1850s, government officials were beginning to recognize the failure of attempts to produce agriculturally self-sufficient residential schools.[40] Mission schools and compounds continued to keep sheep in small numbers. Rather than for weaving fabric, however, these sheep were kept for woollen yarn to knit stockings, mittens, scarves and hats.[41] Knitted woollen sweaters, cardigans and vests were also gaining popularity during this time period.

By the late nineteenth and early twentieth centuries, self-sufficiency was replaced by an emphasis on 'providence', which meant that God would provide for those who exercised foresight and prudent care in the management of resources. Implicit in this view was that those of 'lesser' classes and races would inherently be less provident, which explained why God had not provided for them. At the same time, both American and Canadian governments took control of residential and day-school policy while contracting various Christian denominations to run them.[42] In 1901, the new superintendent of Indians Schools, Estelle Reel, introduced the Uniform Course of Study, which standardized a new emphasis on industrial training in the curriculum across all Indian boarding schools in the United States.[43] The goal was to 'cultivate good habits' and 'self-control' rather than learning 'definitions and important dates'.[44] While not naming Protestantism explicitly, Reed clearly expressed the Protestant ethic of 'providence' in a letter she wrote to introduce the new curriculum to educational administrators and teachers: 'Hoping that better morals, a more patriotic and Christian citizenship, and ability for self-support will result from what this course of study may inspire'.[45] Although in theory students were to receive industrial or vocational training, letters from students, parents and even administrators suggest that they often received very little actual training in these activities.[46]

Changes in Protestant values coincided with a shift in the global textile industry. The goods available in rural North America moved away from imported woollens and towards inexpensive cottons produced in the United States.[47] Exponential growth in the American cotton textile industry, particularly in the southern states, produced an overabundance of low-quality cotton or what was then called 'wash goods'.[48] This material circumstance turned missionary efforts away from teaching the processing of wool and woollen products to those of recycled cotton. Thereby, quilts became a means through which missionaries attempted to counteract what they perceived as Native people's improvidence and wastefulness. Mission schools taught girls quilt making along with other types of sewing and 'handiwork'. Reed's Uniform Course of Study advised that students needed to be taught to 'cut, fit, and make all kinds of wearing apparel and all articles needed for the household, and to be resourceful, using every scrap in some way'.[49] Quilt making was not new in the curriculum of 1901, however. Brenda Child notes that many Amerindian girls first learned to make star quilts at the Carlisle Institute, Carlisle, Pennsylvania, the flagship Indian boarding school in the United States.

Contrary to teachers' and administrators' perceptions, the practice of wasting nothing was inherent in traditional Anishinaabe women's work. This may partially explain their enthusiasm to learn quilt making. Child recalls that her grandmother, who attended Flandreau School in Minnesota in the 1920s, enjoyed the sewing classes at school and spent much time sewing quilts during her adult life.[50] Anishinaabe women also took their own initiative to learn quilt making. As Rebecca Kugel points out, Susie Bonga Wright and other Leech Lake Episcopal Indigenous women organized their own sewing circles as early as the 1880s.[51] When Episcopal missionary Pauline Colby arrived at Leech Lake in 1891, she commented that women in this group 'loved to make quilts or comforts, and do some very nice quilting, also braid rugs, and make sweet grass and birch bark baskets'.[52] Although the sewing circle was concluded with an Episcopalian service, the Indigenous agency in these sewing circles shows that Anishinaabe women desired to learn Euro-American sewing techniques. Moreover, these women's sewing groups became a mechanism through which Anishinaabe women could rise in status through leadership roles. They resembled the 'work groups' that were the characteristic form of women's collective economic activities in their traditional lifeways. They were the social setting in which women gained acclaim for their skills and rose in leadership positions. Kugel argues that sewing circles were a form of Indigenous women's political activity in the new framework of settler colonial 'civilization'. She shows how female Episcopal converts at Leech Lake, Minnesota, organized their own sewing circles in which they not only learned the new sewing skills, but they also engaged in their own charitable distributions within their own communities. In giving goods 'to the needy', they reproduced their traditional reciprocity mode of exchange. Within these work groups, women also discussed political issues and then vetted their views at community councils, contrary to the wishes of the resident missionaries, who were focused on developing individual women's Christian morality.[53]

While missionaries focused on women's virtue in making quilts, it is ironic that Anishinaabe men adopted them in the place of wearing blankets, the foremost symbol of 'heathen' Indians.[54] A studio portrait *carte de visite* shows Newriash, whom a Catholic commentator described as a Lac Courte Oreilles 'medicine man', wearing a quilt and moccasins, while holding a sacred Midewiwin otter bag (Figure 11.1). The repeating geometric patterns of the quilts are

FIGURE 11.1 Photograph of Newriash, Medicine Man, Lac Courte Oreilles, Wisconsin, *c.*1875–1880.

Source: © Photographed in McElroy Studios. Courtesy of the Department of Special Collections and University Archives, Marquette University Libraries (#10883).

reminiscent of traditional Anishinaabe motifs, and their essential form as a blanket, no doubt made them very appealing apparel to replace fur trade point blankets, which were becoming lower quality and increasingly difficult to obtain by the mid-nineteenth century.

Embodied practices: gender assimilation

Whether in Christian communities or at residential schools, missionaries vigorously promoted what Katrina Paxton calls 'gender assimilation'.[55] This refers to the practice of assimilating Amerindians into specific male and female gender roles consistent with Euro-American norms. From about 1830 to 1870, sheep provided practical lessons in Christian gender roles at residential schools: boys tended sheep; girls processed their wool.[56] Within the context of late nineteenth-century residential schools, however, missionary educators promoted a broad range of vocational training programmes they deemed suitable for each gender. This is because, as in the case of class, they believed in essential differences between moral virtues for men and women. As might be expected, sewing figured prominently in the girls' curriculum. It included training on sewing machines, cutting, fitting and sewing women's garments, as well as all manner of quilting, lacemaking and embroidery. Female graduates could apply these skills to sewing clothes for their families or in professional dressmaking.[57] Students gained skills in large-scale manufacturing by producing clothing for the schools' students. A quarterly report from 1904 notes that girls at Flandreau Indian School, in Flandreau, South Dakota, completed 193 dresses, skirts, underwear and sheets.[58] Occasionally, female students were able to sell their handiwork while still in school. Around 1912, a female student wrote that she 'was always doing embroidery or crochet or tatting, making things to sell'. As Michael Coleman notes, her narrative 'reads like a success story of the Protestant work ethic'.[59] Beyond practical sewing skills, instructors instilled embodied sewing practices that encompassed 'not only the correct motion of the arm in taking stitches but also in marching, breathing, calisthenics and games'.[60] Sewing skills and bodily regimes were designed to mould femininity into the everyday practices of female students.

Although one might stereotypically assume that making clothes was women's work, in practice both male and female students gained skills in this field. As David Wallace Adams notes, 'boys enrolled in classes in farming, blacksmithing, carpentry, wagon building and tailoring, girls pursued domestic science courses in the areas of cooking, sewing and canning'.[61] Toward the end of the nineteenth century, tailored suits, which were a mark of respectability, employed a newly emerging scientific approach to apparel construction that involved drafting flat patterns.[62] As such, tailoring was deemed suitable vocational training for boys rather than girls. Simon Otto, a renowned Ojibwa elder and storyteller, related that his father learned tailoring at the Mount Pleasant Indian School in Michigan. Beginning in about 1935, he became the only tailor north of Grand

Rapids and made all the suits for 'people who could afford them'. By the 1940s, he and his wife, whom he met at the Mount Pleasant School, became leaders in cultural revitalization by making traditional regalia for the Hiawatha pageants and naming ceremonies. Otto notes that making these traditional clothes was 'easy for [his] father to do because he was a tailor'.[63]

Shoemaking and shoe repairing were also among the employments of boys in boarding schools (Figure 11.2).[64] This corresponded with the notion that wearing moccasins or going barefoot was a quintessential mark of savagery. The number of photographs that show Amerindian men and women wearing moccasins with 'citizen's dress' well into the twentieth century suggest that these were one of the slowest elements of Indigenous dress to change.[65] Around the turn of the twentieth century, a matron at the Cecilia Jeffrey School in Kenora, Ontario, boasted to her supervisor that, although the 'favorite footwear for girls as well as boys in winter is moccasins', one girl wanted to wear her Sunday boots to serve the staff table. This one instance was considered evidence of the success of their assimilation policies, despite the admittance that everyone else chose to wear moccasins.[66]

As Tim Ingold observed, in eighteenth-century Europe the 'mechanization of footwork' was part of a movement towards modernity that left walking to 'the poor, the criminal, the young, and above all, the ignorant'.[67] The importance of hard-soled footwear in the assimilation programme of Methodist missionaries is apparent in the Mount Elgin Industrial School Day Book expense accounts,

FIGURE 11.2 Photograph of boys in shoemaking shop at St Joseph's Industrial School, Keshina, Wisconsin, c.1900.

Source: Courtesy of the Department of Special Collections and University Archives, Marquette University Libraries (#11665).

1850–1856. Among ready-made items found in the 'clothing department', footwear made up 56 per cent of the total purchases: 35 per cent shoes and boots, plus 21 per cent socks, stocking and hose to be worn with them. As noted above, shoemaking was also the single most frequent category of labour expenses (30 per cent). Among the textiles purchased, 'leather' for shoes was the third largest category (10 per cent) after cotton (46 per cent) and woollens (14.5 per cent).[68] By 1880, the school had turned expense to asset by replacing paid labour with unpaid students. The principal of the school, Reverend Thomas Cosford, boasted that the school's 'shops' produced large quantities of shoes and boots, for which they could turn a profit if they could find a market.[69]

The figures in the Mount Elgin Industrial School Day Book clearly reflect the most salient symbols of Christian 'virtue' – accessories at the extremities such as footwear, handwear, headwear, cuffs and collars. Because Anishinaabe pictographic inscriptions employed a hat to represent European colonizers,[70] one would expect hats to likewise be the focus of ethnic difference for colonizers. What seems unusual in this preponderance of concern over footwear is the extent to which it completely overshadows the frequency of headgear purchases, which composed only 18 per cent of the total ready-wear entries.[71] As Ingold notes, however, nothing better symbolizes the Western value of 'groundlessness' than the combination of the boot and the chair. 'Between them, the boot and the chair establish a technological foundation for the separation of thought from action and mind from body – that is for the fundamental *groundlessness* so characteristic of modern metropolitan dwelling' (italics in original). Ingold suggests that these body practices reflect the Western belief in 'raising human beings above the limitations of nature and establishing the conditions for their control over it'.[72]

In this light it is not surprising that missionaries also focused on eradicating the Anishinaabe practice of sitting on the ground as a symbol of heathenism and encouraged them instead to sit on chairs or to stand as evidence of 'Christian civilization'.[73] Tim Ingold points out that Western parents 'armed with a battery of devices from high chairs to baby walkers ... devote much effort to getting their infants to sit or stand as soon as physically possible'.[74] Likewise nineteenth-century missionaries and Christian converts began the body regime with babies, which entailed getting them out of cradleboards and up and standing as soon as possible. Against a backdrop of a hewn log cabin, a descendant of Mississauga missionary Peter Jones holds her shoe-clad baby upright on a chair in anticipation of his or her future erect posture (Figure 11.3). Not coincidentally, many members of this family married into British settler families, moved away from the reserve and subsequently self-identified as white on government censuses.[75]

In contrast, living in semi-permanent wigwam, teepee and tent structures with outdoor cooking and workspace lends itself most comfortably to sitting on the ground, wearing moccasins, as opposed to hard-soled shoes or boots. Conventionally, the sitting position of Anishinaabe men encompassed crossed legs, both legs bent, one leg bent and the other folded, both legs folded and various semi-reclining positions. Anishinaabe women customarily sat with either or both

FIGURE 11.3 Photograph of the daughter-in-law or granddaughter-in-law of Reverend Peter Jones (Kahkewaquonaby) with baby on chair, Brantford, Ontario, 1916, by Frederick Waugh.

Source: Courtesy of the Canadian Museum of History (#36777).

legs folded to one side, or with both or one leg outstretched in front, especially while performing certain kinds of manufacturing or decorative work. Cradleboards also supported the semi-nomadic life style, affecting the bodily regime of both baby and mother. Carrying cradleboards with burden straps across their chests or foreheads reinforced the stereotype of Amerindian women as "beasts of burden." In Protestant gender roles, strength and mobility were coded male virtues.

Precisely because *groundedness* symbolized heathenism, missionaries took energetic measures to eradicate it. The concept of 'deportment' described a subtle dimension of dressed body practices that inscribed gendered class affiliation upon the body. Emerging Western middle-class society developed the 'cult of domesticity' in which women were expected to manage the extensive duties associated with housekeeping and childrearing.[76] In this role, women were also held responsible for upholding the moral character of men.[77] For this reason, missionary efforts at visual assimilation were levelled more intensively at women than they were at men.[78] Nineteenth- and early twentieth-century missionaries battled against what they perceived as the 'backward' body practices of Anishinaabe women to train them instead to the manners of 'deportment' appropriate for homemaker 'ladies'. Indian school superintendent Philena E. Johnson expressed this view in an 1896 speech: '[We will] make her environments such that the sickly body will become strong, the uncouth, awkward movements will become graceful, the general bearing dignified, and mind intellectual and spiritual, the morals chaste'. In response, one educator enthused that it was the responsibility of the female students to lift the 'Indian race into civilization through the home, with its educated Christian motherhood'.[79] In practice, Reel's standardized curriculum of 1901 encouraged matrons and teachers to instruct girls in 'the correct handling of the needle, the correct motion of the arm in taking stitches, the requisite erect posture and the need to avoid resting an arm on the desk'.[80] To boarding school personnel, this regimentation of the female body coupled with surveillance of female students' dress was justified on the grounds of gendered morality.

During the last quarter of the nineteenth century, the corset was the bodily regime, imposed by boarding schools, which had the most impact on female students. While the radical dress movement gained and waned in popularity among middle- and upper-class European and Euro-American women,[81] female residential school students continued to be corseted. To a much greater extent than did shoes and boots, corsets restricted movement and ensured proper 'ladylike' comportment with straight upright spines and shoulders back. This included controlled sitting, standing and walking practices, as well as restricted movements such as running and stooping. As corset historian Lee Summers notes, whether or not they were designed to shape the growing body, juvenile corsets were 'clearly intended to modify or circumvent activities deemed inappropriate' for female children.[82]

Christian purity: producing whiteness

There was an inherent contradiction in missionary efforts to produce 'ladies' and their view of Indigenous converts as comparable in status to Western lower classes. This class association can be seen in approaches to teaching various kinds of needlework. In Britain, curricula for the poor focused on 'plain needlework' because embroidery 'served no practical purpose' and, for working-class girls, indicated 'sinful laziness' and 'aristocratic decadence'.[83] In Grand Rapids, Michigan, the girls' 'recreation' programme at the school that William Keating observed in 1823 consisted of learning embroidery to counteract their imagined tendency towards 'laziness'. Because 'fancy work' was at that time the increasing prerogative of upper-class women, William Keating felt he had to justify this seeming impropriety of the missionaries' judgment:

> [T]hey were just beginning to embroider, an occupation which may by some, be considered as unsuitable to the situation which they are destined

to hold in life, but which appears to us very judiciously used as a reward and stimulus; it encourages their taste and natural talent for imitation, which is very great; and by teaching them that occupation may be connected with amusement, it may prevent their relapsing into that idleness which has been justly termed the source of all evils.[84]

More important than class associations, however, was the virtue of embroidery as a symbol of feminine Christian virtue. For this reason, embroidery of all kinds remained a component of the boarding school curriculum for girls throughout the nineteenth and into the twentieth century. The variety of sewn products encompassed both practical and decorative items that were destined for use at the school, for sale or for the personal use of the students. It was also common for students to give embroidery as gifts to their teachers and other church officials, or for students to compulsorily give their completed work to their teachers who would then give it to others of their own choosing.[85] In the sewing room of St Mary's School in Odanah, Wisconsin, c.1890s, female students displayed various types of lace along with the quilts they had made.[86] Similarly, in an 1895 photograph, girls displayed a variety of their 'handiwork' in the sewing room of the St Benedict's mission school at White Earth, Minnesota.[87] These students' 'domestic arts' include rag rugs, an embroidered quilt cover, a crazy quilt and a crocheted shawl. The St Benedict's Monastery's online record explains:

> Domestic arts were considered important. So before and after school hours, the girls were taught to card wool and spin yarn with which they knitted their own stockings. They were taught plain and fancy sewing and took turns in assisting the sisters in the kitchen, laundry and dairy.[88]

Additionally, missionaries organized sewing circles for adult women that they believed imparted Christian values as well as practical skills. White lace trim, visible on extremities of the body (collars, cuffs, headgear, handkerchiefs, etc.), and adorning furniture in Christian homes (tables, mantles, counters, etc.), conveyed messages of purity, grace and refinement. This association arose out of an eighteenth-century belief that white linen undergarments cleansed impurities from the body, more so than washing the body itself.[89] Bodily regimes that employed laundered white linens were critical to performing 'civilized' identities. Producing and maintaining such clothes, however, depended upon working-class ethnically diverse labour.[90] In Minnesota, Deaconess Sybil Carter managed lacemaking economic development projects in which church networks activated markets for Native-made lace in Eastern American cities. In 1890s Minnesota, Mrs Fanny C. Wiswell at White Earth and Pauline Colby at Leech Lake taught Anishinaabe women lace work and organized the marketing through Sybil Carter. In this rare photograph of a sewing circle *in situ* as opposed to in a photography studio, participants sit on chairs on the lawn of the mission complex with white aprons over

FIGURE 11.4 Photograph of lacemakers at Leech Lake, Minnesota, 1906.

Source: Courtesy of the Minnesota Historical Society (#N4.4 p. 22).

their everyday reservation-era dress (Figure 11.4). Although the woman in the centre wears a lace collar over a dark bodice, the women on the right wear colourful shawls characteristic of Anishinaabe women's styles of the time. Reverend Francis Palmer explains that the women in Carter's lacemaking programme included not only Protestants, but also Catholics and 'traditionalists' and they often did the work 'at home'.[91]

Lacemaking is a particularly salient symbol of Protestant female virtue because the white colour of the lace demands practical cleanliness. Within nineteenth-century Protestantism, the powerful metaphor between physical cleanliness and 'inner' spiritual purity gained increasing momentum under the movement of 'physical puritanism'.[92] Conversion narratives emphasized the ritual shedding of dirty rags, bathing and donning clean new garments as an initiation into a life of moral virtue, particularly among children, the poor and immigrants.[93] In this theological context, missionaries believed Native peoples possessed 'natural filthiness', as if they genetically inherited it. Pauline Colby found that cleanliness was the most difficult but 'indispensable point' in teaching lacemaking. Elsewhere, however, she admits that she had never had a problem with cleanliness when women took work home with them to complete.[94] In the 1908 report of the Sybil Carter Indian Mission and Lace Industry Association, the president implores members to give generously so that through making lace, Amerindian women can 'be uplifted, taught to become self-supporting, and given habits of thrift, cleanliness and industry'.[95]

For Protestants, the whiteness of lace was a symbol of Western standards of both physical and spiritual 'cleanliness'. This obsession with cleanliness extended beyond the body to the domestic environment. It was a good Christian woman's duty to keep a clean house. Consequently, at boarding schools missionaries inculcated Anishinaabe girls in housekeeping duties with female students sweeping and mopping floors.[96] Girls, and sometimes boys, were also assigned to laundry duty for the entire establishment (clothing, sheets and linens), and in the early years, the girls also had to make the laundry soap.[97] Laundry duty was unpleasant whether it involved scrubbing with washboards by hand or mechanized machines that sometimes resulted in accidents. At Mount Elgin Industrial School in the early 1900s, the laundry facilities were notoriously unsanitary and laundry duty regularly caused illness and possibly the occasional death (Figure 11.5).[98] While cleaning and laundry duties were typically assigned on a rotating basis, they could also be used as punishment.[99] To prepare girls for the 'domestic' labour market, in both private homes and service in the tourism industry, they were trained in both industrial and hand washing methods.[100] Some schools 'put out' female students as domestic servants in middle-class White homes where their duties included laundry, cooking and caring for children.[101]

Not surprisingly, in contrast with the missionary stereotype of Anishinaabek as 'slovenly', Anishinaabe women took an active interest in new washing technologies. Cotton goods, cotton ready-made clothing and washing implements simultaneously became available in Anishinaabe communities through storekeepers and mail order catalogues. At Leech Lake in 1896, concurrently with Colby's lacemaking programme there, a staff photographer for the *Minneapolis Times* captured an image of an elderly Anishinaabe woman returning from a shopping trip with her family and a new washboard.[102] A few decades later in Northern Ontario, a Department of Indian Affairs photographer captured on film an Anishinaabe family with a new washing machine after receiving their annuity payment.[103] This visual evidence is reinforced by accounts by Anishinaabek. Ignatia Broker relates how her mother volunteered to work at the missionary's house to learn the Western forms of housekeeping, including sewing, washing and ironing techniques.[104] Adam Fortunate Eagle relates a similar story: 'Mom is washing all our clothes for us to take to school. Getting us ready to leave for school turns into a real family event when all my aunties show up to help Mom'.[105] When he and his siblings arrived at Pipestone Indian Boarding School, Minnesota, in 1935, they were given a shower and medical examination, and then they were dressed in 'different clothes'. Fortunate Eagle calls this time the 'crying season' because when they emerged from this regime, they were 'all crying'.[106] They were 'lonely, bald-headed', their clothes did not fit and they smelled bad from medicinal ointments. After his first year at the school, he returned home for summer to find that his mother had 'a new husband and a new gas engine-operated washing machine. I like that washing machine best'.[107] In her

FIGURE 11.5 Photograph of pupils doing the laundry at the Mount Elgin Indian Industrial Institute, Muncey, Ontario, *c.*1890s.

Source: Courtesy of the United Church of Canada Archives (90.162P, #11173N).

play, *Path with No Moccasins*, Shirley Cheechoo recounts similar experiences in which she purchased new clothes with money her mother gave her. When she got back to school, however, 'they took them away and they gave me this stupid tunic, again. So I ripped it, see?' Cheechoo makes the metaphor between the cleanliness of white clothes and the white race poignantly clear as she enacts an incident at the residential school:

> I'll just put some Javex on this cloth and wash my skin with it. It should turn my skin real white, like my underwear does, when I wash them in Javex. Ouch! Boy that burns my skin. I'm all covered in a rash. I sure am a red Indian now.[108]

The same 'ritual violence' occurred when generations of students first arrived at boarding schools and when they returned from summer at home.[109]

Conclusion

This study reveals four main findings about Christian cultural genocide programmes: (1) there were major distinctions between Catholic and Protestant approaches to visual assimilation, although these became blurred in the boarding/residential school context that was dominated by Protestant-influenced government polices; (2) they included not only clothing styles, but also perhaps even more importantly, the daily repetition of bodily regimes that 'ungrounded' Anishinaabek; (3) they extended beyond creating and 'reading' clothed appearances to the clothing production and maintenance activities associated with particular dress styles; and (4) the dress styles, their associated bodily regimes and their production and maintenance, were linked to gender-specific practices and societal roles. Resistance to these regimes and indigenization of the dress and lifestyles can be seen in many individual instances, such as repurposing quilts and using sewing circles to maintain traditional reciprocity redistributive and ranked social systems. Due to such decolonization strategies, Protestant visual assimilation programmes did not wholly succeed in their efforts to eradicate Indigenous cultural values and practices. Yet, clothing was an effective 'weapon of colonization'[110] precisely because of its insinuation into the mundane practices of everyday life, particularly in the domains of gender roles and bodily regimes. Whether forcibly or voluntarily donned, Western styles of dress effectively ungrounded Anishinaabe wearers, imperceptibly undermining their relationship with the land and fitting them out for gendered urban dwelling. The relative merit or demerit of this result may remain contested. However, Protestant visual assimilation programmes teach us that First Peoples can reappropriate the power of dress and harness it to effect social change for cultural decolonization, indigenization and revitalization.

Notes

1 Anishinaabe (plural Anishinaabek) is the name in Anishinaabemowin, the Indigenous Algonquian language. This nation is also known as the Chippewa (in the United States) and the Ojibwa (in Canada), also spelled Ojibwe or Ojibway. This nation is not related to the Chipewyan, who speak a dialect of the Athabaskan language group.
2 Robert Hillestad, 'The Underlying Structure of Appearance', *Dress* 6 (1980): 116–125. For a similar concept of 'assemblage', see Ruth Phillips, 'Dress and Address: First Nations Self-Fashioning and the 1860 Royal Tour of Canada', in *The Art of Clothing: A Pacific Experience*, ed. Suzanne Küchler and Graeme Were (London: University College of London Press, 2005), 135.
3 Ralph Linton, *The Study of Man* (New York: Appleton-Century Company Inc., 1936), 93–96.
4 Irving Goffman, *Encounters: Two Studies in the Sociology of Interaction* (Indianapolis, IN: Bobbs-Merrill Educational, 1961), 87, 90–91, 95.
5 Mary Ellen Roach-Higgins and Joanne Eicher, 'Dress and Identity', *Clothing and Textiles Research Journal* 10.4 (1992): 1–8.
6 Judith Butler, *Bodies That Matter: On the Discursive Limits of 'Sex'* (New York: Routledge, 1993).
7 Paulette Regan, *Unsettling the Settler Within: Indian Residential Schools, Truth Telling, and Reconciliation in Canada* (Vancouver: UBC Press, 2010); John T. Warren,

Performing Purity: Whiteness, Pedagogy, and the Reconstitution of Power (New York: Peter Lang, 2003).

8   George E. Tinker, *Missionary Conquest: The Gospel and Native American Cultural Genocide* (Minneapolis, MN: Fortress Press, 1993), 5.

9   Andrea Smith. 'Soul Wound: The Legacy of Native American Schools', in *Boarding School Healing Symposium*, ed. Carolyna Smiley-Marquez and Jill E. Tompkins (Boulder: University of Colorado, School of Law, 2011), 39.

10 For example, Prime Minister Stephen Harper's 'Statement of Apology to former students of Indian Residential Schools on behalf of the Government of Canada' notes that: 'Two primary objectives of the Residential Schools system were to remove and isolate children from the influence of their homes, families, traditions and cultures, and to assimilate them into the dominant culture. These objectives were based on the assumption Aboriginal cultures and spiritual beliefs were inferior and unequal. Indeed, some sought, as it was infamously said, "to kill the Indian in the child". Today, we recognize that this policy of assimilation was wrong, has caused great harm, and has no place in our country.' Truth and Reconciliation Commission of Canada, *Honouring the Truth; Reconciling for the Future: Summary of the Final Report of the Truth and Reconciliation Commission of Canada* (Ottawa: Government of Canada, 2015), 369.

11 Truth and Reconciliation Commission of Canada, *Honouring the Truth*, 319–337.

12 111th Congress, 1st Session, S.J. Res. 14, in the Senate of the United States, 30 April 2009, Section 1. Resolution of apology to Native Peoples of the United States. Quoted in Smiley-Marquez and Tompkins, *Boarding School Healing Symposium*, 40.

13 Protestant missionaries pursued visual assimilation programmes around the world. For Africa see Jean Comaroff, 'The Empire's Old Clothes', in *Cross-Cultural Consumption: Global Markets, Local Realities*, ed. David Howes (London: Routledge, 1996), 19–38. For the West Pacific see Richard Eves, 'Colonialism, Corporality and Character: Methodist Missions and Refashioning of Bodies in the West Pacific', *History and Anthropology* 10.1 (1996): 85–138. Everyday life is theorized as 'an interpretive framework defined in dialectical opposition to the notion of special events'. Giovanna Del Negro and Harris Berger, 'New Directions in the Study of Everyday Life', in *Identity and Everyday Life: Essays in the Study of Folklore, Music and Popular Culture*, ed. Harris Berger and Giovanni Del Negro (Middletown, CT: Wesleyan University Press, 2004), 3–23.

14 Clyde Ellis, 'We Had a Lot of Fun, But of Course, That Wasn't the School Part: Life at the Rainy Mountain Boarding School, 1893–1920', in *Boarding School Blues: Revisiting American Indian Educational Experiences*, ed. C. E. Trafzer, J. A. Keller and L. Sisquoc (Lincoln: University of Nebraska Press, 2006), 66; Tsianina Lomawaima, 'Domesticity in the Federal Indian Schools: The Power of Authority over Mind and Body', *American Ethnologist* 20.2 (1993): 228.

15 Library and Archives Canada (hereafter LAC): MG 24, vol. J51, 1864–1865. Sims, Rev. Jabez Waters, 1842–1869, 'Journal of Missionary on Manitoulin Island', 143, 149, 154, 164, 205; Elizabeth Baird, 'Reminiscences of Early Days on Mackinac Island', in *Collections of the State Historical Society of Wisconsin, Vol. XIV* (Madison: State Historical Society of Wisconsin, 1898), 45–47; Rosamond M. Vanderburgh, *I Am Nokomis, Too* (Don Mills, ON: General Publishing Company, 1977), 27–29.

16 John Pitezel, *Lights and Shades of Missionary Life: Containing Travels, Sketches, Incidents, and Missionary Efforts, During Nine Years Spent in the Region of Lake Superior* (Cincinnati, OH: Western Book Concern, 1860), 29.

17 Joseph-Urbain Hanipaux, 'Letter #1: Hanipaux to Boulanger, Wikwemikong, 1853', in *Letters from Manitoulin Island, 1853–1870*, ed. S. J. Lorenzo Cadieux and S. J. Robert Toupin, trans. Shelley Pearen and William Lonc (Ottawa: William Lonc, 2007), 62.

18 Sims, n.d, 143.

19 Rev. Alban Fruth, OSB, *A Century of Mission Work Among the Red Lake Chippewa Indians, 1858–1958* (Red Lake, MN: St. Mary's Mission, 1958), 12.

20 Michael Coleman, *American Indian Children at School, 1850–1930* (Jackson: University Press of Mississippi, 1993), 116; Adam Fortunate Eagle, *Pipestone: My Life at an Indian Boarding School* (Norman: University of Oklahoma Press, 2010), 31. Fortunate Eagle reports that he was allowed to attend a Protestant Church in town, while the Catholics attended services in the school chapel. At Shingwauk Industrial School, short biographies attached to portraits of students taken in 1878 reveal that many of them arrived at the school already converted to Catholicism or Methodism. Edward Wilson, Shingwauk Project, Algoma University, http://archives.algomau.ca/main/node/17416 (accessed 8 April 2015).

21 Sarah Shillinger, *A Case Study of the American Indian Boarding School Movement: An Oral History of Saint Joseph's Indian Industrial School* (Lewiston, NY: Edwin Mellon Press, 2008), 24–25.

22 Richard Eves, 'Colonialism, Corporeality and Character: Methodist Missions and the Refashioning of Bodies in the Pacific', *History and Anthropology* 10.1 (1996): 86.

23 Rebecca Kugel '"To Work Like a Frenchman": Ojibwe Men's Definition of Métis Men's Ethnicity in the Early Nineteenth Century', paper presented at the American Society for Ethnohistory, Minneapolis, 12 November 1998.

24 Rev. Peter Jones, *History of the Ojebway Indians with Especial Reference to Their Conversion to Christianity* (Freeport, NY: Books for Libraries Press, 1970), 172.

25 Keith R. Widder, *Battle for the Soul: Métis Children Encounter Evangelical Protestants at Mackinaw Mission, 1823–1837* (East Lansing: Michigan State University Press, 1999), 49, 106–108.

26 1904 contract quoted in Shillinger, *American Indian Boarding School Movement*, 82.

27 Cory Willmott, 'Beavers and Sheep: Visual Appearance and Identity in Nineteenth Century Algonquian-Anglo Relations', *History and Anthropology* 25.1 (2013): 28.

28 Cory Silverstein-Willmott, 'Men or Monkeys? The Politics of Clothing and Land within Ontario First Nations, 1830–1900', in *Native Voices in Research*, ed. Jill Oakes, Rick Riewe, Alison Edmunds, Alison Dubois and Kimberly Wilde (Winnipeg: Aboriginal Issues Press, 2003), 127–140.

29 Alice Littlefield, 'Indian Education and the World of Work in Michigan, 1893–1933', in *Native Americans and Wage Labor: Ethnohistoric Perspectives*, ed. Alice Littlefield and Martha C. Knack (Norman: University of Oklahoma Press), 119.

30 Kathleen Waters Sander, *The Business of Charity: The Women's Exchange Movement, 1832–1900* (Urbana and Chicago: University of Illinois Press, 1998), 21.

31 Linda Grant DePauw, *Founding Mothers: Women of America in the Revolutionary Era* (Boston: Houghton Mifflin Co., 1975), 11–12.

32 Willmott, *Beavers and Sheep*, 25–28.

33 Peter S. Schmalz, *The Ojibwa of Southern Ontario* (Toronto: University of Toronto Press, 1991), 158.

34 Soaphy Anderson in Victoria Brehm, ed., *The Women's Great Lakes Reader* (Duluth, MN: The Holy Cow! Press, 1998), 118. Anderson was the daughter of the Indian Agent, T. G. Anderson, who oversaw the 'Establishment'.

35 Sims, n.d., 142–169.

36 Joseph-Urbain Hanipaux, 'Letter #6: Hanipaux to Boulanger, 22 November 1855', in *Letters from Manitoulin Island, 1853–1870*, 91.

37 United Church of Canada Archives (hereafter UCCA): 83.065C Reel 32-2, 'Mt. Elgin Industrial School Day Book, 1850–1856'.

38 Analysis of data found in UCCA: 'Mt Elgin Industrial School Day Book'

39 Willmott, *Beavers and Sheep*, 34.

40 '1858 Report of the Special Commissioners', in Elizabeth Graham, ed., *The Mush Hole: Life at Two Indian Residential Schools* (Waterloo, ON: Heffle Publishing, 1997), 223–224.

41 Thomas Cosford in Graham, *Mush Hole*, 240.

42 Institutionalized education for Amerindian children became mandatory in Canada in 1884 and in the United States in 1893.

43 Mary A. Stout, *Native American Boarding Schools* (Santa Barbara, CA: Greenwood Press, 2012), 50.

44 Stout, *Native American Boarding Schools*, 150–151.

45 Stout, *Native American Boarding Schools*, 151.

46 Brenda Child, *Boarding School Seasons: American Indian Families, 1900–1940* (Lincoln: University of Nebraska Press, 1998), 75; Wilmer Nadjiwon, *Not Wolf, Nor Dog* (Tobermory, ON: Tobermory Press, 2012), 33–34, 50.

47 For example, in 1895 the American mail order house, Montgomery Ward, offered a wide selection of domestically produced cotton textiles that took up 13 out of a total of 16 pages of textiles (81 per cent). Some of the most popular varieties were sateens, ginghams, shirtings and prints. The remaining 19 per cent was composed of the 'flannel department' (9.5 per cent) and the 'woollen department' (9.5 per cent). Since the American 'flannels' were made of cotton unless otherwise indicated, less than 10 per cent of the catalogue's fabric offerings were woollens. The descriptions of 'wash goods', as cotton textiles were called at that time, repeatedly pointed out the high degree of quality for the low amount of cost to the consumer. Obviously, these fabrics were aimed towards low to middle-income consumers. The cotton textiles ranged from 3¢ per yard for plain varieties to 25¢ per yard for very fancy weaves. Boris Emmet, *Montgomery Ward and Co. Catalogue and Buyers' Guide, No. 57, Spring and Summer 1895* (New York: Dover Publications [reprint], 1969), 7–11, 13–22, 30–32.

48 For rapid growth of the southern cotton manufacturing industry see Adrienne Snow, 'Cotton Mill City: Huntsville Textile Industry, 1880–1889', *Alabama Review* 63.4 (2010): 243–281; and T. W. Uttely, *Cotton Spinning and Manufacturing in the United States of America* (Manchester: Manchester University Press, 1905).

49 Stout, *Native American Boarding Schools*, 154.

50 Child, *Boarding School Seasons*, 1, 5.

51 Rebecca Kugel, 'Leadership within the Women's Community: Susie Bonga Wright of the Leech Lake Ojibwe', in *Native Women's History in Eastern North America before 1900*, ed. Rebecca Kugel and Lucy Eldersveld Murphy (Lincoln: University of Nebraska Press, 2007), 176–177.

52 Minnesota Historical Society (hereafter MNHS): MNHS P2085, 'Pauline Colby Reminiscences'.

53 Kugel, 'Leadership within the Women's Community', 176–177.

54 Mason and Hough in Emma Blair, ed., *The Indian Tribes of the Upper Mississippi Valley and Region of the Great Lakes*, 2 vols. (Lincoln: University of Nebraska Press, 1996), vol. 2, 149; Willmott, *Beavers and Sheep*, 33.

55 Katrina Paxton, 'Learning Gender: Female Students at the Sherman Institute, 1907–1925', in *Boarding School Blues: Revisiting American Indian Educational Experiences*, ed. Clifford E. Trafzer, Jean A. Keller and Lorene Sisquoc (Lincoln: University of Nebraska Press, 2006), 174.

56 Willmott, *Beavers and Sheep*, 33.

57 Paxton, 'Learning Gender', 179, 181.

58 Child, *Boarding School Seasons*, 80.

59 Coleman, *American Indian Children*, 114.

60 Lomawaima, 'Domesticity in the Federal Indian Schools', 233.

61 David Wallace Adams, 'Beyond Bleakness: The Brighter Side of Indian Boarding Schools, 1870–1940', in *Boarding School Blues: Revisiting American Indian Educational Experiences*, ed. Clifford E. Trafzer, Jean A. Keller and Lorene Sisquoc (Lincoln: University of Nebraska Press, 2006), 43.

62 MMe Kellogg, *Instruction Book for the Kellogg French Tailor System for Cutting Every Description of Ladies' Garments, System Patent, Revised Edition* (Washington, DC: Library

of Congress, 1880), 1. Insight into the scientific basis and male occupation of tailoring can also be gleaned from the articles and advertisements in the *International Record of Correct Styles*, a circular published by the Cutters' and Tailors' Academy in Chicago, 1882.

63 Tape recorded interview with Simon Otto, 3 November 2009, Little Traverse Bay, Michigan.

64 Child, *Boarding School Seasons*, 75; Nadjiwon, *Not Wolf*, 33–34, 50; Lomawaima, 'Domesticity in the Federal Indian Schools', 233.

65 Silverstein, *Clothed Encounters*, 297.

66 J. R. Miller, *Shingwauk's Vision: A History of Native Residential Schools* (Toronto: University of Toronto Press, 1996), 194.

67 Tim Ingold, 'Culture on the Ground: The World Perceived through the Feet', *Journal of Material Culture* 9.3 (2004): 321–323.

68 Analysis of data found in UCCA: 'Mt. Elgin Industrial School Day Book'.

69 Thomas Cosford in Graham, *Mush Hole*, 238.

70 Willmott, *Beavers and Sheep*, 19.

71 Analysis of data found in UCCA: 'Mt. Elgin Industrial School Day Book'

72 Ingold, 'Culture on the Ground', 323, 325.

73 Morris Davis, 'Early Twentieth Century U.S. Methodist Missions Photography: The Problems of "Home"', *Methodist Review* 2 (2010): 59.

74 Ingold, 'Culture on the Ground', 323–324.

75 Frederick Waugh's field notes state, 'Daughter of Peter Jones and her baby', Wikwemikong, 1916. However, the only possible subjects of this photograph are Maani Jones (daughter-in-law of Rev. Jones) or Edna Maud Jones (granddaughter-in-law of Rev. Jones) with Victor C. Jones, son of the latter, born 6 March 1916. See Jones Family Tree, created by the author based on available census and other data, www.ancestry.com/family-tree/tree/155931964/family (accessed 12 December 2018).

76 Ann Chisholm, 'Incarnations and Practices of Feminine Rectitude: Nineteenth-Century Gymnastics for U.S. Women', *Journal of Social History* 38.3 (2005): 740.

77 Rev. John Potts, ed., *The Royal Path of Life* (Toronto: John B. Magurn, 1880), 67.

78 Lomawaima, 'Domesticity in the Federal Indian Schools', 231.

79 Child, *Boarding School Seasons*, 78–79.

80 Lomawaima, 'Domesticity in the Federal Indian Schools', 233.

81 Leigh Summers, *Bound to Please: A History of the Victorian Corset* (Oxford: Berg, 2001), 75–77.

82 Summers, *Bound to Please*, 71.

83 Vivienne Richmond, *Clothing the Poor in Nineteenth-Century England* (New York: Cambridge University Press, 2013), 100–101.

84 Keating, *Narrative of an Expedition*, 150–155.

85 Sky Blue Mary Morin, 'Number 107', in *Residential Schools: The Stolen Years*, ed. Linda Jaine (Saskatoon, SK: University of Saskatchewan, University Extension Press, 1993), 118.

86 'Making Lace at St. Mary's School', *c.*1890, Department of Special Collections and University Archives, Marquette University Libraries, http://cdm16280.contentdm.oclc.org/cdm/singleitem/collection/p4007coll4/id/943/rec/30 (accessed 25 November 2018). Also see 'St. Mary's Odanah, Wisc., What Our Indian Girls Can Do with Small Pieces of New Material', Department of Special Collections and University Archives, Marquette University Libraries.

87 'Student Sewing Room, St. Benedict's Academy, St. Joseph, Minnesota', https://reflections.mndigital.org/catalog/stbm:295?pn=false#/image/0 (accessed 9 September 2018).

88 'SBM.06m Boarding School Workroom, St. Benedict's Mission, White Earth, MN', http://cdm.csbsju.edu/cdm/singleitem/collection/SBM/id/85/rec/2 (accessed 21 September 2018).

89 Sophie White, *Wild Frenchmen and Frenchified Indians: Material Culture and Race in Colonial Louisiana* (Philadelphia: University of Pennsylvania Press, 2012), 179, 206–207.
90 Kathleen M. Brown, *Foul Bodies: Cleanliness in Early America* (New Haven, CT and London: Yale University Press), 268–272.
91 MNHS: P2085, Rev. Francis Palmer, Introduction to 'Pauline Colby Reminiscences', 1937.
92 Virginia Smith, *Clean: A History of Personal Hygiene* (Oxford: Oxford University Press, 2007), 267–273.
93 Kathleen M. Brown, *Foul Bodies*, 326.
94 MNHS: P2085, Colby, n.d., 48, 86. 'Pauline Colby Reminiscences … '
95 Olivia M. Cutting, 'Sybil Carter Indian Mission and Lace Industry Report', in *Sybil Carter Indian Mission and Lace Industry Association Annual Report, 1908* (New York: Sybil Carter Indian Mission and Lace Industry Association, 1908), 11.
96 See, for example, MNHS: E97.7W, 24, photograph entitled, 'Girls Washroom in Dormitory at White Earth School, 1889'.
97 Fortunate Eagle, *Pipestone*, 50, 93; Littlefield, 'Indian Education', 110.
98 Manass and McVitty in Graham, *Mush Hole*, 255, 272.
99 Bernice Jackson in Graham, *Mush Hole*, 472; Coleman, *American Indian Children*, 113.
100 Littlefield, 'Indian Education', 111.
101 Child, *Boarding School Seasons*, 82.
102 MNHS: E97.1 r39, 'Ojibway Woman Packing Groceries, Leech Lake Reservation, 1896', photography by Edward Bromley, staff photographer *Minneapolis Times*.
103 IAND: 1971-205, LAC, 'Simon Taylor's Family at English River with Their Up-to-Date Washing Machine, 1929'.
104 Ignatia Broker, *Night Flying Woman: An Ojibway Narrative* (St Paul: Minnesota Historical Society Press, 1983), 82–83.
105 Fortunate Eagle, *Pipestone*, 4–8.
106 Fortunate Eagle, *Pipestone*, 4–8.
107 Fortunate Eagle, *Pipestone*, 4–8.
108 Shirley Cheechoo, Path with No Moccasins (Toronto: Talent Group, 1991), 19, 34.
109 Kevin Whalen, 'Finding a Balance: Student Voices and Cultural Loss at Sherman Institute', *American Behavioral Scientist* 58.1 (2014): 139.
110 Term coined by Riley Kucheran, Lecture at the Center for Fashion Diversity and Social Change, Ryerson University, January 2018, www.youtube.com/watch?v=BMzAChVAaKU (accessed 1 September 2018).

12

TAILORING IN CHINA AND JAPAN

Cultural transfer and cutting techniques in the early twentieth century

Hissako Anjo and Antonia Finnane

China and Japan have often been compared in terms of their different responses to the 'impact of the West' in the nineteenth century. A striking representation of the differences is to be found in a coloured woodblock print by Kobayashi Kiyochika小林清親 (1847–1915), illustrating the negotiations between the Chinese and Japanese parties to the historic negotiations in Shimonoseki following the Sino-Japanese War of 1894 (Figure 12.1). On the one side of the room are Chinese officials in their full robes with rank badges and elevated cotton-soled boots; on the other, the Japanese in European-style ceremonial dress, complete with medals, sashes and epaulettes. Not only the clothes, but also the bodily dispositions of the conference participants appear different. The Chinese delegates, with their long history and tradition of sitting down in chairs, are duly seated. On the Japanese side a distinctly European pattern of status differentiation within the delegation is observable. Senior members Ito Hirobumi 伊藤博文 and Foreign Minister Mutsu Munemitsu 陸奥宗光 are provided with chairs while others in the party are left standing more or less to attention.

The print seems the perfect illustration of the now dated paradigm of historical change sometimes referred to as the 'impact-response' model.[1] According to the model, Japan responded to the challenge of the West by modernizing quickly and successfully, while China did so only slowly and reluctantly. Looking at the picture, it is easy to forget both the strident opposition to Westernization evident in Japan following the Meiji restoration in 1868 and the rejection of Manchu dress by Chinese rebels, reformers and revolutionaries from the middle of the nineteenth century onward; and easy, too, to overlook the dynamic relationship between China and Japan in this period. The two Western figures in the print, John W. Foster and Henry W. Denison, respectively advisers to the Chinese and Japanese governments, are not unimportant in the overall composition of the picture but they are not the dominant

FIGURE 12.1 Kobayashi Kiyochika小林清親 (1847–1915), 'Kōwashi Ri Kōshō danpan no zu' 媾和使李鴻章談判之図 [Peace negotiation with Li Hongzhang], woodblock print, 1895.

Source: Author's collection.

presence, either. The Japanese and Chinese delegates look past them at each other, as if in a reminder that the process of Westernization involved more than a simple East–West binary.

The present chapter explores this process via the history of tailoring in China and Japan, a generally neglected area of study and one that deserves attention from the perspective of cultural transfer. While the wearing of Western-style clothes in China and Japan is recognized as a sign of cultural change in the late nineteenth and early twentieth centuries, not much is known about those who made these new sorts of clothes or how they learnt about them. In the Anglophone sphere, there is just one established item of 'knowledge' about tailors in China and Japan and it takes the form of a story about a tailor (either Chinese or Japanese) who copied a Western suit coat (or pair of trousers) so well that he even reproduced the patch on the coat sleeve (or trouser leg or elsewhere, depending on the version).[2] This story naturally posits the West as the site of origin of a form of material culture that was exactly replicated by China and Japan.

As we show in this chapter, the writings and professional activities of tailors in China and Japan in the first half of the twentieth century show that the technical challenges of producing these new styles of garment met with a range of local responses. They provoked debate and inspired the formation of organizations that were critical to the propagation of new technologies of cutting and sewing. Further, although the histories of vestimentary change in the two countries were by no means identical, they were related. Regional migratory movements – especially on the part of Chinese tailors – were a critical part of the cultural transfer process. In this process, London and New York served as sources of professional knowledge, but as points of transfer they were less important than Canton, Shanghai and Yokohama.

Western dress in China and Japan: early developments in comparative perspective

The broad outlines of fashion history in China and Japan from the nineteenth century onward can be summarized on the basis of the existing scholarly literature. Briefly, in Japan, the beginning of the Meiji era in 1868 opened the way to Westernized lifestyles, with the popularization of Western clothing being one of the more visible outcomes.[3] The spread of European fashions among Japanese women was initially limited, but for men, Western-style garments, including uniforms for policemen, postmen, customs officials, railways workers and students, slowly but surely replaced the *kimono*. The Western suit, too, was introduced. It was 'a sort of uniform that is not a uniform' in the words of Nagai Kafū 永井荷風,[4] and in the Taishō period (1912–1925) it became standard dress for male white-collar workers. When haiku poet Takahama Kyoshi 高浜虚子 set up an office in Tokyo in 1923, he found that he was almost alone among office occupants of the building in wearing Japanese dress.[5]

Changes in fashion were linked to changes in economic organization. In the late Meiji to Taishō periods the service sector in Japan grew steadily, with a concomitant increase in the number of office workers. The demand for business suits increased accordingly.[6] Lowly office workers bought their suits through monthly instalments. They were dubbed 'poor people in Western suits' (*yōfuku saimin* 洋服細民), a phrase that denoted their occupational category (office work) while at the same time indicating how closely that category had come to be associated with the Western suit. At home, these same workers would generally wear a kimono.

Circumstances in China were different. The shift to modern, tailored uniforms for the military and police forces was observable from around the turn of the century, when the chastened Qing court embarked on a series of modernizing reforms. After the fall of the Qing in 1912, the new government of the Republic of China approved Western styles for civilian wear, as well. The lounge suit and the morning suit were designated as proper wear for different occasions.[7] The move towards the adoption of Western dress at this time was slowed by a change of political momentum after the failed 1913 revolution but picked up again following the May Fourth Movement of 1919, when there was a general move away from the conservative, Confucian order that had seemed till then the default for Chinese society. In the 1920s, the suit was worn by educated, progressive young men, especially those who had returned from study in foreign lands, including Japan.[8] It continued to have a presence in China thereafter, being worn variously by dandies, businessmen and foreigners, especially in Shanghai, right up until the founding of the People's Republic in 1949. Among progressive young Chinese, however, a rising tide of nationalism meant a decided return to the long gown in the 1930s, while bureaucrats in the new government of Nationalist China, established in 1928, wore the Zhongshan suit.[9]

The different trajectories of vestimentary change in China and Japan were linked. In an overview of the development of the 'Red Group' (*Hongbang* 红帮) tailors of Ningbo, famous for their technical expertise in the making of Western suits, Ji Xueyuan季学源notes the Japanese impact on Chinese tailoring: the Meiji dress reforms, the exposure of young Chinese to Japanese modernity through study abroad, and the migration to Japan of Chinese tailors were all factors helping to shape Chinese tailoring expertise.[10] The Zhongshan suit is a monument to the effects: created for 'Father of the Republic' Sun Yatsen (Sun Zhongshan孙中山, 1866–1925), it was designed on the basis, apparently, of a Japanese military uniform and made by Wang Caiyun 王才运 (1879–1931), a Red Group tailor whose father Wang Ruimo王睿谟 (1846–1924) had set up a Western tailoring business in Shanghai after his return from working in a Western clothing shop in Japan.[11]

The flow of influence was by no means all in the one direction. Chinese tailors were early exposed to the clothing requirements of foreigners due to the presence of Westerners in Macao and Canton in the late eighteenth and early nineteenth centuries. When Japanese ports too began to open up in the 1850s, Chinese tailors took their expertise to Japan. Japanese heading abroad for study in the early Meiji years typically sought out Chinese tailors in Yokohama to fit them out if they could afford the cost, or else had their Western suits made en route in Hong Kong.[12] Among foreigners, the Chinese tailors in Japan were long held in high repute. In Yokohama around 1890, Eliza Ruhamah Scidmore found only one reputable Japanese dressmaker; the trade was otherwise dominated by Chinese tailors: 'Cock Eye, tailor, Ah Nie and Wong Fai, ladies' tailors, are the Poole, Worth, and Felix of the foreign community'.[13] The Japanese government recognized Chinese strengths in this area of enterprise and in 1903, with war looming on the Manchurian front, contracted Hong Kong tailors to supply 20,000 khaki uniforms with red facings.[14]

Hong Kong, a British colony from 1842 and increasingly important as an international port, was a rewarding market for Cantonese tailors.[15] It is probable that the early migrant tailors in Japan, too, were mostly from Guangzhou (Canton) or Macao. Certainly Cantonese natives accounted for a majority of Japan's Chinese population.[16] Among tailors, however, the Cantonese were increasingly challenged by a growing number from Zhejiang province, often travelling from bases in Shanghai. These were the Red Group tailors mentioned above, all originally from villages around the port city of Ningbo. They had a virtual monopoly on Western tailoring in Shanghai, allegedly acquiring their collective name from the fact they made garments for the 'red-haired' ones, as Europeans were known.[17] By the 1930s, natives of Zhejiang and Jiangsu provinces (Ningbo was in Zhejiang, Shanghai in Jiangsu) were reportedly in an overwhelming majority among Chinese tailors and dressmakers in Japan.[18]

The career of Wang Ruimo shows how time spent in Japan might provide a critical turning point in a tailor's career. Wang's early training, probably as an apprentice, was in a standard or native tailor shop in Shanghai, making Chinese-style garments. He left Shanghai for Japan in 1885, learnt suit making at a Western clothing store, and returned five years later to set up his own tailoring shop. This provided the foundations for a second and larger business, the iconic Rongchang-xiang 榮昌祥 woollen suits store in Nanjing Road. In the hands of his son Wang Caiyun, Rongchangxiang became the most noted tailors in Shanghai, employing more than 100 employees at the peak of its fortunes.[19]

It is not clear whether Wang Ruimo's training in Japan was in a Japanese or a Chinese tailor's shop, but given that Chinese tailors were well established in Yokohama at the time and were the tailors of choice for Westerners and perhaps for well-to-do Japanese as well, the latter seems more likely. In time, the balance of skills shifted. In the Taishō period, Japanese tailors were meeting, debating and subsequently disseminating new technologies of drafting and cutting. Chinese tailors may well have been going to Japan to exploit greater economic opportunities, but it is clear that they came back from Japan equipped with new forms of knowledge and experience and ultimately also new qualifications from the newly established academies of tailoring.

Patterns

The social history of clothing in East Asia sheds light on the cultural contexts within which Chinese and Japanese tailors acquired and demonstrated their skills in Western garment making. It does not in itself explain what skills were entailed and how they were developed and transmitted. To tailors from non-Western clothing cultures, cutting tailored garments posed special challenges. Unlike in the West, where garments were cut to fit the human form, clothing in Asian societies consisted for the most part of loose garments that were hung on or draped around the figure. In both Japan and China, measurements of the customer were taken preparatory to making up a garment, but clothing was typically cut on a generous scale and could be gifted or bequeathed and then worn by someone other than the original owner with no adjustments necessary. With so little experience among tailors of cutting to the shape of the individual body, it is no surprise that in Japan the first-generation of Western-style tailors came from the ranks of *tabi* makers, the manufacturers of traditional Japanese socks, modelled on the feet.[20]

For these reasons, patterns emerged early as the *sine qua non* of Western tailoring in the East. Commodore Perry, visiting the south coast of China in 1853, observed that in Canton and Macao, tailors ('male-milliners', to use his term), 'generally require a muster or pattern, which they, with their usual Chinese imitative skill, reproduce exactly … and adapt it to any shape or size'.[21] Bayard

Taylor was in China around the same time (he there joined Perry's expedition to Japan) and likewise found 'there were none but Chinese tailors in Shanghai, who work entirely from ready-made patterns'.[22]

Perry's use of the word 'muster' points to British India as a possible source of patterns as well as of vocabulary, for 'in Calcutta and some other parts ... the word *Muster* [was], strangely, a common English synonyme [*sic*] for the words *Sample* and *Pattern*' (original emphasis).[23] The term was in use on the China coast at least by 1830. Harriet Low, a young American woman living in Macao around that time, complained about the many grievances of getting dresses made up by the local tailors, but had to admit that 'if they have an exact muster, they sometimes do pretty well'.[24] The actual phenomenon of the 'muster' was probably introduced to India from London. By the end of the eighteenth century, according to Joy Emery, 'there were tailors who were teaching cutting ... to anyone who could afford the fee'.[25] Among these, a Mr Dietrichstein of Rathbone Place was making his name as a producer of paper patterns, which were sold all over Britain – and perhaps all over Britain's empire as well.[26]

Perry's arrival in Japan in 1853 gave local residents their first opportunity to observe the peculiarities of Western dress. Perry and his companions found their clothing to be of great interest to their Japanese hosts, who unabashedly 'fingered the broadcloth, smoothed down the nap ... pulled a lappel [*sic*] here, adjusted a collar there' and furthermore, 'showed a peculiar passion for buttons'.[27] The principle of a pattern made of paper was probably unknown in Japan at that time. In an account published in its English translation for the first time this same year, Russian navigator and explorer Vasily Golovnin described the clothing made for him and his party when they were being held captive in Hokkaido. They had provided their captors with a coat by way of a model of what they wanted made up for the winter. A tailor was brought in, duly shown the coat, and 'proceeded to take our measures', but when the garments arrived, made of wadded cotton, they proved to be 'singularly shaped, being neither cloaks, great-coats, nor Japanese loose gowns'.[28] The 'measures' were presumably of height and bulk, to ensure that the garments would not be too large or small.

Early paper patterns used in both China and Japan may have suffered from poor drafting in the first instance or from loss of detail through replication. In *A History of the Tokyo Association of Merchants and Manufacturers of Western Clothing*, published by and for the Association in 1941, the writer recalled the circumstances of tailoring *c*.1889:

> Tailors [at that time] still cut the fabric incorrectly by using a paper pattern that they bought or they were given. Therefore, it was common for Japanese wearing Western clothing not to be able to rotate their shoulders or move their arms forward freely; also, their legs would feel uncomfortable when walking up stairs. Many tailors [simply] obtained and used paper patterns that had been drafted and cut out by more skilled tailors.[29]

The implication is that many tailors cut the fabric using patterns designed for physiques different from that of their customers. In fact, in the first half of the 1910s, the Japan Wool Textile News Company 日本毛織物新報社 sold paper patterns to tailors who were not able to draft patterns themselves.[30] We do not have the personal memoirs of any tailor to reveal the evolving sense of dissatisfaction with these practices, but by the middle of the Taishō period, it must have been palpable. In 1916 and 1917 the *Japan Woolen Textiles News* promoted a series of meetings aimed at redressing the problem.

Cutting: the great challenge

How to cut the cloth to suit the figure was the greatest challenge that Western garments posed to tailors, East or West, but in the East it took a while for tailors to come to grips with what it meant. In his *Tailors' Guidebook*, published in 1906, Iwamura Hidetarō 岩村秀太郎 wrote that Japanese tailors were no worse than their Western counterparts in sewing, but 'they do not understand the principle of cutting. Consequently, even if they take great care with sewing, the clothes [they make] cannot be beautiful'.[31] In fact, as he further noted, Japanese tailors placed significantly greater emphasis on sewing than on cutting. In other words, not only did they not understand cutting techniques; they had not yet grasped how important cutting was.[32] Historians of fashion and style generally tend to fall into the same error, paying more attention to surface appearances than to construction.[33] Yet cutting is central to explaining the reception of Western clothing in China and Japan.[34] In the beginning, the very scissors used to cut the cloth differed from those used in Europe.

From the perspective of tailors in China and Japan, it is important to note that their acquisition of skills in measuring up, drafting and cutting took place in a period when tailoring in the West, too, was in a dynamic phase. Winifred Aldrich has noted the variety of approaches taken, including direct measurement, where cloth or tissue paper was moulded around the body; the proportional principle based on a theory that chest measurement would indicate all other measurements; and the divisional principle, based on measurements of defined areas of the body.[35] Overall, the tailor needed to resolve tensions between the style of the garment (with its ideal proportions) and the shape of the body. In the course of the nineteenth century, tailors in England and France responded to this challenge with 'anatomical' drafting systems'[36] that contributed to the improvement of paper patterns and the development of ready-to-wear garments as well as to the refinement of bespoke tailoring. Critical to advances in the both the tailoring profession and garment manufacture was the development of anthropometric charts, which made allowance for variety in body proportions and underpinned the emergence of standard sizes.[37]

There was plainly a long prehistory to the technical adaptations to Western standards among tailors in China and Japan, and also a continuous process of adjustment, as new theories and trends were popularized in the West. Prior to the two Conventions on Techniques of Tailoring 洋服技術大会 held in Tokyo in 1916 and 1917, the documentary record is thin. Nonetheless, a number of professional cutting manuals were published in the years leading up to the first convention, showing that new means of communicating skills within the profession were already in play.[38] From the various prefaces to these works, it seems likely that in the early 1910s, tailors were studying cutting methods from a range of sources and presenting lectures to share the results of their study with other tailors.[39] Wada Eikichi 和田栄吉, well known for his 1916 publication, *The Imperial Japanese Wada Cutting Manual*, is an example.[40] According to the preface written for this manual, Wada presented a lecture on his cutting method at an event held in Shiba ward on 22 July 1916. Fukuda Nakajirō 福田仲次郎, vice president of the Tokyo Association of Merchants and Manufacturers of Western Clothing, was impressed by the clarity of the presentation and invited Wada to give a ten-day series of lectures in Kanda. Kanda, later incorporated into Chiyoda ward, was the neighbourhood with the greatest concentration of tailors' shops in Tokyo.[41] It was shortly in wake of his Shiba address that Wada spoke at the first of the two tailoring conventions, also held in Kanda.

Presentations at the two conventions by tailors like Wada, who were already experimenting with new techniques, show that the conventions were a watershed in the history of technological advances in Japanese tailoring. The first convention, held 14–16 August 1916, was marked by controversy, as discussed further below. The second, which took place in Akasaka 10–15 March 1917, was an outcome of this controversy and showed efforts to resolve it.[42] A partial record of the two meetings is available in the *Conventions Memorial Book*, published by *The Japan Woolen Textiles Journal* in 1917. In an informative introduction, editor Yoneda Suekichi set out the aims and scope of the meetings:

> Earnest study of drafting and division [necessary for] cutting of Western clothing commenced four or five years ago. However, can we say immediately that our cutting techniques have consequently progressed? ... If there are ten skilled tailors, they use ten drafting methods. What is the point of departure for these ten methods? What path do they follow? Where do they end up? In other words, what type of methods does each tailor use in taking measurements, dividing, and altering? How does he accomplish his work?[43]

The primary concern of the conventions was to elucidate various drafting methods with the aim of identifying best practice and standardizing procedures. The programme for 15 August 1916, the second day of the first convention, shows that some tailors had already adopted British and American drafting methods.[44] Shibata Ichirō 柴田一郎 demonstrated how to draft a morning suit pattern, based on the American short measure system; Numata Hiroshi 沼田弘 presented a comparative study of high-shoulder and low-shoulder fittings, explaining how to draft a morning suit pattern based on the Thornton system;

and Nomura Gorō 野村五郎 showed how to draft a suit pattern for a stout man.[45] Interestingly, Japanese garment making was not neglected. A tailor named Hara Sentarō 原仙太郎 addressed the audience on the subject of the kimono sleeve.

The meetings were well attended and lively. Photographs show a throng of tailors in attendance, and they had travelled to Tokyo from far and wide (Figure 12.2). There were participants from the Korean Peninsula and Karafuto (Sakhalin), both of which were under Japanese colonial rule until 1945.[46] The participants were intensely engaged in the proceedings. One speaker was booed and jeered for explaining his method obscurely.[47] The first meeting moreover featured a robust debate between advocates and critics of 'principles of cutting' 裁断原則. The critics held staunchly to skills and experience as the bedrock of tailoring. They defended what in the Anglophone world was known as the 'rock of eye' method, whereby the tailor sized up the client at a glance, measured directly and cut and sewed accordingly. The *Japan Woolen Textiles News* aired the controversy by publishing a number of letters from the two camps.[48]

Wada Eikichi was on the progressive side of this debate. A professional tailor who had turned to dedicated study of cutting techniques, Wada was the founder of the Imperial Japanese Wada Cutting System School.[49] The imperial Wada cutting system was a typically Japanese combination of Western technology with

FIGURE 12.2 The first Tailoring Techniques Meeting, Kanda, 1916.

Source: Yoneda Suekichi 米田末吉, ed., *Yōfuku gijutsu taikai kinenchō: shotaika saidan kessakushū* 洋服技術大会記念帳:諸大家裁断傑作集 [Tailoring techniques conventions memorial book: collection of skilled tailors' best cutting works] (Tokyo: Nihon Keorimono Shimpōsha, 1917).

Japanese essence. In Wada's view, it was meaningless to study British and American drafting methods for Westerners because their 'height, arm length, leg length, and skeletal proportions' were completely different from those of the Japanese.[50] The Wada cutting system accordingly presented a Japanese drafting method suitable for a supposed Japanese body shape (Figure 12.3). Since Wada gave a number of presentations in 1916 and spoke at both the tailors' conventions – twice at the first and once at the second – it can be surmised that his system became widely known at this time.[51]

Again on the progressive side was Kimura Keiichi 木村慶市, the manager of a well-known woollen textile company called the Stock Company.[52] It is unclear whether Kimura had experience of working in a tailor's shop, but he was well versed in cutting techniques and in later years wrote his own manual on cutting.[53] The *Conventions Memorial Book* contains two articles by him, one on the British Inverness coat and the other on the British circular cape. Like Wada, he showed a consciousness of the particularities of the Japanese body, showing how the climax system of drafting, developed by Minister and Co. in London, could be used to adapt the Inverness coat pattern to accommodate the

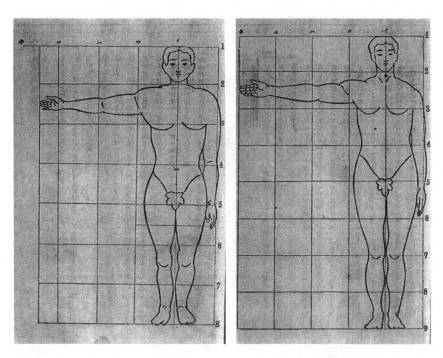

FIGURE 12.3 Illustration of the difference in body shape between Japanese and Westerners.

Source: Wada Eikichi 和田栄吉, *Dainihon wadashiki yōfuku saidansho* 大日本和田式洋服裁断書 [The imperial Japanese Wada cutting manual] (Tokyo: Dainihon Wadashiki yōfuku saidan kōshūjo, 1916), pp. 81 and 85.

Japanese body shape.[54] In discussing the circular cape, Kimura made it apparent that he was familiar with materials such as the magazine published by the Minister Academy and technical works such as Leggatt and Hodginskon's *The 'Climax' System for Cutting Gentleman's Garments*.[55]

The final lecture at the second of the two conventions was delivered by Tsuji Masamichi 辻正道, head teacher at the School of Western Clothing Manufacturers and Commerce, who drew a large crowd. The hall was packed with tailors, so that 'there was no place to stand', and heated discussion of cutting principles was underway even before the start of the lecture. As this lecture is the only one to have been reproduced in full in the *Conventions Memorial Book*, it would appear to have been the most significant, in the eyes of the publishers at least. It is noteworthy for its engagement with new theories of knowledge and action.

Tsuji commenced his address expressing his surprise that 'principles of cutting had become a matter of controversy'. He went on to explain the problem, making explicit reference to science and theory:

> Not only cutting but everything is naturally controlled by some principles or some theories. Using the new term 'principle', we have felt doubts and fears. However, you have already been unconsciously controlled by the principles … There are scientific theories in all civilized societies … Everything can be explained by the theories. Needless to say, there is also a theory to explain cutting. Poor understanding of cutting theory is the reason why a tailor cuts with difficulty. I often hear the irresponsible argument that theory and practice are completely different, but we cannot call a theory that differs from practice 'theory'.[56]

By way of illustrating the relationship between practice and theory, he used the example of drafting for non-standard bodies (*hentai* 变体), pointing out that without a pattern for standard bodies, there would be no basis for comparison and alterations.[57] Importantly, the standard pattern was also the basis for the manufacture of fashion:

> It would be wrong to look at this pattern with eyes attuned to other styles and immediately conclude that it has gone out of fashion … With precise alterations, this pattern is usable for all body shapes, and for adjusting to fashionable suits. Moreover, altering also has its principle and its order.[58]

Progressive tailors such as Wada, Kimura and Tsuji were in lockstep with their counterparts in London and New York. Wada's use of Minister's climax system has already been mentioned. Two other systems, the Thornton system and the American short measure system, were introduced at the 1916 tailors' meeting. Tsuji's emphasis on the standard coat pattern echoes J. P. Thornton's advice:

As a basis for the construction of any system of cutting, the frock coat is beyond dispute the most appropriate. Its outline exactly follows the natural formation of the body ... It is also a standard style of garment, changing slowly but slightly in its details.[59]

A distinguished tailor and educator in the industry, Thornton had made a name for himself through the publication of a series of guides to measuring, drafting and cutting.[60] These were among the publications to which tailors in Japan (and no doubt also in China) looked for guidance in developing their skills.

The various systems promoted through tailoring academies and publications in Britain and the United States met the interest of Japanese tailors in how to draft patterns to suit the body shapes of particular clients. During the question and answer session, at a request from the audience, Tsuji Masamichi extemporaneously drafted a suit pattern for Takahashi Yasujirō 高橋泰次郎, who was overweight and had one shoulder higher than the other – in other words, whose physique was not standard.[61] This was probably a textbook demonstration. Both Thornton and Mitchell devoted attention to non-standard figures, including the corpulent or very thin, over-erect and stooping, necks long or short, even hunchbacks. The case of Takahashi, with one shoulder higher than the other, was explicitly covered by Mitchell's guidelines for 'difference of shoulder height'.[62]

All in all, the record of the conventions shows a high degree of intellectual and even emotional investment by tailors in the technological revolution underway in their profession. The discussion of techniques was robust, suggesting an underlying philosophy of clothing in relationship to the body, one that was expressed in the artisanal practices of the traditional tailor and that was now coming under challenge. New ways of measuring both the body and the fabric meant a change in philosophy. The debate over 'principles' in particular shows a turn towards an explicitly scientific understanding of how to draft a pattern and cut the cloth. These principles were in the end not confined to making suits. They were taught as well in dressmaking schools, where women learned how to make a kimono the modern way.[63]

Professional institutions and professional development in tailoring

From the vantage point of these meetings, it is worth considering the relative positions of Chinese and Japanese tailors in Taishō Japan. That Chinese tailors in Yokohama continued to enjoy some sort of competitive advantage is suggested by comments by Stanhope Sams, US Trade Commissioner in the Far East 1913–1915. Sams had an extended stay in Japan in 1915, his visit covering the coronation of the Taishō emperor, which was attended by members of the diplomatic corps and their wives. Chinese tailors were employed for the occasion, and in Sams' view '[succeeded] so well' that it was 'hard to tell which of the [ladies'] gowns had been made in Paris, New York, or Yokohama'. Japanese labour also went into the making of these gowns, but only in the area of embroidery, a task undertaken for very small return. Ladies' gowns and gentlemen's suits are of course different categories of dress, but the relative positions of Chinese and Japanese craftsmen (or women?) in this production process nonetheless points to sustained Chinese ascendancy in the making of Western garments to this date. This conclusion is supported by a US government report of 1916, in which the reputation of Chinese tailors of Yokohama is reported to be second only to that of their peers in Shanghai.[64]

It is possible that the high level of visibility of Chinese tailors in Western accounts was due to their domination of the niche market of tailoring for Westerners. Evidence of a symbiotic relationship can be found in reports following the destruction of Yokohama in the Kanto earthquake of 1923. The death toll exacted by the earthquake was proportionally heavy for Chinese residents. Yokohama's Chinatown was flattened; of a registered 5,721 residents, 1,700 died.[65] Despite the devastation and some resulting violence against Chinese, the next 18 months saw a steady resumption of business by Chinese shopkeepers and service providers alongside the many British, American, French and Indian firms that had likewise resumed operations. Around one third of all 'pre-quake companies', including 88 Chinese businesses, are reported to have returned to the port by May 1925.[66] It can be assumed that these small businesses, reportedly consisting mostly of grocers and tailors, were servicing the larger British and American outfits.

In the immediate post-quake years, moreover, Chinese tailors popped up in Karuizawa. This inland town had emerged as a resort for foreign missionaries in the late nineteenth century and in the wake of the Kanto earthquake was increasingly popular as a holiday site for foreigners who might otherwise have stayed in Yokohama. Where the foreigners went, the Chinese tailors followed. Small-time Japanese entrepreneurs were also drawn to Karuizawa by the foreign market, but they tended to be curio dealers.[67] In reporting this occupational breakdown the *Japan Times* may have been indulging in some stereotyping, but the association between Chinese tailors and foreign patrons remains clear. In 1935, H. Vere Redman observed that Chinese tailors did not cater to the needs of someone like 'Suzuki' (his fictional Japanese everyman). Their customers were Suzuki's Japanese 'betters', along with foreign residents.[68]

On the Japanese side, however, institutional developments in the early twentieth century provided solid foundations for the creation of a modern sector in garment making. These reveal some instructive contrasts between Japan and China. The first was the development of department stores, central to the development of fashion and fashion-related consumption in the modern world. Department stores, or 'universal providers' as they were known in Britain and its outposts, had their origins in haberdasheries and draperies. Given the trend they showed towards combination of goods and services under the one roof, it seems appropriate that they should have eventually have provided a home for tailors. In Tokyo, Mitsukoshi, founded in 1904, positioned itself at the forefront of providers of Western clothing when in 1906 it invited Alexander Mitchell to serve as technical adviser for its tailoring department. The store paid him a handsome salary, higher than that of its own executive officers in the first instance with a promise of more again. The *Yomiuri Newspaper* reported in astonishment, 'A year hence, [Mitchell's] annual salary will be 5,500 yen, and two years hence, and 6,500 yen – 500 yen higher than that of a certain minister!'[69] In the May 1912 issue of *Mitsukoshi* he is described as the 'director of cutting', suggesting that Mitsukoshi may have invited him to obtain his advice on cutting techniques specifically.[70]

A second important development was the appearance of special publications on cutting and drafting. Tsubota Sentarō 坪田仙太郎 reportedly studied British and American books on cutting at Mitchell's side over a period of nine years, periodically submitting the results of his studies to Japanese professional magazines.[71] These magazines are difficult to locate now, but appear to have included the *World of Western Clothing* (*Yōsōkai* 洋装界) and *Materials for Western Clothing Bulletin* (*Yōfuku Zairyō Tsūshin* 洋服材料通信), in addition to the *Japan Woolen Textiles News*.[72] A related development was the formation of associations such as the Tokyo Western Clothing Society (Tōkyō Yōsō Kenkyūkai 東京洋装研究会), which, at a time when Western clothing was still not accepted for subjects of the Qing dynasty in China, was disseminating technical knowledge about how to cut the cloth for the Western suit.[73]

A third important development was the establishment of training institutes or specialist schools for the instruction in drafting, cutting and eventually machine sewing. As indicated above, several of the speakers at the two tailors' conventions were involved in teaching at or actually founded such schools. Schools for dressmakers were simultaneously being established. The renowned Sugino Yoshiko (1892–1978), author of many extant pattern books, founded a dressmaking college for women in Tokyo in 1926, the forbear of the present Sugino Fashion College. Perhaps just as importantly, there was an awareness at this time of a need for a better infrastructure for tailoring. 'There are no complete training institutes and very few orderly tailor shops in Japan', complained Maruyama Kōsaku in 1926. 'Under these circumstances, how can we master tailoring techniques and acquire useful experience?'[74]

In all these respects Japan was well ahead of China. The first of the big Chinese department stores on Shanghai's Nanjing Road was not built until 1917.[75] Fashion magazines or magazines featuring fashion began making an appearance in the 1920s, but professional guides to drafting and cutting and industry magazines hardly existed before the 1930s, and even then were very few in number.[76] Specialist literature in Chinese collections from these decades is more likely to be in Japanese than in Chinese. One plausible reason for this is that Japanese tailors were operational in Shanghai, Qingdao and elsewhere, serving expatriate Japanese communities, but another is that Chinese tailors brought them back from Japan. Not until after 1949 did sewing schools and associated types of literature such as pattern books and machine sewing manuals begin to proliferate in China.[77]

Chinese tailors: Japanese contexts

It is worth asking whether any of the many Chinese tailors living in Japan attended the tailoring conventions of 1916–1917. One possible participant is the author of the earliest known guide to cutting and drafting in Chinese, a tailor who had spent years in Japan. A native of Ningbo, Gu Tianyun 顾天云 (b. 1883), served his apprenticeship in Shanghai where he also worked for two or three years, before leaving for Japan in 1902. He established his own business in Yokohama, the Hong Tai Western Clothing Store, advertised under the English name 'K. Tomas'. Like many others, he felt the impact of the Kanto earthquake in 1923, and after 21 years abroad ended up back in Shanghai, relocating his business to a site in Nanjing Road. The 1920s were a period of unprecedented cultural effervescence in Chinese history, and when Gu Tianyun set about writing his *Guide to Western Tailoring* (Xifu caijian zhinan 西服裁剪指南), he was undoubtedly responding at some level to the frisson of modernity experienced by residents of Shanghai in those years.

The introduction to the *Guide to Western Tailoring* is notable for its ethical and patriotic concerns. Gu was at pains to establish the dignity of tailoring as a profession, pointing out that one American president had started his working life as a tailor. He stressed the importance of 'hard work, integrity, and modesty' in the pursuit of success. Noting the backward state of the Chinese economy and the humiliations to which the country was subject from external forces, he pointed out the obligation on every citizen to improve productivity in his or her own line of work. These essentially moral preoccupations were not unusual in a Confucian business environment,[78] but their particular inflection in Gu's preface is attributable to the specific historical conditions of China in the 1920s and 1930s, when intensifying Japanese aggression was fuelling Chinese nationalism. Shanghai itself was occupied by Japanese forces for nearly six weeks in early 1932.

No doubt on account of the intensity of anti-Japanese feeling in this period (often directed against Ningbo merchants on account of their trade in Japanese goods[79]), Gu was careful to avoid too direct a reference to Japan in his introduction. Nonetheless, he pays tribute to the influence of the years he spent there:

> I was overseas for twenty years, quietly observing foreigners engaged in this profession. They were invariably meticulous in their study, achieving great proficiency in tailoring. Winning over the hearts of their clients, they looked forward to the future growth of their businesses.[80]

These foreigners (*wairen* 外人) can only have been Japanese. In a later passage Gu refers to working in 'the Eastern Isles' (Dongying 东瀛, a literary name for

Japan), to his extensive experience with foreigners there and in Shanghai and to the importance of learning foreign languages, something that he felt was 'even more important [for our profession] than sewing'.[81] At the time of the tailoring conventions in Tokyo, Gu had already spent 15 years in Japan and was probably able to speak Japanese. His guide shows familiarity with Thornton's 'shoulder measure' principle, as indicated in Figure 12.4:

> In measuring up, it is of the utmost importance to attend to whether the shoulders are high or low … Paying attention to high or low the shoulders means that when it comes to cutting, the results will be entirely satisfactory.[82]

The same illustration shows another standard variable covered in Western tailoring guides: stooping, standard or over-erect posture as indicated by the neckline. Despite the title, the contents of the book prove to include Chinese as well as

FIGURE 12.4 Gu Tianyun's instructions on 'The Study of Physique: The Height of Shoulders, and the Line of the Neck'.

Source: Gu Tianyun 顾天云, *Xifu caijian zhinan* 西服裁剪指南 [Guide to Western tailoring] (Shanghai: Gu Tianyun, 1933), 8.

Western-style garments, but the approach is uniform: measurements had to be taken in accordance with the proportions of the individual body. A tape measure and a set square were utilized. An appendix lists English words related to tailoring. Whether or not Gu was introduced to these techniques at the tailors' meetings in Tokyo, it seems at least likely that he acquired the knowledge while in Japan.

This is not to say that considerable advances in drafting and cutting had not already been made in China. To the contrary, however piecemeal the advances made by the Red Group tailors in the early decades of suit making, there had clearly been a consolidation of skills by the early twentieth century. Without this, the Red Group would not have enjoyed its enviable reputation. Further, even if the communication of skills within the Red Group remained dependent on the old apprentice system, new values were forming around the cluster of new skills in garment making.

Both the transmission of skills and the shaping of values are evident in the experience of Manchu tailor Yin Changrong (印常荣, b. 1903). The son of an impoverished Manchu family in Beijing, Yin grew up far from the stamping ground of the Red Group tailors in Shanghai but was drawn into their world when in 1916 he began an apprenticeship in Zhou's Women's Wear shop (*Zhouji nüzhuang dian*周记女装店), in the eastern part of Beijing. Tailor Zhou was from Ningbo. Under his tutelage, the young Changrong learnt to speak Ningbo dialect and to cook Zhejiang food. He also became a skilled tailor, 'practicing cutting with old newspapers while everyone else was sleeping'. This description by his grandson attests to the importance increasingly accorded to the art of cutting as the age of the tailored wardrobe dawned in China: many tailors were sewers, but only the truly skilled were also cutters. Yin Changrong eventually became proprietor of his own extremely successful women's clothing shop in Beijing. Established in 1938, it had 60 employees and a turnover of 5,000 yuan at its most prosperous, during the period of Japanese occupation.[83]

Yin's story draws attention to the traditional apprentice system in China. In Japan also, despite a few professional schools of tailoring in the 1920s, it was mostly the case that tailoring was taught through an apprenticeship system.[84] In China, however, the scale of urban apprenticeships was phenomenal. The system soaked up surplus labour from the countryside and churned out more tailors than could possibly have been needed. In Shanghai alone, there were around 45,000 tailors in 1946.[85] Given the strength and stability of the apprenticeship system, and also the dearth of professional training schools within which published teaching materials might have been disseminated, a publication such as Gu Tianyun's guide – now an extremely rare book – could hardly have been a big factor in the evolution of Western tailoring in China. Nonetheless, it has unique importance as documentary evidence of principles and practices in the Western tailoring in a Sino-Japanese context at a time when technical publications of this nature were uncommon in China.

Gu's Japanese experience was not untypical of Red Group tailors. In 1929, in all Japan, there were 165 Chinese tailoring businesses and 641 Chinese tailors.[86] Of these, many must have been of the Red Group. Researchers at the Ningbo Costume Museum have located around 30 tailoring businesses run by Red Group tailors variously in Yokohama, Tokyo and Kobe.[87] A notable example is Tom Sung Tailors (*Tangmusen shanghao* 汤姆森商号), established in 1926 by Zhang Youxian (张有宪, d. 1947). Zhang arrived in Japan in 1900, a couple of years before Gu, and set up his first business in 1905. His son, Zhang Fangguang 张方厂, was born in Japan in 1916. The family left Japan following the Kanto earthquake, but returned in 1926, settling there permanently. Zhang Fangguang emerged as a leading member of the overseas Chinese community in Japan, with his son carrying on the business.[88]

Apart from those drawn to Japan by employment and business opportunities, aspiring tailors may have been attracted by the possibility of learning their trade at the vocational training schools that were springing up in the 1920s. Zhang Fang-guang attended just such a school in Yokohama, probably in the 1930s. A younger contemporary, Lin Zhengbao 林正苞, graduated from Tokyo Western Sewing School in 1942. Lin was at the forefront of the wave of Chinese tailors who established sewing schools in the 'New China' of the 1950s. His publishing and pedagogical activities were a response to the new government's call for sewing schools to be established for training housewives to become productive citizens of New China. His training in Japan was undoubtedly responsible for the professional presentation of his *Guide to Cutting* (Figure 12.5). With 118 pages, smart cover design featuring a set square ruler and business logo, and multiple fonts, this state-of-the-art pattern book offered readers the scientific set-square chest-measure (or as originally known in English, the 'breast-measure') method, by which it was hoped students could advance from a 'more-or-less' approach to precision in cutting clothes to fit the wearer. The chest-measure method was early developed and widely used by British tailors, and was one of the methods taught in the Japanese system. Lin's manual contains tables of sizes, conversion tables for calculating size of garment based on half-chest measurement, measure-ment tools, amounts of cloth for particular garments and colour combinations. Although cheaply produced compared to Japanese manuals published in the same period, it well exceeds any other contemporary Chinese publication of this genre for attention to technical detail and excellence in graphic design.

An interesting aspect of Lin's manual is its documentation of his training in Japan. His two diplomas in tailoring – one for women's and children's clothes, the other for gentlemen's high-class wear – are featured in the opening pages. Both diplomas were signed by the principal, Imai Masanori 今井正紀. In an advertisement for a new handbook by himself, the author is again presented as having studied in Japan and being a graduate of the Tokyo Western Sewing School. For a tailor to parade his Japanese credentials so soon after the end of a devastating war might seem surprising, but it is consistent with Japan's sus-tained reputation in China for quality craftsmanship.

FIGURE 12.5 Cover page of Lin Zhengbao 林正苞, *Caijian zhinan* 裁剪指南 [Guide to tailoring] (Shanghai: Meilin caijian fengxiu zhuanxisuo, 1954).

Japan was not the only place where Chinese tailors received overseas training and experience. Hong Kong tailor Bok Chen (Bo Zhen 卜珍) documents a different route. From tailoring college in London in 1936 he made his way to Malaya where he opened a sewing school, returning after World War II to Hong Kong where he set up the Lingdong School of Scientific Tailoring and Cutting. His school had one branch in Hong Kong, two in Guangzhou and one in Macao, all registered as vocational schools with the Chinese and British governments. Like Lin Zhengbao, Bok Chen was keen to emphasize his qualifications. One photograph in the opening pages shows him wearing a mortarboard, another shows the diploma he held from the Tailor and Cutter Academy in London and a third shows the diploma awarded by the Lingdong School itself.[89]

This life trajectory followed a parallel course to the professional journey undertaken by many progressive Japanese tailors. Like Tsubota Sentarō, Bok Chen came home with a diploma from a leading London school of tailoring.[90] Like Wada Keiichi he went on to found schools and provide professional training to a new generation of tailors and dressmakers. And like Tsuji Matsumichi, he was keen to establish underlying principles. Fashions might change the appearance of garments, he wrote, but 'the principles of tailoring and cutting are iron-clad'.[91] Bok Chen's tailoring expertise could be described as a product of British–Chinese cultural transfer without too much controversy, but considered in regional context it seems better viewed as the outcome of a much more complex process, which in these later times would probably be talked about as globalization.

Conclusion

During the Cold War, tailoring in Japan and China followed different lines of development. The Japanese took a relatively short path from 'subsistence fashion' in the immediate post-war years to a mass fashion system that allowed diversity, individualism and experiment.[92] In China, the Communist revolution led to the flight of tailors from Shanghai and Guangzhou. They set up shop in Hong Kong, Taiwan and even in Japan itself. Gu Tianyun was among those who returned to Japan. In the China they left behind them, a truly 'mass' system of clothing developed. It was characterized by a low level of diversity and a deteriorating quality of design, cut and assemblage.

By the 1980s, there was a yawning gulf between Japan and China in terms of the skills sets in clothing manufacture. The situation was the reverse of the 1880s, when Chinese tailors were well in advance of their Japanese counterparts in the mastery of Western-style tailoring. Yet the same general mix of cultural cross-currents is observable. It is common to begin the tale of the transformation of Chinese fashion in the 1980s with a reference to Pierre Cardin's visit to China in 1979, overlooking Hanae Mori's visit in the same year.[93] A resumption of the movement of money, enterprise and talent between China and Japan in the 1980s was critical to narrowing the skills gap between the two countries. To draw attention to this fact is not to detract from the significance of Cardin in China, but rather to restate a point made at the beginning of this article: cultural change in modern East Asia involves more than an East–West exchange.

Looking back at the tailors' conventions in Tokyo in 1916 and 1917 enables an unpicking of the process of cultural transfer. The conventions were a significant means of disseminating information about new tailoring techniques. They also shed light on the sources of information and inspiration. London's J. P. Thornton and New York's Jonathan Mitchell were given particular prominence in presentations by master tailors, showing the significance of Western imports – in this case of ideas and technologies – in the transformation of Japanese dress in the early twentieth century.

The term 'import' can, however, be misleading if read too simply as meaning relocation *tout court* of an idea, a practice or even an object from an external source to an internal site. In a thoughtful exploration of the idea of cultural transfer in relationship to China, Heiner Roetz points out that 'if cross-border influences did not fall on receptive "internal" ground, they would remain futile'.[94] One way of reconfiguring what is often written about as a bilateral process (whether United States–Japan or Europe–China), would be to think of it as a matter of 'chain transfer', involving multiple nodes of transshipment, both actual and figurative.[95]

The complexity of transactions at these nodes needs to be borne in mind. The transfer is a negotiated process and the end product will necessarily be a little different from the original export. 'Chain transfer', like 'Chinese whispers', will see a slight change in variables along the way. It seems clear that one variable in the Japanese reception and management of imported fashions might have been competition offered by Chinese tailors on Japanese soil. Chinese tailors only rarely cooperated with their Japanese counterparts, but they must have been very visible to them.[96]

The core issue at the conventions, and the focus of innovation and debate, was how to cut. As the proceedings of the conventions showed, this was in turn related to how to take measurements and thence how to draft patterns and alter them. The most progressive tailors took up the challenge with enthusiasm, embraced the theory of cutting and embarked on the study of the latest methods emanating from London and New York. Others disputed the significance of the cutting principle, leading to Tsuji Matsumachi's spirited defence of theory as the bedrock of all things, and specifically of cutting. The problem of the relationship between theory and practice addressed by Tsuji was simultaneously being aired in other areas of East Asian life. Chinese medicine in Japan, and medical or forensic law in China are two examples.[97] An epistemological revolution in biology and the related field of medicine was then underway in East Asia, and seems relevant to the tailors' debate over cutting. The attention paid to the relationship between body parts – neck to back, chest to belly – and to precision in measurements of these parts meant that improvements in tasks of drafting and cutting were not too far removed from a generally better understanding of anatomy. In London, indeed, training in anatomy was fast becoming part of the tailor's education.[98]

In Japan, the debate over cutting showed a shift from an essentially artisanal to a scientific approach within the profession. Since Chinese texts, too, eventually showed an explicit commitment to a scientific approach in tailoring, it can be concluded that this was part of a larger discursive shift evident across East Asia. Although there were differences between, as well as similarities in, the tailoring professions in the two countries, how best to cut the cloth became a common concern. Although the history of technological exchange on this question needs further research for a clarification of communications between East and East as well as East and West, the evidence to date at least shows that the history was a shared one.

Notes

1 This oft-employed phrase expresses a paradigm that has been critiqued in the cases of both China and Japan. See Paul A. Cohen, *Discovering History in China: American Historical Writing on the Recent Chinese Past* (New York: Columbia University Press, 2010); Paul A. Cohen, 'Nineteenth-Century China: The Evolution of American Historical Approaches', in *A Companion to Chinese History*, ed. Michael Szonyi (Chichester: John Wiley & Sons, 2016), 155; Stefan Tanaka, *Japan's Orient: Rendering Pasts into History* (Berkeley: University of California Press, 1995), 31.

2 Published examples are legion. For an early reference, see Anon, 'The Anecdotist', *American Museum, or Universal Magazine: Containing Essays on Agriculture, Commerce, Manufactures, Politics, Morals and Manners* (December, 1790): 288.

3 Toby Slade, 'Neither East Nor West: Japanese Fashion in Modernity', in *Modern Fashion Traditions: Negotiating Tradition and Modernity Through Fashion*, ed. M. Angela Jansen and Jennifer Craik (London: Bloomsbury, 2016), 25–50.

4 Nagai Kafū 永井荷風, 'Yōfukuron 洋服論' [Essay on Western clothing], *Bunmei* 文明 [Civilization], 1.5 (August 1916): 40–42. Reprinted in Kafū Bunkō 荷風文藁 [Kafū collection] (Tokyo: Shunyōsha 1926), 178.

5 Takahama Kyoshi 高浜虚子, 'Marunouchi 丸の内', *Tōkyō Nichinichi Shimbun Yūkan* 東京日日新聞夕刊 [Tokyo Nichinichi evening newspaper] (15 March 1927): 1, reprinted in *Dai Tōkyō hanjyō ki: Yamanotehen* 大東京繁昌記山手篇 [A contemporary history of the thriving great Tokyo: Yamanote], ed. Tōkyō nichinichi shimbunsha 東京日日新聞社 [The Tokyo Nichinichi Newspaper Company] (Tokyo: Shunjūsha, 1928), 42.

6 Louise Young, 'Marketing the Modern: Department Stores, Consumer Culture, and the New Middle Class in Interwar Japan', *International Labor and Working-Class History* 55.1 (1999): 52–70.

7 Henrietta Harrison, *The Making of the Republican Citizen: Political Ceremonies and Symbols in China, 1911–1929* (Oxford: Clarendon Press, 2000), 59.

8 Robert E. Harrist, Jr., 'Clothes Make the Man: Dress, Modernity, and Masculinity in China, ca. 1912–1937', in Wu *Body and Face in Chinese Visual Culture*, ed. Hung and Katherine R. Tsiang (Cambridge, MA: Harvard University Asia Center, 2005), 171–196.

9 The Zhongshan suit is also known as the Sun Yatsen suit or, in its later manifestation, the Mao suit. See Antonia Finnane, *Changing Clothes in China: Fashion, History, Nation* (Columbia: Columbia University Press, 2008), 182–185.

10 Ji Xueyuan 季学源, 'Hongbang fazhanshi gangyao 红帮发展史纲要' [Outline history of the development of the Red Group], in *Hongbang caifeng pingzhuan* 红榜裁缝评传 [Biographies of Red Group tailors], ed. Ji Xueyuan季学源, Zhu Xiaoen 竺小恩 and Feng Yingzhi 冯盈之 (Hangzhou: Zhejiang daxue chubanshe, 2011), 3–88.

11 Wang Yilin 王以林 and Li Benting李本伫, eds., *Hongbang yanjiu suoyin* 红帮研究索引 [Research index to the Red Group] (Ningbo: Ningbo chubanshe, 2016), 17–18; Finnane, *Changing Clothes in China*, 182.

12 James Thomas Conte, 'Overseas Study in the Meiji Period: Japanese Students in America, 1867–1902' (Unpublished PhD Thesis, University of Princeton, 1977), 128.

13 Eliza Ruhamah Scidmore, *Jinrikisha Days in Japan* (New York: Harper & Brothers, 1891), 20. See also Frank G. Carpenter, 'Asiatic Travel', *Deseret Weekly*, 4 May 1895, 610.

14 *North China Herald*, 14 May 1903, 920.

15 David Field Rennie, *The British Arms in North China and Japan: Peking 1860; Kagosima 1862* (London: John Murray, 1864), 32.

16 Eric C. Han, *Rise of a Japanese Chinatown: Yokohama, 1894–1972* (Cambridge, MA: Harvard University Asia Center, 2014), 113, 116–17.

17 Ji, 'Hongbang fazhanshi gangyao'; Hanchao Lu, *Beyond the Neon Lights: Everyday Shanghai in the Early Twentieth Century* (Berkeley: University of California Press, 2004), 255.

18 B. Haiko, 'The Chinese in Japan', *China Weekly Review* 71 (26 January 1935): 303.

19 Wang and Li, *Hongbang Yanjiu Suoyin*, 17–18, 186–187.

20 Ōsaka Yōfukushō Dōgyō Kumiai 大阪洋服商同業組合 [Osaka Association of Western Clothing Merchants], *Nihon Yōfuku Enkakushi*日本洋服沿革史 [History of Western clothing in Japan] (Osaka: Ōsaka Yōfukushō Dōgyō Kumiai, 1930), 29–33. For a description of the correspondence between *tabi* and Western clothing, see Katō Ekisaburō 加藤益三郎, *Saishin kan-i yōfuku saidanhō* 最新簡易洋服截断法 [The latest simple method for cutting Western suits] (Osaka: Okamoto Igyōkan, 1903), 1.

21 Matthew Calbraith Perry and Lambert Lilly, *Narrative of the Expedition of an American Squadron to the China Seas and Japan: Performed in the Years 1852, 1853, and 1854, Under the Command of Commodore M. C. Perry, United States Navy ...* (New York: D. Appleton & Company, 1856), 342.

22 Bayard Taylor, *A Visit to India, China, and Japan: In the Year 1853* (New York: Putnam, 1860), 362.

23 Anon, *The Anglo-Hindoostanee Handbook*, vol. II (Calcutta and London: W. Thacker & Co., 1850), 619.

24 Harriet Low Hillard, *My Mother's Journal: A Young Lady's Diary of Five Years in China: 1829–1834*, ed. Katherine Hillard (Boston: G. H. Ellis, 1900), 182.

25 Joy Spanabel Emery, *A History of the Paper Pattern Industry: The Home Dressmaking Fashion Revolution* (London: Bloomsbury, 2014), 8.

26 Emery, *A History of the Paper Pattern Industry*, 8.

27 Perry and Lilly, *Narrative of the Expedition of an American Squadron*, 417.

28 Vasiliĭ Mikhaĭlovich Golovnin, *Japan and the Japanese: Comprising the Narrative of a Captivity in Japan, and an Account of British Commercial Intercourse with That Country* (London: Colburn & Co., 1853), 173.

29 Tōkyō yōfuku shōkō dōgyō kumiai kandakubu 東京洋服商工同業組合神田区部 [Kanda District Office of the Tokyo Association of Merchants and Manufacturers of Western Clothing], *Tōkyō yōfuku shōkō dōgyō kumiai enkakushi* 東京洋服商工同業組合沿革史 [History of the Tokyo Association of Merchants and Manufacturers of Western Clothing] (Tokyo: Tōkyō yōfuku shōkō dōgyō kumiai kandakubu, 1941), 79–80. A description of tailors' cutting problems can also be found in Tsuji Kiyoshi 辻清, *Yōfukuten no keiei toranomaki* 洋服店の経営虎の巻 [The bible of the Western clothing business] (Osaka: Yōfukutsūshinsha, 1926), 112.

30 Yoneda Suekichi米田末吉, ed., *Yōfuku gijutsu taikai kinenchō: shotaika saidan kessakushū* 洋服技術大会記念帳□諸大家裁断傑作集 [Tailoring techniques conventions memorial book: collection of skilled tailors' best cutting works] (Tokyo: Nihon Keorimono Shimpōsha, 1917), 2.

31 Iwamura Hidetarō 岩村秀太郎, *Yōfuku saihōshi hikkeisho* 洋服裁縫師必携書 [The tailors' manual] (Tokyo: Yōfuku saihōshi hikkeisho hakkōsho, 1906), 1.

32 Iwamura, *Yōfuku saihōshi hikkeisho*, 1.

33 But see Emery, *A History of the Paper Pattern Industry*; and also Winifred Aldrich, 'Tailors' Cutting Manuals and the Growing Provision of Popular Clothing 1770–1870: "Falling Apart like a Ready-Made"', *Textile History* 31.2 (2000): 163–201.

34 For a treatment of the Japanese experience, see Anjo Hissako 安城寿子, 'Meiji sue kara Taishōki niokeru saidan gijutsu no kōjō wo hakaru ugoki nitsu'ite: dansei yōfuku no seisaku teki sokumen nimiru Nihon fukushoku no kindaika no isō' 明治末から大正期における裁断技術の向上を図る動きについて:男性洋服の製作的側面に見る日本服飾の近代化の位相' [Practices for the development of cutting techniques from the end of the Meiji era to the Taishō era: an aspect of the modernization of Japanese clothes], *Dezain Riron* デザイン理論 [Journal of the Japan Society of Design] 58 (September 2011): 19–34.

35 Aldrich, 'Tailors' Cutting Manuals'.

36 Aldrich, 'Tailors' Cutting Manuals', 164.

37 Aldrich, 'Tailors' Cutting Manuals', 176.

38 See e.g. 畠山兼吉, *Jitsuyō yōfuku saidanhō* 実用洋服裁断法 [The practical cutting manual] (Tokyo: Jitsuyō yōfuku saidanhō hakkōsho, 1910); Tōkyō yōsō kenkyūkai 東京洋装研究会 [Tokyo Western Clothing Society], *Shinshiki yōfuku saidanhō* 新式洋服裁断法 [The new cutting manual], (Tokyo: The Tokyo Western Clothing Society, 1910); Nanshū Namie 浪江南洲, 簡易ミチヨル式洋服裁断図鑑, *Kan-i Michiyorushiki yōfuku saidan zukan* [The easy picture book of Michiyoru cutting system] (Takamatsu: Mimura Shōtarō, 1912); Keizō Hirayama 平山桂蔵, *Yōfuku*

saidanjutsu 洋服裁断術 [Cutting techniques] (Tokyo: Yūbunsha, 1915); Ōta Eitarō 太田栄太郎, *Īōshiki yōfuku saidanhō* EO式洋服裁断法 [EO cutting manual], (Osaka: Naigai orimono shimpōsha, 1917); 佐伯猪八郎, *Esuaishiki yōfuku tachikata no minamoto: Jicchi sūgaku* SI式洋服裁ち方の源:実地数学 [SI cutting principle: practical mathematics] (Osaka: Saeki Ihachirō, 1922).

39 For example, *Shinshiki yōfuku saidanhō* 新式洋服裁断法 [The new cutting manual], published in 1910 was the result of studies by Tōkyō yōsō yenkyūkai東京洋装研究会 (Tokyo Western Clothing Society), which seems to have held lectures.

40 Wada Eikichi和田栄吉, *Dainihon wadashiki yōfuku saidansho* 大日本和田式洋服裁断書 [The imperial Japanese Wada cutting manual] (Tokyo: Dainihon Wadashiki yōfuku saidan kōshūjo, 1916).

41 Wada, *Dainihon wadashiki yōfuku saidansho*, n.p.

42 Home to the great lords of the shogunate in the Tokugawa period, Akasaka had become 'one of the great geisha quarters of the Meiji'. Edward Seidensticker, *Tokyo Rising: The City Since the Great Earthquake* (Cambridge, MA: Harvard University Press, 1991), 244.

43 Seidensticker, *Tokyo Rising*, 3.

44 J. P. Thornton, *The International System of Garment Cutting: Including Coats, Trousers, Breeches and Vests* (London: Thornton Institute, 1911); The Jno. J. Mitchell Co., *The Standard Systems of Cutting Coats, Vests and Trousers: A Short-Measure Method of Drafting All Kinds of Coats and Vests and a Reliable Trousers System*, 8th ed. (New York: The Jno. J. Mitchell Co. 1911).

45 Yoneda, *Yōfuku gijutsu taikai kinenchō: shotaika saidan kessakushū*, 7–8.

46 Yoneda, *Yōfuku gijutsu taikai kinenchō*,1.

47 Yoneda, *Yōfuku gijutsu taikai kinenchō*, 7.

48 Yoneda, *Yōfuku gijutsu taikai* kinenchō, 7. As copies of *The Japan Woolen Textiles Journal* before July 1917 have been lost, it is difficult to confirm the content of these letters.

49 Yoneda, *Yōfuku gijutsu taikai kinenchō*, 5.

50 Yoneda, *Yōfuku gijutsu taikai kinenchō*, 1–5, 78–91.

51 Yoneda, *Yōfuku gijutsu taikai kinenchō*, 6–7.

52 Yoneda, *Yōfuku gijutsu taikai kinenchō*, 12. We also find his name in the Stock Company's advertisement that appeared in the *Asahi Newspaper* 朝日新聞 (20 May 1925), 10.

53 Kimura Keiichi木村慶市, *Saidan kenkyū* 裁断研究 [A study on cutting] (Tokyo: Nihon keorimono shimpōsha, 1926).

54 Yoneda, *Yōfuku gijutsu taikai kinenchō*, 42–44.

55 Yoneda, *Yōfuku gijutsu taikai kinenchō*, 44; William Leggatt and Thomas W. Hodgkinson, *The 'Climax' System for Cutting Gentleman's Garments* (Minister, 1910).

56 Leggatt and Hodgkinson, *The 'Climax' System*, 82.

57 Leggatt and Hodgkinson, *The 'Climax' System*, 85–86.

58 Leggatt and Hodgkinson, *The 'Climax' System*, 88.

59 J. P. Thornton, *The International System of Garment Cutting*, 4th ed. (London: Thornton Institute, 1913), 21.

60 Sometime editor of *Minister's Gazette of Fashion* and then of *The West-End Gazette*, Thornton was known on both sides of the Atlantic from at least 1892, when two articles by him were published in *The American Tailor and Cutter* (Jno. J. Mitchell Company, 1892).

61 Yoneda, *Yōfuku gijutsu taikai kinenchō*, 8.

62 Mitchell, *The New Standard Coat System*, 90.

63 See for example Yoshimura Chizuru 吉村千, *Gendai saihō kyōkasho* 現代裁縫教科書 [Teaching materials for modern dressmaking] (Tokyo: Tōkyō kaiseikan, 1929).

64 *Special Agents' Series* (US Government Printing Office, 1917), 104.

65 Han, *Rise of a Japanese Chinatown*, 108–109.

66 'Foreign Firms in Yokohama', *Japan Times*, Saturday, 3 May 1925.

67 'What Karuizawa people are doing', *Japan Times*, Friday 31 July 1924, 2. See also *Japan Times*, Saturday 7 July 1924.

68 H. Vere Redman (Sir) and H. Vere Redman, *Japan in Crisis: An Englishman's Impressions* (London: G. Allen & Unwin, Ltd., 1935), 54.

69 *Yomiuri Newspaper* 読売新聞 (5 April 1907), 2.

70 *Mitsukoshi* 三越 (May 1912), 17.

71 Tōkyō yōfuku shōkō dōgyō kumiai kandakubu, *Tōkyō yōfuku shōkō dōgyō kumiai enkakushi*, 80–81.

72 Tōkyō yōsō kenkyukai 東京洋装研究会 [Tokyo Western Clothing Society], *Yōfuku taizen* 洋服大全 [The encyclopedia of Western clothing] (Tokyo: Tokyo Western Clothing Society 1908), 1. Yoneda, *Yōfuku gijutsu taikai kinenchō*, 1–2. Tsuji, *Yōfuku-ten no keiei toranomaki*, n.p.

73 Tōkyō yōsō kenkyūkai 東京洋装研究会, *Shinshiki yōfuku saidanhō* 新式洋服裁断法 (The new cutting manual), (Tokyo: Tōkyō yōsō kenkyūkai, 1910).

74 Maruyama, *Maruyama shiki yōfuku saidan zensho* 丸山式洋服裁断全書 [The complete manual of the Maruyama cutting system] (Tokyo: Nihon Keorimono Shimpōsha 1926); Maruyama, *The Complete Manual of the Maruyama Cutting System* (Tokyo: Japan Woolen Textiles Journal Company 1926), 10.

75 Wellington K. K. Chan, 'Selling Goods and Promoting a New Commercial Culture: The Four Premier Department Stores on Nanjing Road, 1917–1937', in *Inventing Nanjing Road: Commercial Culture in Shanghai, 1900–1945*, ed. Sherman Cochran (Ithaca, NY: East Asia Program, Cornell University, 1999), 1–36.

76 Chen Wanfeng 陈万丰, *Zhongguo hongbang caifeng fazhanshi* 中国红帮裁缝发展史 [Development of China's Hongbang tailors' group] (Shanghai: Donghua daxue chubanshe, 2007), 33.

77 See Antonia Finnane, 'Sewing Manuals in 1950s China: Socialist Narratives and Dress Patterns from New Democracy to Socialist Transformation', in *Transglobal Fashion Narratives: Clothing Communication, Style Statements and Brand Storytelling*, ed. Anne Peirson-Smith and Joseph H. Hancock II (London: Intellect, 2018), 115–136.

78 See Richard John Lufrano, *Honorable Merchants: Commerce and Self-Cultivation in Late Imperial China* (Honolulu: University of Hawaii Press, 1997), esp. 51–67.

79 Donald A. Jordan, *China's Trial by Fire: The Shanghai War of 1932* (Ann Arbor: University of Michigan Press, 2001), 216.

80 Gu Tianyun 顾天云, *Xifu caijian zhinan* 西服裁剪指南 [Guide to Western tailoring] (Shanghai: Gu Tianyun, 1933), 2–3. Antonia Finnane thanks Mr Li Benting 李本偊 of the Ningbo Fashion Museum for providing access to this book.

81 Gu, *Xifu caijian zhinan*, 4.

82 Gu, *Xifu caijian zhinan*, 8.

83 Ding Yizhuang 定宜庄, *Baqi zidi de zhijie* 八旗子弟的世界 [The world of Bannermen descendants] (Beijing: Beijing chubanshe, 2017), 8–13.

84 Yoneda, *Yōfuku gijutsu taikai kinenchō*, 3. According to Maruyama (*Maruyama shiki yōfuku saidan zensho*, 10): 'There are no complete training institutes and very few orderly tailor shops in Japan. Under these circumstances, how can we master the tailoring techniques and acquire useful experience?'

85 Lu, *Beyond the Neon Lights*, 255–256.

86 Luo Huanghu 罗晃潮, *Riben huaqiao shi* 日本华侨史 [History of overseas Chinese in Japan] (Guangzhou: Guangdong gaodeng jiaoyu chubanshe, 1994), 231.

87 Wang and Li, *Hongbang yanjiu suoyin*, passim.

88 Wang and Li, *Hongbang yanjiu suoyin*, 66–68.

89 Bok Chen 卜珍, *Xiandai caifengxue* 现代裁缝學 [English ed.] *The Modern Theory of Tailor & Cutter*, 1951) (Hong Kong: Shangwu yinshuguan, 1950).

90 *Mitsukoshi* 三越 (May 1912), 17.

91 Bok, *Xiandai caifengxue*, 6.

92 Federica Carlotto, 'Towards the Emergence of Mass Fashion in Post-War Japan: Assessing the Nature and Extent of the American Influence', in *Legacies of the U.S. Occupation of Japan: Appraisals after Sixty Years*, ed. Rosa Caroli and Duccio Basosi (Newcastle: Cambridge Scholars Publishing, 2014).

93 Yiqiu Jiang, 'Zhongshan to Pierre Cardin: 30 Years of Chinese Fashion', in *Contemporary Chinese Visual Culture*, ed. Christopher Crouch (Amherst, MA: Cambria Press, 2010).

94 Heiner Roetz, 'Transfer in Dispute: The Case of China', in *Cultural Transfers in Dispute: Representations in Asia, Europe, and the Arab World Since the Middle Ages*, ed. Jörg Feuchter, Friedhelm Hoffmann and Bee Yun, Eigene Und Fremde Welten, vol. 23 (Frankfurt-on-Main and New York: Campus, 2011), 263–281.

95 Jörg Feuchter, 'Cultural Transfers in Dispute: In Introduction', in Feuchter et al., *Cultural Transfers in Dispute*, 13.

96 'Japanese and Chinese Tailors Combine', *Japan Times*, Thursday 13 January 1898.

97 Daniel Asen, 'The Only Options? "Experience" and "Theory" in Debates over Forensic Knowledge and Expertise in Early Twentieth-Century China', in *Historical Epistemology and the Making of Modern Chinese Medicine*, ed. Howard Chiang (Manchester: Manchester University Press, 2015), 44–45.

98 J. P. Thornton, *Anatomy and Geometry as Applied to the Art of Garment Cutting by Tailors: and Taught at the Polytechnic Institute, Regent Street, London* (London: Thornton Institute, n.d.).

13

GLOBAL FASHION ENCOUNTERS AND AFRICA

Affective materialities in Zambia

Karen Tranberg Hansen

When clothes travel, crossing cultures, nations and continents, they do not necessarily carry ready-made meanings along with them. Depending on the context of circulation, diverse meanings may be mobilized.[1] This became clear to me in the early 1990s at the outset of my research into the second-hand clothing trade in Zambia. I had brought along a couple of second-hand wedding gowns for my research assistant and most important local collaborator, who had expressed her desire to set up a bridal rental activity in her township home in one of the many low-income residential areas in Lusaka, Zambia's capital. To acquire them, one of my PhD students and I had gone to the largest Salvation Army thrift store in Chicago, where in a large room full of wedding attire and accessories we selected two wedding gowns that we thought suitable for sale in Lusaka: they had short lace sleeves, nipped waists, A-line skirts and were without décolletage. Yet the bridal rental activity never took off: there were logistical questions about how to run it. Above all, the design of the gowns was entirely wrong. It took me a while to figure out what was at issue. In Lusaka, the bodice of the desired gown should be low cut and without sleeves, it should not highlight the waist and it should have a train, which these gowns did not.

The meanings of dress, as this example illustrates, do not inhere in the garments themselves but emerge in interactions between wearers and viewers in specific contexts. Because dress both touches the body and faces outward to others, it is unlike most other types of material culture. This dual nature of dress is key to Terence Turner's perceptive characterization of the dressed body as a social skin.[2] Approaching it in this way enables us to explore how the dressed body mediates between the self and society. Materiality has an important role, affecting how we experience clothing and make it act with our bodies. That is, we do not wear our clothes passively but are actively involved with them. Thus dress is an embodied practice that intimately entangles bodies and dress with the particularities of time, location and context.[3]

The observation that the meanings of dress do not inhere in the garments themselves is constructive when exploring dress encounters in Africa, both historically and in the present day. The West has tended to see imitations of itself in the global circulation of its garments. As a result, an overdrawn distinction lingers between European-/Western-style clothing conventions on the one hand and local/traditional ways of dress on the other. The distinction is deceiving because it ignores interchanges spanning the globe and it hides the many diverse, and constantly changing, sources and inspirations that are at play in dress practice from within and beyond the African continent.[4] Reflecting on the significance of textiles in Africa and inspired by his long-term observations, art historian John Picton considers it no longer acceptable to contrast the 'traditional' with the 'contemporary'. Writing more than two decades ago, he explained that 'traditions entail histories ... and that in arts as in politics, religion, and so forth, all manner of traditions are contemporary with each other, coexisting, often mutually reflexive, each with its particular temporal status and functional locus'.[5] More recent scholarship on the developing African fashion scene by art historian Victoria Rovine no longer uses the term 'traditional' to refer to the fundamental status of a textile, a garment or an image. Instead she applies the expression 'traditional' to styles or media that make connections with, or evoke, local culture and history.[6] Such views do not involve a search for historical origins but rather invite explorations of the consequences of their transformations.

This chapter explores two aspects of these processes that sometimes appear to be in opposition to one another and at other times to operate alongside each other. The first process concerns local appropriations of Western-inspired clothing styles, while the second deals with constructions of 'traditional' dress. My focus is on central/southern Africa, specifically Zambia where I have conducted most of my anthropological research. Each of the three snapshots I provide serves as springboard for an exploration of contestations over dress in the context of the broader social and historical processes within which they took place.

In this chapter, I consider long-term change over nearly a century, beginning with the development of 'fashion savvy' by Africans pursuing their dress desires in the context of restricted clothing access and assertions of colonial superiority. I turn next to efforts to construct notions of 'traditional' dress in the era of nationalist rule in the wake of political independence in 1964, discussing the popularity of imported second-hand clothing and its creative reuse when markets were liberalized in the late 1980s. Finally I explore the contemporary fashion scene in Zambia in interactions between consumers and tailors and emerging designers who are launching their own brands, incorporating local dress aesthetics and global taste inspirations into new style creations.

Colonial African 'fashion savvy'

Economically and culturally textiles and clothing are important in African history and in contemporary society. The cloth and clothing trade were big business for decades prior to the arrival of Europeans during the fifteenth century and during the slave trade across both the Atlantic and the Indian Oceans well into the nineteenth century.[7] Along with the trade spread new dress conventions: Islamic-inspired dress had already, from around 1000 and onward, spread in the Sahel/Sudanic region and along the East African coast. Although European-style clothing had been known and worn by local elites in coastal areas since the late fifteenth century, it did not become part of ordinary people's dress until in the late nineteenth century.[8] Talking about the backdrop for this transition with reference to southern and eastern Africa, historian Robert Ross identifies a major shift in the material culture of dress: 'between the 1880s – earlier in some parts of South Africa – and the 1950s, though in most parts of the continent it had been completed before then', which according to him 'entailed the virtually complete reclothing of half a continent, and also the remaking of a whole variety of other articles of consumption'.[9]

In colonies with many white settlers such as eastern and southern Africa, labour migration to mines, farms and towns enabled Africans to acquire Western-styled clothing. This they did eagerly, as a visually arresting presentation when one is out and about had, and continues to have, great appeal. The colonial white ruling class had an ambivalent relationship to the dress practices of Africans. On the one hand they insisted that Africans should not go naked. But on the other hand they were vexed when Africans dressed like themselves. In a short biography written in the late 1930s Zacharia Mawere wrote about his older brother Herbert. He describes how Herbert was received when he returned to his home town Fort Jameson (Chipata) in Northern Rhodesia (Zambia) after many years as a migrant worker in Southern Rhodesia (Zimbabwe). 'Everybody was happy', reported Zacharia.

> But some difficulties arose when they came to Fort Jameson, the trouble did not come from his master but from some other Europeans. They hated him because he did not like to wear the cloth[e]s which Europeans used to offer their boys, but he himself used to put on a suit, and he wished always to put on a suit in the Southern Rhodesia style.[10]

The clothes 'boys' wore were shorts.

Zacharia worked as an assistant for an anthropologist who conducted research about the livelihoods of Africans in a small mining town just prior to and during the early years of World War II. It was in field notes written by Zacharia that I found the account of his older brother. At this time in urban areas, some African residents had formed ballroom dancing clubs, which they sometimes invited Europeans to attend in order to watch and to judge both the dancing and the dress style. One evening the anthropologist brought along his wife in order to describe 'the frocks'. Her notes about the dress styles and the dancing include comments she overheard from another European woman, the wife of the district governor. The governor's wife had this to say about the best dressed African woman: 'I never knew they could dance so well. That is a lovely frock – really lovely, I mean. It looks as if she had it made for her'. Yet she wondered, 'but do you think it is good for them. I mean (pause). Surely they feel themselves Europeans now'. Another European woman also present at the event exclaimed, 'Just think, they dress up like this and then they go back to their little *kayas* [servants' quarters in the back of their employers' gardens]'.[11]

Indeed clothing was a contentious topic, as revealed in discussions in the 1940s and 1950s when the colonial administration attempted to assess the cost of living of the rapidly growing African populations in urban areas. A. L. Saffrey, a labour officer in the early 1940s, was in charge of this investigation. When his preliminary findings were presented to the Advisory Board on African Labour in 1943, all hell broke loose. For Saffrey found a high degree of 'stabilization', meaning African commitment to urban living, and suggested that the process was likely to continue. He argued,

> [I]n ascertaining a reasonable standard for clothes and covering it is obvious that one must be guided by the desires of the people but not bound by them. At the same time, one must give due consideration to the changing standards that have come about and are continuing at an increased tempo in the urban areas.[12]

Saffrey's minimum requirement estimates for a family of four provoked irate commentary, especially his suggestion that African urban women needed several dresses. His 'house to house investigations' had revealed that 'most women have at least five or six dresses'. In the preliminary report he explained that

> one of the most difficult items to assess when estimating a reasonable minimum standard is the quantity of clothes ... European type clothes are to the African a sign of prosperity and advancement, and one of the first things the wage earner buys with his first month's pay is, not pots and pans, but a shirt and a pair of trousers for himself and a dress for his wife.[13]

But colonial urban administrators expressed doubts about the accuracy of Saffrey's observations, which a representative from the Chamber of Mines went to great pains to discredit. 'The fact that most women have at least five or six dresses', he argued, 'is surely an indication that their incomes are not inadequate'.[14] In the end, the report was considered to be confidential. It was shelved and never released for official circulation.

To be sure, colonial authorities had trouble understanding African clothing desires. In fact, when discussing African clothing consumption, colonial authorities were talking about another subject, embedded in the political future, but not immediately apparent in the contemporary clothing terms of discourse. Just what and where was the place of the growing urban African population in this rapidly changing society? At this time, clothing comprised a very large proportion of the household budgets of Africans living in urban areas.[15] Low wages, rising costs of living and wartime restrictions on manufactured goods made accumulation of clothing the one sure option. By law, Africans could not buy houses and land, so they invested in clothing. They acquired clothing from small shops, had it made by tailors, purchased it second-hand and bought it from mail-order firms in England. They distributed textiles and clothing to relatives in the countryside, where a well-dressed visiting urban relative attracted considerable attention. Complicating the often drawn distinction between the local and Western in the clothing history of this region of Africa, European-/Western-style clothing had become a standard article of African dress.[16]

The national fabric

In 1964, when Zambia became independent from British colonial rule, it presented itself symbolically to the world of nations with a newly designed coat of arms. The new republic's heraldic imagery features a shield with black and white wavy lines, representing white water cascading over black rock in the Victoria Falls, with a fish eagle on top and a crossed hoe and pick underneath. The eagle stands for freedom, the hoe and pick for farming and mining. To the left and right of the shield are a man and a woman, the man dressed in a bush jacket and shorts and the woman in a cloth tied at the waist, a square necked top with a yoked neck and puffed sleeves. She is adorned with beads and an ivory bracelet. They both wear sandals. At their feet are symbols of the country's natural resources: a maize cop, a mine head-frame and a zebra. At the bottom is a narrow horizontal banner with the political motto: 'One Zambia, One Nation'. The country's many ethnic groups were to be melded into one unitary polity, Zambia (Figure 13.1).

When the ministerial consultative committee for the independence celebration asked Zambian artist Gabriel Ellison to design the new coat of arms, it insisted on human figures as bearers. Considering several suggestions for the dress of the bearers, the consultative committee members settled on dress styles that were common during the two decades prior to independence. The all-male committee members agreed more easily on the male bearer's dress than that of the female bearer. The designer had proposed birds or wild game as bearers, arguing that human bearers were unlikely to withstand the effects of time.[17]

Subsequent developments indicate that Gabriel Ellison was partly right in her argument. The coat of arms has indeed been subject to criticism for the colonial associations, particularly with the male bearer's bush suit. Adult African men

FIGURE 13.1 Coat of arms of the Republic of Zambia, 1964.

Source: Karen Tranberg Hansen, *Salaula: The World of Second-Hand Clothing and Zambia* (Chicago: University of Chicago Press, 2000), 79.

who worked in lowly jobs for the colonial administration commonly wore shorts as did the many men who served in the private households of white employers. Even then, the bush suit of colonial vintage took off as required wear for men in official jobs in the new nation but with an important twist: men now wore long trousers rather than shorts. Called a safari suit in Zambia, in eastern and southern Africa this suit was often referred to as a *Kaunda* with reference to Zambia's first president, Kenneth Kaunda, for whom a safari suit was standard wear during his long-term presidency.

Aside from the missionary-inspired top with puffed sleeves and yoked neck, the woman's dress style on the coat of arms is charged with fewer colonial associations. It showcases a clothing practice that has come to be interpreted as 'traditional'. When Zambia in 1972 became a one-party state, a commemorative stamp was issued, also drawn by Gabriel Ellison, featuring three women in wrappers of colourful printed fabric called *chitenge* in Zambia (*vitenge* in some regions of Zambia and *kitenge* in East Africa and the Congo). *Chitenge*, a factory-produced textile, roller printed on one face, is one of several colourful printed cotton fabrics, including wax prints and *kanga* (East Africa), which are worn widely across the African continent.[18] They are often called African prints with a designation that turns history on its head.[19] Originally produced in India and then in Europe, these fabrics have become Africanized, imbued with meanings whose significance arises from the particularities of time, location and context (Figure 13.2).[20]

During the 1930s, some *kitenge* fabrics imported from Japan reached Zambia from the Belgian Congo,[21] while Europe, India and America served as other sources for fabric. The two textile manufacturing companies that began producing *chitenge* soon after independence (1964) closed before the turn of the last millennium, when market liberalization expanded the importation of textiles.

FIGURE 13.2 Postage stamp designed by Zambian artist, Gabriel Ellison, 1972, featuring three Zambian women wearing *chitenge*.

Source: Author's collection.

Today, the main source of *chitenge* fabrics is China. *Chitenge* is also a sought-after commodity by long-distance suitcase traders, who travel from Zambia to the Democratic Republic of Congo and Tanzania to purchase domestically produced textiles, which are popular with Zambian customers.[22]

Consumers evaluate *chitenge* in terms of fabric quality, design and price. The colourful imagery includes symbolic and geometric motifs, depictions of human beings, animals, mythical figures and masks and a variety of different designs. Some designs copy existing fabrics and graphic art. Diverse aspects of changing everyday life appear on *chitenge* fabrics, among them shoes with stiletto heels, sunglasses and new forms of technology such as mobile phones. There are also commemorative *chitenge* fabrics with both political and religious motifs. When a woman intends to source *chitenge* fabric, she has quite a variety of options, ranging from commissioning *chitenge* manufactured in the Democratic Republic of Congo from a suitcase trader to shopping herself at a market venue that specializes in fabrics. Lusaka has several large urban markets with open and covered stalls displaying African print fabrics and outdoor vendors with piles of *chitenge* on the ground. The oldest of these markets is located in part of the city reserved for African trade during the colonial period. Today this area is still often referred to as the second-class trading area. Many traders of Indian and Pakistani background have their retail premises here. A few sell only fabrics while many offer a mix of fabrics, garments and apparel and household objects, most of it made in India and China.

In the shops, and in other areas where they are sold, the fabrics are generally displayed on shelves lining the walls and hung from lines under the ceiling. In the more exclusive stores, *chitenge* is only sold in the full length (*c.*5.5 meters or approximately 6.5 yards) sufficient for a two- or three-piece outfit while smaller shops may sell cuts of 2 meters (approximately 2.5 yards), the standard length for a wrapper. When a potential customer wishes to scrutinize a fabric, a shop assistant has either to bring a sample from the shelves or remove it from the line of hanging fabrics with the use of a long pole. As this approach does not readily encourage the customer to touch and rub the fabric to assess its quality, it is not surprising that women are fond of shopping in open-air and market stalls where they can engage actively both with the fabric and the vendor. Touch is an important part of fabric selection. If a fabric contains too much starch, for example, the customer knows that it is of poor quality and that the starch will wash off during laundering, making the fabric difficult to fold and leaving it with a tired look. In effect, fabric quality contributes to the sensuous experience of wearing *chitenge* and the embodied materiality of *chitenge* dress practice.

Chitenge fabrics are worn as wrappers and plain dresses for everyday use. In the 1960s, tailored *chitenge* outfits became popular as 'national dress'. Over time, they incorporated style elements from across Africa and spread regionally in southern Africa.[23] When a woman wishes to commission a *chitenge* outfit, she calls on local and foreign tailors (from the Democratic Republic of Congo, Ghana and Nigeria), many of them men, and designers, most but not all women.[24] During the mid- to late 1980s *chitenge* outfits were plain skirts or wrappers worn with tops adorned by contrasting ribbons around necks and sleeves. Tie-dyed cloth became common then, made by women from Ghana and Nigeria who taught Zambian women the technique. *Chitenge* was tailored into loose garments, including trouser and top combinations, with West African-styled embroidery around necks, sleeves and edges. During the early 1990s, the trouser and top combination changed to skirts and tops of *chitenge* or tie-dyed fabric with marked waistlines, peplums and elaborate built-up sleeves supported by interfacing and with collars, necklines and fronts embellished by contrasting fabric, buttons, ruffles or smocking. There were several types of skirts: pencil skirts, plain wrappers and double wrappers. During the mid-1990s, a pencil-tight skirt reaching below the knee with a high front slit became known as *Tshala Muana*, the name of a popular singer from the Democratic Republic of Congo. The late 1990s style was inspired by West African dress practice and referred to as 'Nigerian *boubou*', named after the big robes men wear in Francophone Africa. It consisted of huge gowns of single-coloured fabric, damask or damask imitations, with embroidery in contrasting colours. Elaborate head-ties completed the look. By the turn of the millennium, popular *chitenge* outfits comprised short-sleeved blouses and full-length skirts, one style called *donafish* with a bottom flounce reminiscent of a mermaid's tail (Figure 13.3).

When women in Zambia refer to their *chitenge* outfits as 'traditional', they are talking about an invented tradition that keeps evolving as a result of changing inspirations from across the continent and beyond. It is 'our wear', they say, and indeed *chitenge* is deeply embedded in an ongoing history of global trade and changing national representations. Today in Zambia adult men wear suits and not big robes like in West Africa and along the East African coast. Adult Zambian women's wardrobes hold Western-styled garments like yours and mine, which they wear at work in schools, banks and offices. For festive occasions and special events, women may dress in elaborate *chitenge* outfits. At home and when they go shopping, they often tie a *chitenge* wrapper around the waist. They carry their infants in a piece of *chitenge* on their back. Because *chitenge* fabric is multi-purpose and worn in both town and country, it is unlikely to be replaced entirely by Western-style garments.

Creative repurposing of second-hand clothing

When import restrictions were removed in the late 1980s and in the early 1990s and markets opened up, Zambia's clothing scene changed dramatically. Throughout the 1990s, tailors and their clients benefitted from the ready availability of imported fabrics and clothing, many of which tailored into *chitenge* outfits. And residents in both urban and rural areas eagerly bought clothes for themselves and their families in rapidly growing markets that sold second-hand clothing imported from the West. Gone were the days of the state-run monopoly stores with their drab clothing. The safari suit disappeared almost overnight. The new president presented himself in elegant double-breasted bespoke suits

FIGURE 13.3 Four women dressed up for a party. The one on the left wears a tailor-made office ensemble. The second from the left wears a 'Nigerian *boubou*'. The two women on the right wear *chitenge* outfits.

Source: Photograph by Karen Tranberg Hansen, Lusaka, Zambia, 2002.

with matching silk ties and handkerchiefs. Men from all ranks of society eagerly adopted this style of dress, dubbed 'new culture'. And the second-hand clothing market affordably supplied large-sized jackets, which tailors re-crafted into 'new culture' styles.

Imported second-hand clothing is called *salaula*, a word from one of the local languages (ChiBemba) that means 'selecting from a pile'. What is remarkable about this designation is that the word *salaula* makes no reference whatsoever to the origin of the clothes as used garments from the West.[25] Instead, it captures the enormous choice and the ability to select from an abundant supply of garments. In effect, when used clothing has been sorted and pressed into bales in Europe and North America for export and has arrived in Zambia, it has been stripped of its former social life.[26]

The value of clothes no longer wanted in the West is then redefined in a process through which second-hand clothes come to be considered as 'new'. I have observed this process in transactions between Western clothing recyclers and importers in Zambia. The process unfolds through contacts and communications between exporters and importers, and in on-site visits. It continues in warehouses when local traders purchase the imported bales and in the big markets where people talk about clothing.

And it manifests itself in how people in Zambia dress in second-hand clothes. It is a process through which the meaning of clothes shifts.

All income groups, women and men, young and old, shop from *salaula* markets. They experience such second-hand clothing markets like outdoor shopping malls: some customers look for something to complement a specific garment in their wardrobe; many office workers spend their lunch hour at *salaula* markets on the lookout for garments they need or desire.

What happens to Western used clothes beyond the point of purchase when they become part of their new owners' wardrobes? How do they acquire new lives? To explore this, we need to appreciate local dress aesthetics and cultural norms about dressed bodies. The desired dress silhouette for adults, both women and men, is polished, neat and tidy, with garments and accessories that match and are not too revealing. This is evident in the detailed attention with which they examine the quality of fabric and sewing, design and style, when they go shopping for *salaula* as well as in the care with which they maintain their clothing at home through washing and ironing. Across all of southern Africa people from Zambia are well known for dressing smart and fashionably. They like to dress well and work hard on how they present their dressed bodies in public. The aspired effect is to attract admiring attention to one's overall look, triggering a 'wow' moment when the dressed body cuts straight to our emotions.

Above all, widespread cultural norms influence clothing practice. These cultural norms weigh down more heavily on women than on men. From when they are very young, girls are instructed not to provoke men by their dress. Most important, they are told not to show their 'private parts', which in this part of Africa means their thighs. At home and in public, women watch that their clothes are not too short, tight or transparent when they are in the company of men and members of the older generation. Young people navigate around these norms, reinterpreting them, when they can get away with it. Even then, they appear to dress more formally when they become adults and find jobs.[27]

Within these aesthetic and cultural frames, it is the abundance of clothes from which to choose and the possibilities for variation that make the *salaula* markets attractive in terms of quality, design and the possibility to make a good purchase in terms of value for money. Yet in order to find out how clothes acquire meaning, we have to go beyond the markets, the tailor workshops and the shops. To be sure, a garment is perhaps only a thing, a material, tangible item. But when we dress and wear it, it requires our active collaboration to bring it to life by the body. When we dress, something happens to our entire expression. That is to say that the meaning of dress emerges in the context of its use. The distinction is in the wearing, which involves the body. It is during social interaction that second-hand clothes become new outfits. We notice the results in everyday life, on the street and at social occasions through what and how people dress and in their comments about other people's clothes.[28]

Second-hand clothing is redefined as 'new' in Zambia through a variety of processes that change the meaning of clothes. In addition, anonymous clothes imported from the West are changed into one-of-a kind garments through physical and material changes like repair, alteration and recycling, which take place in tailor workshops in markets and private homes. What is more, *salaula* is repurposed. In the big markets young men search the piles of clothes when traders open second-hand clothing bales they have purchased in the importers' warehouses. With a sharp eye for style, they put garments together in new combinations. They resell these preselected garments to eager customers looking for coordinated ensembles for everyday, work and leisure wear. And around the city, a new generation of fashion-conscious people use their flair and creativity to restyle and put fresh spins on second-hand clothing. Some of them sell from home, others set up pop-up shops or rent spaces where they create events, for example with music, around the sale of *salaula*. Their innovating attitude captures the moment and people's desires about how they like to dress. Such young entrepreneurs find in second-hand clothing a good source of income because the garments appeal to the widespread appreciation of style and fashion throughout Zambian society.

Some observers view the second-hand clothing import as dumping, the dropping of the West's surplus consumption on poor people in Africa, and some describe the popularity of second-hand clothing in a country like Zambia as the flip side of Western fashion.[29] But in seeing only the West in our discarded garments, such narratives reduce local people to passive imitators of our dress conventions. Local consumers are actively shaping the demand, influencing what types of garments the wholesalers import, and this depends in turn on local aesthetics and cultural norms, the season and changing world fashion trends. The creativity people in Zambia have developed around second-hand clothing brings into play both local cultural norms and changing inspirations from many directions, regionally and across the globe.

Designers and new style creations

The design scene is the most recent twist on the ever-changing appreciation of stylish dress in Zambia as it is in many other countries in Africa.[30] In the mid-1990s, downtown Lusaka had several production units with boutique-style outlets, operated by well-educated women, often married to wealthy men. Such women were able to travel abroad where some had taken design and fashion courses. They concentrated on producing 'high quality fashion garments for high-income clients who prefer imported clothing from London, Paris, and New York' to what they perceived as cheap local wear.[31] But when I began to explore the emerging fashion and design scene in 2007, the preferences for Western wear were being challenged. Seasonally changing and creatively styled *chitenge* outfits had begun to take centre stage alongside other dress inspirations in fashionable women's wardrobes.

Between 1997 and today, several up-scale shopping malls have opened in Lusaka. New consumption spaces, clothing stores and boutiques appeal to urban residents with money to spend. Against this backdrop, two processes have helped fuel the growth of a more vibrant fashion design scene. For one, the production potential of the new designers has been greatly improved by the ready availability in recent years of imported sewing machines, dress fabric and sewing notions. Second and above all, their exposure to a global world of fashion and styles has expanded and along with it, so has the scope for local dress entrepreneurship. The Internet and social media have opened up networks of previously unimaginable interchange, spanning the globe.

There is now a formal fashion circuit, complete with organizers, promoters, models and photographers. And dress entrepreneurs view themselves as designers and label their clothing lines; among the recent and carefully watched are Debbie Chu, Dodo Wear Design, Fay Designs, Kamanga Wear and Kutowa. The first organized Zambia Fashion Week unfolded in Lusaka in October 2005 and has taken place subsequently every year except for a brief hiatus between 2009 and 2011. Alongside this, other fashion shows and competitions take place and new events and venues keep appearing. In 2014, a group of fashion professionals established the Zambia Fashion Council to promote locally produced fashion.[32]

Most of these designers are women, although they include a few men. Among them are people of several national and cultural backgrounds, that is, not all of them are black Zambians. What they all share is a keen sense of style acquired from diverse experiences and exposures that do not always include formal training. Some of these designers, in fact, do not sew themselves but hire tailors, mostly men, to carry out the basic tasks. A few put out their work for completion by tailors. Many operate from their own or their parents' homes or rented premises. They use several sewing machines, mostly their own but at times also rented, including in addition to chain-stitch sewing machines, lock-stitch machines and machines for embroidery and knitting. Some have industrial sewing machines as well as old-fashioned treadle and hand-operated machines. Consider Angela Mulenga, for example, whose production of the Queen's Wear label takes place in a tiny workshop in one of downtown Lusaka's old shopping venues, the Central Arcade, with four industrial sewing machines and one embroidery machine. Her mother started Queen's Wear. Angela employs four male tailors of whom the oldest began working for her mother several years ago.

Who are the clients? For a while, My Choice, an up-scale boutique in Lusaka's Manda Hill's shopping mall, sold some garments produced by the new designers. In 2014, Zambia's first designer boutique featuring locally created fashion, Vala Local Design House (*vala* meaning wear in ChiNyanja), opened in a strip mall for commission sales of the clothes by local designers. This new emporium was the brainchild of the Zambia Fashion Council. The new crop of style entrepreneurs design clothes, for example, for beauty pageant and Face of Africa contestants. In 2009, a group of them designed part of the wardrobe for the Zambian participant in the Miss Universe contest in Brazil. Designs produced for such events have ripple effects in the form of referrals. Women of means call on these designers to get special dresses made particularly for kitchen parties (bridal showers) and weddings. Many designers have a special clientele of women in high-level jobs and public positions who are well known throughout Zambian society and regarded as trendsetters when it comes to fashion. Seasonally changing *chitenge* outfits have wide appeal in a dress universe that is strongly inflected by Western-style wear. Although most *chitenge* fabric today is imported from China, it constitutes the currency of women's dress in Zambia.

Contrary to Gabriel Ellison's concern about the human bearers when she designed the national coat of arms in 1964, *chitenge* has indeed withstood the effects of time. As this chapter demonstrates, *chitenge* identifies both a fabric and a dress practice, thus merging on women's bodies the agentive medium of the fabric with dress practice. Propelled by the aesthetic sensibilities of a new generation of Zambian creative designers, *chitenge* dress has developed in new directions with inspirations from many angles. 'Traditionally built' women continue proudly to display their dressed bodies in *chitenge* as occasional and special events wear. And young women, who used to complain that *chitenge* outfits made them look 'old', are increasingly attracted to the new creatively styled *chitenge* fashions.[33] Today's young designers work to change the way Zambian women dress by adding a new edge to *chitenge* as everyday wear in the wardrobes of young, upcoming and professional women with disposable incomes.[34] '*Chitenge*', said Angela Mulenga in 2009 when I interviewed this 21-year-old designer with a background in business administration, 'will stand the test of time'.[35]

Conclusion

In this chapter I have explored the entanglements of Western dress conventions introduced during the colonial period, the invented *chitenge* dress tradition in the wake of independence, the popular imported second-hand clothing from the West in the open market economy from the 1990s on and finally the turn of millennium flourishing of a local design and fashion scene. Though small and mainly oriented toward a local clientele, the emerging fashion scene demonstrates creativity and style with new designs that make their wearers feel part of the world on Zambian terms. Clearly, the wedding dresses I brought my assistant in Lusaka in 1992 did not match those terms (Figure 13.4).

The cultural passion for clothing, which I have introduced here, dresses Zambian bodies through trade and interchanges that span the globe. To be sure, the focus has changed, reflecting the cultural politics and trade regimes of their time. Western-inspired dress conventions influenced the dress practice of African women and men during the colonial period, and today men in Zambia proudly continue to wear suits. While women's dress practice remains strongly Western-styled, it is part of a clothing universe that has invented *chitenge* fashions as 'traditional' at the same time as its chief inspirations come from across the African

FIGURE 13.4 Zambian author, Namwali Serpell, wearing a *chitenge* dress of Kutowa design from Lusaka when receiving the Caine Prize for African writing in Oxford 2015. *Source*: Photograph, courtesy of Ranka Primorac.

continent. In this instance, rather than being in opposition to one another, European-/Western-style clothing conventions and local/traditional ways of dress play out together on women's dressed bodies. The new creative designs that incorporate *chitenge* fabric make a direct link between history, the fashion runway and the dressed body, connecting them to wearers and viewers, making sense of their place in the world.

Notes

1 This chapter draws on my previous work on markets and dress in Zambia as well as on explorations into the developing fashion scene in Lusaka, undertaken in 2007, 2009 and 2014. See Karen Tranberg Hansen, *Salaula: The World of Second-Hand Clothing and Zambia* (Chicago: University of Chicago Press, 2000); and Karen Tranberg Hansen, 'Dressed Bodies, Everyday Fashion Practices and Livelihoods: Perspectives from Africa', in *Haute Africa: People Photography Fashion*, exhibition catalogue from the Photofestival Knokke-Heist, ed. Christophe de Jaeger and Ramona van Gansbeke (Tielt, Belgium: Lannoo Publishing, 2014), 189–206.

2 Terence Turner, 'The Social Skin', in *Reading the Social Body*, ed. Catherine B. Burroughs and Jeffrey Ehrenreich (Iowa City: University of Iowa Press, [1980] 1993), 15–39.

3 Joanne Entwistle, *The Fashioned Body: Fashion, Dress and Modern Social Theory* (Cambridge, UK: Polity Press, 2000).

4 Leslie W. Rabine, *The Global Circulation of African Fashion* (New York: Berg, 2002), *Contemporary African Fashion*, ed. Suzanne Gott and Kristyne Loughran (Bloomington: Indiana University Press, 2010); and Victoria L. Rovine, *African Fashion: Global Style: Histories, Innovations and Ideas You Can Wear* (Bloomington: Indiana University Press, 2015).

5 John Picton, 'Introduction. Technology, Tradition and Lurex: The Art of Textiles in Africa', in *Technology, Tradition and Lurex: The Art of Textiles in Africa*, ed. John Picton (London: Barbican Art Gallery/Lund: Humphries Publishers, 1995), 11. I thank Suzanne Gott for reminding me of this.

6 Rovine, *African Fashion*, 18–19.

7 See Colleen E. Kriger, *Cloth in West African History* (Lanham, MD: Altamira, 2006); Pedro Machado, 'Awash in a Sea of Cloth: Gujarat, Africa, and the Western Indian Ocean, 1300–1800', in *The Spinning World: A Global History of Cotton Textiles, 1200–1850*, ed. Giorgio Riello and Prasannan Parthasarathi (Oxford: Oxford University Press, 2009), 161–179; and Jeremy Presholdt, *Domesticating the World: African Consumerism and the Genealogies of Globalization* (Berkeley: University of California Press, 2008).

8 Elisabeth L. Cameron, 'Republic of Congo and Democratic Republic of Congo', in *Berg Encyclopedia of World Dress and Fashion*, vol. 1. Africa, ed. Joanne B. Eicher and Doran H. Ross (Oxford: Berg), 371–372.

9 Robert Ross, *Clothing: A Global History* (Cambridge, UK: Polity Press, 2008), 121.

10 Karen Tranberg Hansen, 'Urban Research in a Hostile Setting: Godfrey Wilson in Broken Hill, Northern Rhodesia, 1938–1940', *Kronos* 41 (2015): 211.

11 Hansen, 'Urban Research in a Hostile Setting', 210.

12 NAZ/SEC 1/1363, 1943–1949 (National Archives of Zambia), Report by Mr A. L. Saffrey on Cost of Living, cited in Hansen, *Salaula*, 36.

13 NAZ/SEC 1/1363, cited in Hansen, *Salaula*, 44.

14 NAZ/SEC 1/1363, cited in Hansen, *Salaula*, 44.

15 According to Wilson, during the early years of World War II African miners in Broken Hill spent 60 per cent of their cash earnings on clothing. Part of their earnings consisted of cash, another part of food rations. Godfrey Wilson, *An Essay on the Economics of Detribalization in Northern Rhodesia: Part II*, Rhodes-Livingstone Papers No. 6 (Manchester: Manchester University Press, [1942] 1968), 77. See also Hansen, 'Urban Research', 208–212.

16 Ross, *Clothing: A Global History*, 121.

17 Gabriel Ellison interview, 12 September 1997, Lusaka, cited in Hansen, *Salaula*, 78.

18 *African Print Fashion Now! A Story of Taste, Globalization, and Style*, ed. Suzanne Gott, Kristyne Loughran, Betsy D. Quick, and Leslie Rabine (Los Angeles: Fowler Museum, University of California, Los Angeles, 2017).

19 Christopher Steiner, 'Another Image of Africa: Toward an Ethnohistory of European Cloth Marketed in West Africa, 1873–1960', *Ethnohistory* 32.2 (1985): 91–110.

20 Nina Sylvanus, *Patterns in Circulation: Cloth, Gender, and Materiality in West Africa* (Chicago: University of Chicago Press, 2016).

21 Katsuhiko Kitaguwa, 'Japanese Competition in the Congo Basin in the 1930s', in *Intra-Asian Trade and the World Market*, ed. A. J. H. Lantham, Heita Kawakatsa and Katsuhiko Kitaguwa (New York: Routledge, 2006), 161–162. For more on these processes, see the special issue of *Textile History* with a focus on the history of cloth in Eastern Africa introduced by Sarah Fee and Pedro Machado, 'Entangled Histories: Translocal Textile Trades in Eastern Africa, c.800 CE to the Early Twentieth Century', *Textile History* 48.1 (2017): 4–14.

22 Hansen, *Salaula*, 180–182; and Hansen, 'Dressed Bodies', 208–214.

23 For Congolese styles, see *Femmes – Mode – Musiques: Memoires de Lubumbashi*, ed. Violaine Sizaire, Dibwe dia Mwembu and Bogumil Jewsiewicki (Paris: L'Harmattan, 2002).

24 Karen Tranberg Hansen, 'Fabricating Dreams: Sewing Machines, Tailors, and Urban Entrepreneurship in Zambia', in *The Objects of Life in Central Africa: The History of Consumption and Social Change, 1840–1980*, ed. Robert Ross, Marja Hinfelaar and Iva Pesa (Leiden: Brill, 2013), 167–185.

25 Imported second-hand clothes are given many different names in Africa. In some parts of Ghana and Nigeria, for example, their local names mean 'dead white people's clothes'; in East Africa they are referred to in Swahili as *mitumba*, meaning bale; in some regions of the Democratic Republic of Congo, they are called *sola*, meaning to choose; while in Mozambique, they are still known as *calamidades*, referencing the Civil War calamities in the wake of independence.

26 Igor Kopytoff, 'The Cultural Biography of Things: Commoditization as Process', in *The Social Life of Things: Commodities in Cultural Perspective*, ed. Arjun Appadurai (Cambridge, UK: Cambridge University Press, 1986), 64–92.

27 Karen Tranberg Hansen, 'Youth, Gender, and Second-hand Clothing in Lusaka, Zambia. Local and Global Styles', in *The Fabric of Cultures: Fashion, Identity, and Globalization*, ed. Eugenia Paulicelli and Hazel Clark (New York: Routledge, 2009), 112–127.

28 See for example Karen Tranberg Hansen, 'Fashioning. Zambian Moments', *Journal of Material Culture* 8.3 (2003): 301–309; Alexandra Palmer and Hazel Clark, eds., *Old Clothes, New Looks: Second Hand Fashion* (Oxford: Berg, 2005); and Stavroula Pipyrou, 'Cutting Bella Figura: Irony, Crisis, and Second-hand Clothes in South Italy', *American Ethnologist* 41.3 (2014): 532–546.

29 Steven Haggblade, 'The Flip Side of Fashion: Used Clothing Exports to the Third World', *Journal of Development Studies* 26.3 (1990): 505–521.

30 Christine Delhave and Rhoda Woets, 'The Commodification of Ethnicity: Vlisco Fabrics and Wax Cloth Fashion in Ghana', *International Journal of Fashion Studies* 2.1 (2015): 77–97; Joanna Grabski, 'Making Fashion in the City: A Case Study of Tailors and Designers in Dakar, Senegal', *Fashion Theory* 13.2 (2009): 215–242; and Rovine, *African Fashion*.

31 Mwango Kasangele, 'Differentiation Among Small-Scale Enterprises: The Zambian Clothing Industry in Lusaka', in *African Entrepreneurship: Theory and Practice*, ed. Anita Spring and Barbara E. McDade (Gainesville: University of Florida Press, 1998), 96–98.

32 *Zambia Weekly*, week 34 (21 August 2014); and www.zambiafashioncouncil.com (accessed 22 September 2019).

33 Hansen, *Salaula*, 204.

34 Interview of Towani Clarke, designer of Kutowa, 25 September 2014, Lusaka.

35 Interview of Andrea Mulenga, designer of Queen's Wear, July 2009, Lusaka.

INDEX

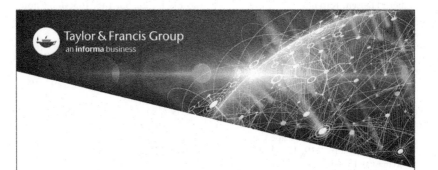